MODERN TIMES

Modern Times is about the emergence of new cultural forms and the experience of modernity over the last hundred years. Its focus is on [what Marshall Berman has called] 'the modernism of the streets' – the perils and possibilities of modern metropolitan life. All the contributions emphasise the instability of modern existance and the complex influence of psychic formation – of fantasy, envy, and denial – for our understanding of twentieth century social and cultural transformations.

Among the themes the book deals with in greater depth are the utopian in popular cinema, the invention of British music, 'camp' as transgressive aesthetic form, migration and the black metropolis, the allure of the city, and the widespread fascination and anxiety about the poor, the hooligan, the new woman, sexual knowledge and shopping in department stores.

The book will be of critical interest to those studying and teaching in the fields of cultural history and cultural theory.

The editors, **Mica Nava** and **Alan O'Shea**, and the other contributors, Sally Alexander, Andrew Blake, Peter Horne, John Marriott and Bill Schwarz, are all based in the Department of Cultural Studies at the University of East London.

MODERN TIMES

Reflections on a century of English modernity

Edited by
Mica Nava and Alan O'Shea

London and New York

First published 1996
by Routledge
11 New Fetter Lane, London EC4P 4EE

Simultaneously published in the USA and Canada
by Routledge
29 West 35th Street, New York, NY 10001

Editorial material © 1996 Mica Nava and Alan O'Shea
Individual contributions © 1996 respective contributors

Typeset in Garamond by
Florencetype Ltd, Stoodleigh, Devon

Printed and bound in Great Britain by
Biddles Ltd, Guildford and King's Lynn

British Library Cataloguing in Publication Data
A catalogue record for this book is available from the British Library

Library of Congress Cataloguing in Publication Data.
A catalogue record for this book has been requested

ISBN 0–415–06932–7
0–415–06933–5 (pbk)

CONTENTS

FIGURES

NOTES ON CONTRIBUTORS

Sally Alexander is author of *Becoming a Woman and Other Essays* and an editor of *History Workshop Journal*. She is currently researching on the relations between psychoanalysis and history.

Andrew Blake is a historian and a musician, and has published *Reading Victorian Fiction* and *The Music Business*. He is currently completing a monograph on language and sport, and has also contributed to this book's companion volume *The Expansion of England: Essays on Race, Ethnicity and Cultural History*.

Peter Horne teaches and researches on sexuality and visual aesthetic practices, and is co-editor with Reina Lewis of *Outlooks: Lesbian and Gay Sexualities and Visual Culture*.

John Marriott researches on the cultural and political history of East London, and has recently published *The Culture of Labourism: The East End Between the Wars*.

Mica Nava was an editor of *Feminist Review* for ten years, co-edited *Gender and Generation* with Angela McRobbie and is author of *Changing Cultures: Feminism, Youth and Consumerism*. She is currently working on consumption and knowledge.

Alan O'Shea is Head of the Department of Cultural Studies at the University of East London and teaches and writes on the politics of popular culture.

Bill Schwarz is an editor of *History Workshop Journal* and *Cultural Studies*, and has written widely on British conservatism, nationalism, the state, popular culture and Latin American history. He is editor of the present book's companion volume, *The Expansion of England: Essays on Race, Ethnicity and Cultural History*.

ACKNOWLEDGEMENTS

We would like to thank our teaching and secretarial colleagues and our students in the Department of Cultural Studies at the University of East London for all their support during the production of this book. Particular thanks are due to Bob Chase and Couze Venn who participated with us in the development of the course from which the book emerged. We are grateful to Dick Hebdige and Jeffrey Weeks for their helpful comments on our early ideas, and to Claire L'Enfant at Routledge for her support and patience.

We wish to thank the copyright holders for their kind permission to reproduce the visual images in this book. Detailed acknowledgements are made with the captions. Every effort has been made to obtain permission reproduce copyright material. If any proper acknowledgement has not been made, we would invite copyright holders to inform us of the oversight.

INTRODUCTION

Modern Times: Reflections on a Century of English Modernity was conceived collectively by all the contributors; it was born out of the experience of team-teaching a final year course in Cultural Studies at the University of East London, which tackles aspects of cultural history (mainly in Britain) from the late nineteenth century to the present day reviewed through the prism of recent debates in cultural theory.

Much is made these days of the relations between research and teaching. But this is usually confined to the notion that lecturers teach more knowledgeably and enthusiastically, and develop a better sense of academic enquiry in their students, if they are active researchers. It is rarely acknowledged that engaged teaching itself stimulates research – particularly where team-teaching is involved. Our experience of team-teaching is that it is time-consuming, often frustrating and combative, but immensely stimulating and educative: it is a process of learning, and of the identification of problems which need further thought and research. Our course planning meetings have been the context, even more than our research seminars, in which we have most directly engaged with each other's interests and perspectives, and where we have read each other's seminal texts and reconsidered our own maps.

The germination of this book can be traced to a point in the mid-1980s, when we realised that we could no longer sustain a historical and theoretical framework based largely on a combination of Marxism and feminism. The debates on modernity and postmodernity were opening up too many questions, particularly about our major formative influences.

We introduced into our course the debate between Marshall Berman and Perry Anderson on how to conceptualise modernity and on the different historicisations of culture which follow from this.[1] We wanted students to be brought up against the highly contested nature of historical interpretation. Berman passionately argues for a general Western modernity and forces attention to popular experience – 'modernism in the streets' – while Anderson insists on the need to distinguish between different historical moments and national trajectories. From this debate we conceived a project

1

which would precisely hold onto both these emphases, and thus attempt, through a series of concrete studies, to specify more adequately the twentieth-century experience of modernity.

As ever, studies of the past are driven by present-day preoccupations. Although we share thematic and conceptual concerns, our different priorities, disciplinary backgrounds[2] and modes of engagement will be apparent. Some studies examine class- or gender-specific responses to new economic and social conditions (Alan O'Shea's first chapter, Mica Nava, John Marriott). Others work mainly on representational strategies; in Peter Horne's chapter, for example, this mode of research is clearly linked to the concerns of contemporary sexual politics. Some (such as Bill Schwarz's study of the hooligan crisis) focus on a particular historical moment; others (Andrew Blake's and Peter Horne's) span the past hundred years. There is no attempt at a comprehensive cultural history. We give particular attention to what we see as the formative moment of the turn of the twentieth century. But beyond that we were more concerned to propose new ways of understanding, to stimulate debate and further cultural and historical analysis, than to work towards a definitive account of the period.

As we wrote drafts, certain themes recurred, and consequent versions picked these out more clearly. Alan O'Shea's opening chapter is not quite an introduction in that it ultimately pursues its own line of argument; but it is introductory in two senses. It sets out why we see the late nineteenth century as constituting a break, a transitional moment within the history of modernity. It sketches the general features of this transition, both more generally in the West and in terms of the particular form it took in Britain. Secondly it reviews our debates on Berman and Anderson, and on the different ways of conceptualising modernity. In particular, it offers the first statement of the need to develop an understanding of the *psychic formation* of modernity. Berman argues that the experience of modernity is contradictory in that 'it pours us all into a maelstrom of perpetual disintegration and renewal, of struggle and contradiction, of ambiguity and anguish'.[3] But this still does not characterise how these 'possibilities and perils' are lived out by individuals or groups. It goes beyond simple notions of 'dominant' or 'bourgeois ideology', but does not get at the subjectivities of the modern experience. Several of us return to Raymond Williams' notion of a 'structure of feeling' as one which might deliver a more complex account of this subjectivity. Alan O'Shea's first chapter considers, among other things, whether it is possible to specify in general terms a structure of feeling which is characteristic of Western modernity in the twentieth century: in order to get at the restless, driven aspects of modern identity and the central role of fantasy, it turns towards psychoanalytic explanations. This is not at all accidental, but reflects the continued influence in the group of Sally Alexander and Mica Nava, and their insistence (in their different ways) that fantasy and the unconscious are essential components of any history of subjective experience. Their own chapters embody this concern: in Sally Alexander's exploration of memory and fantasy in relation to the transmission of sexual knowledge this psychoanalytic dimension is central; in Mica Nava's chapter, it allows her to reread Walter Benjamin's work anew, in the light of his own psychic history. It is not surprising that Peter Horne's contribution, focusing as it does on the construction of sexual identities, is also concerned with psychic formations. This dimension is more unusual in the contributions which are closer to the concerns of more conventional social history. John Marriott draws on Stallybrass and White's influential suggestion of an inextricable relation between disgust and desire in nineteenth-century bourgeois culture[4] to speculate on the unconscious fears and fascinations of the late Victorian bourgeoisie about the 'abyss' of London's East End. And even in his study of the moral panic around 'hooligans' at the turn of the century, Bill Schwarz is drawn to conclude that this phenomenon was partly driven by, and given its particular form by, a psychic energy, an erotics, which points to 'demons residing within the interior self' of the bourgeois commentators. Alan O'Shea's final chapter suggests that those who have been concerned with the politics of popular culture have paid insufficient attention to its often intense investment in 'something else', a fascination with excess, chaos, irresponsibility and risk.

All this points to the unfixity of modern culture, and, at the level of the individual, the impossibility of an untroubled, stable identity throughout this period. This brings into serious question the idea that the unfixing of identity is a defining characteristic of *late* twentieth-century 'postmodernity'. Still less secure is the related assumption that prior to the past twenty years or so, stability best characterised the cultural order.

This is not to say that stability was not sought. One recurrent theme which emerged during our writing was the role of *memory* (in various senses) in attempts to grasp and stabilise present identity. The general flurry to cope with modernity by 'inventing tradition' at the end of the nineteenth century is summarised in Alan O'Shea's first chapter, and explored in greater depth by Andrew Blake in relation to the construction of an English musical tradition. Alan O'Shea's second chapter examines elements of nostalgia in recent popular culture as one of the mechanisms of imagining a better life. Peter Horne explores how nineteenth-century homophile identities become possible by reworking myth, and then how this 'tradition' becomes one of the components of more recent camp identifications. These 'memorisations' all have ideological functions, though their politics vary and are forged in particular historical conjunctures. Sally Alexander uses oral testimony as a way of opening up what official memory represses, while also recognising that such testimony occupies 'that difficult borderline between fantasy and history'. One conclusion is that, within modernity, there is no escape from historicisation; in fact, it is only within

3

modernity that tradition is invented, and that the past is an essential tool for addressing the new.

This instability is inextricably linked to the transitoriness of life in the *city*. Most of the chapters are discussing an urban experience, or, more precisely, representations of that experience. John Marriott explores bourgeois perceptions of the East End of London; Bill Schwarz also investigates bourgeois anxiety – in this case of the urban street crime of the 'hooligans'. As we have noted, both propose that these constructions of urban 'others' suggest instability at the heart of these outwardly confident bourgeois identities. Other less conventional observers of the cityscape, in the figure of Baudelaire's '*flâneur*', the dandified aesthete and intellectual, taking note of the activities of the crowds on the pavement, are examined in some detail by Peter Horne and Mica Nava. The latter points to the implicit masculinity of this gaze, even in the work of that most respected commentator on modernity, Walter Benjamin. She also surveys women's participation in the urban crowd, particularly in relation to the rise of shopping, and the increased autonomy won by many women through this aspect of modernity – yet another cause of (male) bourgeois anxiety.

The history of these new, late nineteenth-century, forms of buying and consuming is related to the rise of publicity and to the imagery of the new mass media, where again a gender-specific experience can be discerned. Both Mica Nava and Alan O'Shea refer to the significance of the cinema as a new social space for women: there they enjoy not just new autonomy but also new representations of femininity – particularly of glamour, with its ambiguous offer of control over appearance, but largely through masquerades which address male sexual fantasy. Against these newly sexualised representations for women should be posed the massive ignorance, uncertainty and fear in matters of sexuality which Sally Alexander points to in the 1920s and 1930s.

The engagement with the new mass media was class-specific as well as gender-specific. Alan O'Shea's two chapters propose that the narratives of the mass media (and particularly those from Hollywood) have been a crucial resource in the formation of identities for the popular classes in Britain. This is not because these narratives stultify people into 'masses', but because they mull over the difficulties and contradictions of living in the modern world: they address the instabilities of modernity outlined above, and also offer utopian glimpses of transcendence over the often harsh and hierarchical bureaucratic rationalism which has dominated the twentieth century, and the hypocrisies which have emerged to patch over its failures. He also suggests that this popular engagement was intensified in Britain as a reaction to the anti-Americanism of its cultural elites, and their construction of an Englishness which excluded popular experience and culture. Andrew Blake's chapter examines precisely this latter process in the sphere of music.

Our writing does not dispassionately observe from the outside these processes of cultural formation. As Bill Schwarz has argued elsewhere,[5] the project of cultural studies itself, with which most of the contributors have been associated over the past two decades, is a modernising project, a critique of the high–popular divide in conceptualising culture, an argument for cultural inclusion – for the serious study of *everyone's* cultures – and for breaking down the barriers of traditional academic disciplines as a way of achieving this. This project has been at least partially successful: serious cultural analysis of this kind can now be found widely on television and in the press, and the interdisciplinarity forged by cultural studies is increasingly gaining footholds in formal education.

But that early work in cultural studies now looks overly insular, attempting to evaluate English cultural forms without paying adequate attention to England's external relations.[6] Firstly, although we are concerned with a nationally specific experience, this cannot be satisfactorily understood without also exploring the 'others' established by any construction of a national identity (whether colonised peoples, brash Americans, the dastardly Hun or 'enemies within' such as the 'hooligans'). Secondly, and paradoxically, a nationally specific history is necessarily an international history. This book's companion volume, *The Expansion of England: Essays on Race, Ethnicity and Cultural History* (London, Routledge, 1996), also written by colleagues in our Cultural Studies Department, and edited by Bill Schwarz, demonstrates how 'England' in the nineteenth century was made, politically and culturally, out of colonial relations. His chapter in the current volume, 'Black metropolis, white England', shows this process still at work in the middle of the twentieth century in the influences of the 'black Atlantic' on the internal structures of English modernity. Peter Horne demonstrates that a history of homophile identities has to escape national bounds (his narrative expands to Europe and the USA); while Andrew Blake points out that not only was Europe ransacked to produce an English classical music tradition, but also that the migration of musics across frontiers is ceaseless, and any notion of an English music, however fiercely policed, is always deeply unstable. And, as Alan O'Shea and Mica Nava both indicate, no account of twentieth-century British popular culture can ignore the central role of American forms and themes. Hence, no good account of the British or English experience can be simply 'internal', but should always bring out these interconnections. This does not mean that English modernity has no distinctive forms or histories, simply that it is not an insular experience, however much certain ideologies argue for this. Here we have strived to identify cultural formations which are specific to an English experience, while at the same time demonstrating the processes of transculturation out of which they are produced.

All the contributions concern themselves, to greater or lesser extent, with historical concreteness – with cultural forms and responses specific to particular moments. But some continuities emerge: social and cultural formations established in the late nineteenth century are seen to maintain a purchase well into the second half of the twentieth century. It is possible to identify a 'structure of feeling', with national inflections, of this phase of modernity. The two chapters that consider in some detail cultural transactions of the past fifteen to twenty years (Andrew Blake on music and Alan O'Shea on popular cinema) both suggest powerful new elements and substantial restructurings. But they also argue for the continuing purchase of earlier cultural legacies – in one case the imagery of 'Englishness', in the other the themes and forms of popular fantasy. If we have embarked upon a new phase in cultural history, the moment of 'modern times' will continue to supply significant parts of its repertoire. For this reason it remains important to tease out the often ambiguous or contradictory politics of these cultural forms and moments.

NOTES

1 M. Berman, *All That is Solid Melts into Air. The Experience of Modernity*, London, Verso, 1983; P. Anderson. 'Modernity and revolution', *New Left Review*, no. 144, 1984; M. Berman, 'The signs in the street', *New Left Review*, no. 145, 1984.
2 Several of us are historians or studied history and literature, but we also include a philosopher specialising in aesthetics, a sociologist, a classics graduate with postgraduate qualifications in cultural studies and a musician.
3 Berman, *All That is Solid*, p. 15.
4 P. Stallybrass and A. White, *The Politics and Poetics of Transgression*, London, Methuen, 1986.
5 Bill Schwarz, 'Where is cultural studies?', *Cultural Studies*, vol. 8, no. 3, 1994.
6 See, for example, Paul Gilroy, 'Cultural studies and ethnic absolutism', in L. Grossberg, C. Nelson and P. Treichler (eds), *Cultural Studies*, London, Routledge, 1992.

1

ENGLISH SUBJECTS OF MODERNITY

Alan O'Shea

> To be modern is to find ourselves in an environment that promises us adventure, power, joy, growth, transformation of ourselves and our world – and at the same time threatens to destroy everything we have, everything we know, everything we are.
>
> (Marshall Berman)[1]

> Take it easy and avoid excitement.
>
> (Psychiatrist's advice to Charlie Chaplin in his film *Modern Times*)

In the course of Charlie Chaplin's film *Modern Times* (1936) our hero works on an awesome, dehumanising production line and is made the guinea-pig for a time-and-motion experiment involving feeding the workers on the job; he is eventually sent crazy by the repetitive nature of his work and committed to a mental hospital. On his release he is told to 'take it easy and avoid excitement'; we are then offered a giddy montage of machinery, cars and jostling crowds, and Charlie is caught up in a freedom march, arrested as a communist agitator and serves a sentence in prison, where he mistakenly takes cocaine and finds himself preventing a riot. He is released into a world of mass unemployment, street riots and crime, and tries to be rearrested into the comparative tranquillity of prison. But he falls in love with an equally destitute young waif and his life is given purpose. He finds work as a nightwatchman in a big department store and at night his beloved sneaks in and they enjoy together the profusion of food, luxurious clothes and leisure goods. After further spells in prison, factory work and jobs as dancer and singing waiter, the couple's past catches up on them and they have to leave town. The heroine is in some despair, but, as the tune 'Smile' swells up on the soundtrack, Charlie persuades her to put a brave face on it; and laughing and holding hands they set off down a long country road into the dawn light, presumably towards a better future.

Throughout his films, the world of Chaplin is characterised by rapidly changing conditions, by repression and brutality, by corruption and hypocrisy, by insecurity and want and by dark despair; but also by the little man's spirit and resilience and an unquenchable aspiration for freedom, love, security, equality, communality, abundance and playfulness. These same themes, and this same tension recur again and again in Western popular cultural forms of the twentieth century. Marshall Berman, as the quotation at the head of this chapter indicates, has described the experience of this tension – between 'life's possibilities and perils' – as the condition of *modernity*.[2]

This chapter will attempt to characterise modernity as a popular structure of feeling and consider how it has been inflected in the context of twentieth-century England. While Berman sets a usefully provocative agenda, his argument also falls short at significant points. I will attempt to extend Berman's argument in two directions. Firstly, while Berman claims to deal with the (contradictory) experience of modernity, he fails to characterise how this is lived as a psychic formation: I will suggest how such a characterisation might be developed. Secondly, he has been rightly criticised for an over-universalistic concept of modernity. I will argue for historical differentiation: firstly, that modernity took on decisive new features in Western societies from the last decades of the nineteenth century; and, secondly, that there are crucial national differences. It is no coincidence that we begin with both a theorist and an instance of popular modernity which are American; the USA has undoubtedly had a paradigmatic role within twentieth-century Western modernity. Berman argues forcefully for a common experience of modernity; his case holds – up to a point – but his specific experience, as a New York left intellectual, inflects his account. I will argue not only that the English engagement with this structure of feeling developed certain unique features, but also that it was internally differentiated for different sections of the population.

MODERNITY

Berman's book did not come out of the blue: it is a contribution to a wide-ranging debate about the nature of modernity which has obsessed social and cultural theorists in recent years – all the more because some have argued that we (in the West) are witnessing a deep transformation best understood as the end of modernity. This is not the place for an exhaustive account of these debates, nor of the particular historical conditions which have given rise to them.[3] Nevertheless, a brief sketch is needed to make clear the particular orientation to modernity adopted in this chapter (and deployed in several of the chapters which follow).

Peter Osborne has usefully distinguished three senses of modernity: 'as a category of historical periodisation, a quality of social experience, and as an (incomplete) project.'[4] We will here be largely concerned with the first two senses and the relationship between them, but these cannot be fully discussed without reference to modernity as a 'project'. In this latter sense, modernity is understood as the visions of the Enlightenment philosophers, with their faith in a science which would enable mankind to harness nature and so remove scarcity and poverty; and in a human reason which would liberate us from the shackles of religious mysticism and superstition and produce a rational moral and political order – which would remove injustice and oppression and achieve universal freedom. These visions played, of course, a crucial role in the French Revolution and the struggle for an independent USA. If we focus on the history of these visions, we can identify the common ground between Liberalism and Marxism, popularly seen as polar opposites, as sharing not just the broad goals of the 'Enlightenment project', but many of the strategies for its realisation – industrialism, powerful economic systems, secular nation states and their expansion through militarism, the destruction of tradition and the rational (bureaucratic) organisation of society.[5]

Much recent debate has been concerned with the fate of this project. There is a powerful tradition of argument which asserts that it has failed: there is Max Weber's thesis that in actuality, the dominant legacy of the Enlightenment is 'instrumental rationality' which, far from liberating humanity, imposes the 'iron cage' of bureaucratisation on every sphere of social life – a scenario vividly portrayed in the labyrinthine nightmare of Kafka's novel, *The Castle*. Adorno and Horkheimer similarly argued that the will to 'master' nature could not be separated from the will to dominate human beings.[6] Lyotard extends these critiques to warn against the dominating tendency of any of the 'grand narratives' of modernity which claim a monopoly of the truth, whether the march of Reason, the class struggle or whatever.[7] Others have stressed their Eurocentrism and complicity with the oppressions of colonialism.[8] Against this, Habermas argues that the project of modernity can be rescued. He acknowledges the critique of such unreflective confidence in Reason and the dominance of an oppressive instrumental rationality, but argues that the progressive, emancipatory elements of the project have not been eliminated and can be reconnected to 'reason', so long as it is understood not as absolute and autonomous, but as a consensus to be achieved through historical struggle.[9]

Berman has some sympathy with such a political direction, but shifts the terms of the debate towards modernity as an *existing* mode of experiencing social life, and one which can be periodised historically. While for Habermas the achievement of the Enlightenment ideal lies somewhere in the future, Berman insists that an unremitting focus on future global achievement produces a deep pessimism which overlooks 'the signs in the street'; here he finds a spirit of modernity which is repeatedly being realised in the emancipatory practices of individuals and small groups, perhaps only local and provisional, but in which participants become the 'subjects of modernity', creating 'meaning, dignity and beauty for themselves'.[10]

Furthermore, while Habermas sees the spheres of science, morality and

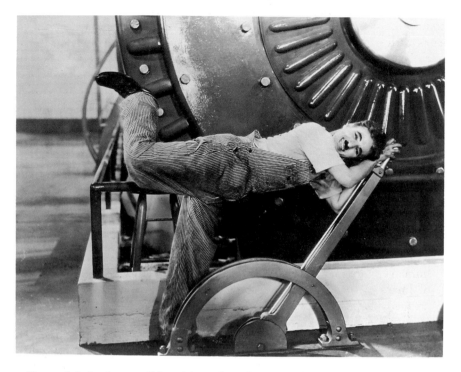

Figure 1.1 An irrepressible subject of modernity? Charlie Chaplin in *Modern Times*, 1936

Source: BFI stills, posters and designs

aesthetics as having been separated since the Enlightenment and the project of modernity as being concerned with their future reunification,[11] Berman's 'signs' are instances of their unification in the present: his categories of 'meaning, dignity and beauty' refer precisely to these spheres. In fact, for Berman the great beacons of modernity have been – Marx aside – artists rather than philosophers: Goethe, Dostoyevsky and Baudelaire, writers who grasped both sides of the dialectic of modernity, its 'possibilities and perils'.

Berman's account also suggests the dangers in conducting a debate, as Habermas and Lyotard do, solely at the level of epistemology and political philosophy. Their argument – particularly over the relative value of consensus versus heterogeneity – is of crucial political importance.[12] But there is a danger of idealism – of reaching political solutions through theoretical debate alone and without reference to complex historical situations and balances of forces. Berman's argument insists on a relation between these two. For him modernity is the experience of living through and making sense of the 'world-historical' social processes of 'modernisation' in terms of the 'variety of visions and ideas' provoked and nourished by these processes ('modernism'). For all our criticisms of Berman's work, it is this conception of modernity that the contributors to this book have chosen to work with – modernity not as an ideal, but as the practical negotiation of one's life and one's identity within a complex and fast-changing world.

We shall not, however, be concerned with 'the world' in general, but with modernity in a particular period and place, and with a particular moment of 'modernisation' – a term which, as the next section explains, needs to be handled with care.

MODERNISATION

Berman's account of *modernisation* is as follows:

> The maelstrom of modern life has been fed from many sources: great discoveries in the physical sciences, changing our images of the universe and our place within it; the industrialisation of production, which transforms scientific knowledge into technology, creates new human environments and destroys old ones, speeds up the whole tempo of life, generates new forms of corporate power and class struggle; immense demographic upheavals, severing millions of people from their ancestral habitats ... rapid and often cataclysmic urban growth; systems of mass communication dynamic in their development, enveloping and binding together the most diverse peoples and societies; increasingly powerful national states, bureaucratically structured and operated, constantly striving to expand their powers; mass social movements of people, and peoples, challenging their political and economic rulers, striving to gain control over their lives; finally bearing and driving all these peoples and institutions along, an ever-expanding, drastically fluctuating capitalist world market.[13]

I have quoted this passage in full for several reasons. Firstly, it begins to specify the economic, political, social and cultural co-ordinates of modernisation within which modernity has to be lived out. These will be scrutinised more closely in due course. Secondly, it offers a gloss on Marx's famous dictum that 'people make their own history but not of their own free will: not under conditions they themselves have chosen but under the given and inherited circumstances with which they are directly confronted'.[14] Berman's elaboration is that the conditions which restrict agency are not necessarily established structures holding us back, but can also be structural *processes* pulling us along pell-mell: it is turbulent movement, not structure, which characterises the condition of modernity, as Chaplin's *Modern Times* illustrates so effectively. This is one way in which a framing concept of modernity could renew and develop existing histories of subordinate groups. Many of these are couched in terms of struggles for change against imposed structures; if we reread that material in terms of

11

understanding such groups as trying to keep abreast of imposed *changes*, new insights will be gained.

Thirdly, though Berman's engagement with Marxism is strong, and the expanding capitalist market is seen as framing other changes, his account of 'modernisation' draws also on the sociologies of Durkheim, Weber, Simmel and Tonnies.[15] One of the benefits of framing historical analyses in terms of modernity rather than more conventional Marxist categories such as 'monopoly capitalism' is an expanded notion of social processes. One of the problems with Marxist historical work has been its unrelenting focus on class relations at the expense of dimensions of experience in which other identities (for example, gender, sexuality, locality, ethnicity, national identity and so on) have been central. More recent neo-Marxist work, drawing particuarly on Gramsci, has attempted to correct this tendency, but is open to a different criticism – that of an overemphasis on short-term political conjunctures.[16] This work, though important, has tended not to be concerned with the broader changes which occupied the classical sociologists – the changing forms of legitimation and belief, slower social and cultural changes in daily life, including responses to urbanisation, the growth of the nation state, bureaucracies and new forms of communication. 'Modernity' offers a framework in which capitalism and its class relations remain an important object of study, but in relation to these other dimensions of social life.

By embracing a notion of the social formation which draws upon these sociological concerns, as well as on Marxist and feminist work, we can achieve a more complex account of social experience. But we must also remember why Marxist and other historians have sharply criticised sociological models of change as idealist, and particularly as oversimplistic and universalistic models of 'before' and 'after', ignoring the often messy and uneven nature of socio-historical change, national and local specificities and the profoundly differentiated experience of different classed, gendered and ethnic social groups. Berman's concept of 'modernisation' has been criticised on these accounts by Perry Anderson – as suggesting an evenly unfolding and undifferentiated 'world-historical' process of development ('modernity can be said to unite all mankind'), and an equally sweeping notion of human evolution through the constant struggle to become the 'subjects as well as the objects of modernisation'.[17] While it is important to acknowledge that there are world-historical tendencies, Anderson is quite right to remind us of Marx's argument that historical change operates simultaneously at different levels and temporalities, and unevenly so, and that there are discontinuities as well as continuities. A model of this kind of complexity is Marx's own *The Eighteenth Brumaire of Louis Bonaparte:*[18] this analysis of a moment of profound crisis in the France of the early 1850s demonstrates the necessity of distinguishing between different levels – day-to-day political struggles, the recomposition of alliances within and between classes, the religious and ideological underpinnings of political struggle, the modification of the structures of the state, phases of economic crisis and recovery, and the longer-term processes of the development of capitalism. (We might now want to decentre capitalism as the only long-term point of reference, and add colonialism and patriarchal relations.) Each of these histories has its own time-scale and rhythm and yet they are articulated to and feed off each other. Starting from the apparent crisis and chaos of the moment, Marx orders his data into these different temporalities while also examining the relation between them. To see the moment simply in terms of 'modernisation' and another instance of the human struggle for emancipation would lose the *politics* of the analysis: Marx demonstrates how Bonaparte can gain power by winning the support of a class (the peasantry) whose demands had not been met by alternative contenders for power – a feat only possible in the context of a particular political, ideological and religious form-ation. And his reason for conducting this analysis is strategic – to reach an understanding of how (in Marx's case) socialist forces can intervene effectively to win power. If we are to learn from history how to achieve changes in our lives, it is not enough to examine what are 'constant' and 'everlasting' processes, we need to examine how, concretely, actions have changed outcomes.

MODERNISATION SINCE THE LATE NINETEENTH CENTURY

Berman traces back the rise of modernity over 400 years. While the structure of feeling Berman characterises has an earlier history, it has a deci-sively new resonance from the late nineteenth century, particularly in the way it begins to address subordinate social strata. This was a period of new or accelerated processes of modernisation – massive transformations in economic and industrial structures, in forms of production and consump-tion, in demographic movements, in communications, in political forms, in the arts and intellectual thought, and in popular culture. This section offers a brief sketch of these co-ordinates followed by a consideration of how they were experienced in more subjective terms.

This was the period in which the power and social significance of the individual ('bourgeois') capitalist industrialist declined before the central-ising tendencies of capital, the bringing together of 'capitals already formed' into cartels and monopolies on an international scale.[19] Lenin argued that this had become the characteristic mode of capitalism by the first decade of the twentieth-century. He also regarded it as inextricably bound up with the political structures of *imperialism* and the wars of the period, the Spanish–American War (1898), the Boer War (1899-1902) and the First World War.[20]

Although in this book, we focus on British/Western experience, this particular process was undoubtedly 'world-historical'. Just as early capitalism had received a kick-start from colonial plundering, this new phase was inextricably tied to imperialism: it depended on secure supplies of cheap raw materials from the colonies, and on international political power to extend and protect world markets. Modernity in fact had always been globalising. A colonial, and then imperial, relation constituted not only an economic condition for 'modernisation': the Enlightenment universalised European thought into an absolute, objective and unquestionable Reason. This is itself an imperialism, as are the related notions of 'progress' and 'development' for they depend on an implicit comparison: 'advanced' Europe against 'backward' colonised peoples. What is not adequately acknowledged by Berman is that 'modernisation' itself is a European perspective on history – it refers to forces set in motion by Europeans (including those who settled in North America and elsewhere) and suggests a periodisation based on these historical processes, rather than others. This is by no means to suggest that modernity is only a European experience: because of colonisation and trade, it constitutes an experience and a consciousness which has been successfully spread to many non-European peoples. As Hobsbawm points out, colonised elites realised very early on that they had to 'Westernise' or be displaced.[21] Is is not therefore surprising that many non-European attempts to achieve their own emancipation have drawn upon Enlightenment philosophies of rights and freedom, or have often been expressed through the discourses of European Christianity.[22]

Another international feature of monopolisation was the establishment of new locations for capitalist production, and the consequent mass migrations of the workforce to these locations, with all the social disruption, cultural displacement and loss, but also new possibilities, that entailed. An associated feature was the concentration of capital – larger-scale production, which in turn encouraged the growth of cities to accommodate the enlarged workforce. Many accounts of 'modern times', both intellectual and popular, lay a central emphasis on the experience of city life – a theme taken up in most of the chapters which follow.

This new epoch of industry was not possible without huge technological advances, and it is the period in which the individual 'inventor' is displaced by corporate investment in 'research and development'.[23] These technological shifts impacted on the modern experience in several ways. Firstly, the developments in electricity, steel production, coal–petroleum and the internal combustion engine helped to expand the scale of production. Secondly, the development of faster road, rail, sea and, eventually, air transport systems speeded up the travel of people and goods. Thirdly, developments in telegraphy, radio, optics, electricity and printing enabled more rapid long-distance communications and the growth of the new mass media, with massive cultural consequences.

David Harvey summarises the effect of these changes as an intense 'time–space compression':[24] lives are speeded up, not just at work, but by faster transport systems and easier communication, so the even leisure activities take less time. In addition, we should remember the process of *change itself* was fast, demanding rapid accommodation to new conditions. Transport and communication also compress *space*: both large migrations and mobility in the community/city are made easier. Increased and rapidly presented information of distant places, via newspaper, telegraph systems and the cinema (and soon radio) shrink the world. But, as far as space is concerned, to compression we have to add *dispersal*. Marcus points out that traditional ethnography has tended to work with a concept of community which mapped shared values and identities onto fixed localities, but that this conception does not operate within the more mobile arrangements of modernity (where we might have to travel, say, to our workplace, to visit friends or organisations to which we belong). Identity is thus dispersed across 'different places of different character', and this throws up new questions as to how people are to relate to space in the construction of their identities.[25]

Within the workplace, the labour process was 'rationalised', often along the lines of the 'scientific management' proposed in the USA by Frederick Taylor ('Taylorism'); that is, its dissection into separable components of specific physical actions, and a reassembly of these into the most efficient use of labour power. As Braverman puts it, capital seeks to displace labour as a subjective element and make it into an objective element in a productive process now conducted by management.[26] This was not just a technical intervention, but a human one: it required a new relation to work on the part of the worker – in Gramsci's terms, a new 'psycho-physical equilibrium'.[27] This meant intervention not just in the rhythm and form of the working day, but also in the process of the renewal of the worker. Both Taylor and Henry Ford, originator of the first large-scale production line, were very aware of this and Ford paid careful attention to the family life and leisure time of the (male) worker.[28] In particular, rampant sexuality and excessive drinking were seen as formidable dangers.

This transition should not be seen as simply the downward imposition of capitalist rationality. The attempts to establish this Fordist regime met with resistance, both organised and individual. It is this attempt to remake the worker that Chaplin is resisting in *Modern Times* – his refusal to abandon the subjective, fallible and funny but 'human' aspects of work and social life more generally. More structurally, inducements were needed to retain those workers whose skills were still required, and within an increased rate of exploitation it was possible to pay higher wages, and for workers to win demands for an improved standard of living. The American labour movement developed its strength in this same conjuncture, as did those of the European nations. The modernisation of capital has therefore to be seen as inextricably linked with the development of the modern aspirations of the working class.

Rationality and bureaucratic management do not only develop within industry. Economic and industrial developments on this scale necessarily involved the *state* – in providing the substructures of distribution and exchange (tariffs, transport, etc.), and in the supply and sustenance of labour (migration, urban planning and training) in investment, in moderating business cycles through fiscal and monetary policies and in managing the social consequences of change both at the level of industrial struggles and in terms of social provision for the casualties of change. In some ways this represents a concentration of state power, particularly if we link it to the development of military forces during the period, necessitated by the ever-intensifying competition for international resources and markets noted above. But we can also chart new phases in the development of 'technologies of the social' – methods of surveillance which disperse power by locating it in apparently objective systems of classification and documentation – what Foucault termed 'regimes of truth'. It is the period of the expansion of the medical profession into new spheres, of the emergence of psychiatry and of the 'scientific' measurement of intelligence, character traits and disorders.[29]

One reason why state power had to become consensual, rather than appear arbitrary, was because many of the long struggles for political inclusion came to fruition at this point: it was the period of the establishment of mass democracies. Again these struggles were fought differently in different countries.[30] In Britain, the franchise was widened in stages, but finally won for working-class men and some women in 1919, and for all women over 21 ten years later. Modernity, in the sense of a liberal-democratic 'project', achieved a big step forward. For the first time in history governments had to address and win the consent of the broad mass of society to secure their position – indeed to conceive of this broad mass as *part of* 'society'.

While in Britain this was achieved within a liberal-democratic framework, and within capitalism, the socialist/communist 'project', also conceived within Enlightenment goals, was embarked upon in the USSR, and almost in Germany too. Even where the socialist route was not taken, this 'other modernity' remained a vision which continued to inspire many on the left and also to perpetuate unease among those in power.

Nevertheless, while the masses achieved political inclusion, it was in many cases other kinds of inclusion that fired their imaginations and their sense of themselves – very often the vision of the 'good life' of a decent standard of living, a pleasant home and time to enjoy it, or perhaps more utopian fantasies of transcendence of hardship and labour – in other words, that aspect of modernity concerned with increased *consumption*. We have noted that the period from 1880 witnessed a decisive transformation into a new stage of capitalist production. However, it is arguable that the consequent transformations in the sphere of consumption constituted an even more fundamental break with the earlier period, for the major new market for the increased numbers of commodities produced was labour itself – the lower middle and working classes. While the new attempts to 'rationalise' capital and intensify labour can be seen as simply *continuing* the process begun by industrialism, this marks a very new relation of the popular classes to the economy. As soon as they become an identifiable market, their needs and desires can no longer be written off. Not only do markets have to respond to those desires, but in the long run the *cultures* which underpinned those needs have to be accommodated. In other words, popular aspirations and pleasures gradually become a concern not just for capital but for 'society' more generally. The significance of this for English cultural history is the theme of the final part of this chapter (p. 26).

This account has so far remained at the level of general tendencies in the advanced capitalist regimes of Europe and the USA from the end of the nineteenth century. But as soon as we begin to look at more specific transformations, national differences open up. For example, the most rapidly modernising nation of this period was widely agreed to be the USA, so much so that Gramsci labelled the processes of rationalisation of industry and the state described above as 'Americanism'.[31] Wollen notes also the Soviet interest in these processes of 'scientific management', and quotes Pirandello's (anxious) perception of America as 'a new beacon of civilisation', concluding that, in general, 'Americanisation stood for true modernity, the liquidisation of stifling traditions and shackling life-styles and work-habits.'[32]

Again, if one probes further the development of state power, specific national histories come into play, particularly as the period is marked by intensely nationalistic ideologies, seen at their extreme in Germany and Italy, but also virulent in Britain. In the light of their very different national histories and cultural traditions[33] It is remarkable that by the 1950s the leading European states, Britain, France, Germany and Italy, had reached rather similar 'mixed economy' models with 'managed' industrial relations plus welfarism.

But before examining the English route into and through twentieth-century modernity, I want to ask whether it is possible to identify a specific 'structure of feeling' across these societies within this period of history.

MODERNITY AS LIVED

It is important to specify what unites the Western 'subjects of modernity' as well as what differentiates them. After all, one of the features of modernity has been its global aspiration; and one of the particular features of this century has been the internationalisation of culture – or rather, of *some* cultures.

The above account of modernisation already necessarily includes reference to the forms of consciousness which accompanied those changes. Firstly, it is important (and difficult from a late twentieth-century perspective) to recover the *optimism* of the early twentieth century – the belief that the emancipatory elements of the 'project' of modernity were achievable through both political and technical means. The confidence in 'instrumental rationality' – the drive for greater efficiencies in the production of what we need to live on and in the ordering of social life to best achieve this – was not simply embedded in economic, industrial and social institutions, it was a conscious and widely accepted value. Moreover, this optimism was not inextricably tied to a capitalist route. We have noted the admiration for the USA as the modernising society *par excellence*. But discourse of 'efficiency' was not seen as particularly capitalist: the British Fabians reconstituted socialism in terms of 'national efficiency', and the British left of the 1920s and 1930s looked to the Soviet rationalisation of the economy as the paradigm of modernisation.

The immense confidence in technology that prevailed at the beginning of the century is hard to imagine after the many technological disasters of the century. Carolyn Marvin documents how electricity, for instance, was not only understood in terms of industrial efficiency, but as transforming communications so radically as to remove all obstacles to human unity, and even invested with magical healing powers.[34] Technological advance won enthused support by feeding futuristic fantasies: the frequency and scale of lavish spectacles of electric light in American cities at the end of the nineteenth century were such that Marvin concludes, 'In sum, the electric light was a public spectacle before it was anything else.'[35] In Britain, Tony Bennett has documented the immense popularity of 'the latest from America' in Blackpool's fairground rides in the same period.[36] This fetishism of technology was severely dented by the experience of the First World War, and dystopian representations begin to proliferate from the 1920s.[37] But even as late as the closing stages of the Second World War, British politicians were able to appeal to a confidence in human reason and sense of justice and in technological advance as the basis for a new kind of 'settlement' for the post-war period.[38]

In Western societies, the discourses of technology and rational progress were powerfully represented in what might be called a petit bourgeois form: the idea of self-improvement, a better standard of living, perhaps also accompanied by upward social mobility. In Britain this dream of stability, comfort and a gradual increase in consumption has been imagined in suburbia; in the USA it was located in the small townships of 'middle America' ('the American dream'). This discourse is closely tied into 'instrumental rationality' – it is the form of happiness to be achieved through it. But this inflection of it is firmly located within capitalism and an ideology of individualism and familialism. It is the discourse which Marxist criticism has understood as the 'bourgeois' or 'dominant ideology' that has sub-ordinated the masses to capitalism. But one of the problems with this conception is that it is an overrationalistic and incomplete account of twentieth-century Western culture. Modernity is not one discourse, but the site of intersection of several, which do not sit easily together.

Even the sense of 'being modern' and embracing the new can come into conflict with the discourse of betterment. Certainly, the modernist artists had no interest in comfort and security. The Futurists, for example, may have celebrated technological innovation, but as heralding in a world of movement and 'dynamic sensation'; they sought to paint 'the simultane-ousness of the ambient . . . the dislocation and dismemberment of objects, the scattering and fusion of details, freed from accepted logic'.[39] Modernist movements embodied what Daniel Bell has called a 'rage against order': the Dadaists, for example, did not just reject traditional conventions and meanings, but asserted the impossibility of *any* sense. However centrally concerned with form, most modernists were also concerned to characterise the society they lived in – often as transitory and fragmented. Particularly influential has been the perspective of Baudelaire's 'observer, philosopher, *flâneur*, call him what you will . . . he is the painter of the passing moment and of all the suggestions of eternity that it contains' – both its exhila-rating aspect and its dark side – 'the savagery that lurks in the midst of civilisation'.[40] 'Modernity', he claimed, 'is the transient, the fleeting and the contingent; it is the one half of art, the other being the eternal and the immutable.' Simmel offers a very similar if more sociological version of the bustling streets full of strangers and of the 'fortuitous fragments' of their encounters. Simmel argued that this experience of metropolitan modernity replaces the individual's inner security by a 'secret restlessness', a 'helpless urgency'.[41]

We are a long way from 'rationality' here – in a Romantic world of excitement, sensation and restlessness – a structure of feeling which does not easily fit with conformity to 'progress'. Artists do not always represent a broader social experience; we have to be cautious about accepting, as Raymond Williams put it, 'the metropolitan interpretation of its own experience as universal'[42] – and particularly that of the metropolitan artists and intellectuals at a time when their lives and values were being trans-formed more rapidly than anyone else's in the aesthetic ferment of Vienna, Paris, Berlin and St Petersburg. No wonder that for these artists 'the fleeting fragment' and 'violent sensation' were all that was left to cling to. Nevertheless it is clear that these formulations caught wider social currents: it was a period of massive immigration into cities and of concomitant urban upheaval; and how to live, and give meaning to your lives, in such conurbations was an obsessive theme of popular culture too. In popular films, for example, we find a repeated focus on the excite-ment and 'restlessness' of the bustling city life and the romance of chance encounters, as well as narratives of degradation and corruption. These images had spread beyond the avant-garde artist and become part of a broader currency.

To explore further these 'unruly' dimensions of modernity – the desire for excitement, risk and the unknown – we will do well to take the instance of the cinema. Its early conception as a 'dream palace' is entirely appropriate: perhaps its major function has been to enable us to 'dream' about how to live in the modern world. Kracauer reports on early German research in behavioural psychology which suggests that the very technology of the cinema (movement on a large, bright screen) induces physiological responses in the spectator which 'lure him into dimensions where sense-impressions are all important' and 'make one renounce the effort to use ones mental and superior capacities'.[43] He goes on to argue that these factors, along with the darkness which reduces our contact with actuality, are the bases for seeing the medium as a sort of drug which fulfils for cinema-goers not a desire to look at a particular film, but 'to be released for once from the grip of consciousness, lose their identity in the dark'. Such a stark stimulus–response model is not sustainable, and yet people do report their experience of the cinema in similar terms – of being 'lost' in a film, as in a dream.

But if people do use the cinema as 'escape', it is important to ask *from* what and *to* what are people are escaping. Kracauer considers the 'safety-valve' argument that the working-class audience went to the cinema to imagine the upward mobility and life free from want which they were unable to achieve in reality; but he is more persuaded by audience research which suggested that the major attraction of the cinema was that it offered us the opportunity to be in 'sensuous and immediate' contact with 'life' – 'life in its inexhaustibility'. He elaborates by quoting two early formulations by respondents: 'the glistening wheel of life which spins around eternally', and 'the pulse of life itself . . . and its overwhelming abundance, so immeasurably superior to our imagination'. This would imply the audiences' sense of their own daily experience as banal, outside the main current, with 'life' passing it by. Kracauer further suggests that the cinema offers, alongside that sensuous contact, some sense of control in the face of 'the increasing difficulty of the individual to account for the forces, mechanisms and processes which shape the modern world, including his own destiny. . . . In the cinema "one grasps all of it" ' (as one respondent put it).[44]

These formulations are full of insight into the different ways in which (Western) modernity has been lived during the twentieth century. The first and the last have already been discussed – the discourse of betterment and the search for control and identity through understanding. But between these we have an echo of Baudelaire's enchantment with the 'life' and 'abundance' of the city, but one which reveals it as an idealised, 'glistening' image. It brings out the *romanticism* of both intellectual and popular images

20

of modernity – the drive towards 'self-infinitisation' (which Berman identified in the figure of Faust – a drive doomed to failure because it is utopian), the reaching after the sublime – that which lies just beyond what we can imagine.[45] It is crucial fact of modernity that this version of 'something better' challenges the more 'sensible' aspiration of betterment: it is a discourse which produces dissatisfaction with the actualities of daily life, and undermines the notion of 'a decent life' as boring, limited, routine, conformist, soulless and to be transcended.

Berman grasps much of this. He speaks of

> the contradictory forces and needs that inspire and torment us: our desire to be rooted in a stable and coherent personal and social past, and our insatiable desire for growth – not merely for economic growth but for growth in experience, in pleasure, in knowledge, in sensibility – growth that destroys both the physical and social landscapes of our past, and our emotional links with lost worlds; our desperate allegiances to ethnic, national, class and sexual groups which we hope will give us a firm 'identity' and the internationalisation of everyday life – of our clothes and household goods, our books and music, our ideas and fantasies – that spreads all our identities all over the map; our desire for clear and solid values to live by, and our desire to embrace the limitless possibilities of modern life and experience that obliterate all values; the social and political forces that propel us into explosive conflicts with other people and other peoples, even as we develop a deeper sensitivity and empathy towards our ordained enemies and come to realise, sometimes too late, that they are not so different from us after all.[46]

This statement persuasively catches the contradictory impulses of modernity. It takes our understanding of twentieth-century Western culture much further than concepts such as 'bourgeois ideology'. Berman's depiction is identifiably Western (particularly the self-infinitising urges associated with European Romanticism), and clearly tied into capitalist consumer culture. But he brings out the *in*stability of modern culture, its discontents and insecurities as well as its unreflective identification with 'Progress'.

What he does not do is develop this initial statement, and explore how people live with these contradictory impulses – that is, explore the *psychic formation* of modernity. Instead, perhaps in an effort to provide hope amidst the gloom of much recent left writing, his instances of personal inventiveness, courage and renewal in the most difficult circumstances smack of a rather undialectical humanism – the celebration of a rather undifferentiated and unquenchable 'human spirit' which appears to belong to a utopian humanism rather than to a historical materialism. I earlier distinguished between modernity as a political 'project' and modernity as a complex mode of experience. Berman manages to (con)fuse the two through this humanism, for the people of his anecdotes embody precisely those Enlightenment ideals of creativity, rationality and a sense of justice! This is not to deny his examples of courage in the face of adversity, but they are better understood as historically achieved, out of determinate circumstances rather than out of an ahistorical 'humanity'. If these values are located in culture rather than human nature, this guards against complacency. They *can* be realised, but there is no guarantee that they will win out in the end; and even to sustain them in the culture requires constant effort.

An influential attempt at greater historical specificity is Daniel Bell's thesis (strongly influenced by the work of Simmel) that since the mid-nineteenth century, Western sensibility has changed from one dominated by rationality, restraint and future planning into one 'open to immediacy, impact, sensation' in which particularly sights, but also sounds, have become central in the production of meaning and identity: 'today, the "dominant outlook" is visual'.[47] This argument depends not just on the proliferation of images produced by the mass media and advertising, but also on broader changes in temporal and spacial relations: modern urban life 'provides a preponderance of occasions for people to *see*, and *want* to see (rather than read or hear) things'; the city itself is an environment of visual impression. Distance is 'eclipsed', physically by the new ability to travel or communicate across huge distances, and aesthetically and psychically by the techniques of modern visual cultures in pulling the spectator into the action or emotion. Thus hedonism displaces the Protestant ethic, the spiritual underpinning of the instrumental rationality of capitalism. For this reason, the massive expansion in the consumption of goods in the Western world is not just a matter of economics: consumption decentres other social activities in the formation of cultures and identities. But in this process a culture has been created which is at odds with competitive, rationalised production. This account at least poses a crisis within modern culture. But, because Bell writes from the side of contemplation and rationality, regretting their decline, he shows little interest in the subject-matter of 'impact and sensation': it is seen as a loss of perspective on modernity, rather than as possibly a different kind of engagement with it.

How then can we explore how individuals and groups live out this tension between the desire for rationality, 'progress', betterment and stability and the urge to innovate and to transcend the everyday? As Berman himself notes, this was precisely the problem Freud tackled in his later writing, particularly from the time of the First World War.[48] He set out to explain the destructive forces which burst out in the heart of 'civilisation', and became increasingly aware that the structures of the unconscious and psychic disorders are formed in relation to the particular nature of 'civilisation' – the social order of modernity. We have seen how the discourse of rationality was increasingly imposed on all spheres of social life. At the level of the individual, this discourse calls for a stable, unified, rational self-identity which requires us to behave in a predictably consistent way within social norms; this expectation becomes embedded in the law, political processes and the institutions of social life. Freud argued that the rationalisation of modern life is only achieved through rigid moralities which require intense repression and internalisation of both sexual and aggressive drives, and thus at great psychic cost. As we have seen (p. 20), this pressure towards a narrow conformity can be resisted culturally – through the romantic, Faustian 'rage against order'. Most of us, however, only have the strength to externalise this mode – to act it out in our daily lives – on rare occasions. Mostly we accept the cost of repression, and only act it out in fantasy, or sublimate it more deeply – with the result that neurosis, guilt and anxiety become typical character traits of modernity.[49]

There have been various attempts to develop Freud's argument and to specify this instability of identity more historically. Richard Sennett argues that during the past 150 years we have witnessed a gradual diffusion of the personal into the public sphere, with the result that a new form of narcissistic individualism has developed.[50] This phenomenon derives from social mobility and the increasing difficulty of sustaining a secure identity in the public sphere – of knowing your social standing in relation to the strangers you meet, and the increasing importance of outward appearance as fixing identity. As a consequence, the public sphere becomes more threatening and 'impersonal' – particularly the large-scale urban developments of concrete and steel. The yardstick against which society is measured becomes personal life – the private sphere, in which personality can be expressed – where one can 'be oneself'. Sennett argues that not only does this terror and evasion of the public sphere have serious effects on social interchange and community, but also leads to an overinvestment in the private sphere, in personal relationships and domestic life – in massive anxiety about whether such relationships are fulfilling.

Christopher Lasch similarly argues that a powerful psychic formation has arisen in which anxiety about personal adequacy dominates – a 'culture of narcissism':[52] even being 'normal' isn't enough; mediocrity has to be shunned – we all have to be special in some way. This sustains the cult of celebrity, narcissistic fantasies of fame and disdain for the banality of ordinary people. This argument usefully helps us to connect the desire for identity with the urge to refuse and transcend even the idealised 'decent' life of suburbia. In this pessimistic reading, the individualism of the Protestant Ethic, the personal relationship with God, has gradually been transformed, over 300 years, into a secular neurosis: contemporary dissatisfactions and desires are seen as the expression of extreme personal anxiety, of the collapse of social relations, rather than of a healthy critique of them. The consumer and advertising industries are understood in terms of feeding off this condition of narcissism and helping to reproduce it. They promote consumption as the solution to anxiety and dissatisfaction, simultaneously validating and accentuating that anxiety. These arguments pinpoint some of the key features of modern societies, and provide useful insights about the widespread unhappinesses to be found in affluent societies. But they are ultimately one-sided and functionalist: the subject is helplessly caught up and reproduced by consumer capitalism.

A psychoanalytic approach need not lead us in this direction. Freud chose to analyse the most depressing features of modern life; he certainly saw living with 'civilisation' as often psychically painful. Nevertheless, for him the subject was never finally fixed, but remained the site of unresolved struggles. In fact, within psychoanalytic theory the drive to consume repeatedly can be understood as a way of living with contradictions, dissatisfactions and desires that we cannot resolve; we tend to consume material which plays across these contradictions, such as fantasy narratives of romance or of male power, or purchases which promise transformation – fashion items, drinks, holidays and so on.[52] It is important to note that the drives Freud posited as repressed by civilisation, the sexual and the aggressive, have been the two most central themes of twentieth-century Western popular culture. For instance, one common way of managing the repetition and monotony of daily work and social routine and investing it with transcendental possibility has been to sexualise it – to imagine the possibility of a romantic encounter which brings one into direct contact with 'life' (as opposed to just plain life). This has been noted of popular narratives for women,[53] but is also to be found in masculine narratives (in both romantic and more erotic forms). Not only does sexuality provide an escape from tedium, it is also the site of greatest anxiety and conflict. Of all the possible ways of challenging social convention, transgressive sexuality has been one of the most disturbing, and, especially for women, one of the most risky. Particularly in male psychic scenarios the sexual and the aggressive become intertwined. Klaus Theweleit's study of male fascist soldiers argues, following Freud, that capitalist modernity has presided over a rigid channelling of pleasure into deep and violent fantasies which, in a patriarchal context, construct the female body as 'other'.[54] Analyses of colonial discourse suggest a similar articulation of aggressive and sexual impulses in relation to the colonised (black) body.[55] James Donald points to related manifestations of 'the impossibility of identity' within modernity: the popular fascination with the boundaries of identity, the 'monstrous', the grotesque, the uncanny – creatures which are neither one thing nor another – vampires, werewolves, cyborgs, Dr Jekyll/Mr Hyde; but also some of the paranoid features of popular culture, 'its racism, its violent misogyny, and its phobias about alien creatures and enemies within'.[56]

These may seem depressing phenomena, but the fact that identity is only ever provisionally resolved means that the social formation is not fixed either. To construct identity we have to establish who we are not, to invent an excluded 'other'; this 'other' not only reassures us about who we are, but also fascinates the more adventurous tendencies within us.[57] Thus these forms do not simply fix us to the existing social formation; they continue to offer glimpses of something else. Our subjectivity is thus never settled: we are never fully socialised,[58] and our incompleteness acts as a drive for continued innovation and transformation. The sublimated 'rage against order' simmers away and can energise the emancipatory activities Berman celebrates as well as feed more negative aggressive acts or impossible romantic fantasies.

Thus, we may embrace modernity in the hope of achieving a more comfortable standard of living, but it could equally be to liberate ourselves, at least at a personal level, from conformity. Or, perhaps most often, an uncertain embracing of both. To return again to the example of the cinema: oral history suggests that many young women of the 1920s and 1930s used the cinema as relief from the mundaneness and labour of daily life; they found the Garbo or Ginger Rogers in themselves, and with a jaunty walk and in home-made imitations of the latest fashion, were able to sustain a more positive sense of self than was available from elsewhere.[59] Michelle Mattelart has suggested that fashion is 'an aspiration and reconciliation of all women, usurping the category of democracy, or using democracy as an alibi'[60] – that is, emancipated fashion can stand in for political emancipation. But we should be wary of passing political judgement. Whether such an enhancement of one's identity contributes, in however small a way, to an eventually more permanent empowerment, or whether it should be seen as a culture of consolation, making powerlessness easier to live with, is never a straightforward question, or one that can be answered in the abstract, but only in the context of other transformations. For example, in Robert Roberts' autobiographical account of Salford life at the beginning of this century, he declares that, with the advent of the cinema, 'for us in the village the world suddenly expanded.'[61] He argues that the constraining Victorian moralism, and the petty ranking of each family and individual along degrees of respectability, which had policed his community since the last decades of the nineteenth century, was decisively 'cracked' in this period. 'Life had broadened in scope; a certain parochialism had gone forever.' He saw women in particular as benefiting: it was a means of getting out of the house both with their husbands and on their own. This change is also found in Ewen and Ewen's research on the experience of immigrant women in New York at the beginning of this century, They note that 'while immigrant parents resisted their daughters' participation in most of the recreational opportunities of the city, *everyone* went to the movies', and that this activity displaced the male sphere of the saloon as the main sphere of cheap leisure.[62] It is clear that the rise of cinema-going had complex effects on existing daily life. In particular, there is a significant shift in the sexual division of how the public and private spheres are occupied. Women gain a broader territory of activity. So do young people: for the cinema becomes possibly the major site for courtship – dark, relatively unsupervised, warm and comfortable.

But Roberts' account also reveals that he cannot isolate this experience of the cinema from that of other significant changes, particularly the impact of the First World War. He also connects this 'broadening' to the upsets in family life caused by the war and the control which passed to many women, to the widening of the horizons of those who went to fight, to the industrial restructuring for the war effort and the improvement in wages this brought. This is not to play down the significance of the mass media or of any of the other powerful new institutions of modernity, but it is to argue that their effects, the way modernity is 'lived' through them, have general and specific aspects, both of which need to be held onto in historical reconstruction.

To sum up this section, we should understand the structure of feeling of modernity as being formed from contradictory discourses: of rationalist modernisation; of personal betterment and a stable life; but also of emancipation from stifling and oppressive structures, often coupled to an adventurous embrace of the new, and sometimes pushed to the limits of self-destruction; all somehow held together in a psychic formation which features (incompletely repressed) aggressive and sexual desires and existential anxiety – an unstable subjectivity in an unstable society.

THE ENGLISH ROUTE

The danger of attempting to characterise a general Western modernity as lived is that one ends up specifying no one's experience concretely enough to be useful. For example, little has been said about fascism: it was not, after all, a general experience; nevertheless, any account German or Italian modernity would have to give an absolutely central place.

If anything, my 'abstract' account may fit the USA best for several reasons. Firstly, I have accepted the view of the USA as the paradigmatic example of modernity. Also I have paid particular attention to consumer capitalism and the popular engagement with American cultural forms. I have also drawn heavily on American theoretical sources – particularly that unapologetic New Yorker, Marshall Berman.

Because of the common language and the particularly close interactions, culturally and politically, it might be assumed that the British experience was close to that of the USA. However the differences are just as striking as the similarities, and stem in part from the *difficult* cultural relation between the two nations. This final section explores the 'peculiarities'[63] of the British route through twentieth-century modernity.

Firstly, a number of commonplaces.[64] Britain's early capitalisation of agriculture and industrialisation, and its annexation of the largest world empire had a number of significant effects for this period. At the turn of the century it was the greatest exporter of industrial products and importer of raw materials and food; it dominated shipping and world financial and commercial services, all protected by a massive navy. This industrial and imperial history, plus the continuity of its political institutions, gave Britain a class structure rather different from the rest of Europe – an incomparably large urban working class, a small peasantry and an aristocracy which had managed to survive better than elsewhere, with footholds in government, imperial administration and business.

But, at least from the 1880s, no aspect of Britain's privileged position was secure. The history of the British state in this period illustrates the profound difficulties of accommodating the changing economic, industrial and political conditions.[65] Internally a modernising rationalism was strongly in evidence, with a drive for 'national efficiency' supported on the left by the new Fabian movement. It was also the moment when Britain's world supremacy came under question, particularly from Germany. The crises in Britain's international and imperial relations are seen in the uncertainties and internal divisions over tariff reform, Irish Home Rule, the Boer War and the First World War.

It has long been argued that the particular cultural response to this conjuncture was decisive in fixing a political and cultural formation which has persisted through the twentieth century.[66] One element of this response was a virulent xenophobia – particularly directed towards European competitors, and an associated 'popular imperialism' – a massive proliferation of discourses claiming the superiority of the English character in its imperial role and representing the colonised peoples as primitive, evil or inscrutable.[67] This strategy of constructing a national unity against external 'otherness' was carefully orchestrated. The British coronation ceremony of 1902 was praised as expressing 'the recognition, by a free democracy, of a hereditary crown, as a symbol of the world-wide domination of their race'.[68] Such discourses of belonging were crucial, particularly as they offered a place within the English nation even to those who had not yet won political franchise, not to speak of economic security. They have also undoubtedly persisted through the twentieth century.[69] But Anderson picks out another aspect of the representation of national identity as more distinctive – the discourse of hierarchy. Here, the monarchy is crucial as the head of a *stratified* social order; in particular, 'the reflux of imperialism at home not only preserved but reinforced the already pronounced personality type of the governing class: aristocratic, amateur and "normatively" agrarian'.[70] The power of this class to define the nation has resulted in a 'suffocating traditionalism'.

More recent research has corroborated this element of his argument. The last decades of the nineteenth century saw many institutions restructured from a local to a national scale. Among these were commercial concerns such as banks, the distributive trades, the press and the new leisure industries, but also churches and voluntary organisations such as the Boy Scouts and the YMCA.[71] It was also the period of the establishment of many key national cultural institutions, for instance, art galleries, orchestras and music colleges, of English as an academic and school discipline, the *Oxford English Dictionary* and the *Dictionary of National Biography*. It has been established that the ideologies of 'Englishness' produced through these institutions constituted an 'invention of tradition' – past greatness, Britain as the cradle of freedom and order and as the repository of maturity and wisdom – and a particularly elitist account of the 'national culture'.[72]

This discourse is just as much a response to the processes of rapid modernisation as the popular excitement with new technologies. Its motivation can be explained in terms of Anderson's argument about the continuity of English institutions, allowing the self-perpetuation of what Gramsci called 'traditional intellectuals' – intellectuals not closely connected to the 'decisive' classes (at this point, the industrial or financial bourgeoisie or the working class).[73] As Raymond Williams pointed out long ago, these intellectuals were diverse in social position and political stance (some were reactionary, others liberal and reforming), but they all tended to be critical of the processes of modernisation, and particularly of the devastation caused by industrialisation; and in most cases they tended to look to the (rural) past for models of a better society.[74] One function of this discourse was undoubtedly, even if often unconsciously, to preserve positions of privilege though this period of change. This can be seen in the way this discursive strategy constructed a national identity through *cultural differentiation*. For example, 'English literature' was installed in the educational curriculum in such a way that it simultaneously constructed an 'Englishness' and prescribed what should and should not be read; that is, it installed a particular 'cultured' form of nationalism. This discourse continues into the twentieth century and can be discerned in the interwar period in Leavis' revaluation of English literature and John Reith's establishment of the BBC.[75] This latter instance is highly contradictory: it is 'modernising' in its embrace of new technologies and its goal of educating the whole nation for democratic citizenship; but it also sought to impose an 'English tradition' as bulwark against *popular* modernism – the popular press, advertising, fashion, film melodramas and detective fiction.

As such material was increasingly imported from the USA, the English culturalism became more virulently anti-American.[76] So While Gramsci and others looked to the USA for the future, little such enthusiasm is evident among English intellectuals, then or since. The view of the USA as a brash, new society without a cultural heritage and as offering a threat to the 'best' cultural traditions was widespread among English cultural elites. Since the English socialist tradition also regarded the USA with hostility, it is not surprising that this anti-Americanism has permeated cultural commentary in England through to the present day.

These discourses of 'Englishness' have been extensively documented, but significantly less attention has been given to their particular effect on the ways in which the popular classes have inhabited modernity. Let us now look at popular and, in particular, working-class routes through the early twentieth century.

The virulence and pervasiveness (and continuing legacy) of the imperialist and xenophobic discourses of the beginning of the century have already been noted. They did not however head off powerful working-class industrial and political movements (though they may well have inhibited the depth of their support). The industrial struggles between the end of the First World War and the mid-1920s were the most intense in Britain's history, and the long struggle for political franchise was won for men over 21 and women over 30 in 1918, and for women between 21 and 30 ten years later. Despite the unrest of this period, it is now generally accepted that the popular classes in Britain did not for the most part live their modernity through a militantly political identity, even while remaining very conscious of class difference.[77] As Hobsbawm puts it, 'what counted for them was not union or class party, but neighbours, family, patrons who could do favours or provide jobs'.[78] But against those accounts of working-class history which have focused either on the activist minority or on the quiescent, apolitical, 'corporate' majority, he stresses that these two modes are never entirely separated: 'the culture of the plebeian poor . . . shaded over into that of class consciousness'.

Thus for most people, for most of the time, their engagement with the modernising world was not through a class politics, but rather through those discourses of modernity identified earlier – particularly the desire for material betterment – for a 'decent life', but also the more romantic idea of transcending the routines of daily life and becoming 'something special'. In other words the desire to consume loomed larger than the desire for political power. However, the process of achieving this kind of inclusion has been extremely slow and is far from completed now. Hobsbawm states that, while there was a gradual, if very patchy, rise in the standard of living for the working class during the first half of this century (by 5 per cent on average) and while industry, unevenly and often belatedly, turned to the production of commodities for the mass market, the working class cannot be said to have entered the 'consumer society' until the 1950s.[79] This may be the case in terms of actual spending on consumer goods, but it can be argued that its *ideological* incorporation was much more rapid: firstly, the widespread *aspiration* for consumer goods can be discerned much earlier (window shopping, for example, was a popular activity); secondly, the working class did, early in the century, become major consumers of the new mass media and capitalised leisure activities – publishing, the cinema, the recording industry, radio, dancing, fashion. It is in these spheres that modernity in the sense of being self-consciously 'modern' comes into its own. And the evidence seems to be that the process of popular inclusion happened more rapidly here than in other spheres of consumption.

Even though the British working class still had its own distinct, uncapitalised and even internally differentiated leisure activities around the turn of the century, the process of commodification proceeded inexorably. Wild's account of this in Rochdale is illuminating.[80] He documents the uneven transition from local, self-made, church- or pub-based activities (outings, parties, sports, concerts, bazaars)[81] to an increasingly commercial organisation of day trips, holidays, dances and, above all, cinema shows. And because of the reduction of working hours and improved transport, there is an overall increase in the amount of time which can be spent on leisure. He notes that the ownership of these enterprises is increasingly oligopolistic, that they tend to be based more and more on the town centre, to be increasingly specialised around one activity (unlike the fairs, circuses and variety shows they displaced) and to be scheduled events with a fixed and known starting and finishing time. The parallels with the modernisation of industry are clear – in other words, concentration, centralisation and Fordism – structured leisure to fit a structured working life. Similarly, the removal of popular control – the shift from *self-made* events to *provided* ones – is homologous to process of deskilling which Braverman has argued is the major tendency of the labour process this century.[82] This reorganisation of leisure, in Britain at least, seems to have been achieved more fully and earlier than industrial modernisation. The Fordist factory was unusual in Britain until the 1930s, and by no means the norm until the Second World War or later,[83] whereas all the above tendencies were fully installed in Rochdale, according to Wild, by 1930. Could it be that the 'psychophysical equilibrium', which Gramsci argued was required by Fordist production, or at least certain aspects of it, had already been widely developed in the populace prior to the establishment of the modern production line?

But it would be a mistake to see these new leisure activities simply as new forms of regulation, particularly if we return to the way these activities were perceived by the guardians of English 'Culture'. Bill Schwarz has suggested that the traditionalist cultural nationalism outlined above may have helped sustain itself by being able to pose itself against a vulgar, 'foreign' popular modernity.[84] But the reverse is also the case: so far from warding off the inroads of mass culture, the stuffy paternalism of the Culture disseminated to the masses drove the popular classes more enthusiastically towards 'Americanism'. This is borne out clearly in Jeffrey Richards study of cinema-going in the 1930s: audiences vehemently preferred the action and glamour of the American cinema to the middle-class 'lifelessness' of British films.[85] Ken Worpole has explored the rather similar attractions of American detective fiction in the same period.[86] And, since the earliest days of a jazz influence, American forms of popular music have been dominant in Britain. Partly because of this and partly because of the energy and slickness of US radio, the BBC was increasingly forced, during the Second World War, towards more 'American' forms of programming in response to competition from the US forces' broadcasting from Europe.[87] In short, large sections of the popular classes in Britain, and the young in particular, have looked to the USA for cultural forms which addressed their experience, and furthermore developed a hostility to English cultural production as either not meant for them or patronising them.

The various forms of this structured opposition between 'English culture' and popular modernism are perceptively traced through into the post-war period by Dick Hebdige.[88] It is a discursive framework which marks out class divisions and will have been very problematic for those who sought upward mobility through educational or cultural routes, rather than simply though the acquisition of wealth: crossing the divide of taste can be more perilous than achieving the necessary affluence (such a passage is hilariously explored in Mike Leigh's films *Abigail's Party* and *High Hopes*, 1988). It may also contribute to the particularly difficult relationship of the English working class to the education system: inseparable from the skills training it offers is a large dose of acculturisation and a dismissal of popular taste. It is difficult not to believe that one of the reasons for working-class disillusionment with English schooling is this repudiation of their pleasures. Ironically, far from recognising this elitism as a barrier to learning, the British government has recently insisted on 'raising standards' by injecting an even heavier dose of this English traditionalism into the national curriculum.

In sum, the particular force of this structured conflict between 'English values' and 'Americanism' has made the kind of modernism represented in Berman – a vigorous, uninhibited but critical embrace of the new which spans intellectual and popular culture alike – difficult to sustain in Britain. We all manage, and make sense of, change in relation to the representations we encounter. But the social groups which have tended to be dominant in producing such representations in Britain have tended to move into the modern world looking backwards. They have also tended (within the cinema, for example) to be unable to represent the working class in terms other than those of comic figures, petty criminal or devoted servants who have no central significance to the narrative – at least until the end of the 1950s. Large sections of the British working and lower middle classes were able to turn to American popular culture for more useful reflections of their experience.

An engagement with the new frequently produces fear and anxiety, with many backward glances to the imagined stabilities of the past. But the forms of these imaginings differ. And the peculiarity of the British route through twentieth-century modernity has been this powerful, *classed* discourse of 'Culture' versus modernisation, framed through *nationalism*.

31

It is a discourse which has spanned the political spectrum and inhibited a left modernism too, and perhaps thereby contributed to the difficulties which British left politicians and intellectuals have had, for most of this century, in addressing popular experience, aspirations and pleasures.[89] Sections of the aspiring, 'respectable' working and lower middle classes have certainly been willing to be 'acculturised', but more have reacted in the opposite direction – towards the 'trashy', the philistine, the bawdy, the glamorous, the American and towards an ironic disrespect for Culture.

This review of the discourses of modernity began with a critique of Berman's formulations; they have provided a valuable basis for exploring the contradictory dimensions of modernity. But while his model has proved extremely useful, it has functioned, at least in the English context, usually in more muted forms than are suggested by his dramatic and romantic formulations (such as the 'insatiable desire' and 'torment'), derived from the great, innovating nineteenth-century intellectuals. Such a mutedness, and indeed a clinging to 'tradition', has long been understood as a characteristic of most English cultural and intellectual elites. More recently the *nationalism* of this cultural formation has been brought out, and particularly its anti-Americanism. Gramsci saw the anti-Americanism of European intellectuals as a last-ditch defence against a tide of modernisation that would sweep away the economic and social base of such groups, a social base with an interest in holding onto older forms of power for which 'Americanism' would have no place.[90] But, in Britain at least, this social stratum has hung on with remarkable tenacity, and in addition has recruited into itself sections of the working class who have secured upward mobility through education.

The debates on postmodernity include the suggestion that this opposition between high and popular culture is breaking down, particularly as elite cultures have themselves been commodified. John Frow argues that 'high culture is no longer "the dominant culture" but is rather a pocket within commodity culture'.[91] It is still attached to the intelligentsia, but, he suggests, 'it is no longer able to exert the same force through the social formation, its authenticity no longer able to secure universal respect'. A number of factors bear out this tendency. It is certainly the case that, since the 1960s, working-class resistance to that 'cultured nationalism' has ceased to be so defensive and subterranean. And Thatcherism has ushered in a new, and rampantly commercial, inflection of 'our heritage'. Furthermore, anti-Americanism no longer dominates English intellectual life. Something of that older taste formation remains in the recent debates over the regulation of broadcasting and the defence of 'quality television' – though this often slides into a defence of a middlebrow traditionalism.[92] But in general the signs are that this particular articulation of English modernity has had its (extended) moment and that a new one is in the process of formation.

But I would claim that what I have called the psychic formation of modernity remains firmly in place. My second chapter in this book seeks this out in present-day popular culture. I have argued that the 'cultured nationalism' of English intellectuals drove the British popular classes towards US culture as a means of thinking through their engagement with modernity, and particularly its discontents – its troublesome, transgressive aspects and its improper pleasures. More tentatively I have suggested another effect: that, because this formation also permeated left political intellectuals and leaders, it opened up a gulf between their cultural formation and those of 'the masses' and inhibited an articulation between popular desires and political movements of the left and centre, with significant consequences for British politics.

NOTES

1 M. Berman, *All That is Solid Melts Into Air. The Experience of Modernity*, London, Verso, 1983, p. 15
2 ibid., pp. 15ff.
3 But see, for example, S. Best and D. Kellner, *Postmodern Theory*, London, Macmillan, 1991; R. Boyne and A. Rattansi (eds), *Postmodernism and Society*, London, Macmillan, 1990; and S. Lash and J. Friedman, *Modernity and Identity*, Oxford, Blackwell, 1992.
4 P. Osborne, 'Modernity is a qualitative, not a chronological, category', *New Left Review*, no. 192, 1992.
5 S. Hall, D. Held and T. McGrew (eds), *Modernity and its Futures*, Cambridge, Polity/Open University, 1992, pp. 2ff.
6 T. Adorno and M. Horkheimer, *Dialectics of Enlightenment*, London, Allen Lane, 1973.
7 J.-F. Lyotard, *The Postmodern Condition: A Report on Knowledge*, Manchester, Manchester University Press, 1984.
8 See Robert Young, *White Mythologies*, London, Routledge, 1990.
9 J. Habermas, *The Philosophical Discourse of Modernity*, Cambridge, Polity Press, 1987.
10 M. Berman, 'The signs in the street', *New Left Review*, no. 145, 1984.
11 See J. Habermas, 'Modernity – an incomplete project', in H. Foster (ed.), *Postmodern Culture*, London, Pluto, 1985.
12 See T. Docherty (ed.), *Postmodernism: A Reader*, London, Harvester Wheatsheaf, 1993, introduction, pp. 25–6.
13 Berman, *All That is Solid*, p. 16.
14 K. Marx, *The Eighteenth Brumaire of Louis Bonaparte*, in *Surveys from Exile*, Harmondsworth, Penguin, 1973, p. 146.
15 For an evaluation of the 'three sociologies' to our understanding of modernity, see A. Giddens, *The Consequences of Modernity*, Cambridge, Polity, 1990.
16 D. Forgacs, 'Gramsci and Marxism in Britain', *New Left Review*, no. 176, 1989.
17 P. Anderson 'Modernity and revolution', *New Left Review*, no. 144, 1984. Quotations from Berman, *All That is Solid*, pp. 15–16. See also Berman's reply: 'The signs in the street'.
18 Marx, *The Eighteenth Brumaire*.
19 E.J Hobsbawm, *The Age of Empire 1875–1914*, London, Cardinal, 1989, p. 10.

20 V.I. Lenin, *Imperialism, The Highest Stage of Capitalism*, Peking, Foreign Languages Press, 1970.

21 Hobsbawm, *Age of Empire*, p. 77.

22 Nevertheless, the colonised peoples caught up in Western modernity might still periodise this engagement very differently. See P. Gilroy, 'It ain't where you're from, it's where you're at . . . : the dialectics of diaspora identification', in his *Small Acts*, London, Serpents Tail, 1993, and his *The Black Atlantic*, London, Verso, 1993.

23 H. Braverman, *Labor and Monopoly Capitalism*, New York and London, Monthly Review Press, 1974, pp. 159ff.

24 D. Harvey, *The Condition of Postmodernity*, Oxford, Basil Blackwell, 1989.

25 G. Marcus, 'Past, present and emergent identities', in S. Lash and J. Friedman (eds), *Modernity and Identity*, Oxford, Blackwell, 1992.

26 Braverman, *Labour and Monopoly Capitalism*.

27 A. Gramsci, 'Americanism and Fordism', in *Selections from the Prison Notebooks*, London, Lawrence and Wishart, 1972, pp. 279ff.

28 See Braverman, *Labour and Monopoly Capitalism* especially part I, for an enthralling account of these processes.

29 M. Foucault, *The Birth of the Clinic*, London, Pantheon, 1973, and *Discipline and Punish*, Harmondsworth, Penguin, 1977; J. Donzelot, *The Policing of Families*, London, Hutchinson, 1980. See also Bill Schwarz's 'Night battles: hooligan and citizen', Chapter 4 in this volume, for a manifestation of the concern with surveillance at this particular historical moment.

30 Hobsbawm, *Age of Empire*, ch. 4.

31 Gramsci, 'Americanism and Fordism'.

32 P. Wollen, 'Cinema/Americanism/the robot', in J. Naremore and P. Brantlinger (eds), *Modernity and Mass Culture*, Bloomington and Indianapolis, Indiana University Press, 1991.

33 J. Joll, *Europe Since 1870*, Harmondsworth, Penguin, 1976.

34 C. Marvin, *When Old Technologies were New*, New York and Oxford, Oxford University Press, 1988.

35 ibid., p. 175.

36 T. Bennett, 'Hegemony, ideology, pleasure: Blackpool', in T. Bennett, C. Mercer and J. Woollacott (eds), *Popular Culture and Social Relations*, Milton Keynes, Open University Press, 1986.

37 See, for example, Aldous Huxley's novel, *Brave New World* (1932), E.M. Forster's short story, 'The machine stops', published in E.M. Forster, *Collected Short Stories*, Sidgwick and Jackson, 1947, and Fritz Lang's film, *Metropolis* (1929).

38 It is a discourse which still has broad currency: we have only to watch the TV programme *Tomorrow's World*, observe how domestic appliances are still marketed or consider the utopian claims which have been made for microchip technologies (see A. Hyman, *The Coming of the Chip*, London, New English Library, 1980).

39 U. Boccioni, C.D. Carra, L. Russolo, C. Balla and G.Severini, 'The exhibitors to the public' (exhibition catalogue, 1912), in H.B. Chipp (ed.), *Theories of Modern Art*, Berkeley, University of California Press, 1968, p. 295.

40 C. Baudelaire, 'The painter of modern life', in his *The Painter of Modern Life and Other Essays*, Da Capo Press, 1986.

41 G. Simmel, 'The metropolis and mental life', in his *On Individuality and Social Forms*, Chicago and London, University of Chicago Press, 1971. See D. Frisby, *Fragments of Modernity*, Cambridge, Polity, 1985. The expression of the

fragmentary and transient nature of experience and this kind of nervous energy is mirrored in the work of the various modernist artistic movements of the early twentieth century: the Futurists' characterisation of the external world as one of violent movement and the inner mental world as one of 'dynamic sensation', the Cubists' more clinical fragmentation of objects into geometric shapes and component colours and so on.

42 R. Williams, *The Politics of Modernism*, London, Verso, 1989, ch. 2, especially p. 47.
43 S. Kracauer, 'The spectator', in R. Hughes (ed.), *Film: Book I*, New York, Grove Press, 1959.
44 ibid., p. 21.
45 For a rethinking of Kant's concept of the sublime see Lyotard, *The Postmodern Condition*; and D. Hebdige, 'The impossible object: towards a sociology of the sublime', *New Formations* no. 1, 1987.
46 Berman, *All That is Solid*, p. 5.
47 D. Bell, *The Cultural Contradictions of Capitalism*, London, Heinemann, 1976, pp. 105ff.
48 M. Berman, 'Why modernism still matters', in Lash and Friedman (eds), *Modernity and Identity*, p. 41.
49 S. Freud, *Civilisation and its Discontents*, London, Hogarth Press, 1963; also included in *Civilisation, Society and Religion*, The Pelican Freud Library, vol. 12, Harmondsworth, Penguin, 1978.
50 R. Sennett, *The Fall of Public Man*, London, Faber and Faber, 1986 (first published in 1977 in the USA).
51. C. Lasch, *The Culture of Narcissism*, London, Sphere, 1980.
52 See, for example, R. Coward, *Female Desire*, London, Paladin, 1984, part 4.
53 See, for example, Ann Barr Snitow, 'Mass market romance: pornography for women is different', in A. Snitow, C. Stansell and S. Thompson (eds), *Desire: The Politics of Sexuality*, London, Virago, 1984.
54 K. Theweleit, *Male Fantasies*, Cambridge, Polity, 1987.
55 See, for example, H. Bhabha, 'The other question – the stereotype and colonial discourse', *Screen*, vol. 24, no. 6, 1983.
56 J. Donald, *Sentimental Education: Schooling, Popular Culture and the Regulation of Liberty*, London, Verso, 1992.
57 There is now a large literature on the psychic formation of 'otherness'. For middle-class constructions of the working class as other see John Marriott's chapter in this volume; and P. Stallybrass and A. White, *The Politics and Poetics of Transgression*, London, Methuen, 1986.
58 A good account of this kind of development of psychoanalytic theory is J. Rose, *Sexuality in the Field of Vision*, London and New York, Verso, 1987, especially ch. 3.
59 S. Alexander, 'Becoming a woman in London in the 1920s and 1930s', in G. Stedman Jones (ed.), *Metropolis: Histories and Representations of London since 1800*, London, Routledge, 1990.
60 M. Mattelart, 'Notes on modernity', in A. Mattelart and S. Siegelaub (eds), *Communication and Class Struggle*, vol. 1, New York, International General, 1979.
61 R. Roberts, *The Classic Slum*, Harmondsworth, Penguin, 1973, p. 175.
62 S. and E. Ewen, *Channels of Desire*, New York, McGraw-Hill, 1982, pp. 86–7.
63 I am alluding to E.P. Thompson's classic essay 'The peculiarities of the English', collected in *The Poverty of Theory*, London, Merlin, 1978, which debates the specifically English route into twentieth-century capitalism with Perry Anderson

(see his 'Origins of the present crisis' and other essays, in his *English Questions*, London, Verso, 1992).

64 What follows is the barest sketch. For excellent recent social histories see J. Harris, *Private Lives, Public Spirit: Britain 1870–1914*, Harmondsworth, Penguin, 1994, and. Hobsbawm, *Age of Empire*. For a longer comparative study, see Joll, *Europe Since 1870*.

65 M. Langham and B. Schwarz (eds), *Crises in the British State 1880–1930*, London, Hutchinson, 1985, particularly ch. 1: S. Hall and B. Schwarz, 'State and society, 1880–1930'.

66 Anderson, 'Origins of the present crisis'; see also his 'Components of the national culture', also in *English Questions*.

67 J. Bristow, *Empire Boys; Adventures in a Man's World*, London, Harper Collins, 1991; J. Springhall, *Youth, Empire and Society*, London, Croom Helm, 1977.

68 Quoted in Hobsbawm, *Age of Empire*, p. 70.

69 See Erroll Lawrence, 'Just plain common sense: the "roots" of racism', in Centre for Contemporary Cultural Studies, *The Empire Strikes Back*, London, Hutchinson, 1977.

70 Anderson, *English Questions*, p. 24.

71 S. Yeo, *Religion and Voluntary Organisations in Crisis*, London, Croom Helm, 1976.

72 R. Colls and P. Dodds (eds), *Englishness. Politics and Culture 1880–1920*, London, Croom Helm, 1986; E. Hobsbawm and T. Ranger (eds), *The Invention of Tradition*, Cambridge, Cambridge University Press, 1983. See Andrew Blake's chapter for the similar invention of a musical tradition in this period.

73 For an elaboration of this argument see Anderson, *English Questions*, p. 34.

74 R. Williams, *Culture and Society, 1780–1950*, London, Chatto, 1958.

75 See Donald, *Sentimental Education*, ch. 3: 'The machinery of democracy'.

76 D. Hebdige, 'Towards a cartography of taste 1935–62', in his *Hiding in the Light*, London, Routledge, 1988.

77 Hobsbawm, *Age of Empire*; G. Stedman Jones, *Languages of Class*, Cambridge, Cambridge University Press, 1983, ch. 4.

78 Hobsbawm, *Age of Empire*, p. 140.

79 This development only took off vigorously in the 1930s and featured a marked *regional* imbalance: the new industries of mass commodity production tended to centre on the Midlands and south east. In the north and west production remained dominated by the faltering 'primary' industries. See E. Hobsbawm, *Industry and Empire*, Harmondsworth, Penguin, 1969.

80 P. Wild, 'Recreation in Rochdale, 1900–1940', in J. Clarke, C. Critcher and R. Johnson (eds), *Working Class Culture*, Hutchinson, London, 1979.

81 To these we can add betting and gambling (Roberts, *The Classic Slum*; Stedman Jones, *Languages of Class*).

82 Braverman, *Labor and Monopoly Capitalism*.

83 Harvey, *The Condition of Postmodernity*, p. 128.

84 Bill Schwarz, 'Englishness and the paradox of modernity', *New Formations*, no. 1, 1987.

85 J. Richards, *The Age of the Dream Palace: Cinema and Society in Britain 1930–39*, London, Routledge, 1984. Richards also records the paternalist surveillance and moral panic around what were described as the 'frequently sordid plots' of American films, and the attempt to promote a British cinema which was more 'uplifting'. See also P. Miles and M. Smith, *Cinema, Literature and Society: Elite and Mass Culture in Interwar Britain*, London, Croom Helm, 1987, pp. 163ff. for a similar argument.

86 K. Worpole, *Dockers and Detectives*, London, Verso, 1982.
87 D. Cardiff and P. Scannell, 'Radio in World War II', Open University course U203, *Popular Culture*, Unit 8, Milton Keynes, Open University Press, 1980.
88 D. Hebdige, 'Towards a cartography of taste'. His argument is developed in D. Webster, *Looka Yonder! The Imaginary America of Populist Culture*, London, Comedia/Routledge, 1988, pp. 193ff.
89 For a striking instance of this, see Stuart Laing's account of a conference of key British intellectuals in 1960 titled 'Popular culture and personal responsibility' in his *Representations of Working-Class Life, 1957–64*, London, Macmillan, 1986, ch. 7.
90 Gramsci, 'Americanism and Fordism', pp. 316–18.
91 J. Frow, 'The concept of the popular', *New Formations*, no. 18, 1992, p. 34.
92 C. Brunsdon, 'Problems with quality', *Screen*, vol. 31, no. 1, 1990.

2

MODERNITY'S DISAVOWAL
Women, the city and the department store

Mica Nava

INTRODUCTION: A GENEALOGY OF ABSENCE

This project started out as an investigation of the position of women in modernity. By focusing on shopping and the emergence of the department store as key iconic aspects of modern urban society my intention was to argue against those theorists who defined modernity of the late nineteenth and early twentieth centuries as a public stage from which women were excluded. However, my attempt to integrate conceptualisations of modernity with questions raised by feminism and the culture of consumption revealed a surprising paucity of theoretical and historical work – a phenomenon which itself required explanation. Increasingly therefore my project was transformed into a genealogy of absence. It became, in addition to an engagement with existing debates and histories, an investigation into the often unconscious motives and priorities that operate in the production of intellectual work and that in this instance have led, I will argue, to the disavowal of a major narrative of twentieth-century life.

MODERNITY AND WOMEN

The argument for deploying the concept of modernity, the organising principle of this book, in order to make sense of the cultural and material changes which were accelerated in the major cities of the Western world towards the end of the nineteenth century and the early decades of the twentieth century has been elaborated by Alan O'Shea.[1] My particular focus is on the experience and representation of women, and, in this context, on the emergence of new forms of social interaction and perception and on the development of a new consciousness about the possibilities that modern urban life was able to offer. Modernity as I use it here – and I have produced a composite account for the purpose of this argument by selecting pertinent features from a range of contributions, both contemporary and more recent[2] – highlights the complexity and danger as well as the richness and excitement of everyday life in the modern city. It draws

38

attention to the texture of commonplace experiences in the metropolis, to an environment characterised by continuous flux and frequent encounters with strangers, in which signs and appearances acquire a new importance and substitute increasingly for traditional narratives of social and geographical belonging. There is a new stress on display and the visual – on looking. Modern urban existence, with its transience and uncertainty, demands new morals as well as new fashions. It produces new aspirations. It generates new enterprises, new languages and cultural forms. But modernity is not only about renewal. As a concept it also emphasises disintegration and fragmentation. It signals the destabilising of many nineteenth-century conventions and highlights the pessimism as well as boldness of the modern imagination. And yet throughout it suggests a kind of *forward-lookingness* and a way, as Marshall Berman has put it, of making oneself at home in the chaos – 'the maelstrom' – of modern life, of becoming the subjects as well as the objects of modernisation.[3]

Modernity of course is a constructed narrative, and, like any other, offers us a *version* of events and the past in that it singles out certain phenomena for investigation or emphasis and ignores others. It is perhaps unsurprising to note therefore that despite the wide range of appropriations of the concept and its fertility in epistemological terms, it has failed on the whole to address the experience of women. In some of the classic accounts the prostitute or actress–entertainer is depicted as the characteristic female figure in the iconography of the urban landscape, in this way shoring up nineteenth-century dualistic thought about virtuous and fallen women as well as mythologies of the sexually licentious city[4] and at the same time ignoring ordinary women. Some of the more recent accounts have been even more neglectful, astonishingly so given the critical climate of the last two decades: Frisby, for example, refers not at all to sexual difference in his study of Simmel, Benjamin and Kracauer as key commentators on modernity, far less even than the authors did themselves when they wrote at the beginning of this century.[5]

The project of academic feminism has been to prise open this sort of narrative and make sense of the marginalisation of women, both theoretically and historically wherever possible. Janet Wolff's influential 'The invisible *flâneuse* and the literature of modernity' has been the seminal piece on this intellectual issue[6] and the argument I develop here was generated in the first instance in response to hers. Wolff's thesis is that women are absent from the critical literature of modernity because its focus is largely upon the public sphere, on the crowded city street and the experience of the *flâneur*, on the world of politics and work – on areas from which, according to her, women were excluded. Hence their neglect by the theorists of modernity. Women's increasing confinement to the domestic sphere during the nineteenth century coincides with the development of the new discipline of sociology, which is concerned to classify and explain the changing phenomena of the modern *public* world. The more literary contributions also understand modernity as uniquely associated with the city and public life. Thus women's activities and labour, even where these are not confined to the home, are largely invisible. 'The literature of modernity ignores the private sphere and to that extent is silent on the subject of women's primary domain.'[7] Although Wolff acknowledges, though almost as an aside, that women are provided with a new public arena as a consequence of the emergence of the department store,[8] her argument is that the characteristics of modernity identified by authors like Baudelaire and Benjamin – 'the fleeting anonymous encounter and the purposeless strolling' – do not apply to women's activities. In sum Wolff's argument is that women were not only excluded from the literature of modernity, but, confined as they were to the domestic sphere and the suburbs, women were also excluded from the *experience* of modernity. no. female equivalent of the *flâneur* can be invented.

Although Wolff's article has made a valuable contribution by opening up the debate, there are nevertheless certain key assumptions in it with which I disagree. My argument will be that women were *not* excluded from the experience of modernity in the public sphere: that, on the contrary, they participated quite crucially in its formation. Indeed women's experience can be interpreted as a quintessential constituent of modernity. So we must look elsewhere if we are to understand the exclusion of women from the literature.

The reason that Wolff has argued otherwise is in part a consequence of her periodisation. The historical focus of her essay is on conditions during the second half of the nineteenth century, on those roughly contemporaneous with the 'early modernity' of Baudelaire, the period which Benjamin called 'the prehistory of modernity'.[9] If she had periodised modernity differently and linked it to the drama of high modernisms, the expansion of mass culture and consumption and the socio-political instability of the late nineteenth and early twentieth centuries, her investigation would have encompassed the moment when women's appropriation of public spaces, in both symbolic and material ways, was growing rapidly. In this case, her argument about women's lack of participation in the experience of modernity would have been harder to sustain.

Another difficulty with Wolff's argument is that she depicts the '*flâneur*' as the archetype of modernity. Here she reproduces the tendency in much of the literature to single out the artist–observer – 'the botaniser on the asphalt' (usually the author himself) – as *the* representative of the modern urban experience. In fact Baudelaire's *flâneur*, 'the painter of modern life', was an observer and recorder of modernity, he did not exemplify it. Wolff's *flâneur* is moreover always a man because according to her argument only men have the freedom to wander at will and 'take visual possession of the city'.[10] My argument will be that Wolff's concept of the *flâneur*, although productive for its emphasis on the ephemeral and the ocular – on looking – is limited insofar as it excludes the everyday spectatorship of ordinary people, and especially ordinary women.

In general Wolff's conclusions are representative of a rich but often pessimistic tradition in feminist historiography which tends to focus on the subordination of women and their marginalisation in mainstream historical accounts.[11] Although these readings have had their political and theoretical importance, they have also inhibited the excavation of other 'truths'. Berman's emphasis on making the world your own, on the heroism as well as the despair of everyday life, offers the possibility of a different kind of interpretation of women's relationship to modernity, despite his own relative neglect of the issues.[12] If Janet Wolff had been readier to focus on the expansion of women's cultural experiences in the city rather than on the constraints, then, paradoxically, she would have been in a position to advance more forcefully the second part of her argument, where she points to the invisibility of women in the *literature* of modernity.

But Wolff's process of deconstruction is not taken far enough. The absence from the literature is read as evidence of a 'real' absence rather than evidence of itself. A different reading of women's participation in modernity would have emphasised the constructedness of this literature. It would have highlighted the *intellectual* exclusion of women and the ambivalence of the authors about cultural change – the androcentrism of most of the texts about modernity. Janet Wolff's own argument about women's invisibility would have been rendered at once more complex and more persuasive.

These are the issues that are going to be developed in this chapter. The focus will be mainly on the department store and shopping in the urban context as an example of the way in which women engaged with the maelstrom of modern life. An exploration of this history will expand our understanding not only of the process of modernity but also, quite crucially, of the way it has been represented to us. In this sense it will be, as I suggested earlier, a kind of genealogy of absence. The question is: how can we make sense of the failure to acknowledge women's participation in the making of modern urban consumer culture – of the disavowal of this pivotal aspect of early twentieth-century life?

One way of addressing this – even if not resolving it – is to look also at some of the formative popular and critical responses to consumerism and mass culture during the first decades of this century and to consider the ways in which the psychic and historical formations of authors inflect the texts that they produce.

WOMEN AND THE CITY

It is important first to explore the symbolic resonance of the city in modernity and register its significance in relation to our objects of concern, to women, the department store and mass culture. More than any other social force of the nineteenth century, the city evoked the freedom as well as the menace that characterised the modern experience. Throughout this period it grew as a territory not only spatially but also in terms of its cultural significations, in the way in which it was understood and represented. The city was increasingly mythologised – albeit in contradictory ways. The British version of this imagined geography tended to stress the disturbing aspects of the urban environment, the chaos and pollution, moral and sexual dissolution and the erosion of traditional order.[13] In this narrative the threatening nature of the city regularly operated as a counterpoint to the ideal of a virtuous and harmonious rural or suburban domestic existence.[14]

This kind of polarisation (splitting and projection, in psychoanalytical terms) can be understood as an attempt to impose a moral and cognitive order on a highly volatile and incomprehensible geopolitical context. It is also linked to the sexualisation of the symbolic register of the city. The position of women in nineteenth-century urban mythologies was particularly charged.[15] Here too classifications of opposition and exclusion operated to maintain order. Disreputable women were associated with the immorality of public life in the city, with the despised prostitute and the unruly and often feminised urban mob.[16] Respectable and virtuous women were connected to the home, and the ideal home was situated outside the city, in the leafy suburbs or village community. The sexual prohibitions and incitement elaborated in these discourses were marked by a deeply rooted conceptual and emotional adherence to the immutability of divisions – the fortified nature of boundaries – between women of different social classes and physical locations, and between the 'naturally ordained' spheres of men and women.

It has already been pointed out that much influential feminist historical research of the last decades (including Wolff's) has been concerned to trace the development of an ideology of separate spheres among the Victorian middle classes and has attempted to show how the cultural entrenchment of such ideas resulted in the social and material exclusion of women from public life and urban areas. This has undoubtedly been the dominant tendency in feminist historiography.[17] However there have also been some dissenting interpretations. Amanda Vickery in her discussion of such positions has suggested 'the stress on the proper female sphere in Victorian discourse signalled concern that more women were active outside the home rather than proof that they were so confined'. Elizabeth Wilson has also argued that women were not easily banished from public places, and Judith Walkowitz and others have drawn attention to the large numbers of middle-class women philanthropists who moved freely around the city streets.[18]

These conflicting versions are evidence not only of current academic debate. They also suggest a much more uneven and contradictory picture of women's experience of city life than can be deduced from a face-value analysis of dominant discourses. Vickery's comment implies (though does not develop in this context) a reading against the grain, a reading which hints that the continuous reiteration of certain ideas might be evidence of anxiety and attempted denial rather than 'reality'. Moreover, there is evidence that, during the closing decades of the century, there occurred increasingly in ideas about femininity and in women's circumstances precisely the instability and unfixing of parameters of difference that the concept of modernity as it has been used here seems to encapsulate so well.

One of the most significant changes that took place during this period was a rapid expansion of what counted as respectable, or at least acceptable, public space for unaccompanied women. The category included the great exhibitions, galleries, libraries, restaurants, tearooms, hotels and department stores (which will be returned to in more detail in the next section) – 'public–private liminal spaces' as Zukin has called them – associated in part with a more general promotion of buildings and events as cultural commodities[19] and in part with the clear demands made by women themselves. A growing number of authors (but still a minority in the context of feminist debate) have described in detail the growth of these places and the ways in which they catered specifically to women visitors and clients. A significant but neglected consequence of this expansion was that middle-class women travelled with increasing freedom through the streets and open public spaces of the city. They took advantage of all available forms of travel: some had their own carriages, others travelled by public transport – on trains, buses and tubes – some rode their bicycles (during the 1890s there was a cycling craze for women) and yet others travelled on foot.[20] Lynne Walker's research on this subject has shown how the private and public spaces that middle-class women frequented were often also within walking distance of each other and movement between them necessarily entailed mingling with the crowd and encountering strangers – possibly disreputable strangers – at close proximity. These forays were conducted on a daily basis for very many women. Several authors have drawn on diaries and correspondence to show the frequency and normality of such excursions, despite in some instances familial opposition and harassment on the streets.[21] So what begins to emerge is a picture in which middle-class women were much closer to the dangers and the excitement of city life than the notion of separate spheres would lead us to anticipate.

In fact middle-class women laid increasing claim not only to 'respectable' public places. Large numbers also visited less salubrious neighbourhoods as part of the proliferation of philanthropic schemes that emerged during late nineteenth century in order to cope with the perceived crisis of the city – with the threat of social disorder, disease, destitution and inadequate housing. Middle-class women, as bearers of a particular kind of knowledge, were involved on a huge scale in the process of disseminating information about morality, domestic economy, hygiene and child care to women of the working class. In 1893 it was estimated that 20,000 women were paid officials and an astonishing half million were voluntary workers engaged in philanthropic projects dedicated to improving the lives of the urban poor.[22]

So it is clear that middle-class urban women were not confined to their homes all the time. Indeed in their pursuit of 'adventure, self-discovery and meaningful work'[23] many would have ventured into slum territory unfamiliar even to their husbands and brothers. These journeys – which involved travel on public transport and on foot along unknown streets, and encounters in insanitary overcrowded housing with strangers possessing quite different life experiences – demanded from these urban explorers a quite extraordinary degree of intrepidity and yielded a rich store of personal and social discoveries. Women charity workers were engaged as much in a mapping of the new social relations of the city as were the more esteemed and recognised historians and poets of the moment. The visionary element in their activities was perhaps somewhat compromised by the fact that their personal freedom from the constraints of late Victorian domesticity was gained in the process of attempting to enforce it elsewhere, on the women of the poorer classes. But this contradiction need not undermine the *modernity* of their consciousness and experience any more than the contradictions of Faust's grand modern project as described by Berman.[24]

The women who travelled in this capacity, purposefully and relatively freely through the notorious streets of London, were unlikely to have lingered in parks and other public places to observe the ephemera of urban life – especially feminine life – in quite the voyeuristic style attributed to Baudelaire's *flâneur*.[25] Nevertheless, charity work established for these women the right to look. It authorised the observation and classification of the homes, lives and even marital relationships of the poor. Middle-class women involved in the philanthropic enterprise were not obliged to conduct their affairs with lowered gaze. They could indulge the pleasures of urban spectatorship – of the voyeur – with a sense of entitlement which is not so easily distinguishable from that of the male *flâneur*. Moreover their participation in increasingly professionalised 'social' work also implicated them in the project of the regulation of populations – in the observation, correction and improvement of the social body – which is the central feature of Foucault's rather differently defined and periodised 'modernity'.[26]

Philanthropy is just one instance of the way in which the Victorian ideal of separate spheres was undermined, if somewhat contradictorily,[27] and in the years around the turn of the century the numbers of women refusing to stay within the confines of the domestic expanded rapidly. Modern women were increasingly, if unevenly, engaged in the public world, in work, in financial transactions, in education and the dissemination of knowledge, and in political action. The movement for women's suffrage represented, perhaps more than any other activity, the spectacular high point of the early twentieth-century challenge to Victorian conventions of femininity. During the years preceding the First World War many thousands of women from all social backgrounds took to the city streets in flamboyant, public and sometimes quite astonishingly violent protest against the injustice of disenfranchisement based on sexual difference. In 1908 it is estimated that as many as half a million people converged in Hyde Park to support (or observe) the struggle. The striking impact of enormously long columns of militant women marchers, progressing from all corners of London, dressed in the suffragette colours of white, green and purple and bearing thousands of boldly designed banners, is described by Lisa Tickner, who argues that the campaign marked a significant turning-point in the modern use of visual imagery and publicity.[28] Moreover, in their articulation of a modernist imagination with political consciousness and a will to change, the protest marches for women's suffrage exemplify with extraordinary vividness the evocative concept of 'primal modern scene' developed by Marshall Berman to describe the archetypal or determining events of modernity in which the city streets become the stage for great moments of mass action and social transformation.[29] Berman, however, does not include the suffrage demonstrations among the historical events he selects to validate his category. So the campaign for votes for women is yet one more instance which demonstrates both the precariousness of nineteenth-century codes of femininity and the narrowness of a notion of modernity which ignores the experience of women.[30]

This period also saw a destabilisation of Victorian sexual mores. There is a rich literature which situates the challenge to sexual conventions within the broader framework of the new woman's pursuit of fresh opportunities and greater social freedom. This challenge was posed not only in relation to choice of partner, courtship patterns and independence of movement. 'Free love' and the idea of sexual pleasure as an entitlement for women as well as men were gradually put on the agenda, albeit mainly in urban Bohemian and intellectual circles, and argued for alongside the need for sexual reforms like contraception and abortion. Despite the dangers of social ostracism and the continuing influence of social purity movements, the old sexual order was increasingly defied.[31] Ideas about 'modern relationships' and new ways of living were slowly disseminated and popularised. Women's magazines and later the cinema were to be among the main sources of information about many of these questions for ordinary women. It was in these fora that women readers and spectators encountered representations of the new femininities, of vamps and independent women.[32] It was here that public discussion took place about the appropriate constituents of women's behaviour.

This section has set out some of the contradictory and unstable elements in city life and women's circumstances during the years around the turn of the century in order to provide a context for the ensuing study of early twentieth-century cultural responses to women as consumers. What has emerged in this account is a dissonance between women's lived experience and the discourse of their seclusion in the domestic sphere. One way of making sense of this discourse is to see it as a form of denial, as a way of attempting to hold back the modern, of resisting – or at the very least of regulating – the encroachment of women, and the 'new woman' in particular. (We will see later that a similar process of denial operated in the public and critical responses to women's involvement in mass culture, particularly to shopping and cinema-going.) The turn of the century did indeed see an accelerating challenge to the rhetorical conventions of public and private spheres and to the distinctions between respectable and disreputable – to some of the major symbolic markers of sex and sexual identity. Insofar as modernity signals a permeability of boundaries and the blurring of categories and difference it seems untenable to argue that women were excluded from it. Furthermore, the women described here, in negotiating urban and political turbulence and challenging social orthodoxies, were engaged in the project of making themselves at home in the maelstrom of modern life, of becoming the subjects as well as the objects of modernisation, however contradictory, painful and uneven the process.

MODERNITY AND THE DEPARTMENT STORE

Alongside these developments in personal mobility, urban spectatorship, political consciousness and social freedoms – and complexly related to them – was women's massive participation in the exploding culture of consumption and spectacle. It is here, in this arena, that the everyday lives of large numbers of ordinary women were most deeply affected by the process of modernity. The department store was from the late nineteenth century central to the iconography of consumer culture; it exemplified the ubiquity of the visual in the new 'scopic regime', and should be read as one of the archetypal sites of modernity which both produced and was produced by the experience of women. Emile Zola, in his carefully researched novel about late nineteenth-century Paris, described such stores as a 'triumph of modern activity'.[33]

Shopping in fashionable city centres as a pleasurable social activity was already established among the upper classes prior to this period, as was the enhancement of social status and identity which derived from the consumption of intricately coded possessions and styles.[34] In the late eighteenth century Oxford Street had already been described as a 'dazzling spectacle' of 'splendidly lit shop fronts' and 'alluring' and 'handsome' displays. In 1807 Robert Southey wrote of their opulence and social importance: 'Shops are become exhibitions of fashion. . . . When persons of distinction are in town, the usual employment of the ladies is to go a-shopping. This they do without actually wanting to purchase anything.'[35] As the century

proceeded a number of factors combined to make the experience of fashionable shopping even more agreeable and to extend it to women of the middle
classes, to 'democratise luxury' as Zola put it.[36] The expansion of shops
and shopping during the latter decades of the nineteenth century and early
years of the twentieth was due in part to a general growth in the economy
and more specifically to developments in public transport, which benefited
manufacturers as well as consumers and altered the spatial relations of the
city. New forms of mass production of non-essential 'consumer' goods and
ready-to-wear clothing also made a crucial contribution, as did the ambi-
tions of individual entrepreneurs. The most significant factor however was
probably growing demand. The aspirations of an expanding and increasingly socially and geographically mobile urban population were inextricably
bound up with the emergence and consolidation of modern forms of
retailing, and the department store in particular.[37]

Department stores were established in all the major cities of the Western
world and reached their zenith[38] during the period identified at the beginning of this chapter as the high point of modernity. Zola depicts the
department store at the centre of his novel as a modern machine which
devours the small outdated commercial enterprises surrounding it. According to him, department stores symbolise the 'forward momentum of the
age: the bold new forms of capitalism'.[39] Their precursors, the covered
shopping arcades of the mid-nineteenth century whose small speciality
shops were unable to compete with mass-produced commodities, are
described by Walter Benjamin in his Arcades Project as an earlier form of
capitalism: part of the 'ur-landscape of consumption'.[40] The new stores
modernised retailing not only by offering a wide range of cheaper, mass-
produced fashionable clothes and other commodities, but also by rational-
ising the use of space, making economies of scale, introducing clear pricing
systems and displaying goods in a safe and pleasant environment so that
customers could look and compare without obligation to buy.[41]

Linked inextricably to these commercial developments – and also a
crucial component of the concept of modernity – was the growing importance of external appearances, of surface impressions. This concern for what
Ewen has called 'armour for city life'[42] was a feature of the specific historical conjuncture under review, which was characterised by an escalating
instability of class and geographical boundaries. This increasing social
fluidity is what fuelled Simmel's preoccupation with the meaning of modern
fashions.[43] The period also witnessed the growing influence of a more open
American culture, brought to Britain by developments in shipping and the
mutual benefits of alliances between New World wealth and European
'distinction'. At such a socially precarious time, new signs were required as
emblems of status and individuality. Dreiser's heroine Carrie (who at the
beginning of the novel *Sister Carrie*, published in 1900, seeks a job in a
department store) exemplifies this in her meticulous acquisition and display

of the codes of social position. Leonore Davidoff has shown how those aspiring to become part of Society in nineteenth-century Britain paid scrupulous attention to dress and comportment. During this period the fashioning of the home also gained significance as a visible indicator not only of rank but increasingly also of choice and 'identity'.[44]

Women played a crucial part in the development of these taxonomies of signification – in the acquisition of goods which conveyed symbolic meanings about their owners – since it was women who went to the department stores and did the shopping. From their inception the department stores provided a particularly welcoming space for women and numerous contemporary accounts indicate that visits to them took place frequently, sometimes several times a week.[45] As institutions the stores made a major contribution to the twentieth-century consolidation of women as consumers and to consumption and consumer expertise as activities that were as gendered as production.[46] During the period we are looking at women were confirmed as arbiters of taste and interpreters of the new – the modern. It was women who first of all encountered new fashions and domestic novelties and decided whether they were worth adopting. As those most literate in the complex signifiers of social hierarchy – a literacy acquired largely from magazines and the stores themselves[47] – it was women who decoded and encoded the changing images of class. Within two or three decades these lessons were to be learned mainly from the movies – indeed Hollywood was to become a major inspiration for shop design[48] – but before the First World War, the principal source of information about the meaning of how others lived and dressed was found in the stores.

So clearly, department stores were more than just places where merchandise was bought and sold. In addition to facilitating the acquisition of 'cultural capital'[49] they formed part of the huge expansion of public space and spectacle which included the great international exhibitions, museums, galleries, leisure gardens and, a little later, the cinema, and they provided an extraordinary range of facilities, entertainments and visual pleasures. People visited them as tourist attractions – as monuments to modernity – for the interest and pleasure they afforded in themselves.

The historians of the most renowned department stores[50] describe them as fantasy palaces. Increasingly purpose-built in the most luxurious styles with the most modern as well as traditional indigenous and imported materials, many had grand open staircases and galleries, ornate iron work, huge areas of glass in domed roofs and display windows, mirrored and marble walls,[51] parquet floors covered with Eastern carpets and furniture upholstered in silk and leather. These emporia were among the very first public spaces to be heated and to use electric light not only for illumination but also for effect. In their display of goods and use of colour, they often drew on the conventions of theatre and exhibitions, continuously innovating to produce new, vivid and seductive environments, with *mises en scène* which combined, or offered in sequence, modernist, traditional and exotic decors (anticipating, or perhaps undermining, late twentieth-century postmodernism). Rosalind Williams describes this constant renewal disdainfully as a 'hodge-podge of visual themes'.[52] However Zola's enthusiastic account of the exhibition of parasols in his (fictional) department store suggests a scenario which has been carefully designed:

> Wide-open, rounded off like shields, (the parasols) covered the whole hall, from the glazed roof to the varnished oak mouldings below. They described festoons round the semi-circular arches of the upper storeys; they descended in garlands along the slender columns; they ran along in close lines on the balustrades of the galleries and the staircases; and everywhere, ranged symmetrically, speckling the walls with red green and yellow, they looked like great Venetian lanterns, lighted up for some colossal entertainment. In the corners were more complicated patterns, stars composed of parasols at thirty-nine sous, the light shades of which, pale-blue, cream-white and blush-rose, seemed to burn with the sweetness of a night light; whilst up above, immense Japanese parasols, on which golden-coloured cranes soared in a purple sky, blazed forth with the reflections of a great conflagration.[53]

These magnificent stage sets also served as backdrop to live entertainment, which was provided on a regular basis. There were live orchestras in the restaurants and tearooms – and even, occasionally, in the grocery departments. Dress shows and pageants were regular occurrences. 'Spectacular oriental extravaganzas' which included live tableaux of Turkish harems, Cairo markets or Hindu temples, with live performers, dance, music and of course oriental products, were also frequent events. It is interesting to note that during this period these exoticised yet commercial representations of 'oriental' imagery and narratives were a major source of popular knowledge about empire, other cultures and other aesthetic formations. Liberty's, which from 1875 specialised in Indian, Persian and Arabic merchandise and themes, was a pioneer in the development of this tradition. An example of Selfridges' 'cosmopolitanism', in which it took great pride, can be seen in Figure 2.1.[54] Another recurring feature in the entertainment provided by the stores was the exhibition and deployment of the most advanced technologies. Rosalind Williams describes how in France new photographic techniques were used for cineoramas, mareoramas and dioramas to create the illusion of travelling not only in exotic places but also by balloon above the sea and to the surface of the moon.[55]

In addition to these visual experiences the department stores provided a vast range of facilities that enhanced the convenience, comfort and pleasure of shopping. These included supervised children's areas, toilets and powder-rooms, hairdressing courts, ladies' and gentlemen's clubs and writing rooms, restaurants and tea-rooms, roof gardens with pergolas, zoos and ice

Figure 2.1 From *The Spirit of Modern Commerce*, 1914, one of the
'cosmopolitan' posters in the souvenir collection published by Selfridge's to
celebrate its fifth anniversary

Source: Selfridges archive

rinks, libraries, picture galleries, banks, ticket and travel agencies, grocery
provision and delivery services. Standards of service were high and customers
were made to feel welcome by obliging liveried doormen and deferential
yet astute assistants. Alison Adburgham cites an article written by Lady

Jeune in 1896 in which she comments on contemporary developments and in particular on the significance of the increase in *women* shopworkers:

> two very important changes have contributed to the temptation of spending money nowadays. One is the gathering under one roof of all kinds of goods – clothing, millinery, groceries, furniture, in fact all the necessities of life. Nearly all the great shops in London are becoming vast stores. Many more people now come to London to shop and they prefer to make their purchases where they can concentrate their forces and diminish fatigue. The other is the large number of women now employed. Women are so much quicker than men, and they understand so much more readily what other women want. They can fathom the agony of despair as to the arrangement of colours, the alternative trimmings, the duration of a fashion and the depth of a woman's purse.[56]

So the department stores provided a source of employment for women as well as a welcoming place for them to shop.

The physical scale of these socio-commercial enterprises was huge. In 1903, Macy's restaurant in New York could accommodate 2,500 in one sitting. Harrods of Knightsbridge, which prided itself on being 'the most elegant and commodious emporium in the world' and 'a recognised social rendez-vous for members of Society' where it is 'perfectly proper for a lady to meet a gentleman', had at the turn of the century 6,000 employees and 36 acres of shopping space organised into eighty different departments.[57] Selfridges, launched by the American entrepreneur Gordon Selfridge in 1909, was the first purpose-built store in Britain and was even larger than Harrods. It distinguished itself from Harrods by targeting a more middle- and lower-middle-class clientele and offered 'bargain basements' from early on. Yet it too was designed to be a social meeting-place and the public was encouraged to come and look without obligation to buy. The publicity slogans invited people to 'spend the day at Selfridges' and they did. 'It's so much brighter than their own homes. This is not a shop – it's a community centre', Mr Selfridge is alleged to have said, and kept the doors open till eight or later and the window displays illuminated until midnight. The store was considered one of the great show sights of London, like Westminster Abbey, which all visitors from the provinces and abroad would expect to see. In the period prior to the First World War, there was a relative scarcity of forms of public entertainment (cinema and radio were to take off later) and partly because the stores were open so far into the evening they did indeed become the entertainment centres and meeting-points their founders envisaged (see Figure 2.2).[58] Some anxiety was expressed by social observers and customers alike about the mingling of social classes within the confines of the stores and there were worries about the difficulties of 'placing' some young women shoppers and shop-workers because of their respectable and fashionable appearances.[59] Concern was also voiced about

Figure 2.2 One of a series of advertisements which appeared in the London daily press promoting the launch of Selfridge's in March 1909

Source: Selfridges archive

Note: See note 58 for a transcription of the text

the possibilities of illicit encounters between men and women. Whiteley's of Bayswater had a 'reputation' in this respect, though what this signified in commercial terms is open to question. It is clear from the inaugural publicity of Selfridge's (as it was then called) that the possibility of 'pleasure' and 'recreation' in the company of a gentleman was deliberately presented as part of the allure of the store (Figure 2.3).[60] So, in general, the blurring of class divisions and the relaxation of socio-sexual prohibitions, though in some respects risky, were considered necessary for the social appeal and commercial success of the stores and were likely to have been justified insofar as they were modern.

Visiting the stores during this period became, then, an excursion, an exciting adventure in the phantasmagoria of the urban landscape. The department store was an anonymous yet acceptable public space and it opened up for women a range of new opportunities and pleasures – for independence, fantasy, unsupervised social encounters, even transgression – as well as, at the same time, for rationality, expertise and financial control. Shopping trips, sanctioned by domestic and familial obligations, justified, as did the philanthropic expeditions referred to earlier, relatively free movement around the city and travel on public transport in the proximity of strangers. The inspection of the merchandise on display in the shop windows was a necessary part of the activity so the streets and pavements in the main shopping centres were monopolised by women, ordinary middle-class women, part of the ebb and flow of the urban crowd, going about their business or indulging their dreams, sometimes alone, sometimes with family or friends (see Figure 2.4). The department store, together with the proliferating women's household and fashion magazines and the popular story papers of that period contributed to the creation of modern female identities.[61] It facilitated the acquisition of consumer knowledge and enabled women to make informed and independent decisions about shopping.[62] It also offered a language to imagine a different and better future, one in which the injuries and wants of everyday existence could be soothed and family lives enhanced. And in addition it provided a spectacular environment in which to stroll aimlessly, to be a *flâneuse*, to observe people, to admire and parade new fashions. This was a context which legitimised the desire of women to look as well as be looked at – it enabled them to be both subject and object of the gaze, to appropriate at one go the pleasure/power of both the voyeur and the narcissist.[63]

To draw attention to the exciting and empowering aspects of women's visits to the stores is not to deny that shopping can also be arduous, that anonymity and desire can be reread more negatively as loneliness and dissatisfaction. It is nevertheless to insist that the stores and shopping be recognised as one of the main contexts in which women developed a new consciousness of the possibilities and entitlements that modern life was able to offer. William Leach in his study of American department stores concludes thus:

SHOPPING at SELFRIDGE'S

A Pleasure—A Pastime—A Recreation

WE aim to make the shopping at "Selfridge's" something more than merely shopping. We would like to think that everyone who spends an hour or day beneath our roof is better for the experience, has seen many "things different," has gathered some new point of knowledge, has discovered a way to do something better and revealed the thought to us.

Such suggestions we will welcome very gratefully and act on to the best of our ability, for by this friendly criticism we can more readily accomplish the work that we have set ourselves, that is, to do every day some one thing better than we did the day before.

This is part of our ambition, and what we know will come about by cordial "entente" between Customers and ourselves.

SELFRIDGE & CO.
OXFORD STREET, LONDON, W.

Figure 2.3 Another of the alluring advertisements in Selfridge's promotional campaign 1909
Source: Selfridges archive

Figure 2.4 Women as part of the urban crowd: shopping in Oxford Street 1909
Source: Hulton Deutsch collection

> In those early . . . euphoric days of consumer capitalism, textured
> so much by the department store, many women thought they had
> discovered a more exciting . . . life. Their participation in consumer
> experience challenged and subverted that complex of qualities tradi-
> tionally known as feminine – dependence, passivity . . . domestic
> inwardness and sexual purity. Mass consumer culture presented to
> women a new definition of gender that carved out a space for indi-
> vidual expression similar to men's.[64]

Leach's article also elaborates on the connections between the department
stores and early feminist organisations. In England, as in the United States,
the high point of the department store coincided with the peak years of
suffragette militancy. The owners of the department stores were well aware
of the importance of the movement and several manufactured, displayed
and supplied a wide range of goods – from tea services to outer garments
– in purple, white and green, the symbolic colours of the struggle.[65] They
perceived their innovations in retailing as part of the same modernising
process as women's emancipation and saw no conflict of interest between
women's growing independence and the economic success of the stores.

Harley Granville Barker's play *The Madras House*, originally published in 1911, includes among its characters an American department store magnate, Eustace Perrin State, who is an avowed supporter of what he refers to as 'the great modern women's movement'. 'A man who is not consciously in that movement is outside history' declares State. Having made a careful study of the issues involved in 'the women's question', he concludes that political claims for the vote constitute only a small part of it. In his opinion, 'the women's movement is [about] woman expressing herself'. His interest is not unrelated to his position as a store-owner because, as he also points out, 'the economic independence of women is the next step [after their political freedom] in the march of civilisation'.[66] There are plenty of 'real' as well as fictional instances of support, or at least acknowledgement, by the stores for the demands of feminism. Most overt was that of Wanamakers, the American store which gave all women employees time off during working hours to march in suffrage parades. Restaurants in a number of stores in England became the meeting places of suffragettes during the period we are looking at. Fenwicks in Newcastle was apparently particularly well known for this. Mr Selfridge was another example of a store-owner who claimed to give support to the emancipation of women: 'I came along just when they wanted to step out on their own. They came to the store and realised some of their dreams', he is supposed to have said.[67]

But consumption of course is about more than emancipation or the realisation of dreams or even politics. It is also crucially about work. Effective retailing is an absolutely integral aspect of modern capitalism. Without efficient marketing, which includes shopping, the production of goods ceases to be profitable. Yet despite the absolute centrality of consumption to modern Western economic life, and despite the cultural and social resonance that I describe in this chapter, consumption as labour – unlike production – has until recently been remarkably neglected, both theoretically and politically. Shopping has been overlooked or trivialised by economists, sociologists, the left and cultural theorists. As Grant McCracken has put it: 'The history of consumption has no history, no community of scholars, no tradition of scholarship.'[68] Shopping is also theoretically insignificant in the literature of modernity. Why should this be? [69]

SHOPPING, THE CINEMA AND PUBLIC ANXIETIES

In order to make sense of this historical neglect we must look at the broader context, at the ways in which shopping and a range of associated mass cultural activities were perceived during this critical period. What emerges is a complex discursive formation composed of different strands – popular and intellectual – held together nevertheless by certain common anxieties which seem inextricably linked to the gendered nature of shopping. This is the context from which the seminal theoretical approaches develop and which goes on to shape the ways these processes have been more recently understood.

First of all, then, it must be noted that the expansion of women's social and economic activity in the public sphere as consumers came at the moment not only of growing suffragette militancy, but also when men's work as producers was increasingly subject to new forms of discipline and rationalisation, particularly in the United States though increasingly in Europe. This was the period of the emergence of 'Fordism', the assembly line, mass production and Frederick Taylor's theories about 'scientific management' which were designed to increase productivity by systematic observation and standardisation of human behaviour in the workplace. The implementation of Taylorism, which entailed a deskilling process as work became more routinised, inflexible and required less thought, was not confined to factories. It was applied increasingly to office work, retailing and the service industries, so rationalisation also affected the middle-classes. The new systematised work processes were often resisted, but the resulting increases in productivity and economic surplus led to higher wages for workers which enabled them to pay for the range of new commodities now available at lower prices on the market.[70] This increased ability to consume acted in effect as compensation for the greater monotony and duress of the workplace.[71] Yet in its turn this compensation was undermined by the contradiction between men's work experiences and those of women, because precisely at the moment that many men were experiencing constraints in their places of employment, women were stepping out. The work that women were doing as consumers, unlike men's, continued to require substantial levels of skill and expertise and remained the one sector of the modern production–retailing cycle that was un-Taylorised and self-regulated. Moreover, this loose, undisciplined activity, although essential in terms of its economic productivity, often took place in the luxurious and symbolically resonant environment that I have already described.

The imagined freedoms and pleasures that these unsupervised excursions to the department stores offered, the ambiguous position of shopping as an activity which was neither clearly work nor leisure, and the financial control and social powers accruing to shoppers, together combined to generate a range of anxieties not only among the 'public' but also among those intellectuals whose ideas contributed to the formation of ideas about modernity and mass culture. Some of the anxieties to which I am referring surface and are easily identifiable in the contemporary accounts excavated by the historians of the stores. Others are more elusive and require different tools of analysis in order to make sense of them. The argument here is that all are associated in one way or another with the feminisation of consumption, with the fact that it was mainly women who did the shopping and that the modern form of consumption was consolidated during a period in which earlier social conventions and boundaries appeared to be rapidly dissolving.

A number of authors have produced work which contributes to the development of a sharper, more textured picture of the nature of the unease that seemed so pervasive and of the way it might have operated to deflect attention away from this particular aspect of commerce. The envy of men confined to routine Taylorised jobs in the face of the expanding liberty and responsibility that the new consumption entailed has already been argued for. Another less historicised way of explaining this envy can be developed by drawing on psychoanalysis. This is the approach of Rosalind Minsky who has explored the unconscious dynamic processes involved in the formation of envy provoked by the fantasised indulgence of desire and has argued that the sense of threat is constituted through the unconscious interpretation of the woman shopper as the pre-Oedipal phallic mother.[72] This kind of account, which draws attention to the fear of dependence as well as greed, goes some way towards explaining the continuing ambivalence of many men, including academics, to the processes involved in shopping. A more historically grounded version (but not one which focuses on gender) is offered by Daniel Horowitz who investigates the shifts in the nature of the anxieties expressed about consumption in the United States between the late nineteenth century and the 1920s. During the earlier period, concern is oriented towards the dangers of profligacy, particularly among workers and immigrants. Subsequently, the emphasis is on the dangers – the vacuity – of mass culture. Underlying both phases, he argues, is the fear of loss of self control in the pursuit of commodities and pleasures; this however sits uneasily with the recognition, current in the same moral discourse, that self-denial is not compatible with the imperatives of economic growth.[73]

Anxiety about the loss of moral and financial control generated by consumption is confirmed by Elaine Abelson who documents the increase in shoplifting by respectable middle-class women from the department stores during the same period. Losses incurred thus were not inconsiderable: in 1905 in New York alone they were estimated to reach thousands of dollars a day. Yet prosecutions were often not carried out since many of the women were also valued customers, wives or daughters of men quite able to afford the price of goods that had been stolen. The inevitable publicity of legal action in such cases was considered counterproductive. The stores had to be careful to maintain their attractive image, to encourage desire, yet at the same time not permit uncontrolled illegal consumption. Men, not surprisingly, were anxious in case their womenfolk succumbed to the temptations of theft or unconsidered buying in the course of their socially sanctioned shopping trips. This is the context from which emerged the construct of kleptomania, considered from its inception to be an illness of middle-class women and associated specifically with department stores.[74]

Interestingly, a popular film of the period entitled *The Kleptomaniac* addresses precisely this issue. It is about a wealthy woman guilty of stealing a decorative item from a store who is not prosecuted and a poor woman, guilty of stealing a loaf of bread, who is.[75] The contradiction inherent in the commercial practices of the department stores which on the one hand endorsed the creation of desire and on the other refused to prosecute 'respectable' customers guilty of theft is an example of the disavowal consumption seems to produce. It is also there in the contradiction highlighted by Horowitz between self-denial and spending.

Yet another reading of the ubiquitous anxieties associated with consumption can be elicited from the work of Stuart Ewen who emphasises the declining authority of fathers and husbands in the early decades of the century as women gradually enter the labour market and as their managerial status in the home is raised. Ewen understands this as a welcome diminution of patriarchal power.[76] Less positive readings of the phenomenon are made by Christopher Lasch and members of the Frankfurt School and will be returned to in the next section.

Expressions of concern about the erosion of men's control over spending and money merge into much more overtly sexualised narratives. Elements of sexual fearfulness and rivalry surface in most of the accounts about women and shopping during this period. The department stores are accused of 'unleashing passions'. 'Temptation' and 'gullibility' become growing preoccupations. Anxieties are voiced about the 'intoxication' caused by the 'sensuous' display of goods. Zola talks about the 'longing covetous gaze' of women customers and the danger of being devoured by the 'erotic' and 'seductive' world of the store. Miller in his account of the *Bon Marché* in Paris tells us of a woman who was alleged to obtain more 'voluptuous sensations' from the feel of silk than from her lover. A few decades later women shoppers in the United States are represented as capricious and emotional, craving glamour and romance.[77] Interestingly these sexual metaphors contain elements of both passivity and activity. On the one hand, they seem to suggest the fear that innocent women will be seduced and ravished. On the other, that the stores will release an unbridled sexuality, an ominous transgressiveness. Zola represents his women saleshoppers in this way, as part of an aggressive and sexually voracious mob:

> The women reigned supreme. They had taken the whole place by storm, camping there, as in a conquered country, like an invading horde. . . .[78]
>
> They advanced slowly . . . kept upright by the shoulders and bellies of those around them, of which they felt the close heat; and their satisfied desire enjoyed the painful entrance which incited still further their curiosity. There was a pell-mell of ladies arrayed in silk, of poorly dressed middle-class women, and of bare-headed girls, all excited and

carried away by the same passion. A few men buried beneath the overflow of bosoms were casting anxious glances around them. . . .[79]

The furs were scattered over the flooring, the ready-made clothes were heaped up like the great coats of wounded soldiers, the lace and underlinen, unfolded, crumpled, thrown about everywhere, made one think of an army of women who had disrobed there in the disorder of some sudden desire.[80]

These descriptions not only refer us back to the fears of uncontainable sexuality that the urban context itself seemed to mobilise during that period (and that are alluded to in the section of this chapter on the city),[81] they also evoke the way in which the crowd – the mob – has been recurringly feminised. Andreas Huyssen makes this point in the following way:

Male fears of an engulfing femininity are . . . projected onto the metropolitan masses, who did indeed represent a threat to the rational bourgeois order. . . . The fear of the masses in this age of declining liberalism is almost always also a fear of woman, a fear of nature out of control, a fear of the unconscious, of sexuality, of the loss of identity and stable ego boundaries in the mass. [82]

It seems therefore that the loss of authority over women shoppers cannot be dissociated from the semi-conscious fear of their untrammelled sexual desire and of the potential eruption of social forces. And in fact some of these connections were fairly explicitly made. The desire of ordinary women for 'finery' in the late Victorian period was perceived not only an indication of sexual immorality but also as an attempt to rise above their station.[83] The decomposition of the visible signs of class distinction that the department store offered, the continuous incitement of desire to possess commodities, the associated discontent and the promulgation of aspirations for a better life, did indeed represent a threat to the social order as well as, at the same time, a modernising force. Berman has pointed to the energy with which the bourgeoisie disrupted the earlier regimes.[84] In this instance the increasing and disturbing disintegration of social boundaries was produced by a contradictory alliance between modern capitalist methods of retailing and women consumers.

The anxieties about consumption and women shoppers that are outlined here have been deduced from a sparse literature. Commerce has not been considered worthy of much intellectual attention, as I have already pointed out, and so is not able to yield a theoretical commentary on the issues which is as extensive as that on other comparable aspects of mass culture. Cinema has produced the richest archive of comment and debate and it is from this source that it is possible to infer further evidence of anxiety about shopping as well as denial of its theoretical significance. Shopping, where it was referred to at all, was quite often associated with cinema-going in the period we are looking at. During the early decades of the century the cinema – like the department store – experienced a remarkable expansion. By 1909 there were over 340 movie houses and nickelodeons in New York City with an estimated 2 million visits per week. Paris had two cinemas in 1907 and by 1913 it had 160. In Germany the number of cinemas rose from two in 1900 to 2,446 in 1914. In Britain in the same year the number of cinemas was estimated at 4,000 with a weekly audience of 7–8 million.[85] The audiences who attended these movie houses – or 'dream palaces' as the agreeable new public social spaces were quickly to be called, echoing the language used about the stores – were composed predominantly of women, young people and children. Seebohm Rowntree estimated in the 1930s that 87.5 per cent of all cinema-goers fell into these categories.[86] During the daytime, audiences would have been almost exclusively made up of women and the young and women often combined their visits to the cinema with their shopping trips on their day excursions to the city centres.

The literature about this period of cinema-going indicates that there was widespread concern about the moral and physical consequences – particularly for the working class and the young – of the content of films and the social and physical environment in which they were shown.[87] Concern about the specific influence of cinema-going on women has been less documented but is also likely to have been extensive, and indeed Miriam Hansen has argued, in relation to this conjunctural moment in Germany, that the resistance to cinema's cultural respectability was a consequence of the threat posed to the organisation of public space by the high proportion of women cinema-goers.[88] Furthermore, women not only went to the cinema unaccompanied by men, once there they were not easily differentiated from each other in social terms: housewives, shopworkers and prostitutes sat as spectators in close proximity, blurring physically and metaphorically the boundaries between the respectable and the unrespectable.

It is certainly the case that 'passivity' and 'excessive excitation' appear as recurring preoccupations in much of the contemporary social comment about movie-going and that these personal attributes contain some of the same gendered and sexualised connotations that are repeated in the discussions about women's visits to the department stores. Some of these connections between shopping and cinema-going are quite explicitly made; others remain more coded, to be uncovered in the course of a closer examination of critical responses to mass culture more generally. The explicit links, made here and there, are what enable us to make the leap into another discourse and assume that the structures of feeling displayed by some of the most influential commentators on cinema and mass culture during the first half of this century have something to reveal to us about how shopping was understood then, and continues to be understood today, in relation to modernity. A few examples from a small selection of key thinkers will trace this chain of cultural associations.

INTELLECTUALS, CONSUMPTION AND MASS CULTURE

Louis Haugmard was among the first cultural critics to concern himself with the new form of cinema. In 1913, in his *Aesthetics of Cinema* (cited by Rosalind Williams) he analyses the specific complexities of film as a medium and elaborates his condemnation of its social ramifications, its escapism and its ability to deceive the naive public. He is among those commentators who consider the movies emotionally overstimulating and intellectually pacifying and he refers repeatedly to the 'excitation' and 'passivity' of cinema spectators. Moreover, and this is why his views are pertinent here, he makes a quite explicit connection between shopping and the cinema: 'the passive solitude of the moviegoer resembles the behaviour of department store shoppers who also submit to the reign of imagery with a strange combination of intellectual and physical passivity and emotional hyperactivity.'[89] Siegfried Kracauer is another cultural critic who, over a decade later, echoes the approach of Haugmard in his piece entitled 'The little shopgirls go to the cinema' and expresses similar fears about emotionality, passivity and receptivity and similarly connects the spheres of shopping and movie-going – not only materially but also symbolically in the very title of his work.[90]

Kracauer was part of a circle of intellectuals, often loosely referred to as the Frankfurt School, which during the 1930s generated a number of seminal critiques of cultural and social issues. Over the last fifteen years, in the context of the emergence of cultural studies as an academic discipline, and with the translation and (re)publication of well-known and more obscure essays, the influence of the analytical approaches and concerns of those associated with the Frankfurt School has been consolidated and is now extensive. In this section I want to sketch out some of the suggestive connections and omissions which appear in this work and which support my general thesis about the anxieties of influential cultural thinkers about consumption. This method will inevitably be deductive, since questions of consumption and shopping are simply not raised in most of the debates about mass culture. So, in order to unravel what might have been thought, consciously or unconsciously, it will be necessary to read texts against the apparent intentions of their authors, to pursue insights across arguments and moments and refocus so that the historical and psychic context from which ideas emerge is scrutinised with as much attention as the ideas themselves.

A useful starting point is Theodor Adorno and Max Horkheimer's critique of the culture industry, partly because of its status as a classic, almost iconic, piece of socio-political comment.[91] Adorno and Horkheimer, drawing on both American and German cultural examples, are deeply disturbed and angered by what they see as the banality of most mass culture

– its dissipating amorphousness and triviality – and they too condemn the 'passivity' and lack of discrimination of the consumer. One way of making sense of what emerges from this text (sometimes only in quite coded form) as a virulent denigration of ordinary audiences, is to turn to the authors' work on the family, much of it written in the preceding decade while they were still in Germany.[92] What emerges from this writing is a surprising nostalgia for an idealised family of the past and a sense of loss about the declining authority of the modern father in relation to his wife and children. Mass culture has threatened the potency of the father and displaced him as the socialising agent to which women and children now submit. The balance of forces within the family has been transformed.[93] Ironically one way of reading these views is to see them as evidence of *men's* passivity as they witness the reorientation of women's desires away from the home to the seductive environment of the cinema and stores. Women's spectatorship in both these contexts is increasingly active and enquiring. Many men – ordinary members of the public as well as intellectuals – are threatened by their exclusion from the pleasures and knowledge that consumption offers.[94] Mass culture emerges then as the despised yet alluring rival of the displaced man. The insistence of the cultural critics on the passivity of the consumer can be reread as denial, as a disavowal of the profound anxiety about loss and displacement that mass culture seems to engender.

Andreas Huyssen, whose indicatively entitled piece 'Mass culture as woman: modernism's other' was referred to earlier in relation to the way the masses have been feminised, explores in the same article the way mass culture likewise has been intricately bound up with pejorative notions of the feminine.[95] Mass culture moreover also takes on the attributes of the (feminised) masses, that is to say it is frequently depicted as engulfing, irrational, sentimental and so forth. Thus it is contrasted not only with masculinity but also with cultural modernism, which is hard, rigorous and rational, and which has always been concerned to distance itself from the popular. Interestingly for my argument here, Huyssen points out that Adorno, Horkheimer and Kracauer each, at different times, explicitly sexualise and engender mass culture. For example, Adorno and Horkheimer argue that mass culture 'cannot renounce the threat of castration'.[96] Adorno, of course, is also known for his defence of modernism and high cultural aesthetics against the encroaching contamination of mass culture. Huyssen's argument about the feminisation of mass culture, and mine about mass culture and consumption as the rival of the male, are obviously different yet they are not incompatible. Indeed, paradoxically, they confirm and complement each other methodologically. Both operate in symbolic registers – as metaphors – and centre-stage the way in which unconscious processes are at work in the formation of intellectual positions. Both insist that these must be rooted in specific historical contexts and narratives.

Walter Benjamin is another influential contributor to the debate about mass culture. His uncompleted and largely unpublished *Passagen-Werk* ('The Arcades Project'), reconstructed and developed with extraordinary insight and elegance by Susan Buck-Morss,[97] is one of the few attempts to theorise the significance of shopping arcades in relation to modernity and commodity capitalism and, in conjunction with his other work on culture and cinema, continues to have a profound influence on contemporary debates. In the context of the argument which is being put forward here, Benjamin must be distinguished from other associates of the Frankfurt School. His criticisms of mass culture are, at least in some places, far more tempered and complex and he argues for the aesthetic and political possibilities of popular cultural forms.[98] He is not only less pessimistic about mass culture and the advent of modernity – about 'modernity's rupture of tradition' – but he also welcomes the decline of 'the antiquarian effect of the father on his son'. Buck-Morss puts it thus:

> In a world of objects that changed its face drastically in the course of a generation, parents could no longer counsel their children. . . . The rupture of tradition was irrevocable. Far from lamenting the situation, Benjamin saw precisely here modernity's uniquely revolutionary potential. . . . The rupture of tradition . . . frees symbolic powers from conservative restraints for the task of social transformation . . . Benjamin insisted: 'We must wake up from the world of our parents.' [99]

Nevertheless, his Arcades Project is also at the same time full of a deeply felt ambivalence about the temptations of the metropolitan world of consumption and spectacle – the urban phantasmagoria – which both dazzles and deceives the crowd. The world of commodities is about *illusion*. Value is eclipsed by representation and display. Benjamin is simultaneously fascinated and guilty, both lustful and repelled by the luxury and decadence of city life. As Elizabeth Wilson has suggested, his views are at once utopian and dystopian.[100] He is also manifestly ambivalent towards women, where he considers them at all.[101] In most of Benjamin's work it is the prostitute who is presented as the key female figure in the iconography of the city, and at the same time, as *the* embodiment of commodification. In *Passagen-Werk* he argues that women use fashion to cover up the 'reality of natural decay', that fashion 'encourages the fetishistic fragmentation of the living body'. We see here the association Benjamin makes between women, commodities and consumption. Women, like commodities, are about surfaces and illusion. Yet among his notes for *Passagen-Werk*, and once more indicative of his contradictory feelings, he suggests also that fashion can be 'irreverent towards tradition . . . and emblematic of social change'.[102]

This major work is a unique yet contradictory and fragmented attempt to understand consumption. The ambivalence to commerce which is expressed throughout can, I think, be traced in part to Benjamin's recurring preoccupation with generational difference and his frequently documented conflicts with his own father, a financier who invested in innovative urban projects, among them a department store and ice-rink. Some of what Benjamin considered his formative commercial and erotic experiences are recounted in his autobiographical essay 'A Berlin chronicle':

> I was most lastingly affected ... when in about 1910 ... my father conceived the idea of taking me to ... The Ice Palace [which was] not only the first artificial ice rink to be seen in Berlin, but also a thriving night club. ... My attention was held ... by the apparitions at the bar. Among these was a prostitute in a very tight-fitting white sailor's suit, who determined my erotic fantasies for years to come. ...
>
> In those early years I got to know the 'town' only as a theatre of purchases, [where] ... my father's money cut a path for us between the shop counters and assistants and mirrors, and the appraising eyes of our mother, whose muff lay on the counter. In the ignominy of a 'new suit' we stood there, our hands peeping from the sleeves like dirty price tags, and it was only in the confectioners that our spirits rose with the feeling of having escaped the false worship that humiliated our mother. ... Caverns of commodities – that was the 'town'.[103]

Hannah Arendt in her introduction to the collection of Benjamin's essays *Illuminations* discusses the insolubility of the Jewish question for Jewish intellectuals of Benjamin's generation 'because all traditions and all cultures as well as all "belonging" had become equally questionable to them'. This refusal of tradition casts additional light on Benjamin's hostility to what his parents represented, to commerce and thence his route to 'commodity fetishism'.[104] Demetz interprets the conflict slightly differently:

> In many Jewish families of late nineteenth-century Europe, gifted sons turned against the commercial interests of their fathers, who were largely assimilated ... to bourgeois success, and, in building their counterworlds in spiritual protest, they incisively shaped the future of science, philosophy and literature. Articulating an insight of far-reaching implications, Karl Kraus, the belligerent Viennese satirist, suggested in his *Magical Operetta* (much enjoyed by Benjamin) that little Jewish family dramas were being played out all over, the stern fathers concerned with ... business and the spiritual sons with ... the less profitable matter of the pure mind.[105]

Among such sons, Demetz includes Freud, Husserl, Kafka and of course Benjamin himself, for whom 'the fundamental pattern reasserts itself with particular clarity'.[106] Benjamin's antagonism towards his parents – and his father in particular (referred to in his own autobiographical work as well as in the biographical accounts of Arendt and Demetz) – contributes to our understanding of his refusal (unlike Adorno and Horkheimer) to lament the decline of paternal authority in the family and helps explain his 'forward-lookingness', his optimism about the possibilities of the modern. A connection can also be made between his ambivalence towards commerce – his simultaneous fascination and repudiation of the 'theatres of purchases' and 'caverns of commodities' that 'create false worship' – and the anti-Semitic climate of central Europe in the 1930s described by Gregor von Rezzori in his *Memoirs of an Anti-Semite* in which 'Commerce per se was embarrassing . . . anything connected with selling in a store was below social acceptance. This was a privilege of the Jews'.[107] The humiliating anti-Semitic targeting of commerce, about which Benjamin must have felt enormously contradictory, was actualised during the period of his immersion in the writing of *Passagen-Werk* by the officially authorised Nazi boycotts of Jewish-owned department stores in Berlin, which, in April 1933, were among the first propaganda assaults of Hitler's newly elected government.[108]

These contextual factors help to make sense of Benjamin's equivocal and uncompleted analysis of consumption as well as his orientation towards the future – his modernism, in Berman's terms. They do not though explain his lack of serious attention to the ways in which consumption is *gendered*, to the ways ordinary modern women might be placed in relation to the modernity and shops he so meticulously represents. This omission, this failure to explore the significance of the feminisation of such a crucial aspect of commodity capitalism and mass culture must also be understood (like the similar omissions of other intellectuals of this and earlier periods) in the context of the broader social and psychic transformations of the period. The shifting balance of forces between men and women in the family and the growing independence of women have already been referred to. This period was also affected by the traumatic and dehumanising slaughter of the First World War. Challenges to the constraints and conventions of femininity reached a particularly frenzied pace during the interwar years and meshed with anxieties about the demographic crisis and the numerical disparity of the sexes resulting from the war. Concerns about 'superfluous' women – who in the popular imagination were also 'new' women: flappers, hedonists, feminists, workers, voters – can be read as evidence of a crisis of masculinity, of men's fear of being diminished, swamped and consumed.[109] Klaus Theweleit has analysed the cultural dread of dissolution and engulfment exhibited during this period in the writing and fantasies of German Freikorps soldiers who were later to become the vanguard of the Nazi Party. He makes the point that some of these fears are articulated by men of the left as well. It would not be surprising therefore – in a context in which additionally, German socialist feminism was still robust and the Weimar Sex Reform movement, designed to address the sexual interests of the new woman, had a membership of 150,000 – to find a certain ambivalence about women and a certain blindness about the feminisation of mass culture and consumption in the work of the cultural critics of the period. [110]

CONCLUSION

One of the innovations of feminist thought has been to alert us to the unpredictable and covert ways of the symbolic world. It has encouraged us to pose different kinds of questions of texts, authors and social processes. In this piece of work, my project has been to excavate the different contexts in which influential ideas about women, modernity and consumption have developed and to refocus theoretical investigation onto gaps and inflections as well as emphases. What has emerged from this research is a history pitted by ambivalence and denial. Modernity as a narrative and experience has turned out to be far more profoundly marked by the material and imagined presence of women than the classic accounts have allowed. Yet, consumption, the sphere in which women's participation has been so culturally and economically definitive, has barely been addressed by the academy.[111] What I have tried to argue here is that this discursive marginalisation must be understood partly as a consequence of the association of consumption with the destabilisation of nineteenth-century femininities and the emergence of the new woman. Public unease provoked by these shifting cultural patterns and the fantasised loss of control incurred in visits to the department stores, meshed in complex ways during the early part of this century with intellectual ambivalence about mass culture and disdain for commerce. This mood, the cultural formation that I have identified here, is deeply implicated in the construction of views about consumption. It has led to the repudiation of shopping and shoppers and a denial of the theoretical centrality of women to the making of modernity.

NOTES

1 Alan O'Shea, 'English subjects of modernity', Chapter 1 of this volume.
2 Among the authors and texts I have drawn on for the purposes of my argument are Perry Anderson, 'Modernity and revolution', *New Left Review*, no. 144, 1984; Charles Baudelaire, *The Painter of Modern Life and Other Essays*, Oxford, Phaidon, 1965; Walter Benjamin, *Illuminations*, ed. Hannah Arendt, London, Fontana, 1973; Walter Benjamin, *Reflections*, ed. Peter Demetz, New York, Schocken Books, 1986; Marshall Berman, *All That is Solid Melts Into Air: The Experience of Modernity*, London, Verso, 1983; Marshall Berman, 'The signs in the street: a response to Perry Anderson', *New Left Review*, no. 145, 1984; Malcolm Bradbury and James McFarlane (eds), *Modernism 1890–1930*, Harmondsworth, Penguin, 1987; Susan Buck-Morss, *The Dialectics of Seeing: Walter Benjamin and the Arcades Project*, Cambridge, Mass., MIT Press, 1989; David Frisby, *Fragments of Modernity: Georg Simmel, Siegfried Kracauer and Walter Benjamin*, London, Heinemann, 1985; Scott Lash and Jonathan Friedman (eds), *Modernity and Identity*, Oxford, Blackwell, 1992; Richard

Sennett, *The Fall of Public Man*, London, Faber and Faber, 1977; Georg Simmel, 'The metropolis and mental life', in his *On Individuality and Social Forms*, Chicago, Ill., University of Chicago Press, 1971; Raymond Williams, *The Politics of Modernism*, London, Verso, 1989; Elizabeth Wilson, *Sphinx in the City*, London, Virago, 1991; Elizabeth Wilson, 'The invisible *flâneur*', *New Left Review*, no. 191, 1992; Janet Wolff 'The invisible *flâneuse*: women and the literature of modernity', *Theory, Culture and Society* vol. 2, no. 3, 1985; Janet Wolff, *Feminine Sentences: Essays on Women and Culture*, Cambridge, Polity, 1990.

3 Berman, 'Signs in the street'.

4 Wilson, *Sphinx*; Christine Buci-Glucksmann, 'Catastrophic Utopia: the feminine as allegory of the modern', in C. Gallagher and T. Laqueur, (eds), *The Making of the Modern Body*, Berkeley and Los Angeles, University of California Press, 1987.

5 Frisby, *Fragments of Modernity*; Lieteke van Vucht Tijssen, 'Women and objective culture: Georg Simmel and Marianne Weber', *Theory, Culture and Society*, vol. 8 no. 3, 1991.

6 'The invisible *flâneuse*: woman and the literature of modernity' was first published in *Theory, Culture and Society* in 1985. A revised version appears in Wolff's collection of essays, *Feminine Sentences*. More recently, in 'Memoirs and micrologies: Walter Benjamin, feminism and cultural analysis', *New Formations*, no. 20, 1993, Janet Wolff affirms her continuing support of the argument initially advanced in 'Invisible *flâneuse*'.

7 Wolff, 'Invisible *flâneuse*', p. 44.

8 The reprinted version of this article in *Feminine Sentences*, includes a slightly longer comment on this subject than the original. See also Janet Wolff's comment in her essay 'Feminism and modernism' in the same book.

9 This is despite the fact that she also draws on theorists whose major concern was with the social transformations which took place later, at the end of the nineteenth and beginning of the twentieth centuries in order to support her argument (for example, Thorstein Veblen, *The Theory of the Leisure Class*, Harmondsworth, Penguin, 1979, originally published 1899; and Georg Simmel, 'The metropolis and mental life').

10 Elizabeth Wilson's phrase in 'Invisible *flâneur*', p. 98. Wilson is more sceptical than Wolff. For her the *flâneur* is a powerless and marginal figure, a loiterer–voyeur in the urban labyrinth.

11 Her reliance on Thorstein Veblen for the development of her comments on consumption confirms this approach. For a critique of Veblen's analysis see Grant McCracken, *Culture and Consumption*, Bloomington and Indianapolis: Indiana University Press, 1990; and Amanda Vickery, 'Women and the world of goods: a Lancashire consumer and her possessions 1751–81', in J. Brewer and R. Porter, (eds) *Consumption and the World of Goods*, London, Routledge, 1992.

12 Lesley Johnson, *The Modern Girls*, Milton Keynes, Open University Press, 1993, has also commented on this.

13 Leonore Davidoff, Jean L'Esperance and Howard Newby, 'Landscape with figures: home and community in English society', in J. Mitchell and A. Oakley (eds), *The Rights and Wrongs of Women*, Harmondsworth, Penguin, 1976; Mica Nava, 'The urban, the domestic and education for girls', in G. Grace (ed.), *Education and the City*, London, Routledge and Kegan Paul, 1984, (reprinted in Mica Nava, *Changing Cultures: Feminism, Youth and Consumerism*, London, Sage, 1992); Nikolas Rose, 'The psychological complex: mental measurement

and social administration', *Ideology and Consciousness*, no. 5, 1979; Gareth Stedman Jones, *Outcast London*, Harmondsworth, Penguin, 1976; Judith Walkowitz, *City of Dreadful Delight*, London, Virago, 1992; Raymond Williams, *Country and City*, Harmondsworth, Penguin, 1975; Elizabeth Wilson, *Sphinx*. See also John Marriott's chapter in this volume. Twentieth-century British versions are also more pessimistic – see, for example, the debate between Marshall Berman ('Signs in the street') and Perry Anderson ('Modernity and revolution') in *New Left Review* in 1984; and the ideology of the garden city and slum clearance movements (Wilson, *Sphinx*).

14 European and American accounts of the city, although often ambivalent and concerned about the destruction of traditional values and modes of living, were also less fearful and more inclined to welcome – even celebrate – the rich and complex phantasmagoria of the modern metropolitan landscape. As Elizabeth Wilson has pointed out (*Sphinx*, 1991), in Paris whole families were likely to enjoy the cafe life on the broad new boulevards, while in the United States the city came increasingly to represent a modern architectural and social ideal. See also, for example, Theodore Dreiser's *Sister Carrie*, Harmondsworth, Penguin, 1981 (first published in 1900).

15 Judith Walkowitz, *Prostitution and Victorian Society*, Cambridge, Cambridge University Press, 1980; Walkowitz, *City*; Wilson, *Sphinx*; Nava, 'The urban and the domestic'.

16 Andreas Huyssen has pointed to some of these associations in 'Mass culture as woman: modernism's other', in his *After the Great Divide*, London, Macmillan, 1986, in which he also quotes Gustave Le Bon: 'Crowds are everywhere characterised by feminine characteristics' (p. 52). On the morality of the rural and domestic, see Sennet, *Public Man*; and Davidoff *et al.* 'Landscape'.

17 Janet Wolff is the one to have made the link to modernity and it is repeated in several of her essays in *Feminine Sentences*; see, for example, 'The culture of separate spheres: the role of culture in nineteenth-century public and private life'. Other feminist historians have also explored the separate spheres of men and women, at least as an ideal: see, for example, the extensive and important contributions of Leonore Davidoff and Catherine Hall who stress the material interdependence of the 'public' and the 'private' during the first half of the nineteenth century in their *Family Fortunes: Men and Women of the English Middle Class 1780–1850*, London, Hutchinson, 1987. See also Jenny Ryan for an example of a feminist historian whose emphasis is predominantly on the constraints of separate spheres and on patriarchal exclusion of women from the public domain in her *Women, Modernity and the City*, Working Papers in Popular Cultural Studies no. 1, Manchester, Manchester Institute for Popular Culture, 1992.

18 Amanda Vickery, 'Shaking the separate spheres', *Times Literary Supplement*, 12 March 1993, p. 6; Wilson, 'Invisible *flâneur*'; Walkowitz, *City*.

19 Sharon Zukin, 'The postmodern debate over urban form', *Theory, Culture and Society*, vol. 5, nos. 2–3, 1988. For details of the expansion of public spaces available to women see Paul Greenhalgh, *Ephemeral Vistas: The Expositions Universelles, Great Exhibitions and World's Fairs, 1851–1939*, Manchester, Manchester University Press, 1988; Elaine Abelson, *When Ladies Go A-Thieving: Middle-Class Shoplifters in the Victorian Department Store*, Oxford, Oxford University Press, 1989; Walkowitz, *City*; Wilson, *Sphinx*.

20 Lynne Walker, 'Women and Victorian public space', paper given at 'The Cracks in the Pavement' conference at the Design Museum, London, 1991. Walker showed a slide of two women in the 1890s travelling on the underground with

their briefcases. Alison Adburgham, *Shops and Shopping 1800–1914*, London, Barrie and Jenkins, 1989, refers to the cycling craze and the new fashions that were required for it.

21 See, for example, Elaine Abelson, *Ladies*; and William Leach, 'Transformations in a culture of consumption: women and department stores, 1890–1925', *Journal of American History*, vol. 7, no. 2, 1984, for the United States; and Adburgham, *Shops and Shopping*, and Walkowitz, *City*, for England, particularly London. See Walkowitz, *City*, pp. 50–2, for a discussion of male pests and sexual harassment.

22 Patricia Hollis, *Women in Public: The Women's Movement 1850–1900*, London, George Allen and Unwin, 1979, p. 226; see also Jane Addams, *The Spirit of Youth and the City Streets*, New York, Macmillan, 1910; Olive Banks, *Faces of Feminism*, Oxford, Martin Robertson, 1981; Mica Nava, 'The urban and the domestic'; Elizabeth Wilson, *Women and the Welfare State*, London, Tavistock, 1978; Walkowitz, *City*.

23 Walkowitz, *City*, p. 53.

24 Berman, *All That Is Solid*.

25 See Elizabeth Wilson's discussion in 'Invisible *flâneur*', of the arguments made by Janet Wolff in 'Invisible *flâneuse*', and by Griselda Pollock in 'Modernity and the spaces of femininity', in her *Vision and Difference*, London, Routledge, 1988.

26 Michel Foucault, *Power/Knowledge*, Brighton, Harvester, 1980; see also Jacques Donzelot, *The Policing of Families*, London, Hutchinson, 1979, who draws on Foucault and explores the shift in philanthropy from the gift of charity to the rendering of advice.

27 This point is developed in Nava, 'The urban and the domestic'.

28 Lisa Tickner, *The Spectacle of Women: Imagery of the Suffrage Campaign 1907–1914*, London, Chatto and Windus, 1987.

29 Berman, *All That is Solid*, p. 163.

30 Banks, *Faces of Feminism*; Tickner, *Spectacle of Women*; Ray Strachey, *The Cause*, London, Virago, 1978; Elizabeth Robins, *The Convert*, London, The Women's Press, 1980.

31 See, for example, Ruth Brandon, *The New Women and The Old Men: Love, Sex and the Woman Question*, London, Flamingo, 1990; Duncan Crow, *The Edwardian Woman*, London, George Allen and Unwin, 1978; Ellen Trimberger, 'Feminism, men and modern love: Greenwich Village 1900–1935', in Ann Snitow, Christine Stansell and Sharon Thompson (eds), *Desire: The Politics of Sexuality*, London, Virago, 1984; Elaine Showalter, *Sexual Anarchy: Gender and Culture at the Fin de Siècle*, London, Virago, 1992; Vita Sackville-West, *The Edwardians*, London, Virago, 1983; Jeffrey Weeks, *Sex, Politics and Society*, London, Longman, 1981.

32 Stuart Ewen and Elizabeth Ewen, *Channels of Desire: Mass Images and the Shaping of American Consciousness*, New York, McGraw Hill, 1982.

33 Martin Jay, 'Scopic regimes of modernity', in Lash and Friedman (eds), *Modernity and Identity*; see also Pasi Falk, 'For your eyes only? The scopic regimes of shopping', in Colin Campbell and Pasi Falk (eds), *Shopping Experience*, London, Sage, forthcoming 1996. The quote from Emile Zola's notes is taken from Kirstin Ross' introduction to Zola's novel, *The Ladies' Paradise*, Berkeley and Los Angeles, University of California Press, 1992 (originally published in 1883).

34 Alison Adburgham, *Shopping in Style: London from the Restoration to Edwardian Elegance*, London, Thames and Hudson, 1979; Colin Campbell, *The Romantic*

Ethic and the Spirit of Modern Consumerism, Oxford, Blackwell, 1987; Neil McKendrick, John Brewer and J.H. Plumb, *The Birth of a Consumer Society: The Commercialisation of Eighteenth-Century England*, London, Europa, 1982; Veblen, *Leisure Class*; Amanda Vickery, 'Women and the world of goods'.

35 Cited in Adburgham, *Shopping in Style*, pp. 71 and 93.

36 Zola, *Paradise*; Michael Schudson, *Advertising the Uneasy Persuasion*, New York, Basic Books, 1984, has suggested that this should be understood as a democratisation of aspiration and envy. But this is another debate. For the expansion of consumer culture into the middle classes see also Abelson *Ladies*; and David Chaney, 'The department store as cultural form', *Theory, Culture and Society*, vol. 1, no. 3, 1983.

37 Campbell, *Romantic Ethic*, has tried to unravel the relationship of production and consumption to 'consumer society' and argues for the rise of a romantic ethic which fuels demand. Dorothy Davis in *A History of Shopping*, London, Routledge and Kegan Paul, 1966, attributes the success of the department store in part to the growth of white-collar workers, small businesses and professional classes.

38 Adburgham's phrase used to describe the stores in the period before the First World War, *Shopping in Style*.

39 Cited in Kirstin Ross' introduction to Zola's *Paradise*.

40 Cited in Buck-Morss, *Dialectics*, p. 83.

41 Chaney, 'The department store as cultural form'.

42 Stuart Ewen, *All Consuming Images*, New York, Basic Books, 1988.

43 Simmel, *On Individuality and Social Forms*.

44 Leonore Davidoff, *The Best Circles*, London, Croom Helm, 1973; Dreiser, *Sister Currie*; Stuart Ewen, *All Consuming Images*; Mike Featherstone, 'Consumer culture', *Theory, Culture and Society*, vol. 1, no. 3, 1983; Adrian Forty, *Objects of Desire*, London, Thames and Hudson, 1986; Michael Schudson, *Advertising*; Georg Simmel, *On Individuality and Social Forms*; Veblen, *Leisure Class*.

45 Abelson, *Ladies*; Leach, 'Transformations in a culture of consumption; Walkowitz, *City*; among the first public toilets for 'ladies' were those provided by the department stores. This was obviously an added incentive.

46 It is generally estimated that 80 per cent of purchasing decisions today are made by women and that this has been the case since the beginning of the century at least, see Martin Pumphrey, 'The flapper, the housewife and the making of modernity', *Cultural Studies*, vol. 1, no. 2, 1987; and Roland Marchand, *Advertising the American Dream: Making Way for Modernity 1920–1940*, Berkeley and Los Angeles, University of California Press, 1986. Women were certainly identified with the internal decor of their homes and were responsible for design and domestic shopping decisions from the mid-nineteenth century onwards: Forty, *Objects*. Men seem never to have been very comfortable in department stores except as sellers, and even here their importance declined from the late nineteenth century onwards: Adburgham, *Shopping in Style*; William Lancaster, *The Department Store: A Social History*, London, Pinter, 1995. Abelson claims that 90 per cent of visitors to the stores in America during this period were women (*Ladies*).

47 Christopher Breward, 'Femininity and consumption: the problem of the late nineteenth-century fashion journal', *Journal of Design History*, June 1994.

48 Charles Eckert, 'The Carole Lombard in Macy's window', in J. Gaines and C. Herzog (eds), *Fabrications: Costume and the Female Body*, London, Routledge, 1990.

49 Pierre Bourdieu, *Distinction: A Social Critique of the Judgement of Taste*, London, Routledge and Kegan Paul, 1986.

50 There were of course regional and historical variations. Not all were as glamorous as those described here. Some were modernised while others were built from scratch. Provincial and suburban stores were oriented towards a different clientele. Yet all were designed to be attractive and make women feel welcome. The account I present here is a composite based on the research of Abelson, *Ladies*; Adburgham, *Shopping in Style*, and *Shops and Shopping*; Rachel Bowlby, *Just Looking: Consumer Culture in Dreiser, Gissing and Zola*, London, Methuen, 1985; Sean Callery, *Harrods Knightsbridge: The Story of Society's Favourite Store*, London, Ebury Press, 1991; Maurice Covina, *Fine Silks and Oak Counters,: Debenhams 1778–1978*, London, Hutchinson Benham, 1978; Davis, *History of Shopping*; Gordon Honeycombe, *Selfridges*, London, Park Lane Press, 1984; Lancaster, *The Department Store*; Leach, 'Transformations in a culture of consumption'; Michael Miller, *The Bon Marché: Bourgeois Culture and the Department Store 1869–1920*, London, Allen and Unwin, 1981; Michael Moss and Alison Turton, *A Legend of Retailing: House of Fraser*, London, Weidenfeld and Nicolson, 1989; Rosalind Williams, *Dream Worlds: Mass Consumption in Late Nineteenth-Century France*, Berkeley and Los Angeles, University of California Press, 1982; Zola, *Paradise*, 1992.

51 The Ladies Club at Harrods was panelled in Brecchi Sanguine, Pavannazi and Levantine marbles and onyx according to Harrods publicity material of 1910 cited in Callery, *Harrods*, 1991.

52 Williams, *Dream Worlds*.

53 Zola, *Paradise*, p. 215. The 1886 translation is not credited.

54 One of the posters in 'The Spirit of Modern Commerce' series produced by Selfridge's to mark the fifth anniversary of its opening which celebrates 'the Romance that lies in Commerce' (held in the store's archive). This poster is also interesting for its text (unfortunately not legible in this reproduction) particularly in relation to the argument I develop later in this chapter. Written by German industrialist Herr Rudolph Hertzog, it is a comment on the important place of the merchant in the life of the people both at home and abroad, and attempts to analyse the lack of regard with which 'princes of commerce' are viewed compared to landowners, even by their own sons. See note 106 below for further discussion of this aspect of Hertzog's comments.

55 Williams, *Dream Worlds*.

56 Adburgham, *Shopping in Style*, p. 159.

57 Adburgham, *Shops and Shopping*; Callery, *Harrods*.

58 See Davis, *History of Shopping*; Honeycombe, *Selfridges*; and Selfridges archive. Figure 2 ('Selfridge's "at home"') was one of a series of full-page advertisements which appeared in the London daily papers in March 1909 to mark the opening of the store (Selfridges archive). The full text reads:

> We are always ready with a welcome to strangers within our gates. We bid them feel at home and endeavour in every way imaginable to create and cherish that comfortable sentiment. Reception Rooms are open to them in which to meet their friends. Name Registers in the National Rooms will enable them to record their own advent and tell them of home acquaintances who may also be in London. The Library is available for correspondence and the Post Office for mailing it. The Silent Room is eloquent of quietude. Retiring Rooms are many and perfectly appointed. If our visitor

is a Gentleman the Smoke Lounge is suggestive of a meditative weed. And these accommodations belong to visitors without fee of any kind whatever and without the remotest obligation in their use to make a purchase.

The Parcel and Cloak Room takes charge of all impediments. The Bureau de Change will negotiate letters of credit. The Information Office will answer accurately any reasonable question. Seats at all theatres can be booked, and Railway and Steamship tickets taken to anywhere without going outside our doors. The Luncheon Hall and *al fresco* Tea Garden serve appetising teas and luncheons in dainty home-like fashion at moderate charges: and from floor to floor, through the hundred or more departments, are displays of Manifold Merchandise incomparable in richness, utility and quality at London's Lowest Prices – always.

59 The stores also provided significant career and income opportunities for women. See Lancaster, *The Department Store*; W. Leach, 'Transformations in a culture of consumption'; Zola, *Paradise.*

60 One of Selfridge's promotional advertisements for its launch in 1909. Selfridges archive.

61 Christopher Breward, 'Femininity and consumption'; Billie Melman, *Women and the Popular Imagination in the Twenties*, London, Macmillan, 1988; Sally Stein, 'The graphic ordering of desire: modernisation of a middle-class women's magazine 1914–1939', *Heresies*, no. 18, 1985.

62 For a discussion of rationality and irrationality in consumer discourse see Mica Nava and Rosalind Minsky, 'Women as rational and irrational shoppers', unpublished (available from authors).

63 See Sean Nixon, 'Have you got the look? Masculinities and shopping spectacle' in R. Shields, (ed.) *Life Style Shopping: The Subject of Consumption*, London, Routledge, 1992, for further discussion of this. See also Rosalind Minsky's section of Nava and Minsky, 'Women as shoppers'.

64 Leach, 'Transformations in a culture of consumption', p. 342. This is a contentious reading of course. Cultural analysis, particularly of the left, has a well established convention of seeing commodity culture as irredeemably bad. Thomas Richards' eloquent critique of advertising and the growth of mass consumption is an example of this, *The Commodity Culture of Victorian England: Advertising and Spectacle 1851–1914*, London, Verso, 1991. See also the discussion in Mica Nava, 'Consumerism reconsidered: buying and power', in her *Changing Cultures.*

65 Tickner, *Spectacle of Women*; Leach, 'Transformations in a culture of consumption', Lancaster, *The Department Store.*

66 Harley Granville Barker, *The Madras House*, London, Eyre Methuen, 1977, pp. 83, 84 and 88. Thanks to Peter Horne for alerting me to this play.

67 Honeycombe, *Selfridges*, p. 24; see also Leach, 'Transformations in a culture of consumption', for information about USA; Lancaster cites David Neville's M.Phil., 'Women's suffrage on Tyneside', University of Northumbria, as a source of information about Fenwicks in Newcastle, *The Department Store*. See also Adburgham, *Shops and Shopping*; Roger Fulford, *Votes for Women*, London, Faber and Faber, 1957.

68 McCracken, *Culture and Consumption*, p. 28.

69 For a discussion of these issues see chs 8 and 10 in Nava, *Changing Cultures*. Consumption as an area of theoretical study is now finally expanding quite rapidly. Among significant contributions to the literature not cited elsewhere in this chapter are: Erica Carter, 'Alice in consumer wonderland' in

A. McRobbie and M. Nava, (eds), *Gender and Generation*, London, Macmillan, 1984; and Erica Carter, *How German is She? National Reconstruction and the Consuming Woman in the FRG and West Berlin 1945–1960*, Ann Arbour, University of Michigan Press, 1995; Meaghan Morris, 'Things to do with shopping centres' in S. Sheridan (ed.), *Grafts*, London, Verso, 1988; Frank Mort, 'Boys own? masculinity, style and popular culture', in R. Chapman and J. Rutherford (eds), *Male Order: Unwrapping Masculinity*, London, Lawrence and Wishart, 1988; Shields, *Life Style Shopping*.

70 Stuart Ewen, *Captains of Consciousness: Advertising and the Social Roots of Consumer Society*, New York, McGraw Hill, 1976, and Ewen, *All Consuming Images*; Antonio Gramsci, 'Americanism and Fordism', in Q. Hoare and G. Nowell Smith (eds), *Prison Notebooks*, London, Lawrence and Wishart, 1973; Bill Schwarz, 'Rationalism, Irrationalism and Taylorism', *Science as Culture*, no. 8, 1991; Peter Wollen 'Modern times: cinema/Americanism/the robot', in his *Raiding the Icebox: Reflections on Twentieth-Century Culture*, London, Verso, 1993.

71 Zygmunt Bauman, 'Industrialism, consumerism and power', *Theory, Culture and Society*, vol. 1, no. 3, 1983.

72 Nava and Minsky, 'Women as shoppers'.

73 Daniel Horowitz, *The Morality of Spending: Attitudes Towards Consumer Society in America 1875–1940*, Baltimore, Md., Johns Hopkins University Press, 1985.

74 Abelson, *Ladies*, 1989; Miller, *Bon Marché*; Zola, *Paradise*.

75 Film directed by Edwin Porter in 1905 referred to in Ewen and Ewen, *Channels of Desire*, p. 89.

76 Ewen, *Captains of Consciousness*; and Ewen and Ewen, *Channels of Desire*.

77 Zola, *Paradise*; Miller, *Bon Marché*, p. 204; Marchand, *Advertising the American Dream*.

78 Zola, *Paradise*, p. 236.

79 ibid., p. 214.

80 E. Zola quoted by Ross in her introduction to ibid., p. xvii.

81 Elizabeth Wilson, *Sphinx*, explores the associations between the city and seductive but threatening sexualities.

82 Andreas Huyssen, *After the Great Divide*, pp. 52–3. Huyssen also elaborates on the contributions of Gustave Le Bon and Klaus Theweleit to this debate.

83 Mariana Valverde, 'The love of finery: fashion and the fallen woman in 19th century social discourse', *Victorian Studies*, Winter, 1989.

84 Berman, *All That is Solid*.

85 Ewen and Ewen, *Channels of Desire*; Annette Kuhn, *Cinema, Censorship and Sexuality 1909–1925*, London, Routledge, 1988; Gerald Mast, *The Movies in Our Midst: Documents in the Cultural History of Film in America*, Chicago, Ill., University of Chicago Press, 1982; Alan O'Shea, 'English subjects of modernity', Chapter 1 in this volume; Ken Ward, *Mass Communications and the Modern World*, London, Macmillan, 1991.

86 Seebohm Rowntree survey reported, in Jeffrey Richards, *The Age of the Dream Palace: Cinema and Society in Britain 1930–1939*, London, Routledge, 1984, that 50 per cent of cinema-goers were young people and children, and of the remaining adults, 75 per cent were women. Such precise information about the earlier period is not available.

87 Kuhn, *Cinema*; Mast, *The Movies*; Ward, *Mass Communications*.

88 Miriam Hansen, 'Early silent cinema: whose public sphere', *New German Critique*, no. 29, 1983, pp. 173–5.

89 Rosalind Williams, *Dream Worlds*, 1982, p. 82. Williams summarises Haugmard's views on pp. 78–84.

90 Siegfried Kracauer, 'The cult of distraction: on Berlin's picture palaces'; Sabine Hake, 'Girls in crisis'; and Patrice Petro, 'Modernity and mass culture in Weimar', all in *New German Critique*, no. 40, 1987; Hansen, 'Early silent cinema', 1983.

91 Theodor Adorno and Max Horkheimer, *Dialectic of Enlightenment*, London, Allen Lane, 1973.

92 Max Horkheimer, 'Authority and the family' and 'Art and mass culture', both in his *Critical Theory: Selected Essays*, New York, Heider and Heider, 1972; Martin Jay, *Adorno*, London, Fontana, 1984; David Held, *Introduction to Critical Theory*, London, Hutchinson, 1980; Mark Poster, *Critical Theory of the Family*, London, Pluto Press, 1978.

93 Christopher Lasch makes exactly the same point in *The Culture of Narcissism*, New York, Norton, 1979, p. 74 and similarly bemoans these transformations.

94 See again Rosalind Minsky's section in Nava and Minsky, 'Women as shoppers'.

95 Huyssen, in *After the Great Divide*,; (this article was originally published in Tania Modleski, (ed.), *Studies in Entertainment: Critical Approaches to Mass Culture*, Indianapolis and Bloomington, Indiana University Press, 1986). For a complementary analysis which also looks at the feminisation of mass culture see Tania Modleski, 'Femininity as Mas(s)querade: a feminist approach to mass culture', in C. McCabe (ed.), *High Theory/Low Culture*, Manchester, Manchester University Press, 1986, reprinted in T. Modleski, *Feminism Without Women*, London, Routledge, 1991.

96 Huyssen, *After the Great Divide*, p.48. Tania Modleski in 'Femininity as Mas(s)querade', makes a parallel point about Jean Baudrillard's ambivalence towards these issues. For him, she says, 'the masses function as a "gigantic black whole", a simile ostensibly taken from physics, but perhaps owing something to (feminine) anatomy as well' (p. 48).

97 Buck-Morss, *Dialectics of Seeing*; and Susan Buck-Morss, 'Benjamin's *Passagen-Werk*: redeeming mass culture for the revolution', *New German Critique*, no. 29, 1983. See also Ben Brewster, 'Walter Benjamin and the Arcades Project', and Walter Benjamin, 'Paris – capital of the nineteenth century', both in *New Left Review*, no. 48, 1968; Benjamin, *Illuminations*; Benjamin, *Reflections*; Angela McRobbie, 'The *Passagenwerk* and the place of Walter Benjamin in cultural studies', *Cultural Studies*, vol. 6, no. 2, 1992; Wilson, 'Invisible *flâneur*'; Daniel Miller, 'Could shopping ever really matter?', in Campbell and Falk (eds), *Shopping Experience*.

98 See for example W. Benjamin, 'The work of art in the age of mechanical reproduction', in his *Illuminations*.

99 Buck-Morss, *Dialectics of seeing*, p. 279.

100 Wilson, 'Invisible *flâneur*'.

101 Susan Buck-Morss makes very little reference to this in either of her discussions of *Passagen-Werk* (*Dialectics of Seeing*; and 'Benjamin's *Passagen-Werk*'). But see, for example, Benjamin's autobiographical 'A Berlin chronicle', in *Reflections*. See also Benjamin's *Moscow Diary*, ed. Gary Smith, Cambridge, Mass., Harvard University Press, 1986, in which he constantly reiterates his ambivalence towards Asja Lacis, the woman he travelled to Moscow to see. The theme of this relationship, according to Gary Smith in his afterword to *Moscow Diary*, is 'drawn as an erotic red thread throughout Benjamin's journal, [it] is one of obsession and denial' (p. 141).

102 S. Buck-Morss, *Dialectics of Seeing*, p. 98. See also Berman, *All That is Solid*; and Jane Gaines, 'Fabricating the female body', in Gaines and Herzog (eds), *Fabrications*, for further discussions of Benjamin's unease.

103 Benjamin, 'A Berlin chronicle', pp. 39–40.
104 Hannah Arendt, 'Introduction: Walter Benjamin 1892–1940', in Benjamin, *Illuminations*, p. 36. See also Buck-Morss, *Dialectics of Seeing*; Peter Demetz in his biographical introduction to the collection of Benjamin's essays, *Reflections*; and Walter Benjamin himself in his autobiographical pieces like 'A Berlin chronicle'.
105 Demetz, 'Introduction', in Benjamin, *Reflections*, p. ix. In order to place myself in relation to this narrative it is worth adding that my father, Marcel Weisselberg, and his brother and sisters, born at the beginning of the century into the Vienna that Karl Kraus describes, also engaged in these domestic intergenerational Jewish struggles about the relative value of commerce and intellectual–political life.
106 Demetz, 'Introduction', p. ix. It is also interesting in this context to refer back to Rudolph Hertzog's comments on the Selfridges fifth anniversary 'Spirit of Modern Commerce' poster (see note 55 above and Figure 2.1). My only information about Hertzog is there in the text: he is the head of one of the greatest businesses in the German empire and here in this letter of congratulation to Selfridge *c.* 1914 rather poignantly regrets that the sons of successful merchants have no pride in commerce and prefer to devote themselves to academic or official careers. 'The merchant is himself to blame if he does not receive the respect he deserves, because frequently he lets his sons choose other careers and gives the impression that he considers other callings of more importance than his own.'
107 Gregor von Rezzori, *Memoirs of an Anti-Semite: A Novel in Five Stories*, London, Pan Books, 1983, p. 86.
108 Bella Fromm, *Blood and Banquets: A Berlin Social Diary*, London, Geoffrey Bles, 1943; Norbert Frei, *National Socialist Rule in Germany: The Fuhrer State 1933–1945*, Oxford, Blackwell, 1987.
109   Melman, *Women and the Popular Imagination*; Marek Kohn, *Dope Girls: The Birth of the British Drug Underground*, London, Lawrence and Wishart, 1992. See also Sally Alexander's chapter in this volume.
110 Klaus Theweleit, *Male Fantasies*, Cambridge, Polity, 1987; Benjamin, *Moscow Diary*; Atina Grossmann, 'The new woman and the rationalisation of sexuality in Weimar Germany', in Ann Snitow *et al.* (eds), *Desire*; Werner Thonnessen, *The Emancipation of Women: Germany 1863–1933*, London, Pluto Press, 1973.
111 As I point out in note 69 above, this has recently started to change.

SENSATION OF THE ABYSS

The urban poor and modernity

John Marriott

FROM PETERSBURG TO SILVERTOWN

Marshall Berman alerts us to the significance of Andrei Biely's *Petersburg* to the modernist project and to the canon of twentieth-century literature.[1] Written in 1913–16 the novel expresses both the failure of the 1905 revolution and its enduring success and creativity in providing what Trotsky described as the majestic prologue to the revolutionary drama of 1917.[2] This it does by exploring the relationship between the son of an imperial officer and a member of the underground who become embroiled in an attempt on the life of the officer. As the narrative unfolds and confusion mounts the two drift into the distinctly modern thoroughfare of Nevsky Prospect which generates a 'new surreality: a vision of itself as a primal swamp in which the anguished modern individual can merge and submerge himself, forgetting his personality and his politics, and drown'.[3]

The street thus becomes a metaphorical site for the modernist psyche sunk in an existential despair from which the individual can emerge with renewed energy and direction. Biely's description of this state of mind is at the same time an affirmation of his vision of modernism: 'Of course, a modernist would call it sensation of the abyss, and he would search for the image that corresponds to the symbolic sensation.'[4] Thus 'sensation of the abyss' is the dangerous labyrinthine oblivion which engulfs the modern mind through experience of direct and immediate symbolic images of the abyss and its human contexts.

This imaginary universe exhibits striking homologies with contemporary constructions of the urban landscape, particularly in its use of the abyss to connote despair. To give two examples from many: in 1902 Charles Masterman, a gifted Liberal politician with a concern for the urban condition, who at the time was MP for Stratford, West Ham, published *From the Abyss*. With perspicacity he articulated middle-class sensibilities of the metropolitan poor as it threatened to encroach on their heartland:

> We are striving to readjust our stable ideas. But within there is
> a cloud on men's minds, a half stifled recognition of the presence of

a new force hitherto unreckoned; the creeping into unconscious existence of the quaint and innumerable populations bred in the abyss.[5]

In the same year Jack London approached Thomas Cook & Son, travel
agents, to find information on the East End and the best means of reaching
there. The firm, which could with ease have sent him to 'Darkest Africa
or Innermost Thibet', could not help, knowing 'nothing whatsoever about
the place at all'.[6] Disguised in rags, he eventually made his way to and
stayed in the East End, subsequently recording his observations in *The
People of the Abyss*. Even if informed by a certain radicalism, his talk is of
a race apart:

> The unfit and the unneeded! The miserable and despised and
> forgotten, dying in the social shambles. The progeny of prostitution
> – of the prostitution of men and women and children, of flesh and
> blood, and sparkle and spirit; in brief, the prostitution of labour. If
> this is the best that civilisation can do for the human, then give us
> howling and naked savagery. Far better to be a people of the wilder-
> ness and desert, of the cave and the squatting place, than to be a
> people of the machine and the abyss.[7]

It would be mistaken, however, to view such constructions as distinctively
novel; in one form or another they had been articulated for most of the
nineteenth century. Nor were they confined to the East End. Chevalier's
study of Paris in the first half of the nineteenth century explores in depth
bourgeois rhetoric on the condition of the urban poor.[8] He quotes from
Hugo's *Les Misérables* on the forces unleashed by the revolution:

> The fauborg Saint-Antoine is a human reservoir. . . . What did these
> shaggy men want, who, ragged, howling, ferocious, with bludgeon
> upraised, pike a-tilt, rushed on the old Paris as it gazed astounded
> on the days pregnant with Revolutionary chaos? They wanted the end
> of oppression. . . . Yes, they clamoured for it, terrible, half-naked,
> cudgel in fist, yells issuing from their throats. They were savages, true
> enough; but the savages of civilization.

Chevalier's comment on this extract is particularly apt:

> This coincidence of descriptions, and especially the choice of the same
> terms, cannot be due merely to chance or literary device. The iden-
> tification of the workers of the fauborg Saint-Antoine with savages
> was more than a bold simile. It simply expressed a fact of opinion.
> Savages, barbarians, nomads, the labouring classes were considered as
> such and for the reasons we have specified, namely, that the terms
> commonly used and recurring or constantly in these works expressed
> the truly racial character of social antagonism in the Paris of this
> period.[9]

Relationships between these urban topographies and the psychic desires of the bourgeoisie during the nineteenth century have been skilfully analysed by Stallybrass and White.[10] From detailed examination of the writings of Mayhew, Engels and Chadwick in particular, they demonstrate how fears of 'the Other' were transcoded into social and geographical boundaries separating high and low, suburb and slum, civilisation and sewage, mansion and sewer, respectable and filthy. In this way the bourgeoisie attempted not only to secure its own sense of self-identity but also to negotiate with carnivalesque forces during its disengagement from popular culture.

Not that the psychic distancing was complete, for the social and geographical Other remained an object of disgust and fascination.[11] The prostitute provided a key site. Baudelaire – significantly, given the place he occupies in the modernist pantheon[12] – wrote that there was 'no exalted pleasure which cannot be related to prostitution'.[13] At the same time, in the Victorian obsession with working-class sexuality, deep concern about class, race, nation and family was articulated to prostitution. It would be difficult otherwise to account fully for the extraordinary detour on the history of prostitution in the first systematic survey of the metropolitan poor, namely, Mayhew's *London Life and London Poor*.

As the nineteenth century progressed so anxieties about the low Other in the metropolis mounted. The docks infrastructure was virtually complete by 1855, and London consolidated its position as the manufacturing and trade centre of the empire. In a desperate search for employment tens of thousands migrated to settle in the already overcrowded slums and rookeries where local authorities, inscribed within archaic administrative structures and *laissez faire* ideologies, proved unwilling and unable to act: that was until the mysterious terrors of cholera which ravaged the metropolis between 1832 and 1866 forced reform. Chadwick's 1842 enquiry into the sanitary conditions of the labouring population set the agenda. Sewage, sanitation and the water supply were singled out as the areas most in need of urgent attention. There followed legislative measures which sought to control house construction, disposal of sewage and the activities of water companies, but which had only limited success. Of more lasting importance was the completion in 1865 of Bazalgette's great sewer system.

While, appropriately enough, public health remained at the centre of concern, other social pathologies received little attention. House-building, substantial as it was in the first half of the nineteenth century, could not meet the demands of a fast growing working-class population. No housing was provided for the casual poor. The word 'slum' first appeared in 1812 to describe a sleepy, unknown back alley;[14] for most of the century slums, despite their aggregation, remained *terra incognita* to the bourgeoisie even before distinct geographical separation.

It was not until mid-century that the problem of overcrowding entered the domain of respectability for the first time. Initially vague, hesitant and timid, reformist zeal gathered pace. And although informed by moral rather than structural imperatives, it promoted a considerable literature within which novel and survey attempted, often in melodramatic and graphic detail, to expose the pathological consequences of overcrowding. 'Sensation' of the abyss assumed a significant ambiguity. The following suggest something of the extent and discursive nature of the concern: G. Godwin (1854) *London Shadows*; J. Greenwood (1876) *Low Life Deeps: And Account of the Strange Fish to be Found There*, (1869) *The Seven Curses of London*, (1874) *The Wilds of London*; J. Hollingshead (1861) *Ragged London in 1861*; A.O. Jay (1891) *Life in Darkest London*; G. Gissing (1889) *The Nether World*; A. Mearns (1883) *The Bitter Cry of Outcast London*; A. Morrison (1894) *Tales of Mean Streets*; W. Gilbert (1858) *Dives and Lazarus; or the Adventures of an Obscure Medical Man in a Low Neighbourhood*.

The spate of legislation this concern engendered did little to alleviate the problem. Some exacerbated it. Slum clearance and street improvement schemes, for example, merely forced the evicted poor to settle elsewhere, thus redistributing and intensifying slum housing. In some areas overcrowding continued to increase well into the twentieth-century until the wholesale destruction of the Blitz provided a solution of sorts.[15]

At the heart of the problem lay the system of endemic and chronic casual labour. 'A slum represents the presence of a market for casual labour', wrote B.F.C. Costello in 1898.[16] However the recognition of the significance and extent of casual labour, not only to overcrowding but to the full range of social pathologies – poverty, crime, drink, prostitution – was a belated one.[17] Until the early 1880s the lot of the residuum attracted little systematic enquiry. Considered as an undesirable vestige of moral, psychological and physical inadequacy, its presence would gradually be eliminated through progress. And yet simultaneously the presence once again engendered fear and disgust.

That this fear erupted with quite dramatic force in the 1880s was due to the perceived threat of the residuum uniting with an impoverished but politically intelligent artisan elite to challenge extant authority relations in the metropolis as it plunged into recession. That this fear subsequently subsided was due to the 1889 dock strike during which casual dock labour under the leadership of artisans schooled in a Marxisant tradition conducted themselves in an orderly and responsible manner rather than one which provoked social unrest.

The discursive realm of bourgeois concern with metropolitan problems in the nineteenth century, therefore, was related less to changing material and structural circumstances of the poor than to its own psychic and political universe. In forging a self-identity, constructions of a low Other articulated disgust, fear and fascination with the specific content of urban geography. This content was no incidental and contingent metaphor in the structuring of the bourgeois Imaginary. It was not a secondary over-coding of some anterior and subjective psychic content. Indeed it participated in the *constitution* of the subject, precisely to the degree that identity is discursively produced from the moment of entry into language by such oppositions and differences.[18]

Here is the significance of Biely's modernist moment. The Petersburg he constructs is infused with familiar images of the cityscape and the shadowy figures that inhabit its outer ring:

Petersburg is surrounded by a ring of many-chimneyed factories.... A many-thousand swarm plods toward them in the morning and the suburbs are all aswarm. All the factories were then in a terrible state of unrest. The workers had turned into prating shady types.... Now were heard the disturbing anti-government cries of street urchins running full tilt from the railway station to the Admiralty waving gutter rags.[19]

Responses of the various characters to this unknown but threatening presence demonstrate the contradictory nature of the bourgeois Imaginary. The imperial officer, insulated from the 'scum of the streets', decides that the islands they inhabit 'must be crushed'. His son, with the spirit of a Jack London and a fascination for the same low Other that his father fears, embarks on a voyage of (self-) discovery. He leaves his cold marble mansion and wanders through 'Petersburg's streets, sordid taverns, underground cellars, in search of an "other world" more vibrant and authentic than his own'.[20] Thus the novel explores the body of the city by articulating social formation to urban topography. In so doing it constructs the 'abyss' as a 'swamp in which the anguished modern individual can merge and submerge himself, forget his personality and politics and drown'.[21] The only way out of the surreal futility which threatens to engulf the city and the mind is to 'do what is morally, politically and psychologically right'.[22] Passage through the abyss offers renewal.

The promise is, however, for the bourgeois psyche alone. What salvation is there for those who do not pass through the abyss but inhabit it? The book provides few clues. For the most part, and in spite of the instrumental role of the Petersburg proletariat in the events of 1905, the workers occupy the same shadowy presence as they do in the officer's mind and in the whole domain of the bourgeois imaginary universe during the nineteenth century. This raises a fundamental issue, namely, to what the extent was the working class engaged by this modernist problematic?

Here we broach a question much neglected by theorists of modernity. Perhaps because modernity as part of the Enlightenment project was driven and shaped by the bourgeoisie, it has come to be associated almost exclusively with them; certainly movements thought best to characterise modernism have been those of an elite. The result is that bourgeois experience has come to represent that of an era in which the working class played no part. It is as if *The Communist Manifesto* stands as a celebration of the brilliant historical progress forged by the bourgeoisie. But it is more than that because it encompasses the impact of capitalism on the industrial proletariat. *Mutatis mutandis* theories of modernity remain incomplete unless they also take due account of working-class experience.

Modernity, Berman writes, is a vital experience that unites all mankind.[23] This unity is one of disunity, however, for the forces are of constant 'disintegration and renewal, of struggle and contradiction, of ambiguity and anguish'. The maelstrom into which people are precipitated has posed a 'radical threat to all their history and traditions' but at the same time 'developed a rich history and a plenitude of traditions of its own'. In the remainder of this chapter I wish to ask precisely how we can begin to locate working-class experience within modernity by exploring the nature of this threat to its history and tradition. I will examine this question through a particular case-study and confine my chronological and geographical boundaries to the late nineteenth and early twentieth centuries – not least because this is generally recognised to be the high point of the modernist moment – and to an area on the perimeter of East London.

CASUAL LABOUR, SPACE AND TIME

Mid-nineteenth-century West Ham was an essentially agricultural community with a population of less than 20,000. By the turn of the century it had emerged as the industrial heartland of the south-east with a population in excess of a quarter of a million. This ascent coincided with the protracted decline of staple industries in the East End, as a result of which London, in defiance of Euclidian geometry, had an industrial centre beyond its circumference.

West Ham retained its industrial base. The mature economy at its peak in the interwar years was dominated by employment in chemicals, transport and the docks, shipbuilding and repairing and the public services of gas, water and electricity. Employment in banking and insurance, public administration and vehicles was low. The social topography of the area reflected this. Data from the New survey of London life and labour indicate that in 1929–30 approximately 107,000 residents worked. Of these 6.4 per cent were skilled manual, 16.8 per cent semi-skilled manual, 53.6 per cent unskilled manual, 8.9 per cent retail, 9.2 per cent clerical and 5.0 per cent other. Such aggregate data disguised considerable variations in localities. The working population of Canning Town in the heavily industrialised south, for example, comprised 66 per cent unskilled labour; that of Forest Gate in the residential north comprised 32 per cent.

The concentration of casual labour in the south engendered widespread poverty. Overall the New survey concluded that the Canning Town and Silvertown areas made up what was perhaps the 'largest part of unbroken depression in East London'.[24] Was this population constituted in any way by the historical experience of modernity? More pointedly, can modernity as a concept illuminate its condition?

The forces of modernisation are complex. Attendant on the expansion of the capitalist global market they are extremely wide-ranging and have a protracted historical lineage. Encompassing scientific and technological advance, capital accumulation, industrial growth and restructuring, demographic change, urbanisation, bureaucratisation, unprecedented productive potential and the formation of nation states, modernisation can be traced back some 500 years, although it is only within the past, say, 150 years that it has accelerated, eclipsing all previous development. No social group could remain immune to such immense change. Its impact, however, was differential. Location of nation states in the capitalist order and position of classes, genders and localities in the relations of production influenced their negotiations with and responses to modernisation, and hence their experience of modernity.

In studying the historical and urban location of the emergent phase of psychoanalysis, Barry Richards has pointed to the seminal role of the modern city.[25] Drawing on the work of Lewis Mumford he argues that cities constituting the sites of early psychoanalytical practice – Vienna, Berlin, London and New York – were precisely those exposed most intensely to the experience of modernity. These were not the cities of the Industrial Revolution, which since the mid-nineteenth century had tended to decline relatively in political, cultural and economic significance, but centres of administration, finance and consumption. They were not built upon organic industrial or religious communities, but were 'shifting aggregations called into being by national and international forces outside themselves' and subject to the discontinuities and fragmentations of modernity. As such they provided fertile ground for a discipline concerned to (re)compose meaning and a coherent sense of selfhood within individual psyches.

West Ham cannot be seen as a modern city. Its industrial structure and social topography may have been created belatedly by the forces of modernisation, but this modernisation was of an earlier age; West Ham remained immune to, indeed actively resisted, the economic and cultural influences of the modernist moment of the late nineteenth century, as a direct result of which a protracted decline set in from which it has never recovered. Nowhere is this better illustrated than in its most pronounced social and economic characteristic, namely, the system of casual labour.

Casualism was a distinctly urban phenomenon. Permanent employment had never been guaranteed in a preindustrial, agricultural economy – harsh winters and failed harvests precipitated many into destitution – but it was not until the vast migrations from the country to the city that casualism became endemic. Migration to the metropolis was promoted by neither seasonality nor climate, nor even by enclosure, but by the wide-scale introduction of capitalist forms of technology and organisation. The tens of thousands displaced from the countryside in the nineteenth century sought work in the docks, on the railways, in building trades and in factories and workshops. The demand for employment could not be met. After 1830 the industrial structure of the metropolis collapsed, throwing thousands of the indigenous workforce onto the casual labour market.[26] The forces of combined and uneven development had acted with rare cruelty.

The Overend Gurney financial empire crashed in 1866, bringing down with it the remains of a once vibrant Thames shipbuilding industry and the speculative boom in railways and building. As industrial production in the metropolis entered into crisis, however, so West Ham embarked on a phase of spectacular growth.[27] Displaced workers now sought refuge in the docks and factories over the River Lea, and casualism, with all its attendant social pathology, found fresh ground.

The whole wretched system of casualism can be seen as part of the historical experience of modernity in that it arose within and was perpetuated by the forces of modernisation. Technological advance displaced and reconstituted workforces and populations. Those made idle in a rural economy migrated to urban environments only to be displaced when competition from other geographical areas undermined the viability of industrial capital in the metropolis. Sectors that remained could sustain growth either by offering regular employment at low wages (for example, the railways), or by having a pool of labour from which they could draw when demand increased, and to which they could syphon off surplus when demand slackened. In industries affected by seasonality such as gas and building, or by the trade cycle such as the docks, casualism provided employers with a convenient and effective solution to the vagaries of demand. But the relation between modernisation and casualism is problematic, in large part because of the contradictory location of the latter in the capitalist market. To develop this point I wish to refer to recent work by David Harvey.

As part of an attempt to explore the relationship between modernisation and the production of meaning within modernity, Harvey has signalled the crucial role of space and time.[28] In a persuasive and overarching account he demonstrates that modernisation perpetually disrupts temporal and spatial rhythms. So deeply embedded in common sense are time and space that they are experienced as fixed and unitary categories. They are in fact both products of human construction and therefore can be organised differently and express various meanings. Capitalism as a distinct mode of production, confers particular qualities and meanings on space and time, and it is through their symbolic orderings that a framework for experience is provided in which social groups are constituted and come to recognise their identity in relation to others. Within the antagonistic social relations of capitalism, temporal and spatial practices become 'imbued with class meaning. . . . They take on their meanings under specific social relations of class, gender, community, ethnicity, or race, and get "used up" or "worked over" in the course of social action'.[29]

Space and time, therefore, are sources of power in hegemonic practices. Capitalism seeks to compress both. Spatial barriers are eliminated to permit the flow of money, information, resources and commodities, and spatial organisation is rationalised to increase production and consumption. Time is reconstituted to accelerate the turnover time of capital through the speeding up of production and circulation, and the intensification of time schedules. At times of profound change in the spatial and temporal order, major shifts occur in representational, cultural and aesthetic forms. One such phase was 1880–1918 when the abrupt time–space compression effected by telephone, cinema, wireless, telegraphy, car and plane constituted a crucial moment in modernity.

Spatial and temporal ordering, however, is subject to struggle and has often met with resistance, particularly when it has threatened traditional customs and practices. Much of the history of the labour movement can be seen as a defensive struggle against the speeding up and intensification of work practices and the dismantling of organic communities, even when these practices and communities were themselves created by modernisation. In this sense, the mass movements of labour, which for the most part represented the interests of skilled and semi-skilled workers, were integral to and worked within modernity. The same cannot be said of the unskilled casual residuum which, because of its ambiguous relation to the labour market and to organised labour, was able more successfully to resist the imposition of temporal and spatial ordering, and hence challenge overarching attempts at control. This unruly outsideness lay at the heart of bourgeois fears of the nineteenth-century metropolis.[30]

Routines of industrial discipline could not easily be imposed on casual labourers. A jealously guarded measure of control over time enabled them rather than employers to dictate when and how they worked. Employment in relatively well-paid industries such as the docks meant that full-time work was not necessary to escape destitution. When not working they had recourse to the poor law for relief.[31] 'Two days on the hook, two days on the book' was both a description of work practice and a social philosophy.

Within work also there were opportunities to challenge temporal ordering, particularly in the docks where powerful subcultures existed. Daily work hours were set but they were nominal for they guaranteed little apart from the physical presence of dockers. The routine and pace of work were controlled entirely by the dock gangs themselves. They decided whether or not to work; 'in general the name of the game was do as little as possible'.[32]

85

Casualism also facilitated resistance to the restructuring of space. No housing was built for casual labourers; even speculative building, which propelled the logic of the intensification of space to its most damaging human consequences, provided accommodation only for those who could afford to pay market rents on a regular basis. Families of casual labourers managed to occupy jerry-built houses, however, by subletting rooms. When rent arrears mounted, they moved elsewhere, often under cover of darkness.

Domestic space itself remained an important symbolic domain for working-class families, in particular mothers, who took responsibility for its organisation. Such home-based cultures had been created in the course of the nineteenth century.[33] Conservative retreats from broader political issues they may have been, but they also served as a means of asserting dignity and an independence from the dominant ordering of space according to middle-class norms. Space within the home took on distinct meanings that consolidated and sustained working-class values.

The 'kitchen', for example, was central to family life. It served as a living room, dining room, kitchen, drying room, nursery, bathroom and laundry. Here a black-leaded range provided heat for the room, for cooking, for drying clothes and for the kettle constantly on the boil. Many of the family's important practical and symbolic articles – the rent book, wedding photographs, tea caddy and candlesticks – were kept on the mantelpiece above.[34]

The 'lav' stood out the back. Visits to it were necessarily conspicuous and noisy. A person had to leave the house, successfully negotiate with an ill-fitting door and lock, return if no newspaper was available, operate a clanking cistern which gushed water and then was filled by a plumbing system that shook violently, and finally re-enter the house. Lack of privacy undermined any attempts to uphold a sense of respectability, and the lav remained a potent source of humour and language.[35]

Appropriation of space, however, was readily extended beyond the private; in part because of severe restrictions in domestic space, families effectively took control of the street. It was a site for children's games, a forum for chats among neighbours and on warmer days an extension of the kitchen as families brought out chairs and sat underneath the windows. Occasionally, in the most visible celebration of collective identity, street parties took this domestication to its logical conclusion. There was less a retreat into domestic space, therefore, than an extension of the domestic into the public:

> The most important house in East London is the street. It contains several rooms, most of them overcrowded, as well as mere passages and the more humble offices of a home. Here is done much of the cooking, most of the amusements, and a great deal of the domestic and political business of the district. . . . Music is also here. At times

everyone in the room seems to be singing or whistling or shouting –
while male-voice choirs pass to and fro.[36]

This appropriation helped build and sustain the locality as a site of resistance. Migrations that originally built communities were complex, but once labour settled in West Ham it tended to remain. Casualism dictated that labourers reside close to potential workplaces, not least to be available for the early morning calls. For most this meant within walking distance; no transport existed. Distinct patterns of residential settlement were forged, establishing strongly rooted occupational communities with a fierce sense of locality and territory, especially in the geographically isolated areas of Canning Town, Silvertown, Tidal Basin and North Woolwich in the south. The New survey reveals that 83 per cent of residents employed at the Royal Docks and 95 per cent of those at Tate & Lyle's sugar refineries lived in Canning Town or Plaistow, while 89 per cent of those at the London and North East Railway locomotive works in the north lived in Stratford or Forest Gate.[37] And these settlements were reproduced over time. Of the unskilled population, 62 per cent of males and 68 per cent of females were born in the borough, with a further 16 per cent in East London. Compressions of space through improved communication had little consequence for a people who considered a visit to East Ham a day's outing and a trip south of the Thames an expedition to a foreign land.

In temporarily acting as a brake against spatial reorganisation of populations such stabilisation both confronted and constituted one of the distinctive features of modernity. Migrants may have been at the vortex of modernity as they walked the streets of Paris, Berlin, St Petersburg and New York, experiencing life as 'transitory, fugitive, contingent ... because it meant personal and social upheaval from the settled peasant existence of agricultural life',[38] but this little resembled the experience of casual labour in the East End, even less so that of West Ham where there was no settlement of Jewish or first generation Irish comparable with Whitechapel and Stepney.

Migrants to West Ham were not peasants, but agricultural labourers who had direct experience of capitalist social relations in the countryside and casual labourers displaced from the East End by collapse of staple economies. They moved not to an atomised, fragmented social milieu, but to relatively stable communities. People from a village settled within easy reach of one another. All brought with them the imprints of an older rural culture, and kinships systems that proved remarkably resistant to urban modernity. The public and private spaces appropriated by members of these communities remained inviolate. Law and order, the civilising influences of bourgeois respectability, municipal reform, employers, the luminosity of the city and newness were resolutely resisted. Here space and place – conceived as the physical location of social activity – were the same as they were in premodern societies.[39] Simultaneously, this strengthening of localism can paradoxically be seen as part of modernity. As modernisation dismantled spatial barriers, it began to explore 'new meanings for space and place that tacitly reinforced local identity'[40] in ways which I shall explore later (p. 92).

PREMODERNISM OF CASUAL LABOUR

Through this dialectic of modernity casual labour in West Ham was able to sustain 'premodern' characteristics well into the interwar period. Local employment structures, patterns of residence and social networks constituted its physical and mental universe; the wireless, car, plane, cinema and telephone simply did not impinge on it.

What were these characteristics? How can we best think about this premodernism? Recent work has testified to the centrality and endurance of the carnival in popular cultural forms.[41] The carnival was the greatest popular festival. Like a gigantic play, it used the town as a theatre and the people as both performers and spectators. All was excess. Massive quantities of meat, pancakes and alcohol were consumed; people sang and danced in the streets, often wearing costumes and masks; bystanders were abused with all manner of projectiles; plays, processions and competitions took place, many symbolically invoking struggles between 'carnival' and 'lent', kings and fools.

Carnival was not, however, merely a festive diversion, but a lived celebration in which the individual became subsumed into the collectivity. It was profoundly oppositional to authority relations for it provided folk with symbolic liberation from political and moral restraint to pursue alternative, utopian visions. Dominant representations were transgressed. Through transgression social norms and structures were inverted or subverted, often by challenging binary, hierarchical oppositions such as low/high, animal/ human and body/mind.[42] Manifest principally in bodily imagery, it provided an anatomical metaphor for a new utopia. Not that transgression can be essentialised; contradictory political specificity was conferred by complex antagonisms at particular historical conjunctures.

From 1500 the assault of church and state on popular recreational forms, the forces of modernisation and withdrawal of the middle classes gradually displaced carnival from the public domain into subcultural and bourgeois cultural forms. The process was an uneven one, tending to intensify at times of profound social and political dislocation such as occurred in England during the Civil War and Industrial Revolution. One of its manifestations was the modern novel, the development of which – as Bakhtin, Foucault and Kristeva have all suggested – was influenced enormously by carnivalesque elements:

> From romanticism through postmodernism we encounter again and
> again the dismembered fragments of the social carnivalesque body –

its symbols, its elements, its members. But now, lodged in bourgeois fictions rather than in social action they are privatised, cut off from social protest and pleasure and assimilated to the subjective unconscious. Less and less the figures of social celebration and communal pleasures, they are the emblems of alienated desire, paranoid fantasy, and the individual will to power.[43]

The novel both reflected and moulded bourgeois constructions of the urban poor as a low Other, an Other that was viewed with disgust and fascination. Simultaneously, these constructions sustained the separateness of the urban poor and thereby subcultural integuments of the carnival throughout the nineteenth century. Public displays of these subcultural forms, as evidenced in the series of bread and unemployed riots, drew upon earlier traditions of collective action, and the 1880 dock strike, which for many was the first union organised response of the urban poor to exploitation, leading directly to new unionism, in fact 'bore as much resemblance to a medieval carnival as to a modern industrial strike'.[44] These subcultural forms were resilient enough to reach well into the twentieth century. As I have argued elsewhere in a study of the political culture of interwar West Ham: 'In street parties, bawdy humour, fairs, street entertainment, the celebration of body over mind, sport, theatre, language, and "crime", elements of the carnivalesque survived among the metropolitan poor.'[45]

Access to this culture is restricted. It was oral rather than literate, and we are forced to rely on accounts – many of which are removed – falteringly to reconstruct its universe. Its most powerful features were a sense of separateness and identity, and a resistance to change:

> Hidden in the cockney soul there is a stubborn, almost sullen resistance to reform; this is based on a deep attachment to environment. . . . Behind his seeing agreement with all that is being said to him, his apparent appreciation of all that is being done for him, there lurks a wilful grip on life as he himself thinks ought to be lived, and as he intends to continue to live it. . . . The social workers in the slums do wonderful things. In the relief of individual hardship they help much, but the essential cockney remains aloof, intangible, unassailable, and, fortunately, safe.[46]

This unassailability made it virtually impossible for those outside the culture to talk of it with understanding. Even settlement workers, many of whom lived in the area and had an intimate knowledge of the youth attending their clubs, viewed it with a thinly-disguised disdain:

> All over this district the narrow, ill-lighted, ill-kept, ill-policed streets, are the drawing rooms of the people and evening after evening, from dusk to far into night, young and old are perforce a wandering street mob. Their entertainment is at best a cheap cinema, at worst a

street fight; a young man's hospitality is given in a Public House or a Coffee Stall, to a girl whose literature is the divorce news on the Sunday press; their art is the posters of bottled beers.[47]

And again:

Opportunities for sport are very limited by lack of time, money and open spaces. Many a boy can only get a holiday by throwing up his job and trusting to luck to find a new one a week later. Music or art of any kind is ordinarily unknown to him – or merely conveys a few dance tunes and a few posters of bottled beers. Left to himself the difficulties of seeing the countryside will probably be too great for it to occur to him as a possible substitute for the nearest broad pavement.[48]

Such accounts reveal more about the persistence of bourgeois constructions and fears than the culture of casualism. Thus a distinct urban geography outside the reach of the law and the civilising influences of middle-class values, dark, charged and violent, becomes a metaphor for the culture which inhabits it. Aspects of this bourgeois psyche are also nicely illustrated by D.S. Brierley in a description of an incident during her work as head of the Ladies Staff at the Docklands Settlement. It is worth quoting at length:

One thing which really terrified me was the drunkenness, especially among the women. There was a particularly lively scrap between two 'ladies' my first night, and I lay petrified in my bed, thinking they must certainly be murdering each other, but later on I confess these brawls fascinated me. I remember one dreadful occasion when another of the staff and I were in my room with the light off, our noses glued to my window watching a particularly fine round, when one of the participants caught sight of us. . . . She let go her opponent for a moment, and shaking her fist up at my window screamed: 'I can see you a'peeking there, yer mission 'ippokrites'. Alas, we had forgotten the landing light was silhouetting us through the open door.[49]

And yet we can also detect something of the nature of this culture from these observations. Denied through lack of material resources the poor were forced into public spaces which they appropriated through their collective presence – no *flâneurs* here.

There was of course more to this culture than fighting, drinking and congregating on street corners. Public spectacle as entertainment, the lineages of which could be traced back to medieval fairs, was popular. Stanley Reed remembers 'Punch and Judy shows, and a strong man at the Greengate on Sunday morning. Also on a patch of waste ground by the railway works at Stratford, a man who bit the heads off live rats.'[50]

90

Sport, in particular football, commanded widespread support. 'West Ham is Syd King', read the headlines of the *East Ham Echo*, referring to the manager of West Ham United Football Club in 1923[51] – the year when the team gained promotion to the first division and reached the first FA Cup final to be held at Wembley. Celebrations became part of local mythology as the club entered popular consciousness far beyond the confines of Upton Park.

The transgressive properties of crime derived from its quite specific status within working-class culture. 'Doing the business' suggested, and continues to suggest, a culture of illicit dealing which actively usurped the practice, ethics and language of bourgeois commerce.[52] 'Business' existed not in open conflict with the forces of capital and the law, but in covert negotiation, often taking the form of repartee. Frequently, transgressive dynamics were conferred on working-class culture by changes in the boundaries of legal activity. Gambling, for example, which in terms of expenditure was probably the most important pursuit, was outlawed in an attempt to drive it off the streets. Football pools and racecourse betting were acceptable, informal sweeps and bookies operating with runners were not. Jack Jones, MP for Silvertown, in commenting on the 1920 Football Betting Bill, suggested the extent to which it criminalised popular recreation:

> If I get a circular from a firm that is running a football sweep, I am a criminal, for according to this Bill the running of a football sweep in the form I am expressing is a criminal offence. But if I get a circular from a speculator in property, I may know as much about property as a Connemara pig does about astronomy; but because I have the money to invest I stand a chance of winning something. Therefore I am a respectable citizen, entitled to become a member of the London Stock Exchange.[53]

It was in the political sphere that casualism had its most decisive impact. The extraordinary growth of West Ham between 1870 and 1910 promoted a distinct political culture. West Ham was the cradle of new unionism, and elected in 1892 the first independent labour MP, Keir Hardie, and in 1898 the first labour council in the country.[54] The Labour Party, however, was unable to secure permanent control until 1919 when it was returned to power. Over the ensuing decade it established hegemony in the formal political arena; after 1926 it was never seriously challenged by oppositional forces from the left or right of the political spectrum.[55]

In few respects could this success be ascribed to the party's ability to command the allegiance of substantial sections of the working-class electorate. The party itself, affiliated organisations such as the Independent Labour Party and the National Socialist Party, the co-operative movement and the trades unions, all of which contributed in one way or another to the success, were led and administered by skilled and semi-skilled workers and those middle-class people around the settlements who had identified with the cause of labour. The majority of the electorate was constituted neither politically nor culturally by Labour's rhetoric. Turnouts at elections were consistently low, especially in the impoverished wards of the south, membership of the party was a fraction of other east and south London boroughs with a tradition of Labour and the party was effectively controlled by the South-West Ham branch of the National Socialist Party, which could muster few more than thirty-five members, but most of these were councillors, and two were MPs.

A case for seeing the Labour Party as modernist cannot be argued fully here, but the party's historical specificity, constituency and the values it enshrined suggest that the case is a good one. Although established initially by the trades union movement in 1900, it was not until the aftermath of the First World War that it emerged as a mass party at the national level. In 1918 there were sixty Labour MPs; these were to increase dramatically to 142 in 1922, and to 288 in 1929, in the process of which the party held office for the first time.

The shock of the war was decisive. Much has been made of the significance of the experience gained by and responsibility conferred on Labour leaders during the conflict – perhaps too much, since this must be tempered by recognition that severely damaging splits between pacifist and pro-war factions in the trades unions and the party reverberated throughout the interwar period. Labour's rhetoric at the end of hostilities, however, did accord with the hopes of a radicalised electorate for a new beginning. *Labour and the New Social Order* was published in 1918. It may have been a pragmatic adaptation of a moderate collectivism, but it laid the foundation for advance in the formal political sphere. Perhaps not surprisingly, in its content and timing it closely resembled the programme of the Cooperative Party, formed in 1917 to promote through parliament the political interests of a national network of local societies.[56]

The Labour Party was universalist, albeit rarely beyond the national. This in part explains why its appeal to a working-class constituency, entrenched at the locality as in West Ham, was limited. Indeed, because of the dialectics of modernity, such universalisation could lead to a reinforcement of local identity:

> By enhancing links between place and the social sense of personal and communal identity, this facet of modernism was bound, to some degree, to entail the aestheticisation of local, regional, or national politics. Loyalties to place then take precedence over loyalties to class, spatialising political action.[57]

The rationalisation of constituency organisation remained a priority for the party throughout the 1920s. In West Ham the constituency party retained a jealously guarded independence from Herbert Morrison's London Labour

Party, enabling it to establish hegemony in the local arena of formal political activity by articulating universalist and particularist rhetoric.

Modernist sensibility was evident among party members. D.J. Davis, ILP, stated at a meeting of the newly formed West Ham Labour Party:

> The Labour Party were leaving no stone unturned and had published 'The New Social Order'. There it had laid down clearly and definitely not only what they aimed at, but how they were going to secure it. . . . The Labour Party had an ideal, and it was the only party which had one and told the people how to achieve it.[58]

And a 1919 election leaflet for W.R. Hughes, a settlement worker who stood as an independent councillor, claimed:

> We want big changes and we want them quickly. . . . We hold, at the bottom of our hearts, the same ideals of justice and brotherhood, and it is this common aspiration that I should like to express and represent. It is because I feel that the impulse that is behind the work of the Labour Party is mainly the same longing for the time when man will be able to live in free and equal comradeship that I find myself in line with that party.[59]

This sensibility – characteristic of a current of political nonconformity which informed the Labour Party at its inception – was tempered by a vigorous assertion of a local working-class identity against incursions from middle-class and foreign influence, rabidly nationalist and virulently anti-communist:

> Carpetbagger political adventurers have joined. Railwaymen were going to object to funds being used to further the political careers of such men. Socialism was not pacifism, nor was it Fabianism with its 'superior person' bureaucratic tyranny and government by experts policy. The bolsheviks they had with them, trying to nobble the Labour Party, were men without a country – mere cosmopolitans, half-baked visionaries without a mission. . . . The workers' control of industry would follow naturally upon the realisation of their industrial and political power. Let them see to it that their power is used effectively in the coming elections for the establishment of a bonafide working-class party, and above all let them beware of the intriguing politics and hypocritical middle-class friends of Germany.[60]

With a most striking alacrity voting Labour became a reflexive act, a tradition:

> People voted Labour because it was traditional. Even today (and it was more so then), if you get into a group and you try to introduce a political discussion you're not on, they don't want to know. . . . As

93

far as they are concerned there is no argument. There is no need for discussion. Labour is the party to represent working class people; the working class vote Labour, finish.[61]

But then modernity needs constantly to invent tradition in order to overcome fragmentation of identity and a sense of historical discontinuity.[62]

From 1919 until the dissolution of West Ham in 1965, Labour dominated local politics, and yet this domination failed to extend to the casual poor. Intense localism, historical continuity and a resistance to temporal and spatial ordering insulated the casual poor from the Labour Party as it did from other mass movements, most notably trades unions. If the party did engage their attention, it was through politics as public spectacle and the festive rather than ideology.[63] Children fought mock battles between Labour and Tory on patches of waste ground and joined marches to chant electioneering slogans. Political rallies and demonstrations provided opportunities for rowdy, often violent behaviour. Regular outdoor meetings were attended to kill time before the pubs opened, and the announcement of election results at Stratford Town Hall attracted large crowds drawn by the theatricality of the event.

RESISTANCE DISMANTLED

In the course of the interwar period this sense of separateness was gradually, almost imperceptibly eroded, and the so-called golden age of East End culture passed. Centralisation and institutionalisation of social and health provision, extension of mass consumerism, widened access to mass communication, residential relocation and secularisation of cultural pursuits were among the more corrosive influences.[64]

The population of West Ham fell after 1924 as outmigration to metropolitan Essex gathered momentum. Barking, Ilford, Basildon, Pitsea and the fast expanding Becontree Estate at Dagenham attracted families by offering modern accommodation. The social cost, however, was considerable; as the warden of the Docklands Settlement noted:

At first sight the new accommodation is excellent – a whole house, bathroom and electric light. But mother finds shops much longer to walk to, misses the Saturday night markets and the old, innumerable familiar things which actually built up for her the old social life. Now she has to find a new panel doctor, new Relieving Officer; the Labour Exchange, where men have to sign on when they are temporarily out of work, may even be a bus fare away; the church, chapel, mothers' meet, or Benevolent Club which she used to frequent must now be a thing of the past for her. The neighbours too with whom she regularly used to 'pass the time of day', and had such enjoyable chats about the street funerals, are now all scattered under the rehousing scheme.[65]

The spatial isolation of West Ham was also being breached by immigration. Foreign workers had been attracted from the early days of industrialisation. The Irish had worked in the docks and construction, the Germans and Lithuanians in the gas, chemical and glass plants by the Thames. There was, however, little of the large-scale settlement experienced by the traditional East End until the interwar years when West Ham's strategic importance as a port began to be realised.

In 1936 West Ham Borough published a pamphlet to promote the advantages of the area. Entitled 'West Ham: London's industrial centre and gateway to the world', it referred to the crucial position occupied by the Royal Docks in the trading relationship between the metropolis and other centres throughout the world, particularly with Britain's colonial empire. Asian and Caribbean seamen and ex-servicemen and their families began to settle after the First World War: soon Canning Town had the largest black community in London.[66]

Few influences, however, could compare with the power of mass communication. Contemporary accounts repeatedly reveal its decisive impact on popular consciousness. George Cooper recalls the excitement of listening to crystal radio sets in the early interwar years. The signal was weak. To obtain any at all an aerial was slung between the house and a pole in the garden. When the wind blew, washing interfered with the aerial and the radio crackled, but it provided entertainment by famous performers for a generation that had made its own. Many gardens sprouted aerials.[67]

The early excitement of radios was soon eclipsed by the cinema, which in the 1930s became the most popular form of entertainment. Picture shows at the Theatre Royal, Stratford, are recorded as early as 1897; used to support stage productions they were described as 'the very latest in fashionable entertainment'. The first film shows took place in converted shops and factories, and from 1909 purpose-built cinemas appeared. By 1921, at least twenty cinemas existed in West Ham, with capacities ranging from the 400 seats of the Rathbone Street Cinema in Canning Town, to the Queens Cinema, Forest Gate, and Grand Cinema, Canning Town, both of which had 1,500.[68] Seat prices ranged from 4d to 2s, making them accessible to all but the very poor. Weekly attendance was 120,000, compared with 10,000 in local churches. By the late 1920s, the massive Premier, Carlton, Broadway and Rex cinemas had been built with capacities of up to 3,000. The impact was soon noted by a Mansfield House settlement worker:

> Though the cinema as a social factor is but beginning to operate, it has already outstripped in popularity and influence every other form of entertainment. . . . It is more readily intelligible to the slightly educated, unimaginative millions. The highly educated have been trained to create mental pictures under the stimulus of language. But words rather confuse than illumine the untrained mind.[69]

Divested of the inevitable middle-class elitism, this does help to explain the universal appeal of cinema to working-class people. The narrative structures, characterisation and spectacle of film were accessible to a predominantly non-literate culture in ways that printed texts were not. Over time audiences developed a skill in reading films quite uncharacteristic of previous generations. Stanley Reed found that the films produced for schools were

> pedestrian, underestimating the sophistication of the thirties generation of children from their experience of commercial cinema and much greater than that of most of their parents and teachers. This curious reversal of roles had been brought home to me by the difficulty on those rare occasions when [my father] went to the cinema in following the plot of the film; it all went too fast he complained.[70]

This new generation was offered and responded to a commercial cinema that was dominated by Hollywood and therefore remote from its own daily experience. A survey of 150,000 children aged 4–14, living in the area of the docks, revealed that cowboy films were most popular, with Shirley Temple coming second. Newsreels, sports items and war films were also liked by over 80 per cent of the respondents.[71]

In a warm, comfortable environment, secure from rent collectors, tallymen, the police, school welfare officers and poor law officials, people could be entertained. Contemporary observers and more recent theorists have tended to emphasise the escapism of cinema:

> People seem to flock to all the shows without regard to the quality ... the countless host of human beings who are condemned to exist year after year in the deadening weariness of ugly slum districts, who spend their days harassed amid the dim and dirt of the factory and the warehouse, and their night wearied in wretchedly furnished, overcrowded houses, require some form of amusement to bring a measure of brightness and stimulus into their grey lives.[72]

Cinema, however, was more than that. By extending the mental horizons of a self-enclosed working-class community, it helped to promote as part of a modernist impulse the dismantling of temporal and spatial barriers. Simultaneously, cinema offered a sense of control over individual identities that were being threatened by these self-same forces.[73] Some viewed its influence with a guarded enthusiasm:

> Alcohol, the age-long ally of the opposing classes, deadens the mind into stolid contentment. The cinema – the 'counter attraction' that Temperance reformers have been long seeking – is drawing more and more from the stupefying public house and is informing and stimulating their minds. The full measure of its far reaching and deep results only time will clearly reveal.[74]

The relationship between the urban poor and modernity was complex and dynamic; put simply, modernisation created the abyss, the abyss structured modernism. The system of casual labour which emerged in and remained specific to the urban environment was the product of forced migration and the necessity of reserve labour. The body of casual labour retained a degree of structural autonomy from the labour market, however, and was able to forge a spatial separateness. Psychically, it was constituted as an outside, low Other within the imaginary universe of the bourgeoisie. Thus casual labour, once established, secured a site of resistance within modernity but simultaneously provoked in the bourgeois mind the sense of fear and fascination that lay at the heart not only of Petersburg but the entire modernist project.

Modernisation readily encompassed the resistance mounted by the urban poor to spatial and temporal ordering; indeed differential ordering of these boundaries is an essential feature of the 'quality of modernity'.[75] Modernity could thus intensify a sense of localism while simultaneously promoting universality. Similarly, the differential temporality internal to modernity promoted not historical continuity but profound fractures. Under such circumstances the weaknesses of chronologically defined conceptions of progress become apparent. We need rather to explore the dialectics of 'homogeneous' and 'differential' historical time within modernity, and the ways in which these are 'tied up, inextricably, with its spatial relations'.[76] Only then can we begin to understand the combined and uneven development of modernity, and the engagement with its multifarious constituencies.

These dialectics have very real material consequences. Vestiges of the culture of casualism and bourgeois sensations of the abyss were finally erased by the Blitz of 1940. Eighty-four per cent of houses in the Tidal Basin area of Canning Town were destroyed or badly damaged. Modernisation, in its most destructive guise, effectively eliminated residual resistance to its onslaught.

NOTES

1 Marshall Berman, *All That is Solid Melts Into Air. The Experience of Modernity*, London, Verso, 1983.
2 Leon Trotsky, *1905*, London, Allen Lane, 1972, p. v.
3 Berman, *All That is Solid*, p. 264.
4 Cited in ibid., p. 266.
5 Cited in H.J. Dyos and D.A. Reeder, 'Slums and suburbs', in H.J. Dyos and M. Woolf (eds), *The Victorian City. Images and Realities*, London, Routledge, 1973, p. 370.
6 Jack London, *The People of the Abyss*, London, Nelson, 1904, p. 15.
7 ibid., p. 328.
8 Louis Chevalier, *Labouring Classes and Dangerous Classes in Paris during the First Half of the Nineteenth Century*, London, Routledge, 1973.
9 ibid., p. 129.

10 Peter Stallybrass and Allon White, *The Politics and Poetics of Transgression*, London, Methuen, 1986.

11 ibid., p. 129.

12 Berman, *All That is Solid*; David Harvey, *The Condition of Postmodernity*, Oxford, Blackwell, 1989.

13 Cited in Stallybrass and White, *Politics and Poetics*, p. 137.

14 Anthony S. Wohl, *The Eternal Slum. Housing and Social Policy in Victorian London*, London, Arnold, 1977, p. 5.

15 John Marriott, 'London over the border. A study of West Ham during rapid growth, 1870–1910', Ph.D. thesis, University of Cambridge, 1984.

16 Cited in Dyos and Reeder, 'Slums and suburbs', p. 369.

17 Gareth Stedman Jones, *Outcast London*, Oxford, Oxford University Press, 1971.

18 Stallybrass and White, *Politics and Poetics*, p. 148.

19 Cited in Berman, *All That is Solid*, p. 258.

20 ibid., p. 260.

21 ibid., p. 264.

22 ibid., p. 265.

23 ibid., p. 267.

24 Data and quotation are to be found in John Marriott, *The Culture of Labourism. The East End between the Wars*, Edinburgh, Edinburgh University Press, 1991, ch. 1.

25 Barry Richards, 'Psychoanalysis in reverse', in B. Richards (ed.), *Crises of the Self*, London, Free Association, 1989.

26 Stedman Jones, *Outcast London*.

27 Marriott, 'London over the border'.

28 Harvey, *The Condition of Postmodernity*.

29 ibid., p. 223.

30 Although most often thought of as a problem of the nineteenth century, the system of casualism persisted far longer. Devastating as it was on the material circumstances of the unskilled, and in spite of various schemes to promote decasualisation implemented by a state concerned over its potentially disruptive consequences, the extent and depth of casual labour in West Ham intensified during the interwar years. It persisted in part because the fluctuations in seasonal demand varied positively with the general level of unemployment, but also because employers and workers resisted reform. Employers benefited from the flexibility that the system offered; for many labourers, casualism offered some control over work patterns, enabling them to adopt work habits and lifestyles denied by the discipline of regular employment.

31 John Marriott, 'West Ham: London's industrial centre and gateway to the world. II Stagnation and decline', *London Journal*, vol. 14, no. 1, 1989, pp. 43–58.

32 For this I am indebted to Ian Olley, an ex-ganger.

33 M.J. Daunton, *House and Home in the Victorian City. Working Class Housing, 1850–1914*, London, Arnold, 1983.

34 Elsie Lewis, 'Family life', in Newham History Workshop (ed.), *A Marsh and a Gasworks. One Hundred Years of Life in West Ham*, London, Newham Parents Centre, 1986.

35 Robert Barltrop and Jim Wolveridge, *Muvver Tongue*, London, Journeyman Press, 1980, pp. 39–40.

36 Mansfield House, *The Story of an English Field*, London, Mansfield House, 1928.

37 Marriott, *The Culture of Labourism*, p. 22.

38 Phillip Cooke, *Back to the Future. Modernity, Postmodernity and Locality*, London, Unwin Hyman, 1990, p. 6.
39 Anthony Giddens, *The Consequences of Modernity*, London, Polity Press, 1990.
40 Harvey, *The Condition of Postmodernity*, p. 273.
41 Peter Burke, *Popular Culture in Early Modern Europe*, New York, New York University Press, 1978; Harvey Cox, *The Feast of Fools*, Cambridge, Mass., Harvard University Press, 1969; Paul Slack (ed.), *Rebellion, Popular Protest and the Social Order in Early Modern England*, Cambridge, Cambridge University Press, 1984; Peter Clark and Paul Slack (eds), *Crisis and Order in English Towns, 1500–1700*, London, Routledge, 1972; David Underdown, *Revel, Riot and Rebellion. Popular Politics and Culture in England, 1603–1660*, Oxford, Oxford University Press, 1987.
42 Allon White, 'Pigs and pierrots: politics of trangression in modern fiction', *Ruritan*, vol. 2, no. 2, 1982.
43 ibid., p. 55.
44 Stedman Jones, *Outcast London*, p. 347.
45 Marriott, *The Culture of Labourism*, p. 176.
46 J. Franklyn, *The Cockney*, London, Deutsch, 1953, p. 45. But note the problematic nature of the 'cockney' as an historical and political figure, explored well by Gareth Stedman Jones, 'The cockney and the nation, 1780–1988', in David Feldman and Gareth Stedman Jones (eds), *Metropolis. London. Histories and Representations since 1800*, London, Routledge, 1989. And Phil Cohen points to the way in which the sense of ethnicity resonant in such sentiments can assume racist dimensions (see *Home Rules. Some Reflections on Racism and Nationalism in Everyday Life*, London, New Ethnicities Unit, University of East London, 1993, pp. 35–6).
47 Mansfield House, *Annual Appeal from Canning Town*, London, Mansfield House, 1920.
48 Mansfield House, *Way Down East*, London, Mansfield House, 1925.
49 Cited in Ben Tinton, *My 25 Years in Docklands*, London, Marshall, Morgan and Scott, 1946, p. 126.
50 Stanley Reed, 'As it seemed', unpublished ms, n.d.
51 Cited in Charles Korr, *West Ham United. The Making of a Football Club*, London, Duckworth, 1986.
52 Dick Hobbs, *Doing the Business*, Oxford, Oxford University Press, 1988, p. 117.
53 Jack Jones, *His Book*, London, Nelson, 1924, p. 78.
54 Marriott, 'London over the border'.
55 Marriott, *The Culture of Labourism*.
56 ibid., p. 44.
57 Harvey, *The Condition of Postmodernity* p. 279.
58 Stratford Express, 28 September 1918, cited in Marriott, *The Culture of Labourism*, p. 34.
59 Cited in Marriott, *The Culture of Labourism*, p. 370.
60 *Stratford Express*, 1 June 1918, cited in Marriott, *Culture*, pp. 32–3.
61 ibid., p. 182.
62 Harvey, *The Condition of Postmodernity*, p. 272. See also Chapters 1 and 8 in this volume.
63 Marriott, *The Culture of Labourism*, c. 5.
64 Cooke, *Back to the Future*, p. 39.
65 Reginal Kennedy Cox, *Through the Dock Gates*, London, Joseph, 1939, p. 161.
66 John Widdowson, 'Immigration', in Newham History Workshop (ed.), *A Marsh and a Gasworks*.

67 George Cooper, 'Memories, torment and torture', unpublished ms, 1975.
68 *Kinematograph Year Book*, 1921.
69 Mansfield House, 'The possibilities of cinema', *Mansfield House Magazine*, vol. 27, 1921.
70 Stanley Reed, 'Notes on a working life', unpublished ms, n.d.
71 Kennedy Cox, *Through the Dock Gates*, p. 184.
72 Mansfield House, *Mansfield House Magazine*, vol. 17 1921.
73 See Chapters 1 and 9 by Alan O'Shea in this volume.
74 Mansfield House, *Magazine* 1921.
75 Peter Osborne, 'Modernity is a qualitative, not a chronological, category', *New Left Review*, no. 192, 1992, pp. 65–84.
76 ibid., p. 74. See also Doreen Massey, 'Politics and space/time', *New Left Review*, no. 196, 1992, pp. 65–84.

4

NIGHT BATTLES:
HOOLIGAN AND CITIZEN

Bill Schwarz

On 26 July 1898 the *Daily News* carried what now appears to be a truly banal comment: 'It is no wonder . . . that Hooligan gangs are bred in these vile, miasmatic byways.' The significance of this report lies only in the fact that it marks the first time the term 'hooligan' appears in print: the sentiment may have been well-worn, the word new.[1] A couple of weeks later, on 8 August, the same newspaper reported a police constable who insisted his 'prisoner belonged to a gang of young roughs, calling themselves "Hooligans"'. Two days earlier the *Daily Telegraph* had referred to one William Lineker who had set upon an innocent man as a 'hooligan'. The August bank holiday of London's hot summer of 1898 produced a rash of such press comment about the apparently new phenomenon of hooliganism. Evidence of an intensification of street disturbances is certainly not hard to find. Conforming to the ritualised choreography of such occasions local ratepayer associations upbraided those in authority. Questions were asked in the House, and the home secretary was called to account. *Lancet*, never slothful in this period to pronounce on any and every hint of social degeneration, was quick to condemn this new manifestation. But whatever the extent of the disturbances it was the press which made the running. Hyperbole tumbled after hyperbole. Well into the swing of things, the *Daily Mail* led its edition of 13 August with its catchy headline: 'HE ATE A POLICEMAN' – a reference, it transpires not to the cannibalistic fantasies of truculent youth but, bizarre enough, to the antics of a wayward crocodile. There was a scatter of sceptical voices complaining that the panic was no more than the usual brouhaha of the 'silly season', while the London Police Court Commissioner described the whole affair as 'press-manufactured Hooliganism'. But by then the momentum had become irreversible.

The etymology of the keyword – hooligan – is now unlikely to be recovered. Various accounts link the term to Ireland, India, Australia or the USA. As part of oral culture it is likely to have had a rather longer history, possibly within the music-hall. The account from the *Daily News* of 8 August suggests the word had a certain popular currency, with groups of youths happy to adopt it for the purposes of self-description. From the very beginning it could carry the connotation of an alien or foreign presence possessing England's urban landscape; from this vantage it could connect with the racialised syntax employed to describe the underclass which inhabited the 'internal orient' of London's East End.[2] The vocabulary of the 'street Arab' was still common, and still relatively recent, and could be pressed into service when explaining the emergence of the hooligan, as could myths about bandits and their locales, allowing the streets of working-class London to be identified with fantasised notions of 'Calabria, Sicily or Greece'. Predictably, it was not long before the idea of the hooligan, seemingly so rooted in the realities of local urban poverty, could be extended to colonial enemies. The arrival of the bank holiday hooligan in East London coincided with the unsurpassed colonial annihilation of Omdurman, the two events converging in the popular imagination. By 15 September the *Westminster Gazette* had appropriated the term to serve in this new context: 'The Khalifa with his 50,000 Dervishes was a powerful foe', it was admitted; 'but . . . the Khalifa was, after all only a sort of Sudanese Hooligan'.[3] Dangers to the social body, from within or without, were thus neatly conflated.

The idea of the hooligan quickly resonated through public life. Examples are legion. An early, substantial rendition came from the American Clarence Rook. Through 1899 he published a series of articles in the *Daily Chronicle* about hooliganism in south London, which appeared later in the year in book form as *Hooligan Nights – Being the Life and Opinions of a Young and Impertinent Criminal Recounted by Himself and Set Forth by Clarence Rook.*[4] In September the previous year Rook, at the height of the hooligan panic, had made his debut as a mystery writer, recounting the exploits of Miss Van Snoop for the readers of *Harmsworth Magazine*. Despite his strenuous affirmations concerning the reality of 'Alf', the hooligan hero of *Hooligan Nights*, the book reproduced some very old literary conventions – reaching back to Defoe and Fielding – resulting in the highly stylised figure of 'Alf' and a recognisable succession of melodramatic, criminal episodes.[5] As in so many other moments in the history of the popular press, we see low life presented for an (imaginary) respectable readership. Rook delighted in reminding his readers that:

When the *Daily Chronicle* published portions of the history of young Alf early in the year the editor received numerous complaints from well-meaning people who protested that I had painted the life of a criminal in alluring colours. They forgot, I presume, that young Alf was a study in reality, and that in real life the villain does not invariably come to grief before he comes of age.[6]

Throughout Rook's story it is the citizen and ratepayer who is addressed, alerted to the possibility that the hooligan is in a state of perpetual readiness 'to pick your pocket, rifle your house, and even bash you in a dark corner if it is made worth his while'. Rook himself wrote for this readership as one of their number:

> Once or twice it crossed my mind that I, an honest citizen, paying rates and taxes, living in a house and serving on juries, having numerous friends . . . should have forthwith handed young Alf over to a passing policeman and demanded that he should thereafter eat skilly and pick oakum'.[7]

Yet the portrayal is by no means unsympathetic. If the young hooligan was a product of dark places at the same time he embodied the exuberance of a popular modernity, openly negotiating and making his own the pleasures of the city. Here the respectable citizen is placed on the defensive:

> Young Alf beckoned; while I hovered on the kerb watching the charging 'buses, the gliding trams, and the cabs that twinkled their danger signals, he had plunged through the traffic and slithered through, dodging 'buses and skirting cabs without a turn of the head. He went through the traffic with a quiet, confident twist of the body, as a fish whisks its way through scattered rocks, touching nothing, but always within a hair's-breadth of collision. On the other side he awaited me, careless, and indeed a little contemptuous; and together we made our way towards Bethlehem Hospital, and thence in the direction of Lambeth Walk. . . .
>
> The Walk, as they term it to whom Lambeth Walk is Bond Street, the promenade, the place to shop, to lounge, to listen to music and singing, to steal, if the opportunity occur, to make love, and not infrequently to fight [sic].

Alf was a self-professed 'leader of Hooligans', devoted to leisure and pleasure, money and spending and to the imperatives of immediate gratification. He was quick-witted, chivalrous and won leadership by force of personality – in this sense, a wayward, proletarian Tom Brown.[8]

Rook's text quickly shifts, however, from recording Alf's exploits to a sociological construction of 'the typical hooligan' and his 'colony'. The hooligan colony comprises 'sturdy young villains, who start with a grievance against society, and are determined to get their own back'.

> The average Hooligan is not an ignorant, hulking ruffian, beetle-browed and bullet-headed. He is the product of the Board School, writes a fair hand, and is quick at arithmetic. His type of face approaches nearer the rat than the bull-dog; he is nervous, highly-strung, almost neurotic. He is by no means a drunkard; but a very small quantity of liquor causes him to run amuck, when he is not pleasant to meet. Under-sized as a rule, he is sinewy, swift and untiring.

The two strands in the narrative are differentially resolved. Alf, a touch abruptly perhaps, 'turns the corner' and determines to marry his sweetheart, Alice: the final vignette is of the two taking their matrimonial vows and racing off to an untroubled future.[9] But the troubling figure of the hooligan, Alf's unredeemed erstwhile self, remains, increasingly fixed in the imagination of a popular readership.

Confirmation of the social ontology of the hooligan arrived, appropriately enough, in a *Times* leader of 30 October 1900. In the view of *The Times,* so long as 'the "Hooligan" maltreated only the "Hooligan"' the problem could be dealt with by 'police arrangements' – a nice encapsulation of high journalistic understatement. However the situation had now become more serious.

> Our 'Hooligans' go from bad to worse; they do not starve and they do not work; they hustle and waylay solitary old gentlemen with gold watches; they hunt in packs too large for a single policeman to cope with. Many of them mature into the professional criminal. Others are certain to become vagrants or paupers. At best they will be brutal husbands, callous to all responsibilities as fathers, and bad citizens. They are an ugly growth on the body politic ... a hideous excrescence on our civilization.

The usual call for the hooligan to be 'flogged freely' made its predictable, punctual appearance. Yet at the same time, in a commendable spirit of open-mindedness *The Times* considered the availability of 'gymnastics, baths, playgrounds, parks and open spaces' – all favoured by the Howard Association – at least to be worthy of further investigation. For:

> The 'Hooligan' is often not irreclaimable. He may be good, of rough raw material rotting. Sometimes ... there is the making of a good football player or cricketer in him. Were he drilled and subject to officers who are merciless to loutish turbulence he might cease to be a pest to society.[10]

In a rhetoric characteristic of the time, athletic discipline of the male body combined with personal hygiene and environmental improvement as the vehicle by which unruly young men might learn the rational disciplines afforded by modern life.

Another slightly later view can be seen in the musings of Arthur Morrison, whose public renown derived from detailed accounts of East End degradation, most notably in his *The Child of the Jago* published in 1896. In 1901 the *Pall Mall Magazine* carried a short piece by him simply entitled 'Hooliganism'. Morrison was identified by the editor as 'an expert in "Hooligans"', one who had 'lived amongst' them in order to verify his reports. Morrison's purpose was to insist that although the term was new it described old habits. He thought the hooligan 'a mere unlicked cub of a peculiarly vicious type ... merely a young criminal'. 'If he had been taken as a child and lifted from out the evil influences about him, he might have grown into a man of credit.' There followed what has now become a familiar lament: too much was being heard of rights rather than duties; punishments were too lenient and severe prison sentencing required 'no cosseting in its regulations'. He advocated, against the 'sentimentalists', more flogging. Failing this, he suggested that young trouble-makers should be incarcerated 'in a town of their own, and wall them in, so that they may Hooliganise each other till no more are left'.[11]

One could go on in this vein a deal longer, surveying explanations of hooliganism which accounted for the phenomenon in terms of an excess of pocket money (the view favoured by Sidney Webb), the evils of smoking, or the allure of sweetshops and ice-cream parlours.[12] By 1901 the problem of the hooligan had been taken up by the National Union of Teachers.[13] Increasingly it became an issue addressed by a new profession of experts, often of Fabian or new Liberal temperament. Educationalists, criminologists and the growing regiment of investigators into the problem of the labour market and the crisis of 'boy labour' all constructed their respective scientific discourses through the protean figure of the hooligan: indeed the epistemological dynamics of these new knowledges were driven by identification of the hooligan phenomenon, which they were designed in part to master and contain. In these contexts, the voice becomes more detached – the protocols of a putative rationality predominating. As a final example we can take one of the foremost experts of the boy labour problem, Reginald Bray, writing somewhat later in 1911:

> it must not be assumed that all boys become hooligans or criminals, but all do suffer from the want of control and the need of a more disciplined life. Hooliganism is merely an extreme type of disease which in a milder form fastens upon the boys who are allowed unrestrained liberty. The disease is the disease of restlessness – the restlessness of the town, the dislike of regularity. . . . This disease . . . leads into unemployment when the age of manhood is reached.'[14]

All this is well documented. The key issues are relatively clear, and can be summarised. The anxieties encoded by the concept of the hooligan are first formed, focused and grounded in the popular press, and then subsequently appropriated and reworked into a stricter scientific or sociological discourse. Although by no means always easy to differentiate, this is a trajectory which moves from common-sense reaction to a more self-conscious, more abstracted rationality. At the same time hooliganism was construed as a social problem, and appropriate ethical and administrative systems – in the eyes of the experts – needed to be devised in order to resolve it. In a sharp break from earlier decades in the nineteenth century criminal disturbances in the streets less readily signified a threat to the political order – even though at particular moments such fears could and did recur.[15]

To a very high degree the figure of the hooligan was located, firstly, as an expression of masculinity and, secondly, as intimately connected to the hiatus for a particular class of boy between school and work when the absence of daily institutional discipline was perceived to be greatest. For some, manifestation of hooligan behaviour was determined environmentally (as with Morrison, for example), for others activated by the protracted slackening of sufficient discipline (as Bray believed), and for others still by some genetic or psychological deformation (in some strands of criminology) – or most frequently, by a chaotic mix of all these. The effect of this in the 1890s, however, was that the new invention of the hooligan assumed the existence of an anti-social *disposition*. The consequent recourse to languages of animality or disease, powerfully adumbrated, implied that notions of wayward or incomplete human development lay at the bottom of the hooligan phenomenon.[16] The force of the central category – the notion of the hooligan – suggests that at its most strident it could function as a mechanism for determining, in a modern vocabulary, characters and characteristics which were not properly part of human society.

Much more could be said about each of these points. But two issues in particular concern me; both concern historical temporality. Firstly, how does one explain the rapidity with which the term hooligan entered the English language and others.[17] What was it about the concept which made it so amenable to widespread appropriation, and which continues to give it life a century later? In Raymond Williams' terms, might the idea of the hooligan operate as one of the keywords of modernity?

The second question is more strictly to do with historical periodisation. Confronted with the kinds of events described by the category of hooliganism there is some reason to suppose, along with Arthur Morrison, that nothing much new was happening. On the face of it this response is justified. I would guess that most people reading this book – those who have passed a certain age at any rate – have at some time or other believed deep in their hearts that a surly destructive abandon is an essential manifestation of young masculinity, an unattractive fact of history which has to be borne with whatever fortitude one can muster. More or less, this is how the most engaging histories are organised, although with less gloomy conclusions. The most notable, because the most imaginative, is Geoffrey Pearson's *Hooligan. A History of Respectable Fears*. Pearson's intention was to emphasise precisely the continuities perpetrated by the mechanisms of social memory, such that childhood – 'thirty years ago' 'a generation ago' – is most frequently recalled as a time of emotional plenitude, broken by an unforgiving modernity which brings with it, among other things, the spectre of young men with surplus sexual energy creating mayhem. With a fine irony and much sympathy Pearson shows how these remembered pasts slip back through history, imaginary premodern childhoods in fact coexisting with and *produced by* modernity itself. This leads him, not unreasonably, to highlight 'a certain constancy of human motive, and of conflicts built around the human meanings that are attached to the social realities of class, physical appearance and territory'.[18] There is plenty of historical and literary evidence to suggest that panics about young men, street disturbances and criminality have a long duration – much longer than the press reports of hooligan behaviour in 1898, or of Mods and Rockers in 1964. There is an entire social history which carries us back to the early decades of the nineteenth century – to the Society for Investigating the Causes of the Alarming Increases of Juvenile Delinquency, for example – and beyond, to the first moment of the early modern period.[19] There is too a commensurate literary history which confirms the central symbolic positioning of shifting ideas of criminality in the making of an enlightened public sphere where ideas of civilisation and nation could be fought out.[20] Yet while we might appreciate the existence of a 'certain constancy of human nature' in these affairs, it is in the end the variant histories which are more interesting and telling; my own view is that, for all his insight, Pearson conflates or collapses distinct historical times, and that it may be precisely around a historical conception of modernity that the problems can best be explored.

Peering behind the immediate events maybe we can get a bit closer to an answer than Pearson allows and suggest some larger cultural shifts which distinguish the particular transformations of the late nineteenth and early twentieth centuries. There are significant social changes – in schooling and the organisation of childhood; in migration, the structuring of domestic life, nutrition and health; in the crisis of masculinity and of sexual relations; in the vicissitudes of rapidly changing labour markets – which (among other things) all bear broadly on the emergent problem of hooliganism, and which also might usefully be thought of as modern.[21] There is too, centrally, the fact of empire which overdetermined the entire range of late nineteenth century discourse on degeneration and efficiency, and which from the earliest days did much to imprint the image of the hooligan on expert and popular opinion. Any one of these themes could open promising avenues of enquiry. But I intend to take a different tack.

My own sense is that if there is something specifically new or modern about the hooligan panic of the 1890s it is less to do with the empirically observed manifestations of young masculinity, which may indeed possess a relatively constant history, and more with the cognitive structures which allowed this to be talked about in a certain way. This requires thinking generally about the issue of crime itself, working back more obliquely to the specificities of hooliganism. But I think the modernity or novelty of the hooligan phenomenon is also related to the institutional recasting of public life under the impact of new popular forms. To put this in less abstract terms: much seems to hinge on the connections between the expansion of state activity into hitherto private social spaces – *creating* more arenas for intensified public concern, as, for example, in the reforming of childhood or the practices of motherhood – and the modernising mission and effects of the emergent mass media, inventing a public vernacular in which competing requirements of modern civilisation could be addressed. This is not to suggest a functional fit between a hesitantly collectivist state and the first generation of press barons (though the connections were there). It is more about the disposition of power in the public sphere; about the actual and symbolic domestication and incorporation of the mass of the population into the matrices of the public nation; and about the circulation of discourses between the official and the vernacular, elite and popular, high and low. The social divisions, in class terms, between high and low may have been widely accepted as a given truth, and the phenomenon of the hooligan may be seen to have worked to keep social distinctions in place, as I discuss later. But it may also be that newly perceived *confusions* about high and low, about the civilised and the degenerate, were also decisive in activating debate and giving it resonance, reflecting not the certainties of the rational commentator about his own steadfast self, but, on the contrary, his unspoken anxieties. In other words, hooliganism might be seen as one symptom of the crisis of the new, indicating the *disjunctions* between the modern public sphere and its popular constituents.

In 1896 the *Daily Mail* was first published, Marconi filed a patent for the radio and the first commercial film ran, at the Empire, Leicester Square: if any single year can be taken as inaugurating the modern mass media, this was it.[22] As ever, criminality appeared as an abiding feature of the popular media, in its novel variants as much as its old. Crime reports were organised in a new structure. At the *Mail* journalists were *trained* in the mysteries of the vernacular, the expanding institutions of print-capitalism reordering perceptions of the nation as an imagined community. The possibility of an abrupt entry of criminal abuse upon the given rituals of everyday life was woven into the experience of modernity itself, and echoed in the mass circulation press: to read the front page of the first issue of the *Daily Mail* we can see, vying for our attention, reports on a war 'in Bulawayo', a murder in Reading and advertisements for Bird's custard and Nestlé's milk. Crime reporting in the popular commercial press both evoked the everyday experiences of its readers and, in its ventriloquist vernacular, distanced and abstracted at the same time. This double movement, in a form still recognisable today, came to be condensed in the constructions of the criminal biography, appearing simultaneously as a lurid, fantasised figure of horror and yet also disarmingly banal and normal. The civilising momentum of the commercial press could cover many a page denouncing criminals and hooligans, and urging a more forceful policing – one of the earliest campaigns of the *Mail*, for example, was its battle to ensure that every police station had a telephone, a quaint reminder of the lack of

material resources which could be called upon by the state in this period
– while at the same moment, with shameless complicity, revel in the grisly
details of each new barbarity.[23]

This was only one aspect. The closing decade of the nineteenth century
witnessed an extraordinary outpouring of literatures of criminality, so much
so that it seemed as if no single form could contain all that needed to be
said, discourses from one institution spilling over into adjacent genres and
forms. Thus the criminal biographies of the popular press could mimic the
rationalism of criminal science while drawing from the aesthetic categories
of gothic and melodrama, producing new forms in the process.

Similar developments occurred in another sector of popular literature –
in the serialised crime stories which dominated popular magazines from
1890 to the beginning of the First World War, the classic age of the crime
short story.[24] The *Strand Magazine*, launched in January 1891 and
publishing its first Sherlock Holmes story the following July, had a circulation of 300,000 by the end of the year. Alongside grew *Pearson's*, *Cassell's*,
Harmsworth's, *Windsor* and the *Royal Magazine* – the romance of the
monarchy clearly driven by a parallel dynamic. It was here, in the sensa-
tionalist literature, that the future experts on hooliganism – Arthur
Morrison and Clarence Rook – first underwent their scientific apprentice-
ships. As many have noted, this is the moment when the image of the
detective cohered in the popular imagination, and when the urban citizen
and sometime *flâneur* also invented a part of himself (and less often, herself)
as detective in order to master the semiotic chaos of the dark city streets:
a fictionalised, mythic London – the metropolis of the age – became the
special locale of detection.[25] Yet crowding in on the image of the detective
was superimposed a different set of motifs drawn from medicine and the
figure of the medical doctor. Medical science also generated its own semiotic system, in its various subdisciplines creating a host of means to distinguish by rational procedures the mental disposition of the wrongdoer from
that of the law abiding citizen. There are moments in the fiction when the
semiotic aspirations of medicine and detection converge in a bid to identify and resolve the single pathology of the criminally deviant. Holmes and
Watson, invented by Conan Doyle who had himself been trained as a
doctor, are the most celebrated instance. In imitation, by the end of the
decade, we see a Miss Cusack – one of the growing band of female sleuths
– teaming up with a Dr Lonsdale.[26]

But perhaps of more interest, where the cognitive boundaries of truth
look more vulnerable, was the fashion for prison medical officers – James
Pitcairn was one, Richard Freeman another – to turn their professional hands
to the writing of crime fiction, imaginatively drawing from the medical
records in their possession.[27] In one sense this can be seen as an old trick:
in the seventeenth and eighteenth centuries the Ordinary of Newgate – the
gaol's cleric – sold in verse a moralised biography of convicted felons on

the eve of their executions, the Ordinary inducing the poor souls to quaff an excess of liquor so as to allow him to gather a modicum of information; the rest he made up.[28] By the late nineteenth century the categories of truth and fiction moved just as freely, from treatise and medical record to fable. In this light the conceptual inconsistencies in the criminal biographies relayed in the press – exhibiting a kind of hybrid gothic rationalism – look less of a singular phenomenon. High (rational) science and low (sensational) literature could speak to the same effect.

New forms of media attention – in the popular press and in popular literature – intensified the public figure of the criminal, in general, and the hooligan, in particular, amplifying his presence within the imaginary life of the nation. But the other side of this was the position of the hooligan or delinquent within the emergent sphere of 'the social' – that is, within those elements of daily life opened up to public scrutiny by state or phil-anthropic activity, which aimed to categorise and publicise certain forms of behaviour, to educate and castigate in the name of civilisation and to force into the light of day those in need of special care and disciplines. A powerful dynamic in this respect was the growing emphasis on the individualisation of the social citizen, on the deployment of specific biogra-phies – in which, in Foucault's terms, every birth could be transformed into an archive, and every pathology or deviance charted.[29]

There were technical developments which were significant in this larger process. Firstly, there was the increasing use of finger-printing, devised as a means to identify individuals without recourse to bodily mutilation. Or more accurately, finger-printing created the means to identify a subject's history within the institutions of the criminal law, determining whether an offender had previous convictions and ensuring that the person indicted was indeed the person his or her record or archive described. The practice originated in Bengal, was appropriated by the British administrator Sir William Herschel, systematised in Britain by Francis Galton and commonly introduced from the late 1880s. Secondly, alongside this, was the devel-opment of photography and the mugshot. This has a history lodged deep in the disciplinary institutions of the nineteenth century, crossing back and forth between the lunatic asylum and *Lancet*, emerging again at Dr Barnado's and becoming an established part of policing in Britain in the 1860s, with Galton playing an important part here too.[30] Thus Clarence Rook, in thinking through the configuration of the hooligan, contrasts his own observations to the image in 'the photograph which has been buried somewhere in Scotland Yard'.[31]

Parallel to these external means of identification was the increasing centrality to criminal theory of the idea of the individual psychology. This is a hugely complex area, but one or two generalisations can be extrapo-lated. According to one authority, classical criminal theory deriving from the Enlightenment, constituted in order to fix the limits of arbitrary royal power, was predicated on the relations between law, crime and punishment. Absent was the figure of the criminal. There were transgressions, committed – within the purview of this problematic – by the abstract citizen. However nowhere within the body of criminal theory itself did there exist the cognitive space to elaborate a theory of the specific biography and psychology of the criminal. In the second half of the nineteenth century, by contrast, the object shifted radically and the theories came to be *all about* the criminal 'himself'.[32] Bold lineages like this only rarely conform to the complexities of history, but even so, they focus the mind and remind us of the broader picture. Increasingly in late nineteenth-century Britain, the law was deployed to neutralise anti-social behaviour; and anti-social behaviour, calibrated and subdivided according to any number of measurable criteria, was the work of deviant or incapable people. This is the broad picture, which secures general assent. Beyond this, there is less agreement.

One source of controversy, for example, is over the impact of Lombroso's theories in England. Lombroso's *L'uomo delinquente*, published in Italy in 1876, was the great work of European criminal theory in the late nineteenth century, its fame resting on the intransigence of its principal thesis, which located the causes of criminality in the biological constitution of the individual. It was translated into English by Havelock Ellis, a fact of significance, but one which has attracted little comment.[33] It is clear that the availability of Lombroso in English triggered wide discussion, but it is not at all evident how much influence his work had on the formulation of state or voluntary policies. There appears to have been widespread distrust of the full force of his arguments, though it was perfectly possible to adapt his basic thesis to differing emphases, in which both psychological and environmental factors could explain the emergence of the criminal entity. At the beginning of the century two medical doctors at Parkhurst prison – one a disciple of the British master of eugenics, Karl Pearson – launched a major enquiry, backed by the Home Office, in which nearly 4,000 'criminal men' and apparently comparable groups of soldiers, hospital patients, students, schoolboys and staff of London University underwent an extraordinary gamut of investigations (comprising ninety-six variables) in an attempt to test the validity of Lombroso's propositions. As ever, the findings were open to many different interpretations, though there occurred precious little vindication for the foundations of Lombroso's arguments.[34] Some put the emphasis on hereditary influences, some on environmental. But these differing emphases are secondary. Of greater import is the fact that the Home Office was sponsoring research into the nature of 'the English convict' – a powerful example of the conjunction of the collectivist state and the institutions of social science, overriding the declining influence of the evangelical and utilitarian systems which had dominated the mid-nineteenth century; and whatever the emphasis, what *was* vindicated was belief in the existence of the criminal being.

In this period the Home Office was not accustomed to embark upon such projects: its material resources were meagre and its chief administrators and ideologues, in the main, had little faith either in direct intervention (except where no other options existed) or in the value of research.[35] What prompted this unusual activity was public recognition that there existed a penal crisis – an index of the arrival of the modern if ever there were one. Since the appearance of the penitentiary in the 1830s and 1840s, prisons had largely functioned to incarcerate the refractory labouring poor, operating alongside the workhouse and accommodating indiscriminately many of those who in one way or other fell through the market: those who ended up in debt or were unable to meet fines, or who became vagrant.[36] In an important, determined bid to reorganise this axis of social power, various departments of state, with the Home Office in the lead, sought to reduce the prison population substantially. Between 1883 and 1896 the convict population fell by half.[37] In 1895 the Gladstone Committee proposed the continuation of this strategy, well aware of the problem of recidivism, and aware too that once an offender crossed the threshold and entered prison the likelihood was that the journey would be repeated many times in the future. The figures still remained high. In 1902 some 120,000 men and 52,000 women were imprisoned, the very large majority – as high perhaps as 90 per cent – from the destitute poor. Winston Churchill, as home secretary and in his radical Liberal moment, tried once more to bring the figures down, pointing out that 90,000 people were still being sent to gaol every year for small debts.[38] Further legislation, in 1914, together with the manpower shortages brought about by the war, ensured another great drop in those imprisoned.

Against this trend two developments of significance occurred. Firstly, in what might appear a paradox, between 1880 and 1914 the number of offences on the statute book increased: henceforth it was illegal to be drunk in public, to solicit, to be cruel to animals or children, to fail to send one's children to school or to neglect maintenance of one's family.[39] Intervention by public bodies in what previously had been deemed the private sphere of family life was dramatic. But, secondly, if regulation became more intensive it also became more selective and this was reflected in the proliferation of strategies to deal with transgressors. Probation, in various forms, began experimentally in the late 1890s, and was written into statute by the Probation of Offenders Act of 1907. Reformatories and industrial schools became more common, borstals appearing in 1900. The purpose behind these developments was to ensure that for each specific form of deviance there existed an appropriate institution, with its own special administration and knowledges, to allow the redemption of the individual concerned. It is significant, for example, to see that borstals appeared on the scene just two years after the first big panic about hooligans. Underlying these shifts, in recognition of the psychological determinants which now received such attention, was the move to locate these disciplinary institutions within the larger ambit of 'welfare'. For the true recidivists, more repression was all that could be expected: the 1908 Prevention of Crime Act proposed a substantial increase in sentencing for the *habitual* criminal.

Ultimately changes in penal policies and in the criminal law depended upon the existence of a police force which was both effective in its organisation and, if not winning the permanent affections of the people, for most of the time in most places capable of conducting its duties without coming under persistent attack from the civilian population. In the eyes of its ideologues and defenders, the purpose of the police, in other words, was not merely to catch criminals, but rather to advance and uphold a level of civilisation equally for everyone regardless of status.[40] Thus at its very inception, in 1829, instructions to members of the Metropolitan Police declared that constables 'will be civil and obliging to every rank and class'. Since that moment there has been a prolonged battle inside the ranks of the police between this official, civilising and universalising project, on the one hand, and, on the other, a variety of countervailing forces which includes the profane, macho instrumentalism of police work (determination to get the buggers whatever the cost), any number of bigotries and phobias which seem to be uniform issue, and too ready a dalliance with the other side – which together have been known to account for the emergence of 'the bad apple'.

At the end of the nineteenth century, as regular confrontations between police and civilians for the most part declined, the police slowly moved into working-class districts, 'ever more thoroughly invading the "rough" and "dark" parts of town, setting up new stations and fifteen-minute patrols'.[41] Thus Clarence Rook can refer to the figure of 'the passing policeman' as if it were a natural feature of the urban landscape, and not as something relatively new.[42] As the police became less militarised and crime was viewed increasingly as possessing a 'social' dimension, the ideological work of representing the universalising and civilising functions of the police intensified. This was a protracted process, evident at many moments in late nineteenth- and early twentieth-century society. It is discernible, for example, in the debates about arming the police. In September 1883 *The Times* put its view:

> The policeman, who is in foreign cities regarded as an enemy, not only by the criminal classes but by the working classes generally, and who in times of social disturbance is made the first victim of popular hatred, is in England rather the friend of the people rather than otherwise. It is not only the black-coated respectability that feels at home with him, but the workman and woman of the people – every one, in fact, but the criminal and the street Arab – look upon him as an excellent fellow, who performs a necessary duty with as little

roughness as possible. It is obvious that such a relation between the police and the people is the best of all guarantees of social order, and that to jeopardise it would be a most serious blunder.[43]

Or one can see similar sentiments later in the period, especially when the findings of the Royal Commission on the Metropolitan Police were published in 1908. The Commission – the first since 1829 – was set up partly to determine whether the Metropolitan Police carried out their duties 'in a manner as to deserve the public confidence' (the fact it sat at all confirmed they did not), and partly to discuss the best ways of the police handling 'drunkenness, disorder, and solicitation on the streets'.[44] What linked the two issues was the problem of police corruption and the justified fear that the police, in ostensibly bringing light to the underworld, were themselves in danger of being swallowed up by the dark, degenerate forces of the criminal city. That same year *The Times* was on hand again to remind its readers of higher things:

> The policeman in London is not merely a guardian of the peace, he is an integral part of its social life. In many a back street and slum he not merely stands for law and order, he is the true handyman of our streets, the best friend of the mass of people who have no other counsellor or protector.[45]

The historical record might suggest a different story.[46] But faith that the working class could be drawn into the order of the nation, active participants in civil society and recognising the merits of its civilisation, obviously was of the greatest importance. For all those who refused the requisite public and private duties, who perversely spurned the rewards of civilised conduct, were no better than . . . hooligans.

Maybe these transformations in the relations between state and civil society help us to see how perceptions of fairly ordinary manifestations of street bravado on the part of young working-class men could become condensed into the hooligan panic. But they tell only part of the story. To suppose this was all would assign too much power to the state and to the institutions of official society. Legislation and administrative reform did not merely conjure up one blueprint after another, but rather worked actively to transform – and to 'conform' – what was seen, rightly, as a largely resistant set of forces which existed deep within the culture of the people, and which showed little evidence of responding to exhortations from without, whichever quarter they emanated from.[47] For this reason it is important to emphasise the place of the new commercial press as a parallel civilising institution, sometimes working in the same grain as the state, sometimes against, but all the while attempting to invent a public vernacular in which these issues could be more widely articulated. This subordinate culture, moreover, possessed its own conceptions of law and justice which were not commensurable with more conventional public interpretations. Hooligans – if we can assume that such people ever existed for more than an instant – emerged directly from this plebian, dispossessed culture. They made themselves as much as they were made. If we go back to the *Daily News* of 8 August 1898, at the very start of the panic, we can see that a band of 'young roughs' had taken the scandalous, provocative nomenclature of the hooligan upon themselves, displaying it with pride – a move which, from the vantage point of the late twentieth century, is now familiar.

Sources for such self-definition are not easy to come by. To date, the most fruitful work has come from oral history: I shall focus on just one example – the oral memoirs of Arthur Harding – and suggest a few themes which arise.[48] This documentation only approximates to what we need to know. Harding was born in the notorious Jago on the southern tip of Bethnal Green in 1886, spending his first ten years there until the tenements were demolished. He was 12 at the outbreak of the first hooligan panic: he does not mention it, nor is there any reason to think it necessarily touched his life. From the inside it might well have looked just like any other similar episode, which in a sense it was. Yet he had already embarked upon a steady succession of criminal activities; he was later gaoled for two stretches of five years apiece; and – perhaps most dramatic of all – he was acquitted twenty-seven times between 1901 and 1922. What his memoirs do allow is a glimpse into the lived culture of the wider social world in which 'the hooligan' flourished.

Most of all Harding communicates a compelling account of the mythic notions of good and evil which structured the social mentalities of his childhood, and in which the narrative of his own life assumes the form of latter-day morality tale. There is a fatalism here, but it is offset by a landscape peopled by angels and devils who have a hand in their own destinies. There are the evil bastards – among his own people, and among the police and the bench – who, in his opinion, should properly be excluded from human society. They are the authentic 'villains' in his vocabulary. In part, combating them and their influence constitutes the principal justification for his own violence.

This supposes the existence of a set of internal regulations, in which the influence of the law was neither adopted nor rejected wholesale, but negotiated and so far as possible – which was not much – made to work for the dispossessed themselves. There was a range of activities, formally illegal, which broadly were tolerated. These included all the ingenuities which could be mustered to outwit the not-so-hidden-hand of the market; infringements of public seemliness (gambling, drinking, brawling); and a looser grouping of activities which could be linked to the pursuit of excitement and, in a world possessing precious little privacy, to the theatre of street life.[49] The legacy of this popular sensibility is still present today: it forms, for example, the ground for the comedy of manners between those two modest heroes of the Thatcher epoch, Arthur Daley and his minder. Similarly, we know from other evidence that rules existed for nearly every public occasion, including the protocols of fighting – or perhaps we might say, especially for fighting, as this signalled a moment when a neighbourhood threatened to implode.[50] In turn this supposes the possibility of transgressing the internal rules of a community: here might be included unsanctioned, undeserved assaults, disrupting the relations regulating the exchange of women and thieving from 'one's own'. Thus these conceptions of justice could, in sum, at different moments collide or converge with the law. The divisions between 'us' and 'them' – 'them' constituting the representatives of official society – were clearly powerful. But they were not absolute. To assume they were ignores the internal hierarchies which stratified even the poorest, street by street, tenement by tenement. And it ignores the moment when, to counter some extreme transgression, the law could legitimately be called upon to break the grip of a real villain.[51]

Of course, much depended on variant perceptions of what, or who, constituted villainy. For all his self-justifications there can be little doubt that Harding himself would, at various times, have qualified. Similarly, it would be foolish to suppose that hooliganism represented only a carnivalesque refusal of external authority, happily endorsed by the larger community. More to the point, hooliganism – young men on the rampage – could equally well signify an incomplete internalisation of the more responsible, but necessarily unwritten, rules of the neighbourhood, irritating the hell out of those struggling against the odds to get some order into their lives. This fluid state of affairs raises another issue. Harding presents his story as a catalogue of good deeds, placing himself on the side of the angels. On behalf of weaker neighbours, and abused femininity, he is ever-prepared to 'give a friend a hand', which in less circumspect language adds up to inflicting 'a good hiding'. His symbolic role in the neighbourhood, establishing him in local legend as a man with a reputation, carries duties as well as rewards. By exerting symbolic and, where necessary, real terror he elevates himself into a position where he assumes the role of tribune of the people.

This is a perceived identity. It has nothing to do with the notion of 'social crime' in which stealing, for example, is interpreted as an act of class rebellion. We can think more productively, however, in terms of the *structures* of 'social banditry'.[52] Hobsbawm highlights certain key themes in the emergence of social banditry, albeit in very different historical circumstances: a community existing in relative insulation from the reach of the state; a community on the point of dislocation or threatened by some perceived external danger; the appearance of a chivalrous leader capable of great exploits who determines to defend his people against external threat. This structure, I think, can help explain Harding's sense of his own identity, and – in a later time – the public identities of a generation of local thugs who came to prominence in the 1960s.[53] But here again the critical issue is the fluidity of these relations and identities: 'A man may be a social bandit in his native mountains, a mere robber on the plains.'[54]

I am not saying that 'hooligans' should be recovered as social bandits. What we can see is a complex intersection of state and public interventions, internally sanctioned illegalities which could, among other things, have turned upon the defence of a symbolic territory from some perceived external danger (such as the intervention, internally, of the policeman or Poor Law guardian), and behaviour hostile to any regulations whatsoever. Given the documentation that exists it is not possible to decide which of these at any one moment was in command. But it is also the case that those identified as hooligans in 1898 – or those who chose to identify themselves as hooligans – did play upon a pronounced sense of style. There was a deliberate, fashioned, symbolically nihilist intention of young working-class men to create their own entry into the public sphere and, we might guess, to play up to the susceptibilities of newsmen and social investigators. Reginald Bray showed a deep anxiety about the aimlessness of young men hanging around the streets to no apparent purpose or, if we stretch things a bit, about what might be thought of as the working-class *flâneur*.[55] Hooligans, according to the press reports of the time, sported a distinctive style composed of bell-bottoms, garish scarves, ornamental belts and the prized donkey-fringe haircut. They chose to enter the public world on their own terms, in their own spectacular fashion, and in a style which was designed to upset to the highest degree conventional public opinion.[56]

There are two broad conclusions to be drawn from these conflicting arguments about hooliganism, which draw us back to the question of the English constitution of modernity. The first is to do with the concept of citizenship; the second – connected to this – with the masculine encodings of the reasoning self.

It should be clear by this stage that the hooligan belongs to that category of new social subjects which proliferated in the late nineteenth and early twentieth centuries. He had a whole regiment of kindred spirits: the common prostitute, the male homosexual, the incorrigible loafer, the destitute alien, the recidivist, the feeble-minded, the feckless mother ... and on and on. These new identities, attributed to particular dispositions and biographies, signified a varied netherworld of characters who – for different reasons – were deemed unable to function as capable and efficient participants in the evolving modern world. Excluded from the norms of society, they were condemned to disciplinary controls of varying intensity. A sense of contagion was attached to them all, requiring a degree of insulation from the mainstream of the population so the latter would not cross the divide between the efficient and the deficient, augmenting the mass of the degenerate.[57] For those condemned as hooligans there grew up a whole array of new regulatory institutions to keep them in check. Formally many of these exemplified faith in the modernising disciplines of welfare and psychology; but this rational modernity carried with it a veritable archipelago of new sites (borstals, reformatories, approved schools) where refractory young children were inducted into a regime of unspeakable physical terror – though this did not prevent the *News of the World*, in 1907, from initiating its campaign against the new borstals for being insufficiently rigorous, suggesting that instead of receiving discipline the inmates were 'petted and coddled' by the authorities.[58]

To make sense of hooliganism we would need to read synchronically across the social formation to see how he, 'the hooligan', was positioned in relation to the other Others. But to restrict our vision to the deficient is to miss the point: for the concept of the hooligan was produced by the concept of the citizen, hooliganism working as the discursive Other of citizenship.

Slowly, working-class men were coming to be recognised as real or potential members of the political nation, by securing the vote on the one hand and by receiving the benefits of culture – parks, museums, libraries, colleges – on the other. The 1867 Reform Act signalled the beginning of this process, the institutions of local democracy and civic culture mushrooming from the 1880s. Alongside these transformations the experiments in mass compulsory schooling were steeped in the ideals of citizenship. The structures underpinning the languages of class shifted commensurably: the collective identity of the mob, in which the working class as a whole was indicted as a real or potential political danger, gave way to a more individualistic discourse in which the construct of the respectable working man loomed large while hooligans, as irresponsible and identifiable figures, assumed an axiomatic position within the new political lexicon as the contagious carriers of an anti-citizen disposition.[59] As the political nation was in the process of becoming more inclusive, ever-more inventive – and ever-more encompassing – structures of exclusion were devised, each finely orchestrated, in order to screen out those pathological individuals unable or unwilling to conduct themselves as potential citizens.[60] The power of these new identities was not at all confined to the imperatives of the public sphere, as we have seen. Citizenship itself was a concept resonant with ethical and domestic as well as straightforwardly political meanings. The moral requirements of citizenship demanded private as well as public obligations, encapsulating the whole complex of patriarchal possessive individualism. As *The Times* put it in its editorial on hooligans, quoted earlier: (p. 104) 'At best, they will be brutal husbands, callous to all responsibilities as fathers, and bad citizens.' Hooliganism thus signified a crisis in the potentialities of the new working-class man as citizen, embracing the full scope of his capacities to manage his own self and the selves of those who depended on him.

As the hooligan panic broke, a prolonged and ferocious public struggle was underway to determine the gendered definitions of citizenship which, eventually, reordered the fundamentals of the debate. Much conservative argument, in defending female exclusion, was conducted in terms of appealing to the peculiarly rational capabilities of men. The intensity of the hooligan moment can, I think, be connected to the anxiety that – palpably – not all men possessed these capabilities. Here were feminists mounting a powerful campaign for citizenship; an active element among the anti-feminist forces worked from the belief that reason belonged only to men, and rights to participate in politics should exclude women as the price of their proximity to nature; and all the while there was terrific publicity given to young men who showed every sign of embodying the highest degree of unreason, running amok and raising Cain.[61]

Again, I have made large arguments and relied on describing patterns of development which deserve more nuanced reading. Yet it is striking how often hooliganism, in this early period, was understood as the explicit antithesis to citizenship. *The Times'* notion of 'bad citizenship' was unambiguous. The theme runs through Clarence Rook's pioneering depiction, an entire episode taking place against the backdrop of the Palace of Westminster, allowing both Alf and the fictionalised figure of Rook to dilate on their respective attitudes to politics.[62] But where these arguments appear in their most sustained form is with Baden Powell and his fledgling scouting movement. In *Scouting for Boys*, first published in 1908, Baden Powell presented his ideas of scouting as a counter to the habits of 'hooliganism' which, like *The Times*, he defined in terms of 'bad citizenship'.[63] Within a very short time the full resources of the scout organisations were purveying similar notions, mounting in effect what was an offensive against the deleterious influences of the hooligan.[64] Yet Baden Powell himself – infantile, quirky and constantly railing against the boredom of modern England compared to the adventures of the frontier – was guaranteed to complicate matters: before long he was wont to declare the hooligan 'the best class of boy', meaning precisely a boy with spunk who possessed the wits to become a proper frontiersman.[65] I do not think this predilection for the perverse detracts from the argument, for there were many other occasions when he was the first to denounce the existence of degenerate city lads hanging around street corners, believing them to be a danger to the body-politic. But as I suggest in a moment it may have been more than just a personal idiosyncrasy.

It is the discursive connection to citizenship and constitutionalism which gives the idea of hooliganism its longevity, and which fixes it so effectively in the popular imagination. In the ideals of the respectable citizen we see the nightmare of the hooligan. It condenses with great power a cluster of anxieties which accrue around masculinity and youth, read through the lens of class. It has never remained attached for long periods to young women, though it occurs now and again; and when delinquent males grow up, they become something else. Nor have attempts to turn the concept round been successful, switching the social stigma from the working class to the upper classes. The first attempt at this I have come across is from 1910 when Hugh Franklin, a feminist sympathiser appalled at the spectacle of police beating women demonstrators on Black Friday, first set upon the home secretary, Winston Churchill, in a train with a riding-whip as the latter was heading for the dining-car, then later condemned Churchill and his police in *Votes for Women* as the 'real hooligans'.[66] Exemplary though this may have been, it did not do much to change the meaning of the key term. Nor did the most recent example I have seen, a *Mirror* editorial attacking hooligans 'of all classes. (He can be found at Ascot as well as Hackney.)', inspired in this instance by the decision of the brother of the Princess of Wales (Charles, then Viscount Althorp) to dismantle a restaurant while the patrons were still eating.[67] The persistence of the term and the stability of its meanings is striking – if not a constant presence in British life, then always an available one.

Briefly, one can note a lull following 1914, and what appear to be the limited usages during the interwar period, although there is little research on this.[68] During the Second World War the axis shifted to the figure of the spiv who, despite the parallels, was of a different order.[69] In the postwar moment those golden-haired toddlers cavorting in the sunshine and drinking their milk, which cinema audiences had become habituated to during the war in the gentle propaganda of the Crown Film Unit, mutate at the end of the 1950s into authentic hooligans, slashing cinema seats in the Elephant and Castle and heading *en masse* for bank holiday mayhem. Its intensity appears to slacken again from the mid-1960s, and then flares up from the 1970s and through the 1980s when it becomes principally, but not exclusively, associated with football.[70] When, in the early 1980s, we can hear Conservative MPs calling for hooligans to be publicly humiliated and to be placed in stocks or caged in the local market on Saturday mornings, we know we are on familiar territory, the anxieties of the 1890s are still active a century later.[71]

This brings me to my final point. The pathology evident in such a response and the degree of fantasy underpinning it – the image of the market-place in Britain of the 1980s is clearly unreal – suggest that we would need to look more carefully at the traffic between the men of reason, ostensibly merely describing and prescribing, and the eruption of the irrational which they attribute to the reflexes of low life. For these are less separate, self-contained occurrences than the manifest evidence would suggest. There is, plainly, the erotics of the situation, where repulsion turns in on itself to reveal attraction. This is where Baden Powell ceases to be idiosyncratic and becomes representative, his penchant for unbridled boyhood well known; or where young Oxford men active in the settlement movement in the East End of London developed obsessions of various kinds about the 'rough lads' within their charge; or in more genteel mode, the frisson associated with bringing 'low-life' characters into one's home, parodied by Rose Macaulay's vision of the respectable classes of the 1890s inviting pickpockets to tea.[72]

The psychic energy producing the hooligan panic was extraordinary, the protocols of orderly reasoning straining at every point and the search for the new demons of modernity uppermost. The most respected, and popular, treatise on the psychology of the adolescent could blithely assert that during the years of adolescence 'the young man is fighting the hottest battles of his life with the Devil'.[73] The legacy of Robert Louis Stevenson's *The Strange Case of Dr Jekyll and Mr Hyde* was powerful – a work of fiction, written in response to a media-fuelled panic about sexuality, and thence insinuating itself as the lodestar of scientific rationality.[74] E.J.Urwick, with Bray the foremost scientific expert on the problems of boy labour, believed: 'It is common experience to find a boy a Jekyll in the classroom, and a Hyde in the street', noting too that 'the heart of a boy is half angel, half savage'.[75] What these opinions manifestly recognised was the potential for the character of young working-class men to waver or split between the virtuous and the vicious, the rational and the irrational. The various solutions to the hooligan problem were all predicated on winning the young men to reasonable civilisation, and suppressing the uncivilised instincts of unreason. Yet what these assumptions also convey – and what *Jekyll and Hyde* opened up – was the possibility that the identity of the rational bourgeois observer might equally well split between his civilized self and another irrational self, his persona riven by unspeakable desires: he too, by some unforeseen ruse of history, might also contain within himself a nature and passion incompletely mastered by reason.[76] If this were so hooliganism not only offered a way of identifying the demons out there, but in a deeper sense alluded to the demons residing in the interior self too.

NOTES

1 All the quotes in the first two paragraphs either come from the *Oxford English Dictionary*, or from Geoffrey Pearson, *Hooligan. A History of Respectable Fears*, London, Macmillan, 1983, ch. 5.

2 See John Marriott's 'Sensation of the abyss', Chapter 3 in this volume; also Phil Cohen, *Home Rules. Reflections on Racism and Nationalism in Everyday Life*, London, New Ethnicities Unit, University of East London, 1993.

3 See too Robert Colls, 'Englishness and political culture', in Robert Colls and Philip Dodd (eds), *Englishness. Politics and Culture, 1880–1920*, Beckenham, Croom Helm, 1986, p. 47.

4 Clarence Rook, *Hooligan Nights*, Oxford, Oxford University Press, 1979, pp. 10–18.

5 There is a colossal literature on this. A sharp-eyed focus can be found in Michael McKeon's 'From picaresque to criminal biography' in his brilliant *The Origins of the English Novel, 1600–1740*, London, Hutchinson Radius, 1988, pp. 96–100.

6 Rook, *Hooligan Nights*, p. xxii.
7 ibid., p. 49.
8 ibid., pp. 2 and xxi.
9 ibid., pp. 15–17 and 179.
10 *The Times*, 30 October 1900.
11 Arthur Morrison, 'Hooliganism', *Pall Mall Magazine*, vol. 23, 1901.
12 Harry Hendrick, *Images of Youth. Age, Class, and the Male Youth Problem, 1880–1920*, Oxford, Clarendon Press, 1990, ch. 4.
13 Stephen Humphries, *Hooligans or Rebels? An Oral History of Working-Class Childhood and Youth, 1889–1939*, Oxford, Blackwell, 1981, p. 18.
14 Cited in ibid., p. 10.
15 *Inter alia*, Robert D. Storch, 'The plague of blue locusts: police reform and popular resistance in northern England, 1840–57', in M. Fitzgerald, G. McLennan and J. Pawson (eds), *Crime and Society. Readings in History and Theory*, London, Routledge and Kegan Paul, 1981; and Victor Bailey, *Policing and Punishment in Nineteenth-Century Britain*, London, Croom Helm, 1981.
16 On ideas of animality in the period see Françoise Barret-Ducrocq, *Love in the Time of Victoria. Sexuality, Class and Gender in Nineteenth-Century London*, London, Verso, 1991, p. 37.
17 For example: Joan Neuberger, *Hooliganism. Crime, Culture and Power in St. Petersburg, 1900–14*, Berkeley, University of California Press, 1994. Neuberger notes the outbreaks of commensurate moral panics at this moment in New York, Paris, London and Berlin (p. 3) which, alongside St Petersburg, also function as key locations of Marshall Berman's modernist imagination: *All That is Solid Melts Into Air. The Experience of Modernity*, London, Verso, 1983. Neuberger shows that the term hooligan first appeared in Russia in *Russkoe Bogatstvo* reporting the London disturbances, but took off from 1900 in its own right, the presence of street gangs on the Nevskii Prospekt fuelling endless comment in the 'boulevard press'. See too John Neubauer, *The Fin-de-Siècle Culture of Adolescence*, New Haven, Yale University Press, 1992.
18 Pearson, *Hooligan*, p. 91. For a similar criticism from the mainstream of the historical profession, Hendrick, *Images of Youth*, p. 141. Pearson's reading of historical memory accords with Raymond Williams' critique of 'the escalator view of history' developed in *The Country and the City*, St Albans, Paladin, 1973.
19 J. Tobias, *Crime and Industrial Society in the Nineteenth Century*, Harmondsworth, Penguin, 1972; Kellow Chesney, *The Victorian Underworld*, Harmondsworth, Penguin, 1982.
20 For devotees, Allen J. Hubin, *Crime Fiction, 1749–1980. A Comprehensive Bibliography*, Garland, Allen J. Hubin, 1984. The standard account can be found in Julian Symons, *Bloody Murder. From the Detective Story to the Crime Novel. A History*, Harmondsworth, Penguin, 1974.
21 These, and much else, are elegantly summarised in José Harris, *Private Lives, Public Spirit: Britain, 1870–1914*, Harmondsworth, Penguin, 1994, which also indicates numerous paths for further exploration.
22 Asa Briggs, *Mass Entertainment. The Origins of a Modern Industry*, Adelaide, Griffin, 1960.
23 R. Pound and G. Harmsworth, *Northcliffe*, London, Cassell, 1959, p. 207.
24 Hugh Greene (ed.), *The Rivals of Sherlock Holmes. Early Detective Stories*, Harmondsworth, Penguin, 1971.
25 For important commentaries on epistemological shifts which anticipated the transformations of the 1890s: Steven Marcus on Engels: 'Reading the illegible',

in H.J. Dyos and M. Wolff (eds), *The Victorian City*, vol. 2, London, Routledge and Kegan Paul, 1973; and Jenny Bourne Taylor on Wilkie Collins: *In The Secret Theatre of Home. Wilkie Collins, Sensation Narrative and Nineteenth-Century Psychology*, London, Routledge, 1989. The theme is carried through in Richard Sennett, *The Fall of Public Man*, London, Faber and Faber, 1986.
26 P. Craig and M. Cadogan, *The Lady Investigates*, Oxford, Oxford University Press, 1986, p. 30; and Judith Walkowitz, who sees the figure of the detective as a 'superrational superego', *City of Dreadful Delight. Narratives of Sexual Danger in Late-Victorian London*, London, Virago, 1992, p. 131; and Franco Moretti on Holmes: 'the great *doctor* of the late Victorians, who convinces them that society is still a great *organism*: a unitary and knowable body', 'Clues', in his *Signs Taken for Wonders. Essays in the Sociology of Literary Forms*, London, Verso, 1983, p. 145.
27 Greene, *Rivals of Sherlock Holmes*.
28 Peter Linebaugh, 'The Ordinary of Newgate and his account', in J.S. Cockburn (ed.), *Crime in England, 1550–1800*, London, Methuen, 1977.
29 There is a wide literature on this, dealing with many local instances. The most comprehensive, retaining a conceptual sense of the field as a whole, is Nikolas Rose, *The Psychological Complex. Psychology, Politics and Society in England, 1869–1939*, London, Routledge and Kegan Paul, 1985. The best historical location remains Gareth Stedman Jones, *Outcast London. A Study in the Relationship Between Classes in Victorian Society*, Harmondsworth, Penguin, 1976.
30 Daniel Pick, *Faces of Degeneration. A European Disorder, c1848–c1918*, Cambridge, Cambridge University Press, 1989, p. 165.
31 John Tagg, *The Burden of Representation. Essays on Photographies and Histories*, London, Macmillan, 1988; Dick Hebdige, 'Hiding in the light. Youth, surveillance and display', in his *Hiding in the Light*, London, Comedia, 1988; Walter Benjamin, *Illuminations*, edited by Hannah Arendt, London, Fontana, 1973, p. 228; and Rook, *Hooligan Nights*, p. 35.
32 Pasquale Pasquino, 'Criminology. The birth of a special savoir', *Ideology and Consciousness*, vol 7, 1980.
33 Sheila Rowbotham and Jeffrey Weeks, *Socialism and the New Life. The Personal and Sexual Politics of Edward Carpenter and Havelock Ellis*, London, Pluto, 1977, p. 158.
34 Pick, *Faces of Degeneration*; Marie-Christine Leps, *Apprehending the Criminal. The Production of Deviance in Nineteenth-Century Discourse*, Durham, NC, Duke University Press, 1992. Leon Radzinowicz and Roger Hood, *A History of English Criminal Law and its Administration from 1750*, vol. 5. *The Emergence of Penal Policy*, London, Stevens and Son, 1986, pp. 20–7. And more specifically, John Gillis, 'The evolution of juvenile delinquency in England, 1890–1914', *Past and Present*, no. 67, 1975.
35 Jill Pellew, *The Home Office, 1848–1914*, London, Heinemann, 1982.
36 Michael Ignatieff, *A Just Measure of Pain. The Penitentiary in the Industrial Revolution, 1750–1850*, London, Macmillan, 1978; M.A. Crowther, *The Workhouse System, 1834–1929. The History of an English Social Institution*, London, Methuen, 1983.
37 Martin J. Wiener, *Reconstructing the Criminal. Culture, Law and Policy in England, 1830-1914*, Cambridge, Cambridge University Press, 1990, p. 325.
38 Martin Gilbert, *Churchill's Political Philosophy*, Oxford, Oxford University Press, 1981, p. 48. In a letter to the King on 21 July 1910 Churchill provides a classic example of the civilising mission:

> Over 5,000 lads between 16 and 21 are sent to prison every year for such offences as swearing, stone throwing, gaming, football in the streets. This is pure waste. Mr Churchill thinks a system of defaulters' drills might be instituted – not military (wh would reflect upon the possession of arms) but physical exercises, vy healthy, vy disagreeable; that this might be done at the Police Station; that the boy might do his ordinary work besides, and not be sent to prison unless incorrigible or really dishonest. No lad between 16 and 21 ought to be sent to prison for mere punishment. Every sentence shd be conceived with the object of pulling him together and bracing him for the world: it shd be in fact disciplinary and educative rather than penal.

For an overall assessment of Churchill's impact, Radzinowicz and Hood, *History of English Criminal Law*, pp. 770–5.

39 Wiener, *Reconstructing the Criminals*, p. 261.
40 T.A. Critchley, *A History of the Police in England and Wales*, London, Constable, 1967, offers a classic view in this vein. For a careful survey of early problems in policing in the national context: Carolyn Steedman, *Policing the Victorian Community. The Formation of English Provincial Police Forces, 1856–80*, London, Routledge and Kegan Paul, 1984.
41 Wiener, *Reconstructing the Criminals*, p. 215. On 10 November 1888 the Queen wired Salisbury from Balmoral: 'All these courts must be lit, and our detectives improved. They are not what they shd be' (cited in Bill Fishman, *East End. 1888*, London, Duckworth, 1988, p. 222.)
42 In metropolitan London in 1906 there were 420 civilians to every police officer in 1985 the ratio was 268:1.
43 Clive Emsley, 'The British bobby', in Roy Porter (ed.), *Myths of the English*, Cambridge, Polity, 1992, p. 121.
44 *Royal Commission upon the Duties of the Metropolitan Police*, London, HMSO, Cd. 4156, 1908.
45 Cited in Robert Roberts, *The Classic Slum. Salford Life in the First Quarter of the Century*, Harmondsworth, Penguin, 1974, p. 100. Note too the comments of the Chief Constable of Manchester in his annual report of the same year: 'Police duty bore little resemblance to that of thirty or forty years earlier. Then the policeman dealt largely with the criminal: now he is rendering a public service to all classes' (ibid., p. 99.)
46 Jerry White, *The Worst Street in North London. Campbell Bunk, Islington, Between the Wars*, London, Routledge and Kegan Paul, 1986; and Phil Cohen, 'Policing the working-class city', in National Deviancy Conference/Conference of Socialist Economists, *Capitalism and the Rule of Law. From Deviance Theory to Marxism*, London, Hutchinson, 1979.
47 Michael Ignatieff, 'State, civil society and total institution: a critique of recent social histories of punishment', in Stan Cohen and Andrew Scull (eds), *Social Control and the State*, Oxford, Martin Robertson, 1983, and his 'Total institutions and working classes', *History Workshop Journal*, vol. 15, 1983. And specifically on London culture in this period: Gareth Stedman Jones, 'Working-class culture and working-class politics in London, 1770–1900. Notes on the remaking of a working class', in his *Languages of Class. Studies in English Working-Class History, 1832–1982*, Cambridge, Cambridge University Press, 1983.
48 Humphries, *Hooligans or Rebels*, and his 'Steal to survive. The social crime of working class children, 1890–1940', *Oral History*, vol. 9, no. 1, 1981. The

bulk of this work attempts to show working-class crime as a form of social resistance. In the latter he claims to have uncovered 'a rich seam of deeply embedded class resistance' (p. 26); in the former he instances the death of an Armenian refugee in Bermondsey in 1897 at the hands of local youths, claiming their actions to have been a 'misdirected expression of class feeling and class hostility' (p. 198) – a baleful interpretation. Also: Raphael Samuel, *East End Underworld. Chapters in the Life of Arthur Harding*, London, Routledge and Kegan Paul, 1981.

49 Ross McKibbon, 'Working-class gambling in Britain, 1880–1939', *Past and Present*, no. 82, 1979; Dick Hobbs, *Doing the Business. Entrepreneurship, the Working Class and Detectives in the East End of London*, Oxford, Clarendon Press, 1988.

50 Jerry White, 'Campbell Bunk. A lumpen community in London between the wars', *History Workshop Journal*, vol. 8, 1979 p. 125.

51 Stripped of its English sentimentality *The Blue Lamp* (Michael Relph, 1949) is actually very insightful in this respect, showing a community uniting to contain the danger brought about by the psychotic hooligan, played by Dirk Bogarde.

52 E.J. Hobsbawm, *Bandits*, Harmondsworth, Penguin, 1972.

53 Excellent on the Krays – with an eye to the transposition of Calabria to Vallance Road – is Dick Hebdige, *The Kray Twins. A Study of a System of Closure*, Birmingham, Centre for Contemporary Cultural Studies, Occasional Paper 20, University of Birmingham, 1974. But there is also John Pearson, *The Profession of Violence. The Rise and Fall of the Krays*, London, Granada, 1982; Jimmy Boyle, *A Sense of Freedom*, London, Pan, 1981; and Walter Probyn, *Angel Face. The Making of a Criminal*, London, Allen and Unwin, 1977. For a view from Westminster, Robert Rhodes James, *Bob Boothby. A Portrait*, London, Hodder and Stoughton, 1991, pp. 414–21. A fine attempt to offer some larger sociological explanation can be found in Phil Cohen, 'Subcultural conflict and working-class community', *Working Papers in Cultural Studies*, vol. 2, 1972.

54 Hobsbawm, *Bandits*, p. 18.

55 Cited in Humphries, *Hooligans or Rebels*, p. 5; and for a sharp formulation concerning the reciprocal processes underpinning the entry of the poor into new urban spaces in the second half of the nineteenth century, Berman, *All That is Solid*, p. 153. Relevant here is the simple equation between modernity and degeneration, a common element in many interpretations of the time. Max Nordau's *Degeneration*, published in German in 1892 and translated three years later, was decisive:

> The end of the twentieth century . . . will probably see a generation to whom it will not be injurious to read a dozen or so yards of newspaper daily, to be constantly called to the telephone, to be thinking simultaneously of the five continents of the world, to live half their time in a railway carriage or flying machine . . . It will know how to find its ease in the midst of a city inhabited by millions.
>
> (Cited in Pick, *Faces of Degeneration*, p. 24)

56 Cohen, 'Policing the working-class city', p. 128; and David Robins and Philip Cohen, *Knuckle Sandwich. Growing Up in the Working-Class City*, Harmondsworth, Penguin, 1978.

57 Charles Booth's comments on 'street Arabs' as 'ready material for disorder' are critical here: 'They degrade whatever they touch', *Labour and Life of the People of London*, vol. 1: *East London*, London, Williams and Norgate, 1889, p. 38.

And this goes back further: the famous opening passage of Mayhew's investigation of 'street-folk' contrasts 'the vagabond and the citizen': Henry Mayhew, *Mayhew's London*, edited by Peter Quennell, London, Bracken Books, 1984, p. 29.

58 Humphries, *Hooligans or Rebels*, ch. 8; and especially the recollections of approved-school life recorded by Mass Observation in 1949, cited in ibid., pp. 224–5. *The Times*' call for 'officers who are merciless to loutish turbulence' has many implications. On this see the deeply depressing accounts of 'The birth of borstal' and 'Whipping juveniles' in Radzinowicz and Hood, *History of English Criminal Law*, pp. 384–7 and 711–19. In the House of Commons on 21 May 1900 the home secretary, Sir Matthew White Ridley, justified the flogging of juveniles as a 'short and sharp punishment' (ibid. p. 712.)

59 Asa Briggs, 'The language of "class" in early nineteenth century England', in Asa Briggs and John Saville (eds), *Essays in Labour History*, London, Macmillan, 1967; and for an attempt to look at the relations between citizenship and collectivism in the later period, Stuart Hall and Bill Schwarz, 'State and society, 1880–1930', in Mary Langan and Bill Schwarz (eds), *Crises in the British State*, London, Hutchinson, 1984.

60 Daniel Pick argues that Lombroso conforms to this project, suggesting that he determined 'to formulate the definition of a political subject by elaborating ever more closely the criteria for exclusion' ('Faces of anarchy. Lombroso and the politics of criminal science in post-Unification Italy', *History Workshop Journal*, vol. 21, 1986, p. 76). And for the specific context of British progressivism:

> the concept of the 'residuum' was built into new liberal ideology. This was the logical deduction from their principles. New liberalism re-defined citizenship not simply as a political right but as a moral, social and even aesthetic ideal. This concept of citizenship implied not only an extension of opportunities to the citizen but a reciprocal set of duties on the part of the citizen to the state. Inevitably some failed to reciprocate. There was, in fact, always the possibility of an intractable and undeserving stratum among the poor whose moral character and social life did not live up to these ideals of citizenship. The 'social problem group' fitted this idea perfectly.
>
> (Greta Jones, 'Eugenics and social policy between the wars', *Historical Journal*, vol. 25, no. 3, 1982, pp. 726–7)

61 Brian Harrison, *Separate Spheres. The Opposition to Women's Suffrage in Britain*, London, Croom Helm, 1978. For the 'girl on the streets' see the figure of 'the amateur prostitute' described by Lucy Bland, 'Guardians of race or vampires upon the nation's health? Female sexuality and its regulation in early twentieth century Britain', in E. Whitelegg *et al.* (eds), *The Changing Experience of Women*, Oxford, Martin Robertson, 1982; and with more circumspection, Lily Montagu, 'The girl in the background', in E.J. Urwick (ed.), *Studies of Boy Life in Our Cities*, London, Dent, 1904.

62 Rook, *Hooligan Nights*, pp. 117–19.

63 Robert Baden Powell, *Scouting for Boys*, London, Horace Cox, 1908, p. 264.

64 For guerrilla warfare conducted against organised youth movements by hooligans, John Springhall, 'Building character in the British boy: the attempt to extend Christian manliness to working-class adolescents, 1880 to 1914', in J.A. Mangan and James Walvin (eds), *Manliness and Morality. Middle-Class Masculinity in Britain and America, 1800–1940*, Manchester, Manchester University Press, 1987, pp. 59–60.

For another view, with the pathos of Richmal Crompton:

> Among volumes filched appeared a battered copy of *Scouting for Boys*. After reading it we both felt an overwhelming urge to assist Baden Powell in an organization where, we believed, our own brickhills experience would prove invaluable. We discussed the matter by our corrugated wigwam, Ignatius standing about respectfully.
>
> 'How about me joinin', then?' he asked.
>
> Sydney showed his contempt. 'You! There's a uniform, for a start – fifteen shillings. Where'd you get that?'
>
> Where *we* would get it Syd didn't mention. Not a single troop existed in our area; one had to make do with the Church of England Lads' Brigade, a much less glamorous affair. As easily the most respectable of the trio I went to offer our services at St John's, a troop in a lower-middle-class district beyond the tramlines, and duly reported back.
>
> 'Stuck up!' I said. 'I was the only one with clogs on!'
>
> (Robert Roberts, *A Ragged Schooling. Growing Up in the Classic Slum*, London, Fontana, 1979, p. 87)

65 Pearson, *The Profession of Violence*, p. 110; and for Baden Powell welcoming the rise in juvenile crime in 1933, Pearson, *Hooligan*, p. 34.

66 Randolph Churchill, *Winston S. Churchill*, vol. 2: *Young Statesman, 1901–1914*, London, Heinemann, 1967, p. 400. Filial discretion prevents Randolph Churchill mentioning the fact that Hugh Franklin was subsequently gaoled, went on hunger strike and in the end was force-fed: Sylvia Pankhurst, *The Suffragette Movement. An Intimate Account of Persons and Ideals*, London, Virago, 1977, p. 345.

67 'What is a hooligan?', *Daily Mirror*, 24 May 1984.

68 Victor Bailey, *Delinquency and Citizenship. Reclaiming the Young Offender, 1914–48*, Oxford, Clarendon Press, 1987. It does seem as if children's street life did diminish rapidly in the 1930s: Humphries, *Hooligans or Rebels*, p. 167; Lionel Rose, *The Erosion of Childhood. Child Oppression in Britain, 1860–1918*, London, Routledge, 1991, p. 79; and George Orwell, writing in 1937, remembered a time when 'whole quarters of big towns were considered unsafe because of "hooligans"', suggesting that they had now become 'almost an extinct type', (*The Road to Wigan Pier*, Harmondsworth, Penguin, 1974, p. 110). Rose also points out that in England and Wales in 1911 there were 23,000 'lads' selling newspapers on the streets: one can assume that the arrival of the new popular press *increased* the numbers, a nice irony given the unease expressed in the *Mail* and the rest about laddish street culture (*Erosion of Childhood*, p. 70).

69 Edward Smithies, *Crime in Wartime. A Social History of Crime in World War II*, London, Allen and Unwin, 1982; and for an extraordinary rendering of the relations between hooligan and citizen, see the correspondence in *Picture Post*, 15 September 1945.

70 A key turning-point came in the aftermath of the white riots in Notting Hill and Nottingham in September 1958 when the notion of hooliganism was redeployed to suggest simultaneously both an alien presence and white ethnicity: see the editorial in *The Times*, 3 September 1958.

A large academic literature was spawned around football hooliganism of the 1970s and 1980s. My own favourite occurrences include 'I like football but I like trouble as well' by 'The Hooligan' in the *Guardian*, 19 November 1986; Wolverhampton police's operation GROWTH (Get Rid Of Wolverhampton's Troublesome Hooligans), reported in the *Financial Times*, 30 March 1988; and in the lead-up to the 1990 World Cup in Italy the British police initiated a 'Hooligan Hotline'.

71 The offender in this instance was the Conservative MP for Harrow West, John Page: see *The Times*, 14 March 1982.

72 Contrary positions on Baden Powell, which in my view tell the same story, can be found in Tim Jeal, *Baden Powell*, London, Hutchinson, 1989; and Michael Rosenthal, *The Character Factory. Baden Powell and the Origins of the Boy Scout Movement*, London, Collins, 1986. Seth Koven, 'From rough lads to hooligans. Boy life, national culture and social reform', in Andrew Parker, Mary Russo, Doris Sommer and Patricia Yaeger (eds), *Nationalisms and Sexualities*, London, Routledge, 1992; the theme of homosexuality and hooligans makes its first explicit appearance, I think, in *The Leather Boys* (Sidney Furie, 1963). See Rose Macaulay, *Tale Told by an Idiot*, London, Virago, 1983.

73 G. Stanley Hall, *Adolescence. Its Psychology, and Its Relations to Physiology, Anthropology, Sociology, Sex, Crime, Religion and Education*, vol. 2, New York, Appleton, 1904, p. 458.

74 I have read *Jekyll and Hyde* alongside Walkowitz, *City of Dreadful Delight*; for Oscar Wilde, Stevenson's fable 'reads dangerously like an experiment in the *Lancet*', (Pick, *Faces of Degeneration*, p. 165).

75 Urwick (ed.), *Studies of Boy Life*, pp. 295 and xiii; for Urwick's views on hooligans explicitly, p. 265.

76 On the dialectic of orderly and disorderly masculinity I have found very interesting Lyndal Roper, 'Blood and codpieces: masculinity in the early modern town', in her *Oedipus and the Devil. Witchcraft, Sexuality and Religion in Early Modern Europe*, London, Routledge, 1994. And we might note Freud's comment in a letter of 1897 that 'the story of the devil' was 'gaining significance for me': cited in James Donald, *Sentimental Education. Schooling, Popular Culture and the Regulation of Liberty*, London, Verso, 1992, p. 99.

5

SODOMY TO SALOME

Camp revisions of modernism, modernity and masquerade

Peter Horne

THE GAY BRICOLEUR

Take two images from gay culture of the 1980s. The first is a crack and peel sticker, used to deface advertisements and add to the collage of the city streets. Leaving traces of a presence, these gay calling cards promise the return of those who refuse to fade from view in the spectacle of the modern metropolis. The sticker reworks an image from the 'original' design by Barbara Kruger – itself a pastiche of a salesman's card – a hand proffering the message 'I shop, therefore I am'. In Adam Rolston's gay appropriation, the logo announces 'I am out, therefore I am'.[1] It was produced for the twentieth anniversary of the riots in the Stonewall bar in New York in 1969 when gays retaliated against another of the regular police raids. This event was to become the symbolic moment for the start of Gay Liberation and the coming out of gays from the easily policed bars to become 'street people'.[2] The Rolston logo is also printed on T-shirts, the wearing of which is a performative utterance in the exchange of signs in the city, suggesting not a nature to be deciphered, nor a code for those in the know, but a politicised identity. For Rolston and Douglas Crimp, co-editors of *AIDS Demo Graphics*, it is one of their compilation of city graphics dedicated to the memory of thousands who have died because of government inaction in the Aids crisis and the survival of thousands who are fighting to stay alive. Rolston and Crimp identified the work in their collection as part of what is radical in post-modernist art, since it calls into question issues of identity, authorship and audience, and the way all three are constructed through representation, while resisting the institutionalisation to which postmodern practices have fallen prey.[3]

The second gay image refers back to the nineteenth century through the eyes of radical camp. Neil Bartlett's work frequently sustains and comments on a late nineteenth-century tradition of creating a pantheon of homo-sexual artists, as a way of constructing a sense of identity out of the residues of culture. His play, *A Vision of Love Revealed in Sleep (Part Three)*, is based on the life of the nineteenth-century painter Simeon Solomon. In it, three drag queens, Betty Bourne, Regina Fong and Ivan appear first as a tableau based on Solomon's painting of the fiery furnace in the Old Testament book of Daniel (Figure 5.1). With hair in Pre-Raphaelite style and scarlet robes of floor-length velvet, they descend a stairway – a necessary accessory to glamour – and begin to sing 'In the Still of the Night', an outing perhaps for Cole Porter.[4] Meanwhile Bartlett, naked on the stage, his body shaved to assume the codes of the classic nude, shamelessly asks latecomers whether they can 'see everything'. The play reminds us that we are all latecomers. There is a history to our sexualities. But it will not deliver itself up in ways which unproblematically secure identity. There is no organic nature, tradition or historical community to be summoned up in order to express ourselves or our aspirations. Yet Bartlett's work consistently looks for touchstones of intimacy with the past, and works with the empathetic identification of camp. This is not the empathy of a general response schooled in high culture but that of the contemporary gay man aware of his inscription within a history of power and pleasure in the modern city. It is this sense of an identity inscribed within relations of power that gives bite to the gentle tones of camp which addresses its audience as if it shared complicit pleasures and knowledges.

Both the abrasive public sticker, emboldening bodies on the New York street and Bartlett's nostalgic recall have a feel for the possibilities of a transformative sense of identity through performance and assemblages of appropriated images. This chapter goes in quest of a historical homosexual identity similarly formed as *bricolage* out of the available aesthetic codes. To glimpse such an identity, it is necessary to take seriously the nature of camp as a complex form of life which by the late nineteenth century drew on the aesthetes' masquerade of a femininity constructed in the discourses of the modern city. It is a history which is partly illuminated and partly obscured by two sorts of influential recent writing. On the one hand, there is work which has highlighted the historical construction of the homosexual identity and in the process has rendered problematic the ascription of homosexual identity to past artists or their work. On the other hand, there are writings on modernism which have attached significance to artistic practices in the formation of new identities within the modern city. These have excluded the role of the homosexual because they have focused their attention on the public sphere and a particular formative moment for modernity, the building of the Paris boulevards.

To recover a sense of how a homosexual identity was partly constructed through modern aesthetic discourses, we have to supplement what useful material can be wrested from the above accounts with a new look at the movement of aestheticism which is so often marginalised within accounts of modernism and representations of modern life. We also have to trust the intimations of a camp retrospective vision.

130

Figure 5.1 Publicity photograph for Neil Bartlett's *A Vision of Love Revealed in Sleep (Part Three)*, 1989

Source: Courtesy of Gloria, Theatre Production Company

THE DARK SHIMMER OF SEX

There are different versions of the theory that the homosexual identity is a modern construction.[5] All distinguish such an identity from some previous phenomenon, be it same-sex desire or actions not previously understood

131

as indicators of sexual identity in the modern sense. All versions raise problems in ascribing gay or homosexual identities to figures of the past. As Foucault pointed out, in one of his interviews, the problem is one of language.[6] To call past writers gay, he says would be anachronistic. Yet to call them homosexual, a term of positivistic behavioural identity produced within late nineteenth-century sexological discourses, is to say nothing of the meaning they ascribe to their desires.

The notion of the homosexual artist presents further problems. The conjunction of terms suggests someone whose work is unified in its expression of the author's condition and saturated with his or her sexuality. This fits all too well the discursive construction of the homosexual as a thoroughly sexualised being, a conception which is confirmed, if we identify past artists as homosexual through signs of the homoerotic in their work. Yet these eroticisms, which have been excluded from so many art histories, still need to be explored. There is a difficult path to tread between projecting current identities onto past figures and repeating the excisions of a culture which is compelled to define 'perverse identities' but seeks to exclude traces of the homoerotic.

It was Foucault's purpose to draw attention to the processes whereby we have all, in relatively recent times in Western cultures, found our sense of self in categories of the sexual, in the reflection the 'dark shimmer of sex' offers to our narcissistic gaze.[7] The gay man, looking back with a sense of empathy with past artists, may be seen as compounding the errors of this outlook, searching for the reflection of a modern sexual identity. Yet the desire to find touchstones of intimacy is of particular importance to lesbians and gay men who have been denied their history. The search need not necessarily imply belief in a given transhistorical homosexual nature hidden in the past and 'out' in the present. Fear of such theoretical solecisms has been an inhibiting factor in relating sexualities to aesthetic practices.

In looking back from the present to late nineteenth-century writers and artists who were themselves looking back, we can avoid the imposition of anachronistic gay identities, as well as the medicalised concepts of the homosexual, by employing the term 'homophile'. This term can be kept historically specific, relating, as it does, to its binary opposite, the 'homophobe', a public role of increasing definition and significance in the late nineteenth century, and a figure against whom the homophile created narratives of past artists with whom to identify. Although the term might underplay the sexuality of modern identities, it will nevertheless be used here since it resists, as perhaps the homophiles themselves did, the definitions of the sexologists who have commanded attention in some recent historical work.

Attention to the part played by sexologists in the construction of a homosexual identity at the end of the nineteenth century has been encouraged by theoretical insights about the relationship between power and knowledge. The sense of surveillance has been widened, as in Foucault's brilliant work, to include the role of discourses. Claims to knowledge are deployed within institutions presenting a beneficent face in the cause of 'the management of life'.[8] In what he called the 'perverse implantation' of the late eighteenth century and after, many become objects of new forms of scrutiny for deviant sexual behaviour.[9] This surveillance spread through the home, school and surgery. Within this epistemological outlook, the sense of a more positive self-identity waited upon the emergence of a 'reverse discourse'[10] through which those who were the objects of the late nineteenth-century sexological scrutiny began to redefine themselves, albeit still in terms of a sexual nature, as in the notion of 'a third sex'.[11] But this only happened in response to the way science had gathered together the 'subjects' of the perverse implantation and seen in them the working of the new unified object of study, 'sex' as a hidden inner force. Discovering deeper meanings in aberrant behaviour, new sexualised natures were constructed by the sexologists. One of these was the 'invert' whose sexual attraction to members of his or her own sex was considered to be a congenital condition. This was a preferable term to the alternative 'pervert' which implied being driven by lust alone, and many homosexual men adopted it.

The impact of this work has been to see the formation of identity as consequent on the construction of objects of knowledge and to ignore other expressions of identity. Within this perspective, artistic productions have tended to be seen as fine art reflections of sexological concepts[12] or as contributions to the discourses employed within institutions of care and control, as in the use of photography to create physiognomies for criminal types.[13] This latter work has fitted well within those paradigms in cultural studies which have moved away from the study of elitist taste towards an examination of the codes which construct regimes of representation that cut across categories of high and low culture. But this has excluded a consideration of what certain types of high art might mean to particular groups and to homophile and gay people in particular.

In this chapter, I wish to look at other ways homophiles could construct a form of identity. Material was available in the aesthetic discourses of the nineteenth-century city which existed alongside, and in some ways prefigured, the discourses of the scientific. Such identities did not so much reverse the sexological discourses as challenge the terms of identity in a play with the shifting meanings of androgyny and a masquerade of femininity.

BOTANISING ON THE ASPHALT[14]

If recent cultural theory on the historical construction of homosexuality has drawn attention away from the role of aesthetic practices in the formation of a homophile identity, accounts of modernism have also occluded the place of such an identity within the experience of modernity. This applies even when the relationship of modernism to the emergence of new identities is explored. The absence of the homophile identity has not seemed remarkable since it was formed within the movement of aestheticism which has been regularly positioned outside modernism.

The nature of artistic modernism has been a hotly contested issue. Diverse versions stress the significance of different moments for its formation. Often there is attention to either a moment of bourgeois ascendancy in the 1860s in Paris or the period of crisis in Europe prior to the First World War. Aestheticism is situated differently in the chronology of modern history. The aesthetic doctrine of 'art for art's sake', possibly used first in 1818, became current in France by 1830. As a movement, however, aestheticism flourished from the 1870s in England and France, and is particularly associated with Oscar Wilde who, in the late 1880s and early 1890s, proclaimed his wish to make life live up to art rather than have art be subject to life and its supposedly moral constraints. Wilde's purpose suggests that there might be more to the ways in which accounts of modernism have excluded aestheticism than the incidental effect of emphasis on particular moments. The aesthete who is reputed to have turned his back on the world, who valued the exotic and the fine in art and embraced artificiality, does not fit the image of the avant-garde modernist artist who created abrasive new forms to express the tensions of engagement with the contemporary social world. It is not surprising, then, if histories of modernism and new social identities have overlooked the way the aesthete appropriated modern urban discourses in order to forge a new homophile identity.

In recent years, there has been considerable interest in the relationship of modernist forms of art to the emergence of new social identities in the city. In particular, attention has been commanded by Paris, dramatically modernised by Haussmann in the mid-nineteenth century to create a city of spectacle.[15] Influenced by Benjamin's evocative essays on Baudelaire, accounts frequently figure the *flâneur* as a distinctly modern identity. The precursor of the detective, botanising on the asphalt, he roams the streets identifying other modern types. The streets become a text, the site of new visual pleasures for those who can read the appearances of others. Not all accounts celebrate this. Some feminists have seen the *flâneur* as adopting a masculine role, taking women on the boulevards as the object of his gaze.[16] But more striking is the selectiveness of Baudelaire's voyeuristic gaze which seems to make the deviant woman in particular a figure in a modern allegory. Sometimes, recalling Sappho, she is a lesbian, a prototype of the modern emancipated women, and sometimes she is a prostitute.[17] These women, crossing the boundaries of the public and the private, are significant figures for a city that Baudelaire wishes to see as both modern and an archaic ruin.

The *flâneur* is often represented as either a universal modern type, or fixed in the moment when the boulevards were new.[18] But it is also possible to see the *flâneur* as having evolved out of and reconverged with another of Baudelaire's modern types, the 'dandy', whose sense of self became the self-consciousness of the figure determined to stand out. One may see the aesthete's adoption of this role as an active reconstitution of the *flâneur* whose original fancy was that the city was a visual text for a modern allegory of visual desires. For the aesthete, the city became instead the site for a play in which roles could be adopted as masquerade, as a way of being transgressive in a modern style. To be a dandy in the cafes and clubs of the 1890s was, in any case, to act the role of the aristocrat. But there were other possibilities suggested by the *flâneur* discourse. The fantasised objects of the *flâneur*'s gaze could also be employed in imaginative readings of masquerade in art. The rest of this chapter seeks to explore the radical ways in which the aesthetes, through their use of masquerade, transformed the role of the *flâneur* and the discourses of femininity which it had generated. But this is not easily noticed if the *flâneur* is perceived either as a universal modern figure or as a the dandy artificially carrying on the *flâneur*'s role beyond its historical moment.

To understand the relationship of sexuality to the formation of aestheticism may require a different sense of the relations of power and visibility in the modern city to those featured in most accounts of modernity. However, there is at least one account of the nineteenth-century city which provides a context in which to see how a masquerade of femininity came to be indulged, and yet confined, within the visual relations of the modern urban life.[19] For Richard Sennett, the city of the nineteenth century became a place of spectacle in a particularly gloomy way, where the preserve of one's individuality amounted to becoming a silent spectator. The role of the *flâneur* was learnt at the cost of communication. In the eighteenth century, when masquerade incidentally became a form of entertainment, there was an appreciation of the fact that people dressed up to assume a role in public. While there was a strong new sense of the division between public and private life, the self was not yet identified with the heartfelt intimacies of home. A self was as much to be discovered in one's public performance as in one's private nature. Stage and street were continuous. But in the nineteenth century, as appearances came to be regarded as signs of inner personality, anxiety increased over the way appearances could be understood, leading ultimately to conformity and a distrust of the lavish and excessive. The result was a destructive *gemeinschaft*, a reversal of eighteenth-century life in which people shared a participation in public roles, involving a kind of acting out that neither disguised nor revealed a true inner self. In contrast, the occupants of the nineteenth-century city, fixed in desire rather than active participation, circulated around each other, moved by a mixture of voyeuristic and narcissistic pleasures which equally filled them with dread.

The new insistence on the division of art and life required that performance and excess remained upon a stage, whether in the showmanship of the virtuoso or the masquerade of the cross-dresser. This is illustrated by the trial of Park and Boulton, two 'actresses' who not only cross-dressed but crossed over the divide between the theatre, the accepted sphere of artifice, and the world of the audience. Appreciated for their transvestite performances on the stage, they were arrested for entering the auditorium in full slap and frocks. For Neil Bartlett in his book, *Who Was That Man: A Present for Oscar Wilde*, their trial revealed a debate about the meaning of the signs of homosexuality in public life.[20] Their successful defence was that they could hardly have *really* meant what their outward show implied. Their frocks were signs of frivolity rather than a dark secret. This defence was attempted again during the Wilde trials but failed because, Bartlett suggests, by 1895 there was widespread knowledge of a homosexual subculture and aestheticism had become associated with a transgressive sexuality. Wilde's transgression became all too believable.[21]

Boulton and Park came partly from an old tradition of cross-dressing found in the molly houses, which were places of entertainment and sexual encounter between men from the end of the seventeenth century. These houses were periodically raided, usually in response to the activities of unpopular moral pressure groups, but provided the location for a defensive subculture.[22] In the middle of the nineteenth century, Boulton and Park could cross-dress away from the relative security of the molly house, provided they obeyed the ordinances of the nineteenth century city that such masquerade and excess remained on the stage. Their folly, or their transgressive pleasure, was partly to disregard the new boundaries between the stage and life. At the trial their behaviour was taken as a silly, if shocking, transgression rather than a sincere expression of a deviant sexual nature. Neither alternative seems to leave much possibility for discovering identity through performance and masquerade. Meanwhile, often in a more reserved way, the aesthetes were forming such an identity by exploring identification with representations of woman. This may have been conceived in the closet of the aesthete, away from the public sphere, but it drew upon the discourses of femininity in the representations of nineteenth-century public life. As long as this was done in quiet and coded ways, it escaped the persecution that had been meted out to Boulton and Park. But when Wilde took himself back to cafe and club in the flamboyant persona of the dandy and deliberately made a spectacle of himself, he was jailed and his play *Salome* was banned.

MYTHS OF THE MEDUSA

It is hardly surprising that the aesthete tends to be excluded from discussions of modernity, though there is a fascination with his forbear, Baudelaire, who is a recurring rhetorical figure in the narratives of modernism. In the fictions of decadence, the aesthete is likely to have withdrawn from the *flâneur*'s boulevards into the private sphere (domestic is hardly the word) which becomes a place for the exercise of a fantastic and frequently orientalised taste, determinedly in excess of what might be had from new department stores. The decadent turned his back on the contemporary world and rejected the codes of the realist movement which were intended to find the appropriate forms to represent modern life, often in its harshest forms. Huysmans, the French-born writer who turned from realism to the style of decadence, begins chapter 5 of *À Rebours* (1884), a very influential text for aestheticism, with the description of his hero, Des Esseintes, having 'the desire to escape from a hateful period of sordid degradation, [and] the longing to see no more pictures of the human world toiling in Paris between four walls or roaming the streets in search of money'.[23] He turns instead to a painting of Salome by Gustave Moreau (Figure 5.2) This sort of tone encourages us to see the aesthetes upholding the tradition of the dandy beyond the moment when this role might seem to offer a position from which to speak adequately of modern life. The detachment of the *flâneur* has become an affectedly aristocratic disdain. It suggests a nostalgic fantasy of a lifestyle which, in Wilde's case, might seem to be at odds with his belief in socialism. But recent writing suggests that the implied life of leisure of the aesthetes, a pretence by hard working artists, was disruptive of a new class hegemony within which the ideal of the gentleman was being restyled, in a less exclusive way, as a person who fulfilled civic responsibility through work.[24] The elegant and erudite occupation of leisure recommended by the aesthetes had a precise social edge.

The nostalgic assumption of a lost style and taste had another function. It provided the codes for a modern homophile identity to be fabricated by empathy with assumed homosexual artists of the past, especially those of the Renaissance courts. Richard Dellamora has reinterpreted the works of Walter Pater, the writer whose collection of essays, *Studies in the History of the Renaissance*, had considerable influence on Wilde and the aesthetes in the last quarter of the nineteenth century.[25] Dellamora, in *Masculine Desire: The Sexual Politics of Victorian Aestheticism,* argues that Pater found the key to his criticism of Leonardo da Vinci's work in the *Medusa*, a painting once ascribed to Leonardo.[26] In Greek legend, Medusa was one of the gorgons whose frightening appearance turned those who beheld them to stone. Even after she was beheaded by Perseus, her head, with its snakes for hair, continued to petrify the viewer. Frequently represented in symbolist work, Medusa can be seen to represent a misogynistic fear of the feminine.[27] But Dellamora contends that Pater constructed a positive sense of male-to-male desire out of interpretations of the Medusa imagery. The Medusa's severed head with its phallic hair could represent that 'liminal state that is both masculine and feminine' which Pater was prepared to enter in an abandonment of the conventional masculinity of his time.[28] The context for this was the escalating homophobia which arose out of new homosocial environments of the late nineteenth century.[29] The masculine socialising in institutions

Figure 5.2 Gustave Moreau, *The Apparition*, *c.* 1875; oil on canvas, 106 × 72 cm
Source: Courtesy of the Musée Gustave Moreau, Paris
Photograph: Réunion de Musée Nationaux

such as clubs and schools cemented cross-class alliances against new social and sexual forces, but also created new anxieties about the possible sexuality of male bonding. In reaction to the resultant homophobia, Dellamora claims that the aesthetes, from Pater onwards, used the image of the Medusa to present an ideal, in which the masculine homophile embraced the feminine. The resulting transformation, for which cross-dressing was a metaphor, was signified by androgyny, which, in turn, was a mediating term for the combination of opposites to be found in hermaphroditism. This last association conveyed a particular value, in that hermaphroditism was believed, in an ancient shamanic tradition, to confer prophetic powers. Hence the fascination with the figures in Leonardo's work who are iconographically identifiable as male, but depicted as beings of somewhat indeterminate sex.

The androgyny of the representations had already led some French critics to read paintings of St John and other figures as transvestite portraits, apparently preferring to think that female models had cross-dressed rather than that Leonardo was depicting ambiguous males. But Pater was to see in this androgyny a prefiguration of his ideal homophile identity. A further twist is introduced when Dellamora turns to Pater's famous description of the *Mona Lisa* which contributed to the late nineteenth-century cult around the work. He sees Pater as taking a cue from the French criticism mentioned above, but turning it to different effect. This time an ostensibly female portrait is appropriated by the homophile. Pater sees the *Mona Lisa* as Leonardo's cross-dressed self-portrait, as an androgyne. The conventional romantic notion of a fatal beauty was thus supplemented by a suggestion of the hermaphrodeity which conveys sibylline powers. These powers were also signified by the attributes of the Medusa whose allure and danger permeate the portrait. The result is the summoning of an ambiguous woman to convey the seductive but challenging ideal towards which homophiles could aspire. As evidence that this identity extended beyond the particular case of Pater, Dellamora cites the case of the enigmatic late drawings by Simeon Solomon, such as *The Tormented Soul* (1894), representing a severed androgynous, but apparently male, head with hair transformed into snakes[30] (Figure 5.3). These point to a continuing homophile tradition which drew upon codes of androgyny and the Medusa myth.

Pater seems to have constructed a sense of identity, out of readings of legend and Renaissance culture, which anticipates the idealisation of androgyny in the later works of the homophile utopian socialist, Edward Carpenter. But in his evocation of older ideas of androgyny as an indeterminacy of sex, or as an ideal combination of the characteristics of mixed genders to be achieved by personal transformation, Pater puts forward ideas at odds with the sexologists' notion of inversion as a condition found in one's nature, and which was sometimes thought of in terms of having the

Figure 5.3 Simeon Solomon, *The Tormented Soul,* 1894;
black chalk on paper, 39.5 × 30 cm

Source: Private collection

soul of one sex inside the body of another.[31] Dellamora suggests that this ideal of sexual transformation is represented for Pater by the Medusa as a 'figure of the passage from the conventional male state into the metaphorical state of "being-woman"'.[32] As such, she does not represent femininity so much as the possibility of a marvellous but threatening transformation into androgyny, which Dellamora is keen to distance from the misogyny present in late nineteenth-century iconography of threatening women. Yet, it seems likely that even a 'metaphorical state of "being woman"' would be affected by contemporary notions of the female gender. And in fact, the account of the identity he constructs, through his reading of Pater, might be thought to hover between one which offers the transcendence of sexual difference implicit in older ideas of androgyny, and one which offers identification with a differentiated femininity. Slippage between these two was perhaps facilitated by new discourses of femininity, to which he alludes but without great emphasis, concentrating instead on Pater's retreat from the masculinity on offer. Accessible to the aesthetes were new notions of a moral androgyny, identified with specifically female gender transgression. This was conceived in terms of a mixture of sexual natures within the inner self which was not necessarily reflected in the body. Prior to the sexologists' notion of the 'invert', critics and writers in the nineteenth century began to construct an identity for deviant women whose behaviour did not accord with true femininity and who were represented by a confusion of codes suggestive of both the primitive and the masculine. Sometimes referred to as a moral androgyne, this figure stems from Baudelaire but continued to be reworked throughout the century.[33] For instance, Huysmans, in his later book *Là-Bas* (1891), created such a figure in his character Mme Chanteloue who is variously described as boyish and voluptuous.[34] In her sexual feelings, she is new woman, but her name, Hyacinth, was in use as a code word for the younger beloved of male same-sex desire, derived from the name of the youth loved by the Greek god, Apollo. It would seem but a small step for the aesthetes to identify with such a character or be attracted to the masquerade of the femininity which it offered and onto which desires could be projected. In doing so, they overlaid old beliefs in the prophetic androgyne who transcended sexual difference with a new idea of female androgyny as a moral deviation from one's supposed gender identity.

Acted out in the public spaces of the modern city, cross-dressing attracted a punitive reaction as the case of Boulton and Park had shown. But the aesthete in his closet could continue to identify with portraits of women interpreted as depictions of men whose androgyny signified the hermaphroditism valued in the shamanistic tradition. But this deliberately arcane recall of legend draws upon ideas of androgyny which were being supplanted by newer ones, focused on the female and defined in terms of a mismatch of inner and outer qualities and a hidden gender deviance. It seems possible that this modern construction, fusing notions of a secret identity and gender deviance, provided an image with which homophiles might identify. Equally, the idea of the moral androgyne required that there were clear natural signs of an inner masculinity and femininity, so that, carefully reading outward behaviour, one could identify souls containing qualities of the opposite sex. Novels like *Là-Bas* depended on this for the creation of an enigmatic femininity which the narrative could unravel and reveal as moral androgyny. But the fixing of these signs also created the possibility of a masquerade or playful identification which did not assume an authentic femininity. The next section considers how Wilde's play *Salome* offered a model for such an imaginative and transgressive masquerade.[35] This carries the emphasis in homophile traditions away from older ideals of androgyny as the fusion of genders or lack of gender differentiation, towards a fascination with the spectacle of transgressive femininity upon which desire could be projected. The particular transgression involved was the desiring gaze.

By the 1890s, some symbolist painters were eschewing naturalism in favour of dream-like evocative images. The paintings of women frequently featured the transgressive gaze. In a painting by Franz von Stuck, entitled *Sin*, a woman is voluptuously embraced by a snake which she wears like a stole. In another painting, Fernand Khnopff's *The Blood of the Medusa*, a similar use is made of the association of femininity with the snake which is common to the myth of the Medusa and the story of Adam and Eve's expulsion from Eden. What is striking in both paintings is the dramatic coding in the compositions, whereby both Eve, as the figure of sin, and the Medusa are portrayed with challenging eyes directed out of the pictorial space towards the viewer. It is as if the ease of inscription of the one legend on the other at this period is secured through the coding of a sexualised femininity as transgressive gaze (Figure 5.4).

It is possible that Wilde reworked the Medusa theme in his play *Salome*, drawing upon the coded meanings of the homophile tradition, but appropriating these new definitions of a transgressive femininity in terms of the gaze. Whereas Dellamora wishes to distance Pater from the reproduction of such misogynistic tropes of transgressive femininity as 'the "femme fatale" which merely project male obsessions',[36] it is possible that Wilde adopts them, but as a masquerade. For Pater, cross-dressing was not intended as a masquerade of femininity, but as a metaphor for the transformation which androgyny could represent. While Pater emphasised the androgynous appearance of figures in Leonardo's work in order to point to a homophile ideal, Wilde dispenses with the use of codes of visible androgyny to suggest a transcendence of sexual difference, and seeks other means to convey the transformations which a masquerade of femininity might offer. In doing so, he presents a spectacle of femininity which is like an awesome parody of notions of female moral androgyny and current codes of a deviant female gaze.

Figure 5.4 Fernand Khnopff, *The Blood of the Medusa, c.* 1895;
charcoal on paper, 21.6 × 14.6 cm

Source: Copyright the Bibliothèque Royale Albert 1er, Brussels (Cabinet des Estampes)

143

WALKING IN PURPLE

I like my tragedy to walk in purple.

(Oscar Wilde)[37]

The figure of Salome could well have entered the gallery of homophile icons, alongside Medusa, represented by similar tropes. In his biography of Wilde, Richard Ellman reproduced a picture thought to be of Wilde in costume as Salome, though this has since been disputed.[38] There is a precedent for this cross-dressing as Salome, at least in the imagination of Pater. According to Dellamora, Pater found a drawing of Salome to represent Leonardo's ideal type of female beauty, and to be a portrait of a male transvestite.[39] Whether or not Wilde posed as Salome, his depiction of her represents a masquerade of femininity, which reworks the codes associated with the Medusa. Like Medusa, Salome can be seen as a dangerous and castrating female whose gaze is destructive. Yet, Wilde thought of her as a mystic, having the properties associated with the homophile representations of Medusa which idealised androgyny.[40] But Wilde modifies this tradition. He does not hesitate to portray the transgressive nature of her desire. Nor does he rely solely on the established hermetic homophile meanings of the Medusa to secure an alternative reading of Salome's transgression. Instead, he invokes other classical myths to open up more favourable and erotic connotations.

The imagery in the tragedy associates Salome with the Greek goddess Diana who ravishes the sleeping youth, Endymion, nightly in the form of moonlight. In Wilde's play, Salome acts under the light of the moon and, in the Beardsley illustrations, as Elaine Showalter has pointed out, the moon even appears as a portrait of Wilde himself, suggesting identification with Salome as well as authorial responsibility for her.[41] Significantly, Endymion was sometimes represented in the nineteenth century as an androgynous youth, as in the famous painting by Ann-Louis Girodet, and may have become another mythic figure to be appropriated in a homophile tradition.[42] Simeon Solomon's painting *Moon and Sleep*, 1894, which was later to be exhibited with the title *Diana and Endymion*, has an androgynous figure of Diana gazing at a similarly androgynous man (Figure 5.5).[43] At first, it might not seem that Endymion is recalled in Wilde's play. However, in representations he usually appears as passively illuminated by the moonlight signifying Diana's gaze. And in the play it is Salome's desire to so look upon John the Baptist, or Jokanaan as he is called. Toying with male coyness, the play has two unveilings: the obvious one of Salome's dance of the veils, performed for Herod with the reward of Jokanaan's head; and her earlier bringing-forth out of the cistern of John the Baptist who is first heard as a disembodied voice castigating female depravity and is reluctant to be seen. By the end of the play, in death, as in a parody of Endymion's sleep, Jokanaan becomes the passive object of Salome's gaze.

The theme of Salome's desiring gaze is not new. Guercino, circa 1624–6,

Figure 5.5 Simeon Solomon, *Moon and Sleep*, 1894;
oil on canvas, 51.5 × 76.3 cm

Source: Courtesy of Trustees of the Tate Gallery, London

painted St John the Baptist visited in his prison by Salome whose young
head appears through the railings of a prison window looking at him
(Figure 5.6). His body is revealed to Salome and the viewer, the folds of
his garment slipping to uncover a shoulder as he turns his head away from
the innocent but loving spectator within the frame. By the late nineteenth
century, in Gustave Moreau's water-colour version of the Salome story, *The
Apparition* (*c.* 1875), she has lost the innocence and become a dark avenger,
glistening with jewels and haunted by the head of John the Baptist (see
Figure 5.2, p. 138).[44] But this kind of savagery, which in male misogynist
fears may be thought to reside in femininity, is given other meanings by
Wilde, using codes from classical legend. This is not to deny that Wilde
was enraptured by the idea of Salome kissing the severed head of John the
Baptist, an image which he found in a poem by an American called
Hayward. But various meanings may be condensed in the image of Salome
holding this head on a platter (Figure 5.7). Elaine Showalter has read the
play, through Beardsley's illustrations, as the coded fulfilment of homosexual desire.[45] In this reading, the platter is like a mirror in which Salome
sees her own reflection in the likeness of the Baptist, signifying the desire
of like for like. It is also possible to see the ending as an allegory of
homophile conversion. As well as carrying connotations of the passivity
of male seduction which the myth of Endymion embodies, Jokanaan's death

145

Figure 5.6 Guercino, *St John the Baptist Visited in Prison by Salome, c.* 1624–6; oil on canvas, 81 × 97.5 cm

Source: Courtesy of Sir Denis Mahon

can also suggest his transfiguration into an image of Orpheus as a sign of the homophile identity of prophetic androgyny which Wilde here recalls. This would give some substance to Wilde's complaint that Beardsley's drawings were too erotic and failed to suggest that Salome was a mystic.[46]

Late nineteenth-century iconography of a severed head has the male Orphic version as well as the female form of Medusa. The one legend could be seen as the mirror-image of the other, or even as differently gendered versions of an androgynous unity. Orpheus was decapitated by Maenads and his head continued to prophecy as it floated on the sea, where it was thrown with the poet's lyre as its vessel. The decapitated male head was a recurring Orphic motif in symbolist works, sometimes with imagery which directly recalls the legend of Salome. (See, for instance, Moreau's painting of 1865 depicting a Thracian maid gazing at the head of Orpheus on a platter-like lyre, recovered from the sea (Figure 5.8)). This imagery, already in circulation, could have had a particular significance in the homophile tradition which read the Medusa myth and the Orpheus myths as mirror-

Figure 5.7 Aubrey Beardsley, *The Dancer's Reward* (for *Salome*), 1894;
black ink and graphite on paper, 23 × 16.5 cm

Source: Courtesy of the Fogg Art Museum (bequest of Grenville L. Winthrop), Harvard
University Art Museums, Cambridge, Mass.

Figure 5.8 Gustave Moreau, *Orphée*, 1865; oil on panel, 153.9 × 99.4 cm
Source: Courtesy of Musée d'Orsay, Paris. *Photograph*: Réunion des Musée Nationaux

images of each other. Orpheus was, in any case, associated with homosexuality: in some classical and Renaissance versions of his myth, he is torn apart by the Maenads for introducing homosexuality into Thrace.[47] Here, in Wilde's play, the Medusa in the form of Salome meets John the Baptist and converts him into Orpheus. It is a conversion which is unsettling to the codes of masculinity, constructed in terms of being the viewer rather than viewed and supposed heterosexual immunity to same-sex love.

In allegorical terms, Salome and Jokanaan represent different forms of transfiguration. He is the scourge of desire and the prophet who foretells that the word of God is to be made flesh by the birth of Christ who is to save humankind through suffering. Salome, as a dancer, represents the power of the body to speak, and desires to possess Jokanaan through sight and touch. When she does, he is dead but transfigured in a parodic conversion into a fusion of Endymion and Orpheus. While symbolist imagery was haunted more generally by representations of the female as a Medusa, Wilde draws upon the fusion of the Medusa and Orpheus legends, which featured in a homophile tradition, to turn fear of the female into, at least in part, a story of homophile conversion.[48] In doing so, he evokes old ideals of androgyny, but also draws a new portrait of an excessive woman, onto whom homosexual desire could be projected and which could be adopted as a form of masquerade of the deviant femininity which was constructed in the nineteenth-century city.

The excess of the character of Salome was unsettling to those codes of realism which made potentially dangerous women who strayed from the path of virtue into social victims. Linda Nead, in *Myths of Sexuality*, has shown how the structures of narrative within English painting carefully excluded the representation of desire in woman in order to secure a safer sentimental sympathy.[49] Wilde expressed his opposition to these codes and to the subject positions offered to the reader, including the author as reader, when he attacked the notion of 'sincerity' which he knew had become a key word in the construction of authorial responsibility towards the realist text: 'What people call insincerity is simply a method by which we can multiply our personalities.'[50] In place of sincerity, he suggested we could adopt masks to discover new voices which were unsettling to fixed identities. When he portrayed a transgressive woman it was not according to the codes of realistic fiction in which the narrative is sustained by the revelation of a true hidden nature. Instead he used the symbolist form of an image, which condenses various meanings and invites different readings. In his play *Salome*, Wilde searched for a new order of meaning, to replace the detection of a given sexual personality and to invite the new desires which could be discovered in the play of masquerade which his figure of a prophetic transgressive woman allowed. Although he drew upon the codes of the homophile tradition which interpreted classical myth, his use of it leaves one with less of a sense of a defensive homophile identity constructed out of a residual concept of the androgyne, than a search for a transgressive play with desire which disturbs existing meanings.

Because of the deliberately precious tone, Wilde's critique of realism has perhaps not always been fully appreciated.[51] He turned away from 'life' as: 'a thing narrowed by circumstance, incoherent in its utterance, and without that fine correspondence of the form and the spirit which is the only thing that can satisfy the artistic and critical temperament'.[52] The life which Wilde wished to eschew was one constructed on the streets of the modern city, in which the compulsion was not merely to conform to an outward show of morality, but to express personality sincerely. The result, as Sennett has indicated, was a more oppressive conformity in a society that distrusted masquerade.[53] Wilde's answer was the symbolist inversion of this injunction. He urged that we live up to a mask, but a mask which in its form and beauty gave expression to spirit. This ideal suggests the possibility of utopian transformation in Wilde's sexual aesthetics.

The play with masquerade had a serious purpose. Salome was Wilde's 'tragic daughter of passion'.[54] To bring 'her' back into a revisionist account of modernism would disturb versions which search for the moment when authentic forms for modernity were to be found in either the new public spaces of the boulevard or the cultural disturbances of the early twentieth century. Homosexual identity, formed under conditions of modern surveillance combined with intensified homophobia, was bound to a nostalgia for an imagined past out of which a more positive sense of identity could be constructed. It took older understandings of androgyny and fused them with the contemporary discourses on deviant femininity to yield an identity under the cover of the myth of the Medusa. Pater's cross-dressed identification with the Mona Lisa evokes both older notions of a prophetic androgyny which lacked gender differentiation and emergent ideas of moral androgyny as an internal state. Wilde kept the tropes of a transgressive prophet in his vision of Salome, but created out of her the spectacle of an excessive woman on which to project desires. To continue to ignore this sexual identity in histories of modernism is a depletion of what modern aesthetic practices have been about.

FROM BOULEVARDS TO BLOOMINGDALES

The modern period has seen the emergence of identities which are ambivalent in their relationship to modernity. Homophiles of the late nineteenth century were paradoxically new in their retrospective visions and attempts to construct hermetic traditions of homosexuality. Wilde was also doing something new in rehabilitating the old role of the *flâneur* which, in the changed circumstances of the *fin de siècle*, was more than a nostalgic gesture. With the emergence of the notion of the gentleman as one who worked, the *flâneur*, transformed into a dandy affecting the life of aristocratic leisure, became a transgressor.[55] And the revenge of a new hegemonic order fell upon Wilde for his sexual escapades and class transgressions. His trials led to prison, exile and the death of aestheticism, at any rate in England. Some of his ideas continued to surface in the writings of the Bloomsbury group. But, in spite of the group's own sexual proclivities and ambiguities, the concept of the separation of life and art was pushed by the critics, Clive Bell and Roger Fry, towards a formalist aesthetic, effectively exorcising the scandal associated with Wilde's flamboyant sexualised fulfilment of the role of the dandy.[56] This undermined Wilde and Pater's imaginative use of identifications with past art and artists to forge identities outside the contemporary city represented in the codes of realism.

However, masquerade did not disappear from modern art, though it is consistently marginalised by accounts of modernism which stress the importance of formal values over figurative significance. Hartshorn and Foresta, in their catalogue for the *Man Ray in Fashion* exhibition, describe the Dadaists, members of a modern art movement which aimed to destroy the cult of art by promoting the meaningless and the shocking, 'lining themselves up to be photographed, the dadaists in their Belle Epoque haberdashery, revealed their vanity; spots and capes, felt gloves and snappy fedoras. . . . Attire was their audacity which the audience admired but did not dare to imitate'.[57] Hartshorn and Foresta, intent upon stressing the modernity of this self-presentation, make little of the surprising allusion in the Dadaists' dress to their forbears, the aesthete dandies of the 1890s, who were similarly attracted to masquerade. But the Dadaists struck a more modern note than their antecedents through their interest in popular merchandising. Adopting codes of femininity from advertising, Marcel Duchamp cross-dressed to pose as 'Rrose Sélavy' for a Man Ray photograph, which was printed as the label for a bottle of toilet water, with the title, *Belle Haleine, Eau de Voilette*. In a similar gesture, but with a further twist, Andy Warhol, in the 1960s, posed as a woman whose femininity is emphasised by her fashion-plate style adoption of masculinised dress.

Though influenced by Duchamp, Warhol's work came out of the gay subculture of 1950s New York, in which there was a camp appreciation of the film stills which foregrounded the artifice involved in the production of charming femininity. This pleasurable appropriation of the glamour of mass advertising for fantasies of identification is perhaps in contrast to the Dadaist intention to create a pastiche of the commercial construction of femininity. It is certainly in marked contrast to the condemnation of advertising techniques produced by many straight intellectuals in the 1950s.[58] The same dominant American intellectual culture which fostered these critiques also accepted the critic Clement Greenberg's version of modernism which defined it in opposition to kitsch and the ersatz culture of commercial society.[59] Greenberg's account also dissociated the true formalist tradition of modernism from Dada and the play with masquerade which was to influence strands within Pop Art in the 1960s. More recently, in order to produce a more seamless account of American modern art which includes Pop Art, histories have been carefully constructed linking Warhol to a New York Dada tradition. Though this has its cogency, the attribution of this origin to Warhol's art tends to exclude reference to the more immediate context of post Second World War gay cultures. Dandy qualities in the work are safely subsumed under the mantle of Duchamp whose cross-dressed photograph can be read as a self-distanced demonstration that femininity is itself a masquerade. In one striking variant of the construction of an American tradition, a separation is made between Warhol's adoption of the moribund role of dandy and the meaning of his work which is reconstituted as a critique of alienated consumption.[60] Thus the left, somewhat surprisingly, can make of this indefatigable shopper a severe critic of the consumption of fetishised signs within late capitalism.

It is perhaps more appropriate to look to the nature of Warhol's camp appropriation of popular culture. In this there are continuities and discontinuities with previous homophile cultures. The dandy was always a consumer and what he consumed was a great signifier of identity. Like Des Esseintes, the hero of Huysmans' *À Rebours*, Warhol's home was an assemblage of bric-a-brac. But, unlike Des Esseintes, he was utterly at home in the city and determinedly shopped in the department store. Whereas the nineteenth-century aesthete preserved his difference from the middle classes by despising what they bought in the emporia, Warhol looked for new ways of consuming the ordinary. He demystified the figure of the artist and offered the role of consumer as a form of creative camp identity. Susan Sontag, in her 'Notes on "Camp"', is astute about this, especially when contrasting the old-style dandy's hatred of vulgarity with the new-style dandy's camp appreciation of it.[61] She distinguishes the tender feeling of this camp style from the 'flat and dry' quality of the mainstream of Pop Art of the 1960s. This seems to indicate what is distinctive in Warhol's version of Pop Art which affectionately celebrates the excess and artifice in the selling of consumer goods and stars alike. It comes from the gay culture of New York in the 1950s and 1960s, within which a new identity was being forged through yet another reworking of the camp aesthetics of the dandy.[62]

Attention to the formation of camp culture raises issues of the relationships between sexuality, modernity and modern aesthetic forms which seem to be missing in most accounts of modernism. Sontag attempts to give camp its due, separating it as a modern sensibility from both modernism and the humanism of high culture. But the links with sexuality are not adequately registered by her interpretation of camp as a form of expediency for homosexuals, enabling them as the propagandist vanguard of this sensibility to integrate into society by promoting the aesthetic sense as the solvent of morality. Sontag does not link the formation of camp to homosexual identity, but rather sees it as serving a function for homosexuals who are drawn to it as a means of assimilation. In more recent work by Eve Kosofsky Sedgwick, camp is not just another modern form of sensibility which happens to contest the terms of modernism, but exists as what was necessarily excluded in the formation of a modernism fearful of the accusation of homosexuality.

For Eve Kosofsky Sedgwick, the history of mainstream modernism is inseparable from an account of the homophobia of the late nineteenth century onwards.[63] As homosexuality came to be conceived more in terms of the same-sex object choice than in terms of gender deviance, the pressure to avoid suspicion increased. The modernist adoption of formal experiment, and especially the equivocal viewpoint of the narrator in fiction, became the means of avoiding disclosure of homosexual erotic involvement in the bodies of one's own sex. What had to be excluded most of all was the taint of male homosexuality of which sentimentality was a key sign. For the author, reader or viewer, it became insufficient to condemn sentimentality in order to avoid suspicion. The charge of sentimentality revealed a responsiveness which showed too much understanding. Camp became the appreciation of this excluded sentimentality and a sign of a community.[64] To identify something as camp is to take pleasure in it and envisage others of the same sexuality similarly pleased. While those who appreciate kitsch hold their objects at a distance, as if their taste revealed nothing about themselves, a camp person knows his or her taste is a give-away to others in the know. Camp is a language that offers an identification. Perhaps, for this reason it seduces some and puts others off. This account links the formation of modernism to the emergence of camp and the formation of a sense of homosexual community through aesthetic codes, in ways which draw out relations of power in a culture disfigured by homophobia. As such, it improves upon Sontag's account. But perhaps some of the elements of camp were formed in a moment before the turn-of-the-century modernist experiments which feature in her account. Such elements may have cohered around a sense of identity which played with cross-dressed identifications and masquerade. If such an identity was formed by the homophile, it was constructed as *bricolage* from the elements of high culture, recoded to speak in the discourses of the modern city. At first, excluded from the public spaces, where the signs and codes of modern life circulated, gay identities were fabricated from the iconography of women as the object of the *flâneur*'s gaze, fused with the figure of the androgyne as prophet. Out of this, there emerged the fascination with the image of the excessive woman, with whom identification in imagination or play was possible, and from whom the connotations of androgyny were dropped in favour of the elaboration of the signs of femininity which could be assumed in masquerade. The fascination with a masquerade of femininity continued to play a part in the Dadaist movement in pastiches of advertising, but

153

Figure 5.9 Andy Warhol, *Marilyn Diptych* (detail), 1962; acrylic and silkscreen
on canvas, 208 × 290 cm

Source: Copyright, ARS, NY and DACS, London, 1995. Collection of the
Tate Gallery, London

found a new meaning in the context of the urban gay cultures of the 1950s
and 1960s. Warhol could make new use of films and advertisements of
female glamour in work exhibiting a taste which does not mock media-
produced images, but appropriates them as camp. It came from a community which, as Sedgwick suggests, was constituted in the expression of shared
pleasures of camp rather than any shared sense of place or common history.

Some of the most poignant and enduring of Warhol's images are those
of Marilyn Monroe (Figure 5.9). She is almost a sign for the *bricolage* of an
identity assembled in the modern city. Though the meaning of the images
is not confined to this, the sentimental appreciation of her brash vulnera-
bility and assumed excess of femininity can stand as a signifier of that camp
taste which is a part of contemporary gay culture. The appropriate companion images to these depictions of a masquerade of femininity are Warhol's
late self-portraits. They break with the codes of portraiture which signify
the presence of character and self-revelation. In some, khaki camouflage
overlays the painting of his face (Figure 5.10). In others, the larger part of
the portrait is a shadow, the insubstantial trace of a presence. These images
are darkly suggestive of many things. Among their possible meanings is the
sense that identity lies, not in some inner essence, nor in the sincerity which

Figure 5.10 Andy Warhol, *Self-Portrait*, 1986; acrylic and silkscreen,
203 × 203 cm

Source: Copyright, ARS, NY and DACS, London, 1995
Photograph: Courtesy Anthony D'Offay Gallery, London

will show in the face, but in a performance that can be carried off. Warhol, like Wilde before him, may have thought that we discover more of ourselves in adopting masks than in obeying the command to be sincere.

This chapter has looked at the way homosexual, homophile and gay identities have been, or could be, placed in relationship to modernity. Paradoxically, some formations of these identities are distinctly modern, yet deeply retrospective in outlook. Pater's criticism, drawing upon abstruse readings of Renaissance paintings, as sources for and legitimation of a new homophile identity, hardly strikes one as a fresh way of responding to modern life. But, it was influential in forming a positive sense of male-to-male desire, under conditions of modern homophobia. This sense of identity has not been highlighted by those accounts which contend that the formation of such identities was articulated around sexological discourses alone, or that artistic forms merely reflect these discourses. Nor has it featured in accounts of modernism which discuss the relationship of modern forms of art to modern urban identities. The tendency to neglect

155

aestheticism, and even sometimes symbolism, in accounts of modernism has obviously rendered invisible the emergence of a homophile identity within the codings of these movements.

But the homophile identity was not a static conception. Nor is there a simple continuous tradition of the masquerade of femininity which featured within its codes. The meaning of male appropriation of feminine dress changes in different contexts. From the molly houses on, there has been a popular practice of cross-dressing and its history, as the case of Boulton and Park demonstrates, has had a shifting relationship to surveillance. The aesthete's interest in producing a homophile identity through the codes of cross-dressing was transformed into a fascination with the masquerade of the excessive woman as spectacle. These are moments in a history of camp which need to be treated as a complex changing form of modern life, having an equally complex relationship to homosexuality and constructions of femininity.

The history of an aesthetics of camp is inseparable from the transformation of the dandy, once an elite modern urban figure, who more recently, in the instance of Warhol, has become the gay appropriator of mass culture and a popular artist. The dandy was always distinguished by his tastes in consumer items. But now there are different ways of becoming gay 'street people'. The placard in the New York demonstration says not 'I shop, therefore I am' but 'I am out, therefore I am', while in England, radical drag is again suffused with nostalgia in the search for its own history. Both are part of the exploration of a gay identity now. As in the past, such an identity is forged out of the appropriation of cultural signs and the transformations of meaning to be discovered in performance and masquerade.

NOTES

1 Adam Rolston's sticker is reproduced in D. Crimp and A. Rolston (eds), *AIDS Demo Graphics*, Seattle, Bay Press, 1990, p. 103.
2 This phrase was used by a participant to describe what gay people became at the moment of the Stonewall riots. It is quoted in J. Weeks, *Coming Out*, London, Quartet Books, rev. edn 1990, p. 188.
3 Crimp and Rolston, *AIDS Demo Graphics*, p. 19
4 N. Bartlett, *A Vision of Love Revealed in Sleep (Part Three)*, printed in M. Wilcox, *Gay Plays: Four*, London, Methuen, 1990, p. 91.
5 For a discussion of the varieties, see C. Vance, 'Social construction theory: problems in the history of sexuality', in D. Altman *et al.*, *Which Homosexuality*, London, Gay Men's Press, 1989.
6 M. Foucault, 'Sexual choice, sexual act: an interview with Michel Foucault', *Salamagundi*, special issue: *Homosexuality: Sacrilege, Vision, Politics* 1982–3, vols 58–9.
7 M. Foucault, *The History of Sexuality, Volume One: An Introduction*, London, Allen Lane, 1979, p. 157.
8 '. . . sex became a crucial target of a power organised around the management of life rather than the menace of death' (ibid., p. 147).

9 ibid., ch. 2

10 See especially the discussion in ibid., p. 101.

11 For an interesting version of this, see 'The intermediate sex', in D. Fernbach and N. Greig (eds), *Edward Carpenter, Selected Writings Volume One: Sex*, London, Gay Men's Press, 1984. It is of special interest that Carpenter calls his version of the third sex an 'intermediate sex', given the idealisation of androgyny among homophile artists and writers of the late nineteenth century.

12 See, for instance, E. Cooper, *The Sexual Perspective*, London, Routledge and Kegan Paul, 1986, p. 64.

13 See among others, D. Green 'Veins of resemblance: photography and eugenics', in P. Holland, J. Spence and S. Watney (eds), *Photography/Politics Two*, London, Comedia, 1986; J. Tagg 'The burden of representation', *TEN.8*, no. 14, 1984; D. Green and F. Mort, 'Is there anyone here from education (again)? Radical art and education for the 1990s', *Block*, no. 13, Winter 1987–8.

14 The phrase comes from W. Benjamin, 'The Paris of the Second Empire in Baudelaire', in his *Charles Baudelaire: A Lyric Poet in the Era of High Capitalism*, London, Verso, 1973, p. 36.

15 See T.J. Clark, *The Painting of Modern Life: Paris in the Art of Manet and his Followers*, London, Thames and Hudson, 1985.

16 See for instance J. Wolff, 'The culture of separate spheres: the role of culture in nineteenth century public and private life', in J. Wolff and J. Seed (eds), *The Culture of Capital: Art, Power and the Nineteenth-Century Middle Class*, Manchester, Manchester University Press, 1988. For responses to this, see among others, E. Wilson, *The Sphinx in the City*, London, Virago, 1991; and Mica Nava, Chapter 2 in this volume.

17 See C. Baudelaire, 'Women and prostitutes', in C. Baudelaire, *The Painter of Modern Life and Other Essays*, edited by J. Mayne, London, Phaidon, 1964. For Baudelaire's depiction of lesbianism, see the discussion in Benjamin, *Charles Baudelaire*, pp. 90–6.

18 For instance, Marshall Berman, in a reply to Perry Anderson's criticism of his book, *All That is Solid Melts into Air. The Experience of Modernity*, London, Verso, 1983 evokes Baudelaire's vision as one with which he can readily identify in reading the signs of the present day streets of New York City. M. Berman, 'The signs in the street', *New Left Review*, no. 144, March–April 1984. Alternatively Benjamin, in *Charles Baudelaire*, p. 54, suggests that the *flâneur* belongs to a particular moment, he is a figure of the arcade, not the later department stores which, as Mica Nava argues in this volume (Chapter 2), were public spaces which women occupied as *flâneuses*.

19 This is the account of the *flâneur* offered in R. Sennett, *The Fall of Public Man*, London, Faber and Faber, 1986, especially pp. 205–18.

20 N. Bartlett, *Who Was That Man: A Present for Oscar Wilde*, London, Serpent's Tail, 1988, pp. 128–44.

21 There were three trials, one for Wilde's charge that the Marquis of Queensbury had libelled him, and two in which Wilde stood accused of gross indecency according to the terms of the Labouchère Amendment Act of 1885. As a result of being found guilty at the last trial, he was sentenced to the maximum penalty of two years hard labour.

22 For historical research on the molly houses, see A. Bray, *Homosexuality in Renaissance England*, London, Gay Men's Press, 1982. Also, R. Norton, *Mother Clap's Molly House*, London, Gay Men's Press, 1992. For discussion of the early nineteenth-century uses of judicial means to persecute sodomites, see also

L. Crompton, *Byron and Greek Love: Homophobia in the Nineteenth Century*, Berkeley and Los Angeles, University of California Press, 1985.

23 J.-K. Huysmans, *Against Nature*, trans. R. Baldick, Harmondsworth, Penguin, 1959, p. 63.

24 See R. Gilmour, *The Idea of the Gentleman in the Victorian Novel*, London, George Allen, 1981.

25 Available edition: Walter Pater, *The Renaissance: Studies in Art and Poetry*, London, Fontana, 1971.

26 R. Dellamora, *Masculine Desire: The Sexual Politics of Victorian Aestheticism*, London, University of North Carolina Press, 1990.

27 B. Dijkstra, *Idols of Perversity*, Oxford, Oxford University Press, 1986.

28 Dellamora, *Masculine Desire*, p. 140.

29 E. Kosofsky Sedgwick, *Between Men: English Literature and Male Homosocial Desire*, New York, Columbia University Press, 1985.

30 Several of Simeon Solomon's works including 'The Tormented Soul' are reproduced in J. Christian (ed.) *The Last Romantics: The Romantic Tradition in British Art*, London, Lund Humphries, 1989. There are more in a catalogue, *Solomon: A Family of Painters*, London, Inner London Education Authority, 1985. This also includes a relevant article addressing his sexuality: see E. Cooper, 'A vision of love: homosexual and androgynous themes in Simeon Solomon's work after 1873', in *Solomon*. Solomon was arrested in 1873 on the charge of buggery.

31 The British sexologists, including John Addington Symonds, Havelock Ellis and Edward Carpenter are discussed in various works by Jeffrey Weeks. See, especially, part two of *Coming Out: Homosexual Politics in Britain from the Nineteenth Century*, London, Quartet, 1990. In this work, Weeks argues that the above-mentioned sexologists contributed to a biological model of homosexuality. Although all three rejected the stereotype of the effeminate male homosexual, Symonds and Carpenter were attracted to the notion of an 'intermediate' or 'third' sex, while Ellis opposed this idea. This notion suggested that the bearer of the sexual characteristics of one sex possessed emotional characteristics of the other: ibid., pp. 49, 63 and 75.

32 Dellamora, *Masculine Desire*, p. 137.

33 Baudelaire wrote of Madame Bovary that she was a 'strange androgyne . . . given all the seductive power of a masculine spirit in an enchanting woman's body' (quoted by Benjamin, *Charles Baudelaire* p. 92).

34 J.-K. Huysmans, *Là-Bas*, London, The Fortune Press, n.d. For instance, on p. 82, Dutrin, the central male figure, says of Mme Chantelou that her name is 'a half boyish name that suits her'. At various other points in the novel, there are references to her split personality and to the fact that she is revealed as common prostitute once her sexual passion is released.

35 O. Wilde, *Salome*, in *Plays*, Harmondsworth, Penguin, 1954.

36 Dellamora, *Masculine Desire*, p. 145.

37 Quoted by R. Ellman in *Oscar Wilde*, London, Hamish Hamilton, 1987, p. 321.

38 The photograph, from the collection of the late Guillot de Saix, was thought by Ellman to be of Wilde. But this has been disputed in a letter to the *London Review of Books*, 27 February 1992.

39 Dellamora, *Masculine Desire*, p. 142.

40 In a remark by Wilde, criticising Beardsley's illustrations to *Salome*, quoted by Ellman, *Oscar Wilde*, p. 355.

41 E. Showalter, *Sexual Anarchy*, London, Bloomsbury, 1991, ch. 8.

42 For a discussion of masculinity, sexuality and Girodet's painting, see Whitney Davis, 'The renunciation of reaction in Girodet's *Sleep of Endymion*', in N. Bryson, M.A. Holly and K. Moxey (eds), *Visual Culture: Images and Interpretations*, Hanover, NH, University Press of New England, 1994. Davis points out that, although Girodet originally presented the painting of 1891 as the depiction of the myth of Selene, he was later to identify the moonbeams with Diana. Both Selene and Diana were moon goddesses.

43 See the catalogue entry for *The Moon and Sleep* by Simeon Solomon in *Solomon: A Family of Painters*.

44 This is the painting which is referred to in chapter 5 of Huysmans' *Against Nature*, which Wilde is said to have called his golden book.

45 Elaine Showalter in chapter 8 of *Sexual Anarchy* draws upon Beardsley's illustrations to make the case that the play, *Salome*, is coded for a homosexual audience. In other works, Wilde clearly used terms which would have a special meaning to members of a homosexual subculture, as in use of the term 'Bunburyist' to allude to one who leads a double life in his play *The Importance of Being Earnest*.

46 Wilde's criticisms of Beardsley's drawings for *Salome* are quoted in Ellman, *Oscar Wilde*, p. 355.

47 The classical sources, which include Ovid's *Metamorphoses*, are discussed by Robert Graves in *The Greek Gods*, vol. 1, Harmondsworth, Penguin, 1960, pp. 11–15. A Renaissance version, Poliziano's verse drama, *Orfeo*, is discussed by James M. Saslow in *Ganymede in the Renaissance: Homosexuality in Art and Society*, New Haven, Yale University Press, 1986.

48 Among the many meanings condensed in the play, Wilde could also have been alluding to the Hellenisation of Christian culture. Belief in the need for a synthesis of Greek and Christian cultures was a common theme in nineteenth-century criticism and is discussed by Wilde in his essay 'The critic as artist', in *Complete Works of Oscar Wilde*, London, Collins, 1966.

49 L. Nead, *Myths of Sexuality: Representations of Women in Victorian Britain*, Oxford, Blackwell, 1988.

50 Wilde 'The critic as artist', p. 1048.

51 For a recent account which takes Wilde's critique of authenticity and relates it to his sexuality, see J. Dollimore, *Sexual Dissidence*, Oxford, Clarendon Press, 1991.

52 Wilde, 'The critic as artist', p. 1038.

53 Sennett, *The Fall of Public Man*, ch. 8, especially pp. 67–76.

54 Wilde called her 'that tragic daughter of passion' in a letter, quoted in Ellman, *Oscar Wilde*, p. 353.

55 See Gilmour, *The Idea of the Gentleman.*. For a discussion of Gilmour's thesis in relation to the Wilde trials, see Dellamora, *Masculine Desire*, ch. 10.

56 See, for instance, R. Fry, 'An essay in aesthetics', in his *Vision and Design*, London, Penguin, 1937; and C. Bell, *Art*, London, Arrow Books, 1961.

57 W. Hartshorn and M. Foresta in the introduction to the exhibition catalogue, *Man Ray in Fashion*, New York, International Center of Photography, 1990, p. 15.

58 See, for instance, Vance Packard, *The Hidden Persuaders*, Harmondsworth, Penguin, 1981 (originally published 1957).

59 See, for instance, Clement Greenberg, 'Avant-garde and kitsch', *Partisan Review*, vol. 6, no. 5, Autumn 1939, reprinted in F. Frascina, *Pollock and After: The Critical Debate*, London, Harper and Row, 1985.

60 See, for instance, various essays in G. Garrels (ed.) *The Work of Andy Warhol*, Seattle, Bay Press, 1989, especially, Benjamin H.D. Buchloh, 'The Andy Warhol line'.

61 Susan Sontag, 'Notes on "camp"', in her *Against Interpretation and Other Essays*, New York, Farrar, Straus and Giroux, 1966.

62 The camp enjoyment of popular culture has to be distinguished from interest in popular culture as a source of codes to set against high culture. This latter approach has been identified as a trend within modernism by T. Crow in 'Modernism and mass culture in the visual arts' in Frascina (ed.), *Pollock and After*.

63 E. Kosofsky Sedgwick, *The Epistemology of the Closet*, Hemel Hempstead, Harvester Wheatsheaf, 1991, especially ch. 3.

64 E. Kosofsky Sedgwick finds it unsurprising therefore that, with postmodernism's re-examination of the figurative, kitsch and sentimentality have become matters of contestation again. See *Epistemology of the Closet*, pp. 166–7.

6

THE MYSTERIES AND SECRETS OF WOMEN'S BODIES

Sexual knowledge in the first half of the twentieth century

Sally Alexander

Sexual knowledge is fundamental to the formation of the self; it tells us who we are, man or woman, and what that means in a given culture. The curiosity that drives a child to enquire about the mysteries and secrets of the body, love and reproduction is one of the elements of the self, and the basis of all subsequent curiosities. The questions 'where do I come from?' and 'what is the difference between the sexes?' are among the first and most insistent that all children ask, Freud noticed; two of the starting-points of philosophical enquiry.[1] Autobiographies and life-stories often confirm the urgency behind the pursuit of such knowledge. Understanding how we came by sexual knowledge will tell us something of how the mind works (one proper object of cultural history as Ludmilla Jordanova has pointed out) and how all knowledge is constituted and internalised.[2] Secondly, the ways in which sexual knowledge is transmitted from one generation to another and where responsibility resides in a culture for the skills and practices required for the reproduction of both people and those skills are vexed questions of ethical debate. Sex and ethics are inseparable in public life and private speech. In the 1920s and 1930s, what could and should be said about sex and sexual relations was tried and tested in law, in modernist writings, in the cinema, in the politics of welfare and in conversation. At the same time fertility was declining. Women were choosing to have fewer children than ever before.

Family size fell among all occupational groups between the wars.[3] By 1933, in the trough of unemployment in Britain, the birth rate reached its lowest ebb.[4] Doubts as to whether the population would reproduce itself were fuelled by the death of men in the great war and high levels of male unemployment throughout the 1920s. Anxiety was driven by both government policy-makers and those voluntary and local authority bodies concerned with the health and welfare of the people. The rise of national socialism in Germany after 1933 with its pro-family policies added urgency to the concern.[5] Advice about family limitation, or birth control (Margaret Sanger's phrase), through public provision was unevenly introduced in the context of a debate which oscillated between the contradictory fears of 'race-suicide' or 'underpopulation' and the birth of too many babies among the poor.[6] Poverty was the reason married people, young married women in particular, gave for not wanting children.[7] Although only the most convinced eugenists argued for selective breeding, or compulsory sterilisation, few spoke without reference to the quality of the race or the differential birth rates of rich and poor, the educated and uneducated.[8] At stake in these debates on population and birth control were the conditions of women's lives and the health and education of mothers.[9]

The health of mothers slipped readily into feminist rhetoric. Feminists (of different persuasions) together with neo-Malthusians, anarchists, communists and sexologists, advocated birth control before and during the 1920s.[10] The needs of mothers were the first concern of the Women's Co-operative Guild, the Standing Joint Committee of Working Women's Organisations, the Labour Party Women's Sections and the National Union of Equal Citizenship (NUSEC). Marie Stopes and her Society of Constructive Birth Control was only the most zealous voice demanding birth control for women to improve their health, and – vitally – as a source of mutual ecstasy for husband and wife within marriage.[11]

The spread of knowledge through the birth control movement and feminism may have contributed to the 'fading of the population' (the phrase is from the 1946 Royal Commission on Population) but birth control was only the means not the cause of fewer births, as Eva Hubback pointed out in 1947.[12] Historians searching for explanations for the falling birth rate have emphasised – among the many causes – higher expectations which led the poor and unemployed to reduce family size even when contraception was beyond the family's means. Only Diana Gittins has emphasised women's oral cultures in the formation of sexual knowledge; and Carolyn Steedman's reading of both Kathleen Woodward's *Jipping Street*, and the recounting of her memories of her own mother's life, have placed the 'impossibility of reproducing herself' in the historical imagination.[13] My work here deepens those insights. It was young women's own wishes in the interwar years not to repeat their mothers' lives that lead to the drop in fertility and the changing meaning of womanhood.

If the limitation of fertility was 'the single most important change in women's lives' as the sociologist Richard Titmuss claimed in the 1950s, then women's changing relationship to the properties and pleasures of their own bodies and to the 'sex-relation' was its vital outcome.[14] For a girl, becoming a woman meant fathoming the mysteries and secrets of the mother's body; it meant not only acknowledging anatomical difference, menstruation and eventually the more obfuscating mysteries of childbirth with all its dangerous associations, but identifying with them and living their consequences. In the interwar years, young women's ambivalent identification with the maternal body was one of the driving forces of modernity, if one of the features of modernity is the break with tradition and the imagining of new futures. There is plenty of anecdotal evidence that young women, while they wanted fewer children, wanted love and sex. The war, Irene Clephane wrote in 1935, had released 'franker attitudes to sex engendered by death'.[15] The cinema taught people how to kiss, court, make love. And perhaps, among some well-to-do feminist and medical opinion, psychoanalysis encouraged desire.[16] But 'Not like my Mum' was the phrase heard everywhere among young mothers in the 1930s, according to Eva Hubback, 'who were so often warned by their own mothers not to expose themselves to the fate the latter themselves suffered'.[17] This chapter considers some elements in and implications of young women's ambivalent maternal identifications between the wars; it focuses on women's memories – that difficult borderline between fantasy and history – of sexual discovery. I am interested in 'how history is lived through people'.[18]

MYSTERIES AND SECRETS

Sexuality, female sexuality, was a source of mystery to young women growing up in London in the interwar years if memory is to be believed. A silence covered women's bodies and their functions in everyday speech I was told. There was no word for pregnant, vagina or lavatory, or any other bodily part or function, or none that could be spoken in company, my mother said, when she was a girl in the 1920s. Expecting her first baby in 1940 she kept indoors.[19] May Jones remembers standing at the window of the front room in Stepney, looking out and seeing a woman with a fat belly walking past: 'What's she got in her tummy?' she asked her mother and received in reply a blow across her face. Sex she told me was 'absolutely taboo'.[20]

This memory of taboo, like children without shoes, begging ex-soldiers' or dancing in the streets, is a ubiquitous memory of childhood in the 1920s and 1930s, intended to convey the trials of living in an unenlightened post-Victorian age – a signifier of economic as well as sexual need. The silence about sex was not only a limit in the speech of the poor. The failure ran across public speech. It was not possible to articulate in a language of legitimacy, compassion or pleasure – without prurience – women's bodily or sexual needs or wants. The disavowal of feminine sexuality in the wider culture meant that there was no smooth transition to sexual knowledge for young women growing up between the wars.

It is difficult to unravel in retrospect whether the lack of words in demotic speech for womens' naked bodies and their functions – fecund, aroused –

may be attributed to the embarrassment of speaking across a generation, or whether it reflected a failure of feeling, a lack of knowledge or simply a series of prohibitions whose most insistent object was the body – in particular the woman's body.[21] David Vincent, the historian of nineteenth-century autobiography, and Elizabeth Roberts in her oral history of women, both discovered the emotional reticence of the poor in written and spoken memory.[22] John Burnett reminds us to pay attention to what is not spoken by reading between the lines to 'fill out the emotional gaps': 'sometimes we can recognize that the simple words and phrases in an author's limited vocabulary have to stand for deeper feelings that he is unable to express.'[23] It is a matter of interpretation whether sentences like 'They had a strong affection' or 'The devastating love that we had . . . that love I had (for my mother)' need more words to make their meaning clear. People born in the first two decades of the twentieth century do remark on the lack of demonstrative love between parents and children at that time, sometimes speaking of a necessary austerity – emotional as well as economic – among the poor.[24] Whether we assume an emotional reticence or not, the effect of silence, or the absence of words for parts of the body, was to reinforce feelings of shame about sexuality.

Shame and fear were the two emotions most often remembered by nineteenth-century working-class autobiographers. Many families had something to hide – family secrets not to be spoken even, or especially, among those most concerned. A search through any oral history archive will reveal family romances of illegitimacy; incest was whispered about too, especially when the tape-recorder was switched off.[25] Elizabeth Roberts, questioning more deliberately, discovered a profound pessimism and conservatism about sex and sexual desire among the 160 women she interviewed in the 1970s and early 1980s, even when there was no family secret to be kept from children. Roberts is persuaded that shame, lack of pleasure and inhibition were the effects of an 'all-pervading prudery about sexual matters' among the older women. Underlying the prudery was the conviction among women that sex was necessary but distasteful, and a fatalism about pregnancy and childbirth. Mothers and daughters did not speak about something that was not only not desired by the mothers, but was considered dangerous and shameful.[26] Young women's expectations were different from their mothers, especially in the city which promised escape from the hardship and poverty of previous generations. Nevertheless, I am suggesting that the imprint of their mothers' experience lived disconsolately in the minds of young women, and that the force of secrecy and mystery around sex and childbirth reinforced the intimacy between shame and femininity in the 1920s and 1930s, implying a structure of feeling of foreboding for young women, which is only sometimes recalled, and is often masked in reminiscence by humour and self-mockery.

THE PURSUIT OF SEX

Conversations between mothers and daughters were always difficult, the more so for the young would-be rebel. Angela Rodaway, growing up in Islington, describes her contempt for her mother who, when her daughter eventually plucked up the courage to tell her she was menstruating (she told her schoolfriends first of all; they begged her to tell her mother), merely repeated the information which she had already discarded as myths and folklore: don't eat apples or ice-cream, wash in cold water and so on. Angela Rodaway's contempt or exasperation spills into the stories of her mother's ceaseless energy, lack of book knowledge (Angela had a secondary school education), strict attention to the observances of 'superiority'. And yet Rodaway herself was also determined not to know. When her mother took to her bed in childbirth, Angela's diagnosis – like many other young women's – was pneumonia not confinement. More interesting, when pressed by friends to confirm the account of sexual intercourse described to her by a schoolfriend Harry and disbelieved by the others she 'found that I had no words to say what I meant'.[27]

Others confirm Angela Rodaway's experience of lack of conversation between mothers and daughters. The secrets of sex were put together like a jigsaw puzzle, learned – in a phrase repeated often – the 'dirty way' at school from children whispering in the playground, from sisters, but never it seems from mothers. Celia Wilmot, living with her mother and sister in Drury Lane, learnt about her body and its functions in a common confusion of facts and fantasy. After describing the protective relationship her older sister adopted towards her, she went on:

> I didn't have any knowledge of babies. I assumed listening that a baby popped out like a shell out of me belly, and I had no knowledge of periods and things like that. But my mother never told me anything. My sister . . . where she gleaned it from I don't know. But there was this sort of protection.
>
> . . . Suddenly I had a period and I knew it was going to happen . . . my sister explained it all to me . . . girls even younger than myself started periods very young, and they'd take you and say, and it was a great event in their life, and say 'I've got it' and – not menstruating, we didn't say. 'I've got a period', and 'I've got blood on my knickers' [in a whisper] [laughter], and you'd say say 'ooargh' and you'd hear about it, and knew it had to come. And then when it came, and it was terrible shock, your older sister would tell you. Mums never told you.[28]

In Celia's account, the thrill of discovery – both a 'great event' and a 'terrible shock' – mitigates the familiar equation: menstruation/female body equals dirt. The shock of menstruation prefigures the shock of birth.[29]

For many the mystery was not solved until the 'shock' of birth itself. Young women remained tenaciously attached to the belly-button theory of birth. Ignorance was not confined to the poor or ill-educated. The poet Robert Graves' wife, Nancy Nicholson, was astonished and horrified by the experience of giving birth. Graves attributed her burgeoning feminism to this 'shock'. Margaret Cole, the young Fabian, and Frances Partridge, the Bloomsbury writer, are among those who recall absolute ignorance when they went up to Oxbridge in the early 1920s.[30]

Young women's potential fertility was the reason given for their need of 'protection'. Protection reaches back to the 1840s when women came under the 'protection' of parliament. Women who had something to sell other than their labour, as Sidney Webb the Fabian put it later in the century, and who were unable to speak for themselves in the public spheres of industry or parliament, were in need of men's protection.[31] Or so it was thought. Elizabeth Roberts' argument was that fear of the consequences of sexual knowledge, and the need to protect young women from men, from their own desires, from unclean thoughts, enforced the silence between generations. Mothers knew but did not want their daughters to know because the knowledge might be used. Presumably if it was not spoken then it was not known, and knowledge could be a dangerous thing. For this reason young women were protected or 'kept in hand' – the equivalent among the poor of chaperonage. Both belonged, in the minds of young women, to the Victorian age.

So evidence from mothers was not directly sought, and when it was, – as now – it was often mistrusted. But in the 1920s and 1930s the resistance to knowledge was also a resistance to their mothers' lives, a recognition that if mothers had the knowledge that they the daughters wanted, it was not wanted in the way their mothers seemed to hold it. More reliable was the evidence of one's own body. Angela Rodaway, for instance, discovered sexual desire through pashes at school, sliding down ropes and long conversations with friends. Words, poetry in particular, induced ecstasies.[32]

This empty speech could also be symptomatic of a gap in the vernacular where once very different practices and conventions around sex had been. Those conventions and their articulation fell out of use, swept away by migration, urban development and industrial restructuring. Winifred Foley, for example, recorded the sexual mores of the Forest of Dean at the beginning of the twentieth century, where illicit sex occurred beyond the boundaries of the village in the Forest, and the mothers of illegitimate children were ostracised.[33] These customs – forms of knowledge and regulation – were lost in the move to the cities.[34] London was a city of migrants in the 1920s and 1930s. London's working populations included migrants from the depressed districts of England, Wales, Scotland and Ireland, some tens of thousands exiled from the pogroms of Russia and Central Europe, all of whom grew up alienated or one step removed from the languages and customs of their parents and kin. Even among London families, slum clearance and municipal as well as private housing schemes fractured continuities in the oral transmission of culture.

The newness of migration was reinforced by changes in literacy – England was more or less a literate culture by 1914.[35] Some remember their parents, in particular their mother's illiteracy, or that of their grandparents, and that memory was often a shameful one.[36] Children were using language differently from their parents. Children in school learned by rote and from texts which bowdlerised the English language. School language and its rules may well have been different from that spoken at home. There was no necessary linguistic continuity between mother and daughter, no continuity in meanings and vocabularies.

SEX AND DEATH

And yet, the knowledge most longed for and which mothers had was knowledge of sex. The only subject that approached it in fascination was death, and sex and death were associated. Rose Gamble's older sister was closest to her mother handing over her wages, helping with the younger children, protecting her mother from their father, listening to conversations between her mother and friends. She 'knew about death too' Rose wrote, recalling her sister's words. The one secret Angela Rodaway and her best friend kept from her mother was knowledge of death.[37]

Two childhood memories, both from written autobiographies, underline the uncanny mental association between sex and death. The first is a story from Edith Hall remembering a young lodger, a former munitions worker, in her mother's house in Hayes in Middlesex (then a village, later a suburb of London) in the early 1920s:

> Doris, one of our young lodgers, met a local man and married him and they continued to live in the neighbourhood. While still in her early twenties she had produced five children and was told not to have another as it would be dangerous to her health. She was not told, however, how to avoid 'having another'; when she again became pregnant, we took care of the children while she sat in a hot bath in our through room and mother kept topping up the water from boiling kettles . . . but nothing happened. Then somebody told Doris about 'Knitting Needle Nelly' who helped women 'who mustn't have another'; but Doris died from Nelly's help and she left two sets of twins and an odd one to her husband Ben. Sometime before, I had heard her say to mother, 'The reason why we keep having children is because Ben and I love each other so much.' So that was it, then; that was why so many other women had died like Doris; love had killed them, leaving behind many small children.[38]

167

The second memory is from Doris Bailey's Bethnal Green autobiography. Once, Doris Bailey rushed in on her parents on the sacrosant Sunday afternoon when her three siblings were at Sunday school. She discovered her father smothering her mother ('being cruel . . . just about squashing every breath out of her') and her mother as angry as he was at the interruption. The idea of murder was in keeping with her father's intermittent beatings.[39] Doris appeased her father whom she loved but feared. She earned extra money for his precious cigarettes, and rejoiced when he took the children for an outing in Epping Forest. Rejoiced that is because the Forest had no pubs and drink could lead to brutality towards her mother.[40]

Young girls, seeking an explanation of the mysteries and secrets of their bodies and those of their parents met angry repudiation, a taboo. Listening to their mothers talking, they misheard, or misunderstood what they heard and saw. They heard of love killing, and saw murder between parents. They associated sex with death, an association which inscribed feminine subjectivity – what it meant to be a woman – with traumatic identifications. The fantastic association between sex and death was mirrored in the real conditions of childbirth – a mirroring which alerts the historian to the difficulty of distinguishing, between fact and fantasy in the inner mental world.[41]

The psychic proximity of sex and death met in the statistics of infant and maternal mortality. Childbirth could end in death. About 3,000 childbearing mothers died per year, Sylvia Pankhurst estimated in the 1900s; and 20,000 infants died at birth.[42] Death haunted the imagination in the interwar years, and the deaths of mothers caused public concern because whereas the numbers of infant births were declining, the proportion of infant to maternal mortality was not shifting. Maternal mortality was significantly higher in the poorer districts where stillbirths increased with unemployment (as in the East End in 1920, for instance). Two studies in the 1920s by Dame Janet Campbell found that lack of professional training and expertise were the cause of high maternal mortality and these findings were confirmed by the Select Committee on Maternal Mortality in 1937, which argued that:

> Changes in social life necessary to raise the standard of health and physical development of the women of the nation can only come in time; great advances in medical knowledge must be made before many of the risks of childbirth can be eliminated; even then the factor of human fallibility will remain.[43]

Limited medical knowledge was underlined by the arbitrary cruelties of poverty: households too poor for medical assistance, contraception, adequate nourishment or sterilised equipment.[44] But low male wages, unemployment, overcrowding lent desperation to women's attempts to reduce the size of their families. Given the lack and cost of adequate contraception, and knowledge, the abortionist was the 'dread' of women's lives. Every working-class locality had its abortionist as well as its laying-out woman, its street (or court) of vice where prostitutes, pills and so on were procured, as well as its lying-in hospital. There is no way of knowing how many women resorted to abortion, but its practice was widespread.[45]

Some sexual reformers blamed women's ignorance of their bodies and its functions for women's ill health. Leonora Eyles argued in a series of books on working-class life that too many babies and bad housing drove women to hysteria. Ignorance led to a lessening of desire, argued Eva Hubback, the advocate of birth control; it caused depression according to Irene Clephane, who evoked the loss and uncertainty that unemployment and political instability across Europe brought – her description of the loss of confidence and security recalls Vera Brittain's 'withering frost of grief and loss'.[46] Marie Stopes spoke of a lack of knowledge about sex so 'abysmal, so universal, that its mists and shadowy darkness have affected even the few who lead us, and who are prosecuting research in these subjects'.[47] Feminists wanted to educate women in the workings of their bodies in order to protect them from VD, from men's lust, from too many children. Others wanted to awaken women to the pleasures of sexual desire and love.

Against the combined hearsay evidence of young women's memories of their mothers' and sexual reformers' insistence on working women's ignorance, we must set the letters to Marie Stopes, the reports from the first birth-control clinics and the memories of older women which reveal an emotional economy of the poor suppressed in public speech – the stuff of rumour and women's gossip – its vocabulary was ancient, its emotional economy violent and secret. Letters to Marie Stopes, for instance, release an avalanche of anguish and suffering. The writers blame ignorance and poverty for their pain; they envy the rich their access to information and medical skills. 'I have many of my friends' one wrote in 1923:

> working class women who need and are grateful for the kind help Dr. Marie Stopes has given them. I feel it a great injustice and unChristian like to think that rich women should have this knowledge and a poor woman should live in ignorance of it. . . .

Another wrote the same year:

> I have had five living children and have been seven times pregnant. I belong to the working class and know only too well how bitterly the working classes need the kind of help Dr. Marie Stopes is giving.

Many of the women who wrote to Marie Stopes in response to articles about her libel action published in *John Bull*, *The Penny Magazine* and the *Daily Mail* describe themselves as women of the working class. 'You have won our hearts and admiration', wrote one woman from London in 1920, 'not that it is worth much because we are of the real working class'.[48]

Throughout these letters the anger and despair stems from the belief that the knowledge of the rich is denied to the poor.

Knowledge meant the prevention of conception, cleanly, safely and legally. People wrote to Marie Stopes because there was nowhere else to turn. They wanted 'scientific' knowledge.[49] Most doctors, it seemed, shrugged their shoulders, remained silent or angrily refused advice during the 1920s except to advocate self-restraint. They sometimes advised women not to have more children, but seldom gave information on how to avoid having them. Women listed their income, budgets and housing. One woman lived in a kitchen, others moved into the workhouse for their confinement or moved their children there when a new child was due – the Poor Law was not abolished until 1929. The bitter truth seems to have been that poverty shrivelled emotional lives, overcrowding bred not intimacy but guilt and cruelty. Letters describe incest, abortion (quinine, pessaries, whisky and gin, 'female pills' and medicines), rape by husbands: 'since then he has been very cruel to me because that I will not submit to his embrace, he has often compelled me as he has very, very many times before to submit with my back to him'.[50] Laudanam addiction, and mental hospital incarceration were two responses described in letters. The appeal for help is insistent 'Doctor please help me', 'Doctor do you hold out any hope?' There was love between women and men, but from the surviving records in the 1920s it could be harrowing to live as a woman among the poor.

The intensity and extent of physical and mental ill-health echoes that revealed in *Maternity Letters from Working Women*, written at the turn of the century to the Women's Co-operative Guild.[51] Both this and the letters to Marie Stopes make almost unbearable reading. The letters Marie Stopes received in the early 1920s show that it must have been a struggle not to speak. The writing is vivid. The words and feelings flow from them like the blood and other fluids they describe. Imagery and vocabulary spring from the Bible. The words for menstruation belong to an ancient vocabulary: courses (sixteenth century according to the *OED*), menses (sixteenth century), colours, connections; come together, coitus, were the words for sexual intercourse. The body was a source of dirt, of mysterious emanations, its functioning unpredictable with often horrible effects. Men's lust was an enemy and contrasted with women's lesser desire.

The woman's body recorded here and reiterated in spoken testimony appears not as signifier of male fantasy, of men's desire, but as it was lived: a body coursed with blood and other fluids, the receptacle of men's sperm, the carrier of infants, hard working and resourceful. This body was the other side of Joan Riviere's 'Womanliness as masquerade'.[52] With what relief did the older women don men's hats and set off for the public houses.[53] Virginia Woolf's androgyny, her wish for £500 a year and a room of her own, were not perhaps only the desire of the educated elite, but one woman's response to the implications of her body which is echoed in memories and autobiographies of the 1920s.[54]

I am suggesting that women's memories of silence and taboo have a particular resonance in the 1920s and 1930s because they signal a watershed in the history of sexual knowledge and its transmission from one generation to another, and mark a hiatus in the understanding of femininity. Young women were refusing their mothers' lives even though their own understanding was based on mishearings and misunderstandings. They were enticed by new and different wants – generated by the new housing estates, jobs in the new industries, birth control and the cinema, but also articulated by literacy, new vocabularies of sexual difference and desire in which peer groups and medical opinion became more significant than the words and experiences of their mothers. For generations growing up after the Second World War, sexual knowledge and care became embodied in the institutions and practices of the welfare state which sought, with patchy effect, to replace ignorance and trauma with reassurance. But women's own wish for fewer children was perhaps the most vital element in the generation of a new mentality of modernity.

Sexual knowledge is difficult to historicise. Constituted through fantasy, emotion and the mother's body it belongs to the realm of the imaginary. Surrounded by taboo, the wishes and feelings associated with it are often repressed and always ambivalent. Unconscious ideas and wishes are timeless and symbolically fragmented and displaced. Nevertheless, it seems that the anatomy of memories and fantasies of young women, insofar as they reveal their understanding of and feelings about sexual difference, uncover an emotional economy of the poor which was particularly hard for a woman to inhabit in the 1920s and 1930s. In 1937 Freud remarked on the universal repudiation of femininity; the historical conditions of sexual difference enhance that understanding.[55]

NOTES

1 Sigmund Freud, 'The sexual enlightenment of children', (1907), and 'On the sexual theories of children' (1908), in (ed. and transl.) James Strachey, *The Standard Edition of the Complete Psychological Works of Sigmund Freud* (hereafter *SE*), vol. 9, London, Hogarth Press, 1981 edn, pp. 129–39, 207–26.
2 Ludmilla Jordanova, 'Where is cultural history going?', Annual Conference, Social History Society, York, January 1995.
3 A.M. Carr-Saunders, D. Caradog Jones and C.A. Moser, *A Survey of Social Conditions in England and Wales, as Illustrated by Statistics*, Oxford, Clarendon Press, 1958, p. 27. Information was taken from the Family Census undertaken for the *Royal Commission on Population* in 1946 (full report published in 1954), which showed that 'for marriages contracted in the decade 1870–9 the average number of live births per married woman was 5.8, while for those begun in 1900–9 it was 3.4, and for those of 1925 it was 2.2' (ibid. p. 23).

4 Eva Hubback, *The Population of Britain*, West Drayton, Pelican, 1947, p. 67 The crude birth rate is the number of births per thousand of the population. In 1876 the birth-rate was 36.3; in 1931, 15.8 (William Beveridge *et al.*, *Changes in Family Life*, London, Allen and Unwin, 1932, p. 44). *Changes in Family Life* took the form of a series of conversations between public figures and policy-makers. William Beveridge himself was anxious about the 'unconscious selective breeding' that would occur if we did not understand the relation between nurture and nature. The book introduced a family survey in the attempt to gauge parents' thoughts in order to construct 'a new kind of instrument for social science' (pp. 54, 65).

5 Eleanor Rathbone, 'Changes in public life', in Ray Strachey (ed.), *Our Freedom and its Results, by Five Women*, London, Hogarth Press, 1936, p. 68.

6 Noreen Branson and Margot Heinemann, *Britain in the Nineteen Thirties*, London, Weidenfeld and Nicolson, 1971, ch. 11.

7 Hubback, *Population of Britain*, pp. 46–50; Irene Clephane, *Towards Sex Freedom*, London, John Lane, The Bodley Head, 1938 edn, p. 205.

8 Jane Lewis, *The Politics of Motherhood, Child and Maternal Welfare in England, 1900–1939*, London, Croom Helm, 1980, pp. 206–27. Alison Neilans, 'Changes in sex morality', in Strachey (ed.), *Our Freedom and Its Results*, pp. 229–30, takes issue with the Labour Women's Conference demand for the 'voluntary sterilization of the feebleminded and other unfit people who might transmit their defect to offspring'.

9 Lewis, *Politics of Motherhood*, ch. 1.

10 ibid., ch. 7; Brian Harrison, *Prudent Revolutionaries: Portraits of British Feminists Between the Wars*, Oxford, Clarendon Press, 1987, ch. 10, 'Catalyst and facilitator, Eva Hubback', pp. 280–2. Hubback herself joined the Eugenics Society in 1929, when working in adult education and for the National Union of Societies for Equal Citizenship (NUSEC). A NUSEC deputation to the government in 1932 asked for extension of birth control and sterilisation to the social problem group: Lewis, *Politics of Motherhood*, p. 307. For feminist advocacy of 'preventive checks' or abstinence in marriage as a form of contraception, Carol Dyhouse, *Feminism and the Family in England, 1880–1939*, Oxford, Basil Blackwell, 1989, pp. 166–74.

11 Marie Carmichael Stopes, *Married Love, A New Contribution to the Solution of Sex Difficulties*, London, G.P. Puttnam's Sons, 1926 edn (first published 1918), pp. 7–8. For a valuable recent account of Stopes' work, Deborah A. Cohen, 'Private lives in public spaces: Marie Stopes, the mothers; clinics and the practice of contraception', *History Workshop Journal*, issue 35, Spring 1993, pp. 95–116.

12 Hubback, *Population of Britain*, p. 45.

13 Diana Gittins, *Fair Sex, Family Size and Structure, 1900–1939*, London, Hutchinson, 1982; Carolyn Steedman, 'Introduction', in Kathleen Woodward, *Jipping Street*, London, Virago, 1983 (first published 1928), p. 13; Carolyn Steedman, *Landscape for a Good Woman, the Story of Two Women's Lives*, London, Virago, 1984.

14. Richard Titmuss, 'The position of women: some vital statistics', in R. Titmuss, *Essays on the 'Welfare State'*, London, George Allen and Unwin, 1958. See also, Richard and Kathleen Titmuss, *Parents Revolt: A Study of the Declining Birth-Rate in Acquisitive Societies*, London, Secker and Warburg, 1942.

15 Clephane, *Towards Sex Freedom*, p. 205.

16 Freud himself was famously unenthusiastic about birth control, believing it created frigidity and sexual frustration. He was clearly thinking about coitus

interruptus: 'Civilisation and its discontents', *SE*, vol. 21. A.J.P. Taylor, *English History 1914–1945*, Harmondsworth, Pelican, 1983 edn, pp. 237, 392–6;, for the cinema. Robert Graves and Alan Hodge, *The Long Weekend, A Social History of Great Britain, 1918–1939*, London, Faber and Faber, 1940, pp. 102–3 for psychoanlysis' putative influence.

17 Hubback, *Population of Britain*, p. 67.

18 Nadine Gordimer in conversation with Hermione Lee, Radio 4, 15 January 1995.

19 Vera Brittain has a different memory. Speaking of the condition of the 'super-fluous women' in 1921 she writes in 1933:

> As a generation of women we were now sophisticated to an extent which was revolutionary when compared with the romantic ignorance of 1914. Where we had once spoken with polite evasion of a 'certain condition', a 'certain profession', we now unblushingly used the words 'pregnancy' and 'prostitution'. Amongst our friends we discussed sodomy and lesbianism with as little hesitation as we compared the merits of different contraceptives, and were theoretically familiar with varieties of homosexuality and venereal disease of which the very existence was unknown to our grandparents. We had not quite lost – and perhaps never shall lose – a self-conscious feeling of boldness in our candour; not all our experience could change us from the earnest, idealistic War generation into our flippant juniors, the post-war youth, who had never been taught to think the terms of sex indecent and to see its facts, if at all, through a glass darkly. But we were now capable of the frank analysis of our own natures, and the stoical, if reluctant, acceptance of realistic conclusions.

But she considered her opinions advanced. *Testament of Youth*, London, Victor Gollancz, 1948 edn, p. 401.

20 May Jones (born 1912), first interview, p. 14 (Note: this and subsequent interviews cited without an archival reference were conducted by myself and are in my possession.) Doris Knight was ten years old in 1927 when she first noticed the

> 'unfortunate girls' as they were called. They used to go for walks along Upper Clapton with a Salvation Army lady at the front of the line. I could never make out why they . . . were all the same shape. Of course, they were the unmarried mothers who were then kept in the hostel awaiting the birth of their babies. . . . Most girls then, you see, were turned out of their homes if they became pregnant, but they could have the babies adopted six weeks after they were born and go back to their parents if they would have them. Not many girls kept their babies in those days if the fathers did not marry them. . . . Mind you, plenty of parents kept their daughters at home even if they had 'got into trouble' as they called it, and plenty of it was hushed up, as it was an episode in their lives for which they were ashamed.
>
> (*Millfields Memories*, London, Centreprise, 1976, p. 24)

21 Marie Stopes claimed that her *The Human Body* (1926), was the first popular book on general physiology in which the sex organs were described and illustrated (Marie C. Stopes, *Marriage in My Time*, London, Rich and Cowan, 1935).

22 David Vincent, *Bread, Knowledge and Freedom, A Study of Nineteenth Century Working Class Autobiography*, London, Methuen, 1981, pp. 40–6, attributed the reticence (men's mostly, only six women's autobiographies had come to light) to

the limited sources of emotional expression so that language proved inadequate, or fell back on biblical phrases; private emotions and family life were private and it was not considered appropriate or of interest to the public to speak of love, marriage or family life. Elizabeth Roberts, *A Woman's Place, An Oral History of Working Class Women, 1890–1940*, Oxford, Basil Blackwell, 1984, ch. 3.

23 John Burnett, *Destiny Obscure, Autobiographies of Childhood, Education and Family from the 1820s to the 1920s*, Harmondsworth, Penguin, 1984, p. 17.

24 Mr A.F., tape-recorded interview, Island History Trust, Isle of Dogs, London, p. 3:

> Parents were . . . very much concerned with the business of keeping a home and earning a living and that sort of thing and so life was a bit austere and it was not a common thing to find the sort of bond of affection between parents and children in the 1920s that one finds today.

25 Allen Hutt, *The Condition of the Working Class in Britain*, London, Martin Lawrence, 1933, p. 158; May Smith, second interview, p. 12, mentions incest. Mrs N.B., tape-recorded interview, Island History Trust, for an example of a family absorbing two 'love-children' of one daughter, and the dramatic emotional effects of discovery.

26 Roberts, *A Woman's Place*, pp. 72–80, ch. 3.

27 Angela Rodaway, *A London Childhood*, London, Virago edn, 1985 (first published 1960), pp. 21–3, 142, 52.

28 Celia Wilmot (born 1914), first interview, p. 1.

29 A full discussion of 'the shock of birth' is given in Ellen Ross, *Love and Toil, Motherhood in Outcast London, 1870–1918*, Oxford, Oxford University Press, 1994, ch. 5.

30 Robert Graves, *Goodbye to All That*, Harmondsworth, Penguin, 1929, pp. 228, 237; Margaret Cole, *Growing Up into Revolution*, London, Longman Green, 1949, p. 35; Frances Partridge, *Memories*, London, Victor Gollancz, 1981, p. 63.

31 Sidney Webb, 'Women's wages', in Sidney and Beatrice Webb, *Problems of Modern Industry*, London, Longman, 1902, pp. 78–9.

32 Rodaway, *A London Childhood*, p. 96.

33 Winifred Foley, *A Child in the Forest*, London, Futura, 1974, chs 10, 11.

34 ibid.

35 In the sense that 99 per cent of brides and grooms had 'gained sufficient command over the technology of communication at least to sign the marriage register': David Vincent, *Literacy and Popular Culture, England 1750–1914*, Cambridge, Cambridge University Press, 1989, p. 1, and p. 19 for literacy's limits.

36 May Jones, first interview, p. 11. Rose Gamble, *Chelsea Child*, London, Ariel Books, 1979, p. 12, describes her father taunting her mother for her 'ignorance'.

37 Gamble, *Chelsea Child*, p. 59; Rodaway, *A London Childhood*, p. 38.

38 Edith Hall, *Canary Girls and Stockpots*, Luton, WEA, 1977, p. 15. Another girl, Olive,

> cried when her soldier boy was reported missing. She admitted that she was in trouble but said she was glad in one way that she would have something to remember him by. She later bore her dead lover a son and, in bearing, died.
>
> (ibid., p. 22)

Pre-First World War memories were as traumatic. Love figured less often, and poverty was grimmer. Kathleen Woodward's mother in *Jipping Street*, London,

Longman's, Green and Co., 1928, bequeathed to her daughter a terrifying memory of the birth of a dead child,

> 'Pulled this way and that with that dead child I was; pulled inside out; everybody in the room bobbing up and down: "For the sake of God Almighty let me die!" They said I tore the doctor's coat in shreds. Fifteen weeks I was in bed after that dead child; had to crawl down the stairs on my back when I got better. . . .'
>
> (p. 6)

39 Doris M. Bailey, *Children of the Green*, London, Stepney Books, 1981, p. 46. S. Freud, 'On the sexual theories of children' (1908), *SE*, vol. 9, p. 221, for the sources of reality in children's imaginings.

40 Bailey, *Children of the Green*, p. 46; p. 18 for her father's brutal 'thumpings' when drunk.

41 Jacqueline Rose, *Why War, Psychoanalysis, Politics and the Return to Melanie Klein*, Oxford, Blackwell, 1993, pp. 89–110 problematises the distinctions between the inner and outer worlds through the relation of violence to sexual difference.

42 Sylvia Pankhurst, *Save the Mothers, A Plea for Measures to Prevent the Annual Loss*, London, A.A. Knopf, 1930.

43 'Report of an investigation into maternal mortality', cond. 5422, *PP*, vol. 11, 1936–7, p. 3. Chapter 2 gives a brief review of earlier investigations.

44 Nicky Leap and Billie Hunter, *The Midwife's Tale, An Oral History from Handywoman to Professional Midwife*, London, Scarlet Press, 1993, ch. 1, gives an account of the Midwive's Institute (1881) whose aim was to replace the informal care of maternity by local women with trained midwives. In 1918 the Maternal and Child Welfare Act encouraged local authorities to set up maternal and child welfare centres with provision for antenatal care.

45 Norman E. and Vera C. Himes, 'Birth control for the British working classes: A study of the first thousand cases to visit an English birth control clinic', reprint from *Hospital Social Service*, xix, 1929, p. 578, claims, for example that 52 per cent of all pregnancy losses recorded at their clinic were due to abortion of some type (p. 589). Some mothers of large families could not easily remember how many pregnancies they had had (pp. 586–7).

46 Leonora Eyles, *The Woman in the Little House*, London, Grant Richards, 1922, p. 15; Hubback, *Population of Britain*, pp. 57–9; Clephane, *Towards Sex Freedom*, pp. 203–5; Brittain, *Testament of Youth*, p. 409.

47 Stopes, *Married Love*, p.10.

48 Ruth Hall (ed.), *Dear Dr. Stopes, Sex in the 1920s*, Harmondsworth, Penguin, 1979, pp. 13–14 and throughout.

49 Hubback, *Population of Britain*, p. 51, writes of the interest and growing faith in science.

50 Hall (ed.), *Dear Dr. Stopes*, p. 15.

51 Margaret Llewelyn Davies (ed.) *Maternity Letters from Working Women, Collected by The Women's Co-operative Guild*, London, Virago, 1978 (first published 1915).

52 Joan Riviere, 'Womanliness as masquerade', in *The Inner World and Joan Riviere, Collected Papers, 1920–1958*, edited and with a biographical chapter by Athol Hughes, London, Karnac Books, 1991, pp. 90–102.

53 Bailey, *Children of the Green*, p. 42.

54 Woodward, *Jipping Street*, p. 48, for example.

55 S. Freud, 'Analysis terminable and interminable' (1937), *SE*, vol. 23, p. 250.

7

BLACK METROPOLIS, WHITE ENGLAND

Bill Schwarz

Some time in the mid-1930s C.L.R. James was outside the British Museum when he spotted Paul Robeson. They'd known each other since James had first arrived in London in 1932. Despite a politics which divided them – Robeson was loyal to the official Communist movement, James at this point to Trotskyism – they got on well. As James later recounted, on 'this day Paul was bothered'. The problem was that the press was speculating about a liaison between a black male singer and a female member of the royal family and Robeson was anxious lest people believed it to be him. 'It is not me', he declared with force. James was tickled by the passion of Robeson's denial, and (as the story goes) replied:

> Paul, you are a Negro from the United States; you are living in England and you say that people are linking your name to a member of the British royal family. That, my dear Paul, for you is not a scandal, it is not a disgrace. I laugh because you seem so upset about it.

And through the years this is how he says he always remembered Robeson: '*James, it isn't me.*'[1]

The charged, overdetermined construct of black masculinity echoes through these words, for in a wider public discourse the image of black men in dalliance with white princesses – English roses all – carried mythic resonance; and in many more local occasions, in backstreets and in posh suburbs, this mythic repertoire was to be called upon again and again in the years to come. Characteristically, James' response was relaxed. Robeson's wasn't. In part, this may have been to do with their distinct cultural origins. For Robeson, the memory of slavery was immediate. His father had been a slave. Born and brought up in New Jersey he always later claimed that Princeton – where he spent the bulk of his childhood – was 'spiritually located in Dixie'.[2] Despite his impressive personal authority – friends and acquaintances universally agreed on this – throughout his adult life he maintained a character founded on deference and discretion which a private rage never undid. He also knew the perils which could attend intimacy with white women. He had had a succession of white lovers, including women

176

prominent in the public eye. The year he had first met James he had been embroiled in a press scandal in which he had been accused of first sleeping with Nancy Cunard, and then with Lady Edwina Mountbatten; and later, in New York, he was to have a rendezvous interrupted by the arrival of a husband, a lawyer and an armed detective, marking, in Robeson's mind, a new and intensified moment of surveillance on the part of those who wished to destroy him. Robeson was a courageous man, but he was also wise enough to see the forces stacked against him.

James on the other hand had been formed in a different cultural milieu. Born a few miles outside Port of Spain in Trinidad at the beginning of the century, he had been inducted through the elite structures of colonial education into an institutional culture in which – nominally – race was only of secondary importance. Although, as everyone knew, the entire culture turned on the most slender refinements in ethnic appearance it was not until relatively late in his life that he was directly confronted with humiliations deriving from racial oppression – in stark contrast to the experience of Robeson both at high school and at Rutgers. James, punctilious in his courtesy, was also defiant in a way that Robeson never could be, and he excelled in making the culture of the white empire his own, turning it against those who ruled him with audacity and sophistication. When he travelled to the United States in 1938 both blacks and whites were curious – slightly bemused – for he 'didn't act like a black man'.[3]

I do not mean by this to make judgements about the relative capacities of either man: I simply think it worth keeping in mind the differing cultural worlds which formed each of them. But another issue crosses this. I like to think, sixty years on, that they were both *there*, James and Robeson chatting in Great Russell Street, where today vendors make a packet selling soft ice-cream and the memorabilia of Old England. That they were both there suggests they were a presence in English modernity, and one which would be worth exploring: in this sense their visibility becomes the precondition for historical enquiry, like the image of a photo slowly taking shape as it is printed.[4]

In the England, and more particularly the London, of the 1930s and 1940s they can be taken as representative of the larger diaspora: uneven though the geographical existence of the black metropolis was, it possessed both a reality and a powerful symbolic register. James himself, on his return from Nelson in Lancashire, spent much of his time living in Boundary Road in Swiss Cottage, temporarily holidaying in Brighton to draft his mighty denunciation of the Third International. His old friend from Trinidad, George Padmore, started out in Vauxhall Bridge Road and then moved to Guilford Street, just off Russell Square, where he was regularly visited by Eric Williams. Slightly later, Nkrumah, whom James had first met in Harlem, and then introduced by letter to Padmore in London, spent two years in Burghley Road in Kentish Town, and Seretse Khama, while outwitting mendacious Labour ministers in order to regain his chieftain-ship of the Bamangwato in Bechuanaland, lived in far from salubrious style at 34 Adolphus Road in Finsbury Park. Cold, privation and a seemingly endless lack of colour punctuate these stories as much as they do those of a later generation of black immigrants. In Manchester a less anomic life flourished, thanks to the acumen of Ras Makonnen who during the war – in between studying Anglo-Saxon history at the university – opened first his Ethiopian Teashop, followed by a chain of restaurants and then by the celebrated Cosmopolitan Club on the Oxford Road. The latter initially was run by Kenyatta, who at other times during the war found himself in the heart of the Sussex countryside in Storrington, and later still, as a lecturer at Selly Oak College in Birmingham.[5]

To think in this pointillist manner is not to everyone's taste, but it serves a purpose. In an obvious way it brings the empire 'home', to everyday and familiar locations, indicating the degree to which the colonised were positioned inside the structures of the metropolitan culture. It suggests too that the metropolis functioned not only as the administrative centre for the ruling bloc, but at the same time generated the resources for the creation of a rich array of subaltern networks of the colonised: indeed, the capital itself worked as an intellectual organiser, allowing West Africans to talk with West Indians, North Americans from Harlem with black British, fash-ioning what can only be called an effervescently hybrid political culture.[6]

In the 1930s formal resources were modest – harangues at Speaker's Corner, the movement of bundles of cyclostyled pamphlets, the inevitable meetings at Conway Hall or the Friends' Meeting House in Euston, sparing use of international airmail or telegrams.[7] But even so the traffic in people and ideas was prodigious, both within the capital and in linking London to other cities of the black world.

London still worked as the globe's premier imperial centre: vast flows of commodities passed through its docks; thousands upon thousands of white-collar workers served to manage and maintain the international law of value in the institutions of the City; official couriers carried their diplomatic bags to all corners of the earth; and even by this time 'London' could speak directly to colonial peoples on the airwaves. This complex of human communication – a dimension of the larger processes of modernisation – inevitably produced its countervailing forces. This is a difficult history to reconstruct, but we can still catch the occasional glimpse:

> In a remote village in the north of Ceylon many years ago, a group of boys, playing truant from school, crowded into the village bakery to look at their first wireless. The owner twiddled the knobs with a flourish, showing his audience how he could bring the world to his doorstep. And suddenly he stopped – at an English song – though he understood not a word. A man was singing what sounded like a

song of his people that sounded so much like their own – and he sang as though the big heart of the radio itself would break. And they fell silent, as though in prayer.[8]

The voice was Robeson's, as one of the boys who was listening discovered much later. Even when the cultural power of the empire was at its most highly centralised the black metropolis could still be heard.

In this way, in the 1930s, two dissident negroes – indeed, two different histories – could meet unexpectedly in the shadow of that great institution of imperial learning and plunder, the British Museum: the one the son of an ex-slave pastor from New Jersey, the other the son of a schoolmaster from Tunapuna in Trinidad. My purpose here is to reflect upon the impact of black cultures on the formations of English modernity. Robeson and James provide a way into this, even though they carry us at times far from England itself. We need to look a bit more closely.

Robeson's first contact with England, apart from a brief but important acting debut in July 1922, began in 1925 and continued on a regular basis until the beginning of the war. Initially he found England less racially oppressive than the United States. Through the earlier years, as befitted a West End star, he lived the high life – Chelsea and Mayfair rather than the anonymous streets of north London. Flats were rented complete with servants and silver, trips organised to Maidenhead and Ascot in the custom-built Daimler; ostentatious parties brought together US entertainers with English high society.[9] At the same time Robeson was paid handsomely – by Beaverbrook among others – for singing at private dinner parties.[10]

There was though a more radical presence in these early years – the friendship with Emma Goldmann, for example, gives a clue (they went together to see Chaplin's *The Gold Rush*); or it is significant that it was a delegation of Labour MP's who took him to the House of Commons (where he heard Stanley Baldwin). Clearly, from the start, he was one of those quintessentially modern figures – a star with progressive sympathies. And choices too were made for him. In 1929, when accompanied by Lady Colefax, he was refused entry to the Savoy, a pattern of discrimination which heightened over the next few years and which broke his illusion of a universally tolerant England. (Marcus Garvey, on his third visit to England in 1928, also testified to a deterioration in tolerance in this period.) Increasingly Robeson was thrown back on his own resources.

There is, in European terms, an orthodox element to this shift in outlook which encompasses his realisation of the historic significance of fascism, an understanding which carried him into the mainstream of conventional left politics. In his own telling he came back to two particular episodes. There is the account of him in 1933 dining (in what was then the relatively modest establishment of L'Escargot in Greek Street) with a US newspaper correspondent fresh from Berlin, and of Robeson's increasing horror the more he heard. The second episode took place a year later, *en route* to the Soviet Union. He and his – very light-skinned – wife, Essie, changed trains at Berlin's Friedrichstrasse station: such apparent racial mixing proved an outrage, and both were terrified by the looks of hateful contempt on the faces of the police and citizens – Robeson feeling in his bones the prox-imity of the lynch-mob. Whatever the complexities, by the time of the Spanish Civil War Robeson had become a militant on the left.

More pertinent to my theme, though, is the fact that he brought Harlem to London and that – in one of those imaginative leaps which makes cultural history so enticing – it was in London that, in his own words, he 'discovered Africa'.[11] Notwithstanding the ironies, singing negro spirituals in the drawing rooms of upper-class England was not entirely an innocent activity.

In order to understand Robeson's position in English culture we have to see what formed him. This requires brief discussion of Harlem, with a detour via Paris. It might appear as if I stray too far from the settled shores of England. But this is necessary: only by making such moves outwards do the inner forms of English modernity come fully into sight.

Robeson moved to Harlem in July 1919, just at the moment it was poised to become the black capital of the world. During the war it had become the focal point of rapid migration, black families choosing to uproot themselves from the small town or rural South, and from further afield in the Caribbean, drawn by the lure of jobs, wages and city life. James Weldon Johnson once witnessed a tiny moment in this continuing movement of population in Jacksonville, Florida: 'For hours they passed steadily, carrying flimsy suit-cases, new and shiny, rusty old ones, bursting at the seams, boxes and bundles and impedimenta of all sorts, including banjos, guitars, birds in cages and what not.'[12] Three years before Robeson arrived, Garvey – racing at ever greater speed from the milieu of his early Jamaican Methodism – had made the journey from Kingston to Harlem, and the effective headquarters of his Universal Negro Improvement Association made the move with him. And Garveyism, as Ras Makonnen put it, was a strategy for 'inciting you into blackness'.[13] From whichever angle one looks, Harlem betokened a new black modernity in which, for the first time, black men and women could hope to enter the modern world on their own terms. Commerce and black entrepreneurship provided one impetus. There was the Harlem of beauticians and tea-parlours, fraternal lodges and sports clubs, a lived culture in which the most knowing of a new generation made style their own. Or in rather different register, the rituals and regalia of Garveyism itself could also provide a vehicle for fash-ioning an acute consciousness of the possibilities of modern life in the urban centre of the black diaspora.

The more formal aesthetic properties which composed the cultural renaissance of Harlem in the 1920s were contested at the time, and have been contested ever since. Historically, Harlem was formed in the vortex of the uneven transitions from rural to urban, slave to citizen, folk to commercial, even – in some views – from Africa to America. The varied consequences of these antinomies are reflected in the scholarly contentions about the rediscovery of folk and oral cultural forms, and their self-conscious reinvention in an urban, modern environment.[14] Certainly, we should not be inveigled into supposing folk forms were antithetical to a modernist aesthetics. To read Alain Locke's 1925 collection, *The New Negro*, it indeed becomes clear that a European folk expressionism functioned as a kind of model, and that the theme of Africa itself remained somewhat subdued – as likely to be refracted through the conventions of European high modernism as appropriated in less mediated form.[15] But for all the fascination for European modernism among a minority, the pulse of Harlem's cultural renaissance was characteristically more vibrantly vernacular in form.

The place of folk culture is clearly central in a discussion of Harlem more generally and Robeson in particular, but is too restricted a term to encompass the range of aesthetic strategies in play: the creation of a public literature from long repressed – whispered, coded, dislocated – oral traditions inevitably resulted in many contradictions and surprises. In the founding text of the new black sensibility W.E.B. Du Bois devoted a chapter to the place of 'sorrow songs' in the making of black society – and he was present in Harlem too, in April 1925, when Robeson gave his first public performance.[16]

Yet it was precisely about the place of these older popular traditions, historically tied so powerfully to the middle passage and the plantation, that contention was most fierce. Despite the speed of Robeson's success he was not without his critics. There were objections to the revival of 'slave songs' on moral and historical grounds – that they represented a shameful past which should be transcended by the imperatives of the present and future – and there were aesthetic objections as well, dwelling on their putatively archaic or primitive forms. In 1933 Zora Neale Hurston wrote to Robeson: 'One night, Alain Locke, Langston Hughes and Louise Thompson wrassled with me nearly all night long that folk sources were not important . . . but I stuck to my guns.'[17] Yet at the same time she was also suspicious of Robeson for capitulating to commercial pressures. Two years later she was writing:

> Robeson sings Negro songs better than most, because, thank God, he lacks musical education. But we have a cathead man in Florida who can sing so that if you heard him you wouldn't want to hear [Roland] Hayes or Robeson. He hasn't the voice of either one. It is the effect.[18]

For Hurston, Beaverbrook's drawing room effectively ended the matter.

The foremost protagonists of Harlem's renaissance consistently articulated their quest in terms of the search for new aesthetic forms which would genuinely function as a new – American – universal, meaningful to white as well as to black.[19] This in part explains the difficulties surrounding an imagined Africa.[20] But one of the historic ironies arising from Harlem was that this new universalism was in fact to resonate less from the spirituals than from the more unabashed commercial forms propagated from the 1920s through the distribution of 'race records': from, in other words, the development of jazz and its transmutation into swing.

Underlying these debates – and unresolved – was the question of the proximity of black culture to nature, or (a significantly different argument despite a frequent elision) the degree to which white culture had become reified by Cartesian abstraction. The uneven and protracted process of breaking from inherited, naturalised discourses on race shadowed even the most adventurous advances in black intellectual life in these years, and these ambivalences are inseparable from the white take-up of Harlem.[21]

White patronage was a significant factor in the making of Harlem in the 1920s, and in opening up external lines of communication, first to downtown Manhattan, and then further afield – notably to Paris. Driven by many contending forces, a common element in white appropriation was the belief – or hope – that black cultures in their very workings, in their everydayness, deployed a practical critique of the imperatives of white civilisation, constituting an enclave in the modern world in which magic predominated over reason and the libido over work discipline. This, I think, was more than a voyeurism, although that was there too. If one thinks of Carl Van Vechten in New York, or Nancy Cunard in London, it is clear that the fantasies which fuelled and sustained these overtures of white to black were intense. A single taxi-ride could carry the white tourist from the inner loneliness of his or her calling to the maelstrom of modernity itself, dancing – so it might seem – on the precipice of chaos. But even so such fantasies could also be justified – intellectually – by the philosophical ambivalences in the black celebrations of blackness, which often could fall back on the habit of affirming the natural passions of the negro.

In Europe the most direct influence was on the cosmopolitan intellectual culture of Paris. 'The cream of Harlem was in Paris', as Claude McKay famously put it.[22] From the 1920s to the post-war moment of Richard Wright and James Baldwin the cultural proximity of Paris and Harlem was renowned, inviting in its later manifestations all manner of rather fanciful journalistic comment on a Left Bank conjunction of 'jazz and existentialism'.[23] If in the later years a characteristic image which comes to mind is of Wright as part of Sartre and de Beauvoir's circle immersed in philosophical debate, in the earlier period – when Robeson first settled in England – blacks from the New World were still more conveniently accommodated in the imagination of those more self-consciously modernist European intellectuals as representatives of a laudable pre-rational – or primitive – elan.[24] This was the Paris of Josephine Baker – as Claude McKay discovered when he arrived in town as a poet and earned his money by posing naked as an artist's model, as Robeson before him had done in New York.

From the perspective of pre-war Paris, Harlem could all too easily signify another strand of the modernist obsession with the primitive. The re-discovery of folk cultures which were deemed to have escaped the full impress of modern civilisation could be appropriated by a political aesthetic hostile to reason, in which there appeared a perceived, natural affinity between the irrationalism of the metropolitan avant-garde and the lived cultures of indigenous folk.[25] The most influential exponents of this thinking, in the 1930s, were the surrealists, and Breton most of all. A more isolated representative, in the English context, was Lawrence, as his excursion to Mexico shows.[26]

However, it is also valuable to see that these transactions could be turned the other way. Thus, for example, late in life Aimé Césaire insisted that one of the founding impetuses for the invention of *négritude* was not only Harlem but surrealism. It was surrealism, he claimed, which first broke the foundations of French civilisation – 'It was a weapon that exploded the French language' in his words. By this route, for him and others of his generation from the francophone Caribbean, came an imagined Africa and the belief that 'if we plumb the depths, then what we will find is funda-mentally black'. In this way, in Césaire's pithy formulation, surrealism comprised 'A plunge into the depths. It was a plunge into Africa for me.'[27]

Robeson's discovery of Africa was rather different, and remained more strictly within the vernacular forms he had first become acquainted with in Harlem, even if the final conceptual destination was rather similar to Césaire's. I think the route from Harlem to London also produced its own distinctive traits, although some broad motifs of the more general experi-ence recurred.

Throughout his time in London it was common for all those who came across Robeson to remark on the elemental qualities of his persona and physique, as if he personified a culture unsullied by the mechanics of moder-nity. As his biographer, Martin Bauml Duberman, likes to point out, male theatre critics in England invariably called upon a barely suppressed homo-erotic vocabulary to describe his performances, which consistently had him baring his torso. The critic for the *Daily Graphic* stated in May 1931, when Robeson was in *Othello* with Peggy Ashcroft, 'That Mr Robeson should be stripped to the waist is my first demand of any play in which he appears' – and thirty years later notices still expressed disappointment that, this time under Tony Richardson's direction, his natural passions as Iago had been curbed.[28] Yet the spell of the primitive never quite faded from his public persona, and was most probably a factor which contributed to the destruction of the private self. But this was different in tone from the intellectualised rapture of a white avant-garde for the primitivism of black.

In Robeson there is nothing quite as tantalising as Césaire's regard for surrealism. His engagement with the avant-garde was restrained. He did, it is true, participate in an experimental film made by Kenneth Macpherson and the *Close-up* group. This was shown at the Academy cinema in 1930: the public response was hostile, although G.W. Pabst, on the point of directing *Kamaradschaft*, was a lonely enthusiast. Essie, who acted with Robeson in the film, described it as 'one of these very advanced expressionistic things in the Russian–German manner', and claimed that their involvement in it was 'a lark'.[29] This was, for Robeson, more memorably the time of Hammerstein and Kern's *Show Boat*, which had opened in London in 1928 and which was about as far removed from a purposively avant-garde modernism as one could imagine; and it was in *Show Boat* that he sang his most famous, all New York, slave song.

There is a tangle of issues here. From his very earliest days in Harlem Robeson had condemned the commercialisation of black culture, and for the greater part of his life remained suspicious of jazz, believing it represented no more than the commodification of the negro in the age of mass culture.[30] Frequently he denounced his own impresarios and, as much as any 1970s supergroup, incessantly vowed that he would perform for these sharks no more. But not only was he a commercial artist, he was also the most prominent black entertainer performing for white audiences. That Robeson lived out these contradictions in a state of peculiarly public exposure imposed heavy costs on him. But I think what held the conflicting demands in place was a powerful sense of the impact of popular forms, a conviction which carried a political faith in the vernacular which had dominated the debates in Harlem and which, intellectually, had shaped him.

As he moved closer to Communism through the 1930s, so at the same time he came to be increasingly preoccupied with Africa. Between 1934 and 1936 he wrote a number of key articles on black culture, the most significant of which were published in the *Spectator* – which may indicate a sense of the more unexpected routes by which Harlem came to be known in England. With enviable energy, he and Essie devoted themselves to serious research: he at London's School of Oriental and African Studies, where with apparent ease he picked up a clutch of new languages, and she at the London School of Economics, where she studied anthropology. Carrying the provocative title, 'I want to be an African', in one of the sharpest of these articles Robeson declared: 'in my music, my plays, my films I want to carry always the central idea: to be African'.[31] As James recalls, this is what Robeson was always talking about at the time. To him the connections binding Africa to the black experience of the New World were direct: as he became increasingly knowledgeable about African languages, the learning brought with it revelation. 'It was to me like a home-coming, and I felt that I had penetrated the core of African culture. I began to study the legendary traditions, folksong and folklore of the West African Negro.'[32] For a short moment, Africa – in Robeson's imagination – served as the principal, perhaps even the sole, source for black civilisation wherever it was to be found in the geographies of modernity.

At the height of this enthusiasm for Africa Robeson became involved in the making of Alexander Korda's *Sanders of the River*. Initially he was excited by Korda's serious engagement with the African themes – demonstrated by the vast amount of footage devoted to ethnographic reconstructions of various central African peoples, and a commensurate amount of recorded music. Kenyatta too, who had a bit part in the film and who was conducting his own anthropological studies in East Africa, shared this excitement.[33] In the event, like many of Robeson's commercial ventures, it all went horribly wrong. The final cut represented little more than a vindication of the colonial authority of the white man, although it also looked as if the domestic mores of Guildford or Godalming – intense discussion of the appropriate schooling to allow one's offspring to 'get on' in life – had universal appeal in the mud huts of the inevitable 'African kraal'.

There is a photograph of Robeson and Kenyatta on set. Kenyatta, the black African statesman in the making, is dressed in the attire of thirties smart-casual – impeccably Western; Robeson, from New Jersey, wears the simulated costume of an African prince deemed appropriate by the conventions of the film industry of the time – basically, Tarzan wear – and looks mightily uncomfortable.[34] For a black North American in London, 'penetrating the core of African culture' was a more perilous business than it had first appeared.

Robeson's discovery of Africa imperceptibly transmuted into a rather different sensibility. Maybe this was due to the fiasco of *Sanders of the River*, or maybe it reflected shifts in the larger political world.[35] But from the mid-1930s his repertoire expanded to include songs in Chinese, Russian and Hebrew, and thence an ever greater diversity. Through the invention of a politically charged folk internationalism he overrode – to a degree at any rate – the inherited fixity between folk culture and a single, irreducibly conceived national–ethnic identity. And through this medium he was, in the local institutions of the labour movement and in the wider media created by the expansion of mass culture, able publicly to affirm the dignity of the racially oppressed. Though vulnerable to critique from the desiderata of current high theory, all those who ever heard him sing insist time and again how moving an experience it was: the being, the voice and the history combined to produce an emotional force not easily transcribed into appropriate conceptual categories.

The theorisations underpinning Robeson's views in this period were fired by some pretty simple faiths. When, in June 1934, he identified the culture of West Africa as his own, he also stated too that the negro was 'radically different from the white man in his mental and emotional structure'. In the course of the next couple of years this primordial division, separating white from black, was opened up in his writings. He became more explicit in recognising structures of exploitation inside the white cultures of Europe – and became as likely to refer to women and Jews alongside the working class. And he identified a historical moment in which the contemporary origins of exploitation could be sought. This was less slavery itself than the form of civilisation which gave rise to it. With increasing focus the enemy assumed the disposition of 'Western bourgeois man', as he put it in an article of 1936 which took the title 'Primitives'. On the one hand, he positioned the European renaissance and the concomitant structures of rationality and abstraction; on the other, those vernacular cultures of non-European peoples which had managed to resist the servitude imposed by white civilisation, and from which the white man must now learn. His was a reading of capitalism with race placed at the centre: the consequence of the European renaissance, he argued, 'has been a race which conquered Nature and now rules the world'.[36]

In fact, the rationale which organised his judgement about various folk or popular forms, and often his own place within them, derived less from any formal aesthetic criteria than from a principled but fast-moving conception of cultural politics. Within these terms apparently heterodox forms could be combined – black and white, folk and commercial. There were limits to this in theory, as his condemnation of jazz suggests, and in practice, as his role in *Sanders of the River* confirms. Even so he could embrace Eisenstein, whose experimental cinema brought to light the aspirations of the peasantry of Russia, and in that respect was for him a qualitatively different project from the conventional avant-garde of Paris or London. Robeson's first visit to Moscow was in order to meet again with Eisenstein – they had first met in a Harlem club – and to prepare C.L.R. James' *Touissant L'Ouverture* for the cinema. But with equal enthusiasm, if strangely to a contemporary English sensibility, he could laud the 'folk-culture of Lancashire which has given to England and the world the artistry of dear Gracie Fields'.[37]

It is tempting at this point to carry the story forward to Robeson's return to the United States and to his increasingly outspoken attacks on what he deliberately termed American fascism, both at home and abroad. To do this justice it would be necessary to look also at the subjective dimensions, for as you read his writings of the 1940s you can almost feel him internalising the terror which he saw all about him, the lynchings and the labyrinthine administrative forces of the Cold War crushing the life out of him. It is indeed telling that the figure heralded as the apogee of 'socialist man' should have ended his life doped with largactyl and paraldehyde, his brain broken by ECT. If the experience of modernity brings with it a maelstrom of perils and pleasures, Robeson knew each in abundance.

But this still leaves one or two questions. The first concerns recognition of Robeson's place within the culture of English modernity. I have hinted at this already. It could be reconstructed empirically, from the poll of 1937, in which he was voted the most popular singer on British radio, through to later television appearances on *Sunday Night at the London Palladium* and *This is Your Life*. Or to shift the ground slightly to a more qualitative mode of enquiry, it seems certain that for a particular generation, especially but not exclusively for those active in the labour movement, a perception of Robeson commonly provided a potent means by which – for white English men and women – the possibilities of the modern world came to be internally recognised, known, judged and felt. Even today, individual memories remain extraordinarily sharp: *Othello* at Stratford; the CND rally in Trafalgar Square; 'Joe Hill' at Harry Pollitt's funeral. English memories of becoming modern, and of first becoming aware of race, can still work through the figure of Robeson. Time and again conversation reveals those born, say, in the 1920s or 1930s, to have stashed under the stairs their old Robeson 78s; or in more public form, those habituated to *Desert Island Discs* can soon spot the moment when he will be called upon. What all this means, especially in terms of race and ethnicity, remains open. (We

Figure 7.1 Paul Robeson leaving Waterloo Station on the boat train, *The Majestic*, 1935

Source: © Hulton Deutsch Collection Limited

187

should remember that the capacity of folk to imagine a primal past – any primal past – does not necessarily require affiliation to *particular* roots in order to have an effect, as canny TV producers in the 1950s and 1960s appreciated.) My own sense is only this: unevenly, perhaps temporarily, Robeson the public star interrupted the usual flow of narratives which served to make up the complexions of English ethnicity.[38] Historically, this represented an early moment when black concerns first began moving directly to the centre of the internal culture of England itself. What followed could take many forms.

In other respects argument can be made on surer ground. A peculiar feature of Robeson's life which carries him out of any national – certainly any English – frame was his capacity to cross cultural boundaries. We might think of him on *Val Parnell's Sunday Night at the London Palladium* or eulogising Gracie Fields; but he was also close to Nehru and Kenyatta, and knew Nkrumah and Manley; he met on social occasions Khrushchev and many leading Soviet figures; his paths crossed those of Gertrude Stein, Virginia Woolf, Rebecca West and Vera Brittain; Dizzy Gillespie and Thelonious Monk were friends, as were Noel Coward and Peggy Ashcroft; at his death in 1976 the high command of the Labour government in London felt obliged to wire their condolences; and one could go on. To his detractors, perhaps this is no more than the privilege accorded to a charming socialite. But this misses too much. (Dinner with Tukhachevsky, the great Soviet commander killed by Stalin, did not normally appear in the social calendar of London's high society.) It could be better argued that Robeson exemplified the cultural radicalism of the 'black Atlantic' – that his capacity to leap over the givens imposed by national forms derived from a deeper history, but one largely concealed from view in the English optic.

The argument here, invoking the idea of the black Atlantic, is Paul Gilroy's.[39] His is a powerful book, rich in insight both in detail and across a larger canvas. In summary terms, for the purpose of this chapter, I will extract only his most general thesis. Although conventionally disregarded, the experience of the black Atlantic – the middle passage and slavery – lies at the heart of the making of the modern world and more specifically at the heart of the making of the West. The intellectual co-ordinates which gave meaning to this history – the philosophical projections of modernity and its associated ideas of progress, the coming of a more rational, higher civilisation – can be maintained only if the black experience is repressed. The black Atlantic has been an active part of modernity since its very formation, but simultaneously it has been positioned outside the given ethical, universal norms of the West: it has more properly functioned (as Zygmunt Bauman put it in a different context) as 'the counter-culture of modernity', both within and without at the same time. In turn, this has given rise to a 'double-consciousness' among blacks of the Atlantic culture. The inspiration here lies directly with W.E.B. Du Bois, who coined the term at the start of the century to describe the 'two souls' – the American and the negro – of blacks in the USA. This black counter-culture of modernity has many virtues. It is, in its very formation, diasporic, hybrid and impure, dissolving all pretensions of a culture which creates for itself imperious myths of ethnic absolutism: it *works* by mixing and miscegenation. It is a culture characteristically based on the vernacular, where the complex cultural practices of the everyday contain within them an implicit critique of the abstractions of the ideologues of modernity. And potentially at its most creative this black counter-culture – 'gifted with second sight', in Du Bois' words – can offer a peculiarly privileged vantage point from which to see and understand the larger culture of modernity by which, and against which, it was made.[40]

Even from such a summary extrapolation it would seem to follow that a confident, sealed amalgam such as 'English modernity' may be found wanting. The logic of Gilroy's argument questions the self-evidence of each of these terms and would seem to favour the disconnection – rather than the connection – of the two. Vernacular or counter-cultural modernities ('modernism in the streets' to put it another way) in his reading would at least formally be inimical to an enclosed national or ethnic form.

These suspicions are well grounded. There is, though, a desperate confusion in terminology which now runs through this entire debate, which is as well to clear up. On the one hand the metanarrative of the West (if temporarily I can resort to such abstraction) has frequently been dubbed the project of modernity realising (or attempting to realise) the dreams and fantasies – in Robeson's terms – of 'Western bourgeois man'. Yet in authors like Marshall Berman the counter cultural forms which unleash new energies and new projects are now often described as a vernacular modernism, or modernism in the streets, or the popular experience of modernity.

The distinction which Berman and others are trying to make is crucial. But the proximity of the terms also suggests their historic interdependence, with popular forms constituted in the interstices of the larger project of the West, but simultaneously trying to imagine a new and more expansive vision which would transcend the philosophical foundations of the European bourgeois order.[41] Thus when Paul Gilroy implies that the counter-cultures of modernity in some profound manner fail to conform to the requirement of a single national or ethnic form, there is surely a truth in this. Or to put this another way: visions which subvert the drive of Western modernisation have been formed in the 'contact-zones' between the forces of modernisation and the production of its various Others – where the two intersect.[42] This is both internal (the dissident modernist cultures of women or Jews or homosexuals) and external (the moment when the empires directly confront their ethnic Others). This is I think the import of Berman's discussion of modernism in the street, or Gilroy's of the black Atlantic.[43]

Gilroy himself is alert to these complexities, as he demonstrates most clearly in his closing discussion of Judaism. But there is a temptation, from the English point of view, when thinking in these terms to hypostatise a new dichotomy between a strongly centred white England, on the one hand, and a strongly decentred black Atlantic, on the other.

At one level there is an inescapable historical truth in this opposition: if the black Atlantic works by miscegenation, the official culture of white England certainly proclaims it does not. But there are a number of caveats. Firstly, the concentration of the external determinations in the making of England is commonly underestimated. Arguably, the culture of insular England was formed as much by its overseas possessions as by the island territory; and in its own — often resoundingly reactionary — way white English ethnicity is, despite all protestations to the contrary, a hybrid, the expansion of England producing innumerable versions of England in many different locales, which have fed back and transformed the metropolis. The expansion and contraction of England require its transformation. To suppose that white English identity is fixed, nurtured in England's land-scape, is to meet the official ideologies on their own terms. The amalga-mation of variant white identities under the master-sign of England may have been conducted in the pursuit of racial truth, but the practice has always been promiscuous. Nor, given the extent of imperial England, could the culture of the colonisers ever be properly policed: its very breadth, apart from anything else, made it vulnerable to those bearers of empire who (one way or the other) 'went native', at 'home' as much as on the frontier. These observations are hardly contentious: they point only to the fact that for all its breathtaking conservatism English culture has at the same time been extraordinarily dynamic, its very dynamism generating new spaces, new contact zones, inside its own field of sovereignty.[44]

Secondly, following from this, the formation of the black Atlantic is not wholly external to the structures of English culture: its presence, seen or unseen, reverberates inside the metropolis. Thus Robeson in the 1930s, for example – as I have suggested – became part of English culture. Principally, though, this is not an empirical problem, counting the passengers from Harlem as they disembarked down the gangways, for the crucial issue is *how* at any moment the components of the black Atlantic are worked into the culture of white England, comprehending not only transaction but repression. Nor should the diasporic dimensions be underestimated. When Robeson first came to England he believed he had found a 'home' – a location where there was no racism; disillusioned, he later turned to the Soviet Union, and was sufficiently enamoured to insist that his 9-year-old son be schooled in Moscow; later still, he looked to Spain. His home-lessness, in his own imagination, could not be resolved. To say that the black Atlantic is partly lodged in England does not mean that rights of domicile are freely given.

Thirdly, there is a question of the particular national and linguistic configurations which compose the black Atlantic, and the particular routes between different centres. The intellectual traffic from New York to Paris is renowned, the connection well-travelled. For all the specificities of the black Atlantic, though, there is also something very American about the way that Paris dominates: it is characteristic that James Baldwin, with his knowing but deft perversity, discovered he was an American – 'as American as any Texas GI' – in Paris.[45] The visibility of this one, essentially northern, route should not conceal others – I am thinking especially of the Portuguese or Hispanic axis. There is too the francophone dimension, as we can see from Césaire's engagement with surrealism, or – slightly later – Fanon's with existentialism and psychoanalysis. Clearly these are intellectual as much as geographical categories, and as such they do not always remain easily contained within their national forms.[46] But nor is national form obliterated: Césaire or Fanon may have been wrestling with the heirs of Descartes; C.L.R. James, in his English idiom, was making a similar journey by reading Thackeray and studying cricket.[47]

This brings me to James, who becomes a larger figure the more I read him. He was never a media star like Robeson – unless one counts his public visibility as a cricket commentator – but as a theorist of English culture, located in the matrices both of the black Atlantic and England, he was indeed 'gifted with second sight' to a remarkable degree. From early on, he saw W.E.B. Du Bois and Richard Wright as 'people who are in Western civilization but yet are not completely a part (made to feel and themselves feeling that they are outside)' and who 'have a unique insight into their society'.[48] He too exemplifies the historic significance of a specifically black Atlantic: born in Trinidad; the boat to Britain; a fifteen-year sojourn in the United States ('I did not really understand the question of race or what real race prejudice was until I went to the United States in 1938'); deportation back to Britain; political activity in Ghana and Trinidad; Brixton; and his posthumous journey home, back to Port of Spain and Tunapuna.[49]

But unlike Robeson he never succumbed to the enticements of the putatively indigenous cultures of blacks in the West. Maybe the specificity of the Caribbean is an issue here: he was never convinced that the Caribbean represented a pure cultural antidote to the West, of either indigenous or African hue. To the contrary, from the time of *The Black Jacobins* on, he insisted that the contemporary Caribbean had been born in the interstices of modern industry, and that its peculiar features rested above all in its combination of backwardness and modernity. This is a constant theme. The West Indies, he claimed, have no 'indigenous civilization and culture'; they are located inside the structures of Western modernity; and yet the legacies of national backwardness, 'the very limitations of the past', might still 'enable us to go further'.[50] Or as he put it in a letter to John Arlott

– the two were discussing Shakespeare and James, in typical mode, was breezily debunking the authority of Granville Barker and Wilson Knight – 'West Indians are a modern people in an underdeveloped society'.[51] For James, retrieval of the primitive or indigenous credentials of black culture in the West short-circuited the legacy of the European Enlightenment – hence the import of his own emphasis on the dramatic, historical significance of *black* Jacobinism.

Yet though this position singled James out in the 1930s he nevertheless maintained that there was something intrinsic in black vernacular cultures which in itself could valuably be counterposed to the traditions of philosophical abstraction embodied in the Enlightenment. This is one of the most difficult areas of James' thought. He never sustained the argument theoretically, and his genuine radicalism is not always distinguished from hyperbole. He loved to show that he – Nello from Tunapuna – possessed a greater command of the intellectual culture of the English than the English themselves: invariably he did, but delight in his own iconoclasm could turn in on itself. At the same time he always remained the political militant, a didacticism – explaining the higher abstractions to the masses – never quite leaving him. This meant, conceptually, that corners were cut and consequently he can appear as a theoretical innocent. This is deceptive. For James' unequivocal insistence on the *modernity* of black life in the Americas signalled the decisive break from the prevailing identifications of blacks with magic, libido or primitivism; if the forms of black popular experience carried within them particular insight into the imperatives of the larger world, it was precisely because they were modern, poised – as James always thought – to make an extraordinary historical leap into the future. If he cut corners in formal philosophical argument this was partly because this is how he read the masters (Hegel especially), and partly also how he believed history moved. What lies behind this is his unparalleled prescience in grasping the increasing, irreducible centrality of the popular in constituting the organisation of modernity.

Thus when Richard Wright told him that reading Kierkegaard brought no surprises, or when James himself argued that the novels of Wilson Harris embodied within them, in practical form, the insights of Heidegger, they were paying testament to the dislocations of the black experience of modernity which from the beginning had been forced into an existence stripped of transcendental faith, stripped of metaphysics, and nourished only by its own local practices, by its own unassuming everydayness.[52] In this reading Melville's Ahab becomes the all-consuming, self-destructive figure of Western modernisation – 'living entirely in abstraction' and bringing to bear on late modernity all the terrors of totalitarianism.[53] The concreteness of James' proposed cultural–political alternative implies above all an expansion of the idea of the aesthetic – popular culture is too tired a term to describe what he means – which includes not merely the conventional artefacts of the imagination, but the body and the very principles which organise popular life; or for James the West Indian, cricket pre-eminently.[54] With characteristic flair, in a futurist recovery of the past, he looked back to classical times – to Athens and its drama – for a vision of the popular–aesthetic life of the future.

When James first arrived in England in 1932 he was headed for Nelson in Lancashire to meet up with the Trinidadian cricketer, Learie Constantine. He brought with him a deep and erudite knowledge of English Victorian culture and, appropriately, the manuscript of his first novel. Although very quickly moving to a firebrand version of Marxism, his life as a cricket correspondent for the *Manchester Guardian* and his orbiting of the Bloomsbury network made him a very English intellectual: accounts suggest that he struck a pose as a gentlemanly English aesthete, attracted to the good things in life. His first piece of writing in England, very soon published back home, recorded an encounter with Edith Sitwell, and displayed some strikingly conservative views on aesthetic matters. Somewhat later his publisher, Fredric Warburg, had this to say of him: 'Immensely amiable, he loved the flesh-pots of capitalism, fine cooking, fine clothes, fine furniture and beautiful women, without a trace of the guilty remorse to be expected from a seasoned warrior of the class war.'[55] James' Englishness is not the whole story, but there is a truth here.

As I see it, an important metamorphosis occurred when he re-crossed the Atlantic and settled in the USA: this is when the English James came irretrievably to be displaced by the James of the black Atlantic. A number of transformations took place. He became more conscious of himself as black; the intensity of his Englishness declined, and with it went his earlier disdain for Americanised mass culture; and he jettisoned his Trotskyism and vanguardism. Arguably, by seeing black America, he could see with new eyes the co-ordinates of his own Caribbean culture. If this were so it would make him a paradigmatic figure in the constellation of the black Atlantic.

But there is a further complication: if the discovery of black America allowed him to reappraise his own bearings, in a contentious move he transposed these insights to the workings of vernacular cultures in general.

Thus in his long unpublished manuscript, written at the end of 1949 and the beginning of 1950, which now takes for its title *American Civilization*, James laid out an agenda for study which anticipates in every detail the current preoccupations of cultural studies.[56] Running through the manuscript is the insistence that the institutions of mass culture – black and white – allow the expansion of subjective life from which any larger social transformation must work. The popular *itself* – even in its most pathological North American forms – becomes reconstituted for James as the arena of politico-aesthetic possibility, the only counter-cultural location from which latter-day Ahabs might be stopped in their tracks.

The clash of periphery and centre, black and white, England and America, made James. *His* 'double-consciousness' turned on the intellectual culture of England: as he wrote in the Preface to *Beyond a Boundary*, 'If the ideas originated in the West Indies it was only in England and in English life and history that I was able to track them down and test them.' Yet 'the frame of reference' that he adopted as his own was one 'that stretches east and west into the receding distance, back into the past and forward into the future'.[57] His life became an exploration of these ambivalences in which, for all their cultural power, the givens of England dissolved and new possibilities cohered.

Again, as with Robeson, an empirical response to this problem cannot take us very far. James, too, appears in many different sequences in the variant histories of English modernity, and seems to have stepped from one to the other with agility. Yet though less easily visible than Robeson his place in contemporary English culture runs much deeper. Above all, I think, it was James who brought together the raw materials of an identity which – after 1981 especially – came to be known as 'black British'. He was organic to the histories from which this culture emerged, connecting the experiences of the diaspora of the 1930s with the aspiration of new black generations in the 1970s and 1980s. In January 1981, on the eve of a succession of angry inner-city rebellions, James told an audience: 'The first thing I want to get out of your mind is that you are not visitors here . . . you belong here. You are living here, part of English society.' As he emphasised, this was not to cancel a diasporic identity with the conventional formulae of the national culture: he was, rather, connecting the given realities of location with the radicalism of the historic experience of the black Atlantic, imagining an indigenous black population propelling England into a future which otherwise would have remained unimaginable.

The theme underlying James' lecture suggests it is only the black presence which allows the formerly imperial nation fully to see itself, and thereby (in his terms) to realise its own modernity. In its own way, this is a classic Hegelian formulation elegantly turned inside out – the slave finally settling accounts with the master, forced by a profane history to do his job for him and imagine a better future for humanity at large.[58]

There is one concluding argument to develop. In order to reflect on relations between black and white in constituting the experience of modernity in England I want to look briefly at the post-war moment, and think more carefully about the mentalities of white Britain. There is much to be said here and what follows is necessarily only a sketch. James' observations were based on the existence of an indigenous black people in Britain. When he left for the United States in 1938 there was, outside a few pockets, no such *social* presence; on his return fifteen years later migration had irrevocably changed the nation's internal ethnic structure.[59]

During the war and in its immediate aftermath the black Atlantic entered a moment of precipitous transformation. Even within the United States, the collapse of the sharecropping system in the South resulted in black migration to the North of such magnitude that its most recent historian has called it 'one of the largest and most rapid mass internal movements of people in history – perhaps the greatest not caused by the immediate threat of execution or starvation', altering forever the culture of the United States.[60] To some degree, black emigration from the Caribbean to the United Kingdom paralleled this demographic shift, highlighting the continuing exodus from rural to urban which works as one of the preconditions of modernity.

The transformation in Britain was based on three distinct processes: the arrival of black colonials as either service personnel or civilians during the war; the temporary presence of black GIs from 1942 to 1945; and the first decade of immigration from the Caribbean, from 1948 to 1958. In these years the reverberations of the black Atlantic inside insular Britain became *visible* to all, with cataclysmic consequences. In an immense, protracted effort of labour, white England was forced to renegotiate – and, in most instances, to intensify – its internal frontiers, inventing a domestic culture which affected to reproduce the accommodating neighbourliness of the English, while simultaneously working to exclude the newcomers within their midst. (We might ponder the wider significance of one such encounter which derives from reports, repeated time and again, of white landladies refusing black tenants on the grounds that it was *the other* tenants who would object.) If the reflexes of English modernity quickened in the post-war world under the impact of increased prosperity and the greater commercialisation of popular culture, they were at the same time fixed by a largely regressive ethnic sensibility.

In the 1940s and 1950s black Britain came into being. There was a marked discontinuity from the black experiences of the 1930s – from those who had once huddled in front of the gas fires of their north London rooms and who, after 1945, journeyed back to their home territories for a spell in prison before taking office. The high point of this exiled culture occurred in October 1945 when the Pan-African Congress convened in Manchester (thanks again to the skills of Ras Makonnen), bringing together Du Bois, Nkrumah, Padmore and many others.[61] Thereafter they went their separate ways and Britain ceased to function as their meeting-point.

In wartime London a new black culture cohered, less cerebral than its predecessor, based on clubs and dance-halls and pubs in Soho and on Tottenham Court Road, and flourishing on hotter, more commercial black musics.[62] Transatlantic lines of communication remained active, touching not only London but pulling anonymous English towns into the wider world of black America.[63] It can be assumed that until the war the great majority of white English people would have never seen a person of colour in their lives. Many confusions followed. One West Indian, for example, encountered a group of evacuees who yelled 'Nazi! Nazi!' at her: she was struck by the realisation that they believed all Germans to be black.[64] But we possess no anthropological study of the broader reaction of white England to this transformation, and we really know very little.

Yet there are some indications of how mental maps were changing. From the very earliest moments the energy expended by government officials in attempting to determine what was acceptable gives a clue to the degree of anxiety. For example, in the autumn of 1942 – at a critical moment of the war, when Stalingrad and El Alamein were in the balance, and the popular response to the Beveridge Report galvanised the home front – the war cabinet met twice to discuss the issue of black GIs and segregation within the US troops stationed in Britain. The question of segregated latrines was debated, while Harold Macmillan supported the idea, originating from the Colonial Office, that British or empire blacks should sport a little Union Jack on their lapels in order to distinguish them from the Americans.[65] That such pedantry should preoccupy the commanding institution of the wartime state, in this critical moment, is revealing. In fact, it is indicative of a whole range of cabinet discussion on race, from the opening moments of the war in 1939 right through to the drafting of the Commonwealth Immigration Bill of 1962 which was devised with the sole purpose of restricting coloured immigration.

Or we can look at this from another perspective. At the start of the war the armed forces in Britain were still subject to an official colour bar. This was lifted – for the duration of 'the present emergency' – on 19 October 1939. In practice not very much changed, especially when it came to commissioning black service men or women. The War Office was nervous about the response of white subordinates to black officers; about potential conflicts between black and white officers, the former lacking the 'European' or 'social' traditions of the mess; and it feared too that there might be 'incidents' in the married quarters and suggested that black officers would be unable to solve the 'family and personal problems' of the men or women in their charge.[66] Or later, after the war, we find Winston Churchill worrying that the Post Office was employing too many blacks: he sent a minute to the postmaster general suggesting that this situation might entail 'some risk that difficult social problems would be created'.[67] Later still, in the early 1960s, we can witness white English people expressing doubts about the advisability of there being black milkmen, while taxi-drivers in Warwick resisted West Indians joining them because cabbing was an 'intimate business' and 'the general public would prefer to be driven by a white man'.[68] Or lastly, from the same period, there developed a wider public discourse organised to discourage the appointment of black police officers to which, in suitably equivocal form, Rab Butler lent his voice.[69]

Army officers, postal workers, milkmen, taxi-drivers, police officers – perhaps this is all depressingly obvious enough. But a number of things are suggested. Firstly, this indicates the massive psychic resistance of white England to the new black population – or more abstractly, to the culture of the black Atlantic – a resistance which could erupt often enough in explicit racial antagonism, but more frequently was articulated through more mediated processes of displacement. Secondly, it suggests the degree to which ethnic differentiation was determined by a pathological precision, in which even the post office counter could come alive in a theatre of racial imaginings, transmuting into a new frontier. And thirdly, the barely coded allusions to the erotics of race – incidents, social problems, personal problems, intimacy – illustrate what the mechanisms of British civility were unable to repress: the fear of miscegenation.

In the England of the 1940s and 1950s the language of miscegenation was the central issue in terms of white perceptions of race, defining the boundaries of England and signifying its inviolate centre which could brook no impurity. The concept itself has a long history, the notion an even longer one.[70] In domestic English culture it began to assume a new prominence from the 1930s (as we might suppose from the press attacks on Robeson), focusing particularly on the children of mixed marriages.[71] From the mid-1940s it dominates. Every autobiographical account of black migrants to Britain in this period which I have come across testifies to the fact that all pretence of English civility collapsed at the point when black men were seen to be with white women. It was in this moment, precisely, that sanctions would be unleashed and abuse and beatings begin. According to one researcher:

> The near-universal hostility towards interracial sexual relations in Britain before and during the war varied only in the vehemence of its expression. It cut across all shades of political opinion and class to such an extent that it was accepted as a fact of life that needed little or no explanation.[72]

These highly fantasised fears turned on a conception of three imagined figures: the active black man who had stepped out of place, the sexually active white woman wittingly or unwittingly courting danger, and the innocent victims of these turbulent liaisons, the children who through no fault of their own – due in fact only to the unregulated passions of their parents – belonged nowhere, and who were destined to become the lost offspring of a displaced England.

Contending images of black masculinity were at work here, deriving ultimately from a splitting within the white imagination. We can see this happening. On 22 June 1948 the *Empire Windrush* docked at Tilbury. Film footage shows stylish, exuberant West Indians, dressed in their best, ready to make their way in the world – images which were to be repeated at Victoria Station or in Southampton customs hall, where the new immigrants donned their smartest suits, their hats and gloves, to cut a dash as they crossed the final boundary.[73] The ambivalence of the response in England was there from the start. While the London *Evening Standard* carried the headline 'Welcome Home' – about one-third of the passengers on the *Windrush* were returning servicemen – those on board heard the BBC announce that were there any 'disturbances' *HMS Sheffield* was on hand to turn them back.[74] No trouble occurred and the passengers disembarked. Nearly half of them were then transported to an old bomb shelter under Clapham Common (which partly explains the later popularity of Brixton). This produced very different photographic images: domesticated black men, in their striped flannel pyjamas and slippers, neatly unpacking their cardboard suitcases deep below the English landscape.[75] These contrasting positionings – above and below, active and passive, foreign and English – were to have great effect. But even at 'his' most domesticated, immured deep within English culture, in the popular discourses of the time 'his' dangerous passions lay close to the surface, and constituted a perpetual danger to English womanhood.

Even when passive and in place, white women posed a potential threat to the extent that (like the negro) they were perceived as closer to nature and only incompletely subject to rational controls. Thus the meeting of the two subjectivities – black men and white women, each in their own way *already* problematic – could prove an explosive combination. The sexualised, abusive epithets which followed white women going out with black men were predictable, indicating the *inherent* perversity of such relations, and marking the most resonant frontier of all.

The force of all this was encapsulated, with stunning economy, in the question: 'Would you let your daughter [sister] marry a Negro?'[76] It was a formulation which condensed and skewed all the issues, and was sufficiently mobile to cross with ease the full gamut of cultural institutions, high and low alike. It underpinned discussion of national policy, recurred in the media and (so far as one can tell) appears to have had a ready purchase in the everyday cultures of lived England, opening and closing the argument in the same move.

And even when public debate slowly was being cast in cultural, rather than biological, terms – as it was from the 1960s – older nineteenth-century racial notions died hard. Suspicions of racial mixing which struggled to find a liberal sentiment, and which recognised the power of cultural difference, could still fall back on concepts of blood. Thus, for example, in a serious intellectual survey of immigration, published by a prestige publishing house well into the 1960s, the colonial writer Elspeth Huxley – having had her say on 'Would you let your daughter . . . ?' – concludes:

Each human body can take so much of someone else's blood and no more. If you overdo the transfusion, and the patient's body cannot absorb so much alien blood so quickly, reactions are set up which can, and do, prove fatal. On the other hand, the same quantity dripped in gradually will strengthen the patient. It is the same with host and immigrants.[77]

The force of such images, and their common currency, must at some level confirm the notion of an England so centred that the idea of any cultural mixing – at least on a scale sufficient to disturb what already was in place – simply could not be countenanced. Indeed, so positioned within their culture were many English men and women that even the most curious could not comprehend that black Others had an identity at all.[78] It could also be argued that racial attitudes were hardening in the 1940s and 1950s: or as George Lamming commented, 'race ceased to be a liberal speculation about life in America or South Africa and became instead a fact like the milk on your doorstep'.[79] The white riots in Nottingham and Notting Hill in September 1958 further confirm this view. (The riot in Nottingham began as a result of 'a Jamaican' opening conversation with a white woman at the bar of the Chase Tavern in the St Ann's district.) Further research is bringing to light other incidents of rioting.[80] Opinion polls and sociological surveys, from the late 1950s to the mid-1960s, tell the same story, with attitudes towards mixed marriages particularly becoming more hostile.[81] Indeed, to put this in abstract terms, one could conclude that in these years England was 're-racialised'.[82]

Certainly, from the late 1940s and through the 1950s, the internal geography of England became more intensively racialised as the colour bar developed and became more pervasive.[83] To follow Zygmunt Bauman, racism inside the polity intensified at the moment when formal (political) barriers to assimilation fell.[84]

And we should note that the rediscovery on the part of English people in this period of themselves as 'white' is as forceful a historical fact as any of the other more conventional ethnic discoveries of the 1950s and 1960s. This conscious positioning and invention of the self, with its concomitant expansion of subjectivity, marks another rendition of the popular experience of modernity. *Becoming modern* works in part by plundering the past for appropriate narratives of our selves, fabricating our contemporary selves from old stories.[85] Thus decisive here is the modernity – not the apparent archaism – of the discovery of ethnicity and of a popular white racism.[86] 'Modernism in the streets' can be transgressive in many different ways, not all of which are attractive.

As ever, the components of English modernity display a number of paradoxes: in this instance, the properties commonly associated with a popular modernism serve to hold together the imagined location of Old England, but in new conditions.[87] But this is only part of the issue. To stay within the discursive world of the debates on miscegenation and the rhetorical 'Would you let your daughter . . . ?' is to remain locked within a world with no exits, held in place by the imperatives of a (fabricated) ethnicity. And yet we know that even if hostility to mixed marriages was hegemonic or 'nearly universal' in the 1940s, by our own times things have shifted: the world still moves, and something has happened. It is important to note that the description of ideologies of miscegenation and racial mixing I have offered is dependent on a largely formal or abstract interpretation of the ways in which they worked. In a rather obvious way we can be sure that the eruption of various panics around this issue arose from responses to real incidents, either in word or deed.[88] In other words, for all the hostility and all the massing on the frontiers, men and women from different races were getting on with it: meeting, talking, dancing, making love. The fears of racist fantasies were not only imaginary.

To see the culture of the colour bar cohering in the England of the 1950s is also to see the conditions in which that culture unravelled. The new counter-cultures which arose took many forms and had many sources, but it was particularly within popular life that a more imaginative, 'phantom history' of race – of the relations between black and white – was played out: in which, in more generous spirit, modernity took to the streets once more.[89]

NOTES

1 C.L.R. James, 'Paul Robeson: black star', in his *Spheres of Existence*, London, Allison and Busby, 1980, pp. 263–4.
2 Martin Bauml Duberman, *Paul Robeson*, London, Bodley Head, 1989, p. 6. Many of the details of Robeson's life which follow have been culled from this exhaustive biography.
3 Paul Buhle, *C.L.R. James. The Artist as Revolutionary*, London, Verso, 1988, p. 74.
4 I will restrict my remarks here to the Afro-American influences: the story would of course look very different if other dimensions were present.
5 C.L.R. James I come to in a moment. Padmore, the son of an education official who converted to Islam, was a tireless worker for Pan-Africanism: first from within the Kremlin, thence from a position deeply hostile to Soviet Communism. According to James, Padmore 'had more knowledge of African political movements and more personal contacts and relations with African politicians than any man living',('Notes on the life of George Padmore', in Anna Grimshaw (ed.), *C.L.R. James Reader*, Oxford, Blackwell, Oxford, 1992, p. 289). He was born in Trinidad in 1904 and died in University College Hospital, London in 1959. Eric Williams, a third Trinidadian, was born in 1904, the son of a post office official; he won a scholarship to Oxford and then studied in the more congenial environment of Howard University. In 1956 he became prime minister of Trinidad and Tobago, and six years later led the nation to independence. He died in 1981. (As James recollected: until the arrival of Nkrumah in June 1945 it was the West Indians 'who made the African question a live question in British politics' 'Notes on Padmore', p. 293).) Kwame Nkrumah (1909–72) was first prime minister and president of independent Ghana. On the eve of independence he was coached by Louis

Armstrong's wife so he could lead off in a quickstep with the Duchess of Kent at the state ball. Jomo Kenyatta (1891–1978) was elected first president of Kenya, an office he held from 1964 until his death. Nkrumah and Kenyatta were jailed by the British, Padmore by the Nazis, and James placed under house arrest by Eric Williams.

6　An indication can be found in Hollis R. Lynch, 'Pan-African responses in the United States to British colonial rule in Africa in the 1940s', in Prosser Gifford and Wm. Roger Louis (eds), *The Transfer of Power in Africa. Decolonization, 1940–1960*, New Haven, Yale University Press, 1982; and more ambitiously, Martin Staniland, *American Intellectuals and African Nationalities, 1955-70*, New Haven, Yale University Press, 1991. Alternatively, we might reflect on a photograph of 1924 which shows a Garveyite parade on Seventh Avenue in Harlem in which a banner is carried with the inscription: 'England Would Do Well To Let Gandhi Go'.

7　Hybridity does not imply harmony – the collision of distinct histories is more likely: in August 1937 James and Padmore went to town heckling Garvey at Speaker's Corner for refusing to take a stand on the strikes in Trinidad. Rupert Lewis, *Marcus Garvey. Anti-Colonial Champion*, London, Karia Press, 1987, p. 269.

8　A. Sivanandan, 'Paul Robeson', in his *A Different Hunger. Writings on Black Resistance*, London, Pluto, 1982, pp. 79–80.

9　Robeson was not alone in these predilections. Jack Johnson, the world heavy-weight boxing champion – a black man from Galveston, Texas – fled to England in 1911 having trounced all white rivals. According to an account published in 1922, he entered 'a kingdom of high speed automobiles, white women, diamond necklaces, chicken and champagne, on each and every day'. Quoted in Michael Herbert, *Never Counted Out! The Story of Len Johnson, Manchester's Black Boxing Hero and Communist*, Manchester, Dropped Aitches Press, 1992, p. 17.

10　Radclyffe Hall's *The Well of Loneliness*, first published in 1928, represents such a scene: London, Virago, 1982, pp. 365–9.

11　Philip S. Foner (ed.), *Paul Robeson Speaks. Writings, Speeches, Interviews, 1918–74*, London, Quartet, 1978, p. 351.

12　James Weldon Johnson, 'Harlem: the cultural capital', in Alain Locke (ed.), *The New Negro*, New York, Johnson, 1968 (first published 1925), p. 305. See too his *Black Manhattan*, Salem, Ayer, 1988 (first published 1930).

13　Ras Makonnen, *Pan-Africanism from Within*, Nairobi, Oxford University Press, 1973, p. 31; and C.L.R. James, 'All of us stand on the shoulders of Marcus Garvey', ('Immigrants to Britain: formerly colonial peoples', in his *80th Birthday Lectures*, London, Race Today Publications, 1984, p. 58).

14　For long the conventional view, emphasising the conservatism or even perhaps failure of Harlem artists in their perceived desire to copy conventional European forms, has been Nathan Irvin Huggins, *Harlem Renaissance*, New York, Oxford University Press, 1971. A more interesting position came from Houston A. Baker, *Modernism and the Harlem Renaissance*, Chicago, University of Chicago Press, 1987. In emphasising speech, sound and music Baker argued that a distinct consciousness of modernity was formed, 'an enlargement of the discursive field of Afro-American possibilities', p. 73. In this reading what is too easily designated as 'folk' assumes a new pertinence. See too Kathy Ogren, '"What is Africa to me?" African strategies in the Harlem Renaissance', in Sidney Lemelle and Robin Kelly (eds), *Imagining Home. Class, Culture and Nationalism in the African Diaspora*, London, Verso, 1994.

15 Alain Locke was the first black Rhodes scholar to attend Oxford.

16 W.E.B. Du Bois, *The Souls of Black Folk*, Greenwich, Conn, Fawcett, 1961 (first published 1903).

17 Cited in Duberman, *Robeson*, p. 170. For one appealing view of Hurston: 'She provides a funky footbridge between lofty pronouncements of a public racial self-consciousness and a private (ordinarily anonymous) collective black sensibility, a sense that somebody/women had another view of things' (Michele Wallace, 'Who owns Zora Neale Hurston? Critics carve up the legend', in her *Invisibility Blues. From Pop to Theory*, London, Verso, 1990, p. 178).

18 Zora Neale Hurston, *Mules and Men*, Bloomington, Indiana University Press, 1978, p. xix.

19 See especially Alain Locke, 'The Negro spirituals', in Locke (ed.), *The New Negro*.

20 See here especially LeRoi Jones, *Blues People. Negro Music in White America*, New York, Morrow Quill, 1963, which highlights 'The one peculiar referent to the drastic change in the Negro from slavery to "citizenship" in his music' (p. x.). Jones' emphasis throughout is on the specifically black, *American* culture which emerged. Or as James Weldon Johnson put it: 'Harlem talks American, reads American, thinks American' ('Harlem: cultural capital', p. 309).

21 I am thinking especially of the concept of *négritude*, influenced by Harlem and formed in the passage between the French Antilles and Paris. The most prominent contemporary critique can be found in Edward Said, *Culture and Imperialism*, London, Chatto and Windus, 1992.

22 Claude McKay, *A Long Way From Home*, London, Pluto, 1985 (first published 1937), p. 311. See too Langston Hughes' 'When the Negro was in vogue', in his *The Big Sea. An Autobiography*, London, Pluto, 1986 (first published 1940).

23 Most recently: James Campbell, *Paris Interzone*, London, Secker and Warburg, 1994. Or as this has been put with some bite by Eric Hobsbawm (a.k.a. Francis Newton): 'jazz in America is a common language and not merely, as in France, a form of upper class slang' (*The Jazz Scene*, Harmondsworth, Penguin, 1961, p. 142).

24 The classic discussion can be found in Robert Goldwater, *Primitivism in Modern Art*, New York, Vintage, 1967 (first published 1938).

25 For suggestive reflections and considerably more detail: James Clifford, 'On ethnographic surrealism', *Comparative Studies in Society and History*, vol. 23, no. 4, 1981. This should be read alongside J. Ayo Langley, 'Pan-Africanism in Paris, 1924–36', *Journal of Modern African Studies*, vol. 7, no. 1, 1969. In terms of anthropology in the US, the influence of Franz Boas was critical. One of his students, Ruth Bunzel, declared that the only choice for those coming of age in the 1920s was to flee to Paris, sell the *Daily Worker* or study anthropology: Elazar Barkan, *The Retreat From Scientific Racism. Changing Concepts of Race in Britain and the United States Between the World Wars*, Cambridge, Cambridge University Press, 1992, p. 128.

26 Fantasies of the primitive run through the work. But *Mornings in Mexico*, Harmondsworth, Penguin, 1972, is worth consulting, as is the long review of Carl Van Vechten, published in *The Portable D.H. Lawrence*, Harmondsworth, Penguin, 1977, pp. 637–45, where he argues that the black primitive in America has been subsumed by mechanisation.

27 This is Césaire interviewed in Havana in 1967, reproduced in his *Discourse on Colonialism*, New York, Monthly Review Press, 1972, pp. 67–8. In the interview he emphasises the importance for him of both the Harlem renaissance and Paris. Alongside this we might think of Carpentier in the 1920s redis-

covering the African rhythms of Cuban popular life by listening to Stravinsky: Timothy Brennan, *Salman Rushdie and the Third World. Myths of the Nation*, London, Macmillan, 1989, p. 59.

28 Duberman, *Robeson*, p. 148, quoting from the *Daily Graphic*, 23 May 1931; and Richard Dyer, *Heavenly Bodies. Film Stars and Society*, New York, St Martin's Press, 1986, pp. 77–8.

29 Duberman, *Robeson*, pp. 130–1; and see Don Macpherson, *Traditions of Independence. British Cinema in the 1930s*, London, British Film Institute, 1980, pp. 35–9 and 167–8.

30 Foner (ed.), *Robeson Speaks*, pp. 72 and 217.

31 ibid., p. 91.

32 ibid., pp. 86–7.

33 Jomo Kenyatta, *Facing Mount Kenya. The Tribal Life of the Gikuyu*, London, Secker and Warburg, 1938. He was studying anthropology with Bronislaw Malinowski.

34 Dyer, *Heavenly Bodies*, pp. 91–2.

35 Dimitrov's role at the Seventh Congress of Comintern is important here, calling upon anti-fascist forces to appropriate for their own ends their respective national–popular traditions. However, it should be remembered that this larger shift in Communist strategy drove Padmore out of the official movement. To him it signalled an accommodation with comprador elements in colonial countries, and thereby served to reproduce the structures of imperialism. See James R. Hooker, *Black Revolutionary. George Padmore's Path from Communism to Pan-Africanism*, London, Pall Mall Press, 1967.

36 Foner (ed.), *Robeson Speaks*, pp. 87–111.

37 ibid., p. 409.

38 The impact of jazz is important here as well, and would offer a different perspective – if one were to think, for example, of Duke Ellington's tour in 1933. The creation of a specifically British jazz aficionado is imaginatively told by Simon Frith, 'Playing with real feeling: making sense of jazz in Britain', *New Formations*, no. 4, 1988, where he persuasively argues the centrality of the suburbs, and that black American music 'stands for a simple idea: that everything *real* is happening elsewhere' (p. 23).

39 Paul Gilroy, *The Black Atlantic. Modernity and Double Consciousness*, London, Verso, 1993.

40 Du Bois, *Souls of Black Folk*, pp. 16–17.

41 See especially Stuart Hall, 'The West and the rest: discourse and power', in Stuart Hall and Bram Gieben (eds), *Formations of Modernity*, Cambridge, Polity, 1992; and his 'What is this "black" in black popular culture?', in Michele Wallace and Gina Dent (eds), *Black Popular Culture*, Seattle, Bay Press, 1992.

42 This term I take from Mary Louise Pratt, *Imperial Eyes. Travel Writing and Transculturation*, London, Routledge, 1992.

43 Marshall Berman, 'The signs in the street: a response to Perry Anderson', *New Left Review*, no. 144, 1984, p. 114.

44 See Bill Schwarz (ed.), *The Expansion of England. Race, Ethnicity and Cultural History*, London, Routledge, 1996.

45 James Baldwin, 'The discovery of what it means to be an American', in his *Nobody Knows My Name. More Notes of a Native Son*, New York, Dell, 1961, p. 17. The story of white America in Paris in the 1920s is told in Malcolm Cowley, *The Exile's Return. A Literary Odyssey of the 1920s*, New York, Viking, 1974. On the other hand, the *American* pleasures of America also should not be lost. Thus Claude McKay, a Jamaican, could say:

I was in love with the large rough unclassical rhythms of American life. If I was sometimes awed by its brutal bigness, I was nonetheless fascinated by its titanic strength. I rejoiced in the lavishness of the engineering exploits and the architectural splendours of New York.

(*A Long Way From Home*, p. 244)

46 For a telling cameo, Manthia Diawara, 'Afro-kitsch', in Wallace and Dent (eds), *Black Popular Culture*.

47 I have found little evidence of white English people travelling to Harlem or other black centres outside the empire. To everyone's consternation Nancy Cunard was one: she thought Harlem resembled the Mile End Road (Anne Chisholm, *Nancy Cunard*, Harmondsworth, Penguin, 1981, p. 240). Mention must be made of Cunard's *Negro Anthology*, published by Edgell Rickword of Wishart's in 1934. This is a stunning artefact on any grounds, weighing in at some 3.5 kilos, and bringing together Harlem, high modernism, documentary accounts of racial terror and anti-colonial manifestos, laced with obeisance to Stalinism: here you can see Samuel Beckett translating from the French the latest reports on hot jazz.

48 C.L.R. James, 'Africans and Afro-Caribbeans: a personal view', *Ten:8*, vol. 16, 1984, p. 55.

49 ibid., p. 54. Here he relates his time in South Carolina, where he was identified as a black man 'but not a Negro'.

50 C.L.R. James, *The Black Jacobins. Touissant L'Ouverture and the San Domingo Revolution*, London, Allison and Busby, 1980 (first published 1938), and his *Party Politics in the West Indies*, San Juan, Trinidad, Vedic, 1962, p. 40. I have developed these themes in Bill Schwarz, 'C.L.R. James in America', *New Formations*, no. 24, 1994.

51 C.L.R. James to John Arlott, 29 December 1962, in James's *Cricket*, London, Allison and Busby, 1986, p. 110.

52 C.L.R. James, 'Black studies and the contemporary student', in his *At the Rendezvous of Victory*, London, Allison and Busby, 1984, and his *Wilson Harris. A Philosophical Approach*, St Augustine, Trinidad, University of the West Indies, 1965.

53 C.L.R. James, *Mariners, Renegades and Castaways. The Story of Herman Melville and the World We Live In*, Detroit, Bewick, 1978, p. 17.

54 See Sylvia Wynter, 'In quest of Matthew Bondsman: some notes on the Jamesian journey', in Paul Buhle (ed.), *C.L.R. James. His Life and Work*, London, Allison and Busby, 1986. Put simply, Wynter draws here from Bakhtin to read James.

55 C.L.R. James, 'An encounter with Edith Sitwell', in Grimshaw (ed.), *C.L.R. James Reader*; and Buhle, *James. Artist as Revolutionary*, p. 63. We might also think of Robeson in Harlem dressed in tweeds.

56 C.L.R. James, *American Civilization*, Oxford, Blackwell, 1993.

57 C.L.R. James, *Beyond a Boundary*, London, Hutchinson, 1986 (first published 1963), preface and p. 17. This should be read alongside LeRoi Jones, *Blues People*, published in the same year: they both turn to a practical, vernacular aesthetic to understand the transition from slavery to citizenship. Although I cannot pursue it here, James's writings on the 1963 cricket test between England and the West Indies are particularly revealing about the forms of this 'double-consciousness'. He comments on the linguistic mix of dialectic and cockney among the West Indian spectators in London. And not only does he argue that the West Indies arrived at national self-consciousness through cricket;

more problematically he suggests that West Indians needed to be recognised in the metropolis before they could recognise themselves. James, *Cricket*, pp. 115–65.

58 C.L.R. James, 'Immigrants to Britain: formerly colonial peoples', in his *80th Birthday Lectures*, p. 48. But note also the enigmatic formulation which follows, transcribed as: 'You are living in another country and you belong here.' See too Alrick Cambridge, 'C.L.R. James: freedom through history and dialectics', in Alistair Hennessy (ed.), *Intellectuals in the Twentieth-Century Caribbean*, vol. 1: *Spectre of the New Class: The Commonwealth Caribbean*, London, Macmillan, 1992.

59 Pedants may like to note that Len Johnson's father, a black seaman from Sierre Leone, worked as a waiter in Hunslet's Prince Albert Hotel: his experience of Hunslet was rather different from Richard Hoggart's. Herbert, *Never Counted Out!*, p. 4.

60 Nicholas Leman, *The Promised Land. The Great Black Migration and How it Changed America*, London, Macmillan, 1991, p. 6. In 1940 77 per cent of US blacks lived in the South; by 1970 this had dropped to 50 per cent.

61 Len Johnson was also present, as was Kenyatta as the Abyssinian delegate. See George Padmore (ed.), *History of the Pan-African Congress*, London, Hammersmith Bookshop, 1963 (first published 1947); Immanuel Geiss, *The Pan-African Movement*, London, Methuen, 1974; 'Africa speaks in Manchester', *Picture Post*, 10 November 1945, which identified Padmore as an extremist.

62 For a nice insight, Val Wilmer, 'First sultan of swing', *Independent on Sunday*, 24 February 1991. Ken 'Snakehips' Johnson was born in British Guiana, schooled in Marlow in Buckinghamshire and had his head turned in Harlem in 1935: he and his – appropriately diasporic – West Indian Dance Orchestra were in the forefront of transforming London's swing culture into something feistier and sexier.

63 See, for example, the impact of the Detroit race riot of June 1943 on black GIs based at Bamber Bridge in Lancashire, centring on the Olde Hobb Inn: Graham Smith, *When Jim Crow Met John Bull. Black American Soldiers in World War II Britain*, London, I.B. Tauris, 1987, pp. 141–4.

64 Lilian Baker's tale is recounted in Ben Bousquet and Colin Douglas, *West Indian Women at War*, London, Lawrence and Wishart, 1991, p. 130.

65 Smith, *When Jim Crow Met John Bull*, pp. 83–6.

66 Marika Sherwood, *Many Struggles. West Indian Workers and Service Personnel in Britain, 1939–45*, London, Karia Press, 1985.

67 D.W. Dean, 'Conservative governments and the restriction of Commonwealth immigration in the 1950s: the problem of constraint', *Historical Journal*, vol. 35, no. 1, 1992, p. 183. In September 1954 he sent a memo: 'Please let me have a one page minute as to what happened to 70 Jamaicans who came over 6 months ago in one ship' (p. 183).

68 Clifford Hill, *How Colour Prejudiced is Britain?*, London, Gollancz, 1965, pp. 110–13.

69 Sheila Patterson, *Dark Strangers. A Study of West Indians in London*, Harmondsworth, Penguin, 1963, p. 82. The first coloured policeman was sworn in as a 'special' in Gloucester in 1964. In the aftermath of the Notting Hill riots in 1958 George Roberts, the MP for North Kensington, suggested there should be black detectives so they could enter 'coloured clubs and houses to catch trouble-makers and halt vice rackets' (*Daily Mirror*, 2 September 1958).

70 See especially Robert J.C. Young, *Colonial Desire. Hybridity in Theory, Culture and Race*, London, Routledge, 1995.

71 In the 1930s sociological studies took off: see Paul B. Rich, *Race and Empire in British Politics*, Cambridge, Cambridge University Press, 1986. Cedric Robinson, close to Robeson and present in Manchester in 1945, described this in purple prose: 'For the bourgeois libido is agreeably excited by experts who deposit coloured horrors on the very doorstep of Balham – licentious buck niggers and sinister celestials menacing Tooting hymens and the security of roast pork and apple-sauce' (*Half-Caste*, London, Secker and Warburg, 1937, p. 14).

72 Smith, *When Jim Crow Met John Bull*, p. 188.

73 Stuart Hall, 'Reconstruction work', *Ten:8*, vol. 16, 1984.

74 Lambeth Council, *Forty Winters On. Memories of Britain's Postwar Caribbean Immigrants*, London, Lambeth Council, 1988, p. 8.

75 ibid.

76 The most widely referenced include 'Would you let your daughter marry a Negro?', *Picture Post*, 30 October 1954; and Daniel Farson's television programme, *People in Trouble*, shown in 1958. But see Michael Dutfield's account of Seretse Khama's marriage to Ruth Williams, and the extraordinary consequences: *A Marriage of Inconvenience. The Persecution of Seretse and Ruth Khama*, London, Unwin, 1990. And one might note too James Baldwin, 'In search of a majority. An address', in his *Nobody Knows My Name*.

77 Elspeth Huxley, *Back Street Worlds. A Look at Immigrants in Britain*, London, Chatto and Windus, 1964, pp. 66 and 158.

78 Thus in the summer of 1965 BBC television screened a discussion between James Baldwin, Colin MacInnes and James Mossman. The latter asked Baldwin: 'But, therefore, I still ask: who are you? You're clearly not an American in the ordinary sense of a White American, are you? You're not an American Negro; that's not an identity really.' Baldwin replied in reasonable and modest mode: 'Then I can't answer it. I'm part of a totally incoherent people at the moment, of African origin, with Indian, Spanish and European blood in my veins. I'm part of a country which has yet to discover who and what it is' ('Race, hate, sex and colour', transcribed and reproduced in *Encounter*, July 1965, p. 57). With this exchange in mind, it is little surprise that intellectuals from the diaspora have been in the forefront of advancing the concept of identity within contemporary cultural theory. See, *inter alia*, *ICA Documents 6: Identity*, London, Institute of Contemporary Arts, 1987.

79 George Lamming in the *West Indian Gazette*, 13 February 1962, quoted in Buzz Johnson, *'I Think of My Mother'. Notes on the Life and Times of Claudia Jones*, London, Karia Press, 1985, p. 84.

80 Edward Pilkington, *Beyond The Mother Country. West Indians and the Notting Hill White Riots*, London, I.B. Tauris, 1988; and David Taylor, 'The Middlesbrough race riot of 1961', *Social History*, vol. 18, no. 1, 1993.

81 Hill, *How Colour Prejudiced is Britain?*, pp. 21, 28, 31 and 38.

82 I have argued this in Bill Schwarz, '"The only white man in there". The re-racialization of England, 1956–68', in James Donald and Stephanie Donald (eds), *Identity, Authority and Democracy*, Research Papers in Media and Cultural Studies, University of Sussex, 1995.

83 Learie Constantine, *Colour Bar*, London, Stanley Paul, 1954.

84 Zygmunt Bauman, *Modernity and the Holocaust*, Cambridge, Polity, 1991.

85 In this context we might think of Phil Cohen's account of the formation of skinhead cultures in the 1960s: 'Subcultural conflict and working class community', *Working Papers in Cultural Studies*, vol. 2, 1972.

86 'The project of ethnicity is to recover something which never existed in the first place through the means of representation which are themselves responsible

for the historical discontinuities which are being denied' (Phil Cohen, *Home Rules. Reflections on Racism and Nationalism in Everyday Life*, London, New Ethnicities Unit, University of East London, 1993, p. 25).

87 Bill Schwarz, 'Englishness and the paradox of modernity', *New Formations*, no. 1, 1987.

88 Thus the phenomenon of 'the postbag', when irate racists write to complain of particular transgressions and provide an extraordinary insight into the inner workings of racist fantasies: see sections of Cunard, *Negro Anthology*; Hill, *How Colour Prejudiced is Britain?*, pp. 218–20; and arising from a different occurrence, but illuminating the same phenomenon, Diana Spearman, 'Letters of blood', *New Society*, 9 May 1968, which analysed the *hundred thousand* letters of support received by Enoch Powell in the fortnight following his so-called 'Rivers of blood' speech.

89 Dick Hebdige, *Subculture. The Meaning of Style*, London, Methuen, 1979, p. 45.

8

RE-PLACING BRITISH MUSIC

Andrew Blake

It may seem a paradox that we often experience, and even define, the modern through an increasing ache for a past which we have ourselves constructed. The invention and reinvention of tradition have been constant companions of the urge within nineteenth- and twentieth-century states to modernise: to industrialise, to electrify, to build and rebuild. As all that is solid in our metropolitan environments melts into air, we turn to a set of representations which can give us, however fleetingly, a feeling of connection with time and space. As modernity's roadscapes, factories and factory farms destroy the countryside, a landscape drawn from an imaginary past becomes increasingly important. The Victorian (or older) house, the landscape art of a Constable, the fiction of a Jane Austen, eighteenth- and nineteenth-century opera and concert music are a few of the favourite things of the English professional classes who perforce inhabit modernity but by choice also inhabit 'tradition'.[1] It is by no means, therefore, a paradox that post-industrial Britain is also Heritage Britain, a land of castles and cathedrals, country houses and agricultural theme parks, of art exhibitions and of the music festival. Music is often claimed to be among the most important of the national treasures: it is very much part of the solidities of Heritage Britain. And yet music, above all else, melts into air. . . .

Any account of music within twentieth-century British culture must confront these seeming paradoxes, and this chapter will do so by examining the continuing re-creation of a set of traditions of musical production (composition, performance, reception and associated sales and marketing activities). This is, then, a narrative, tracing cultural interaction and change through time. But the trace is not a single line. Although, for the sake of analysis, terms such as traditional, modern and modernist will be used, they do not form an account of musical 'progress'. And although classical and popular musics will be discussed, no hierarchy of musical forms or genres is constructed. Indeed the emphasis will be on the difficulties of assembling a single narrative from the multiplicity of events which constitute music within British culture. Exemplary in this regard, and one of the focal points of this chapter, is the moment of 'Thatcherism' – the ideological and political changes of the 1980s – and the contradictory impacts this has had, and continues to have, on the place of music in Britain.

A 'CLASSICAL MUSIC' TRADITION?

The tradition we now refer to as 'classical music'[2] is a conceptual product of the period of consolidation of the first industrial settlement. In Britain this was a long process of economic and social change dating from the early eighteenth century,[3] and climaxing politically in the years around the 1832 reform which restructured the political elite to include elements of the industrial bourgeoisie. These changes included the making of new relations with the past, and among them the manufacture of a musical tradition: an idea of past musics forming part of the continuous musical present. Before the nineteenth century, almost all music was contemporary; music was written and performed for specific occasions, and seldom revived. Where some forms of popular music remained strongly centred in traditions of apprenticeship and oral tradition, the music of the courts and townships, though written, was ephemeral. The eighteenth-century British revival of interest in the music of the sixteenth-century church and court, and continuing interest in the work of eighteenth-century composers like Archangelo Corelli, J.S. Bach and G.F. Handel, began to create a 'great tradition' of canonic works and associated compositional techniques. After the death of Beethoven this notion was normative throughout Europe. Mendelssohn and Weber, two of its continental instigators, were often performers in London, where organisations like the Academy for Ancient Music and the various Handel Societies had done much to establish the norm.[4]

A new tradition of concert-going was created along with this newly historicised repertoire; these connected traditions were always, as they remain, part of a modernising urban capitalism. Capital was exchanged on two levels: the cultural and the economic. Entrepreneurs, paying musicians on a freelance basis, sold tickets for events which gave the audience purchasing the tickets (including many of new wealth and status) some guaranteed cultural capital. Older forms of patronage of musicians – by individual aristocrats, the church or the town council – became less important; the rise of the freelance composer was paralleled by the rise of the middle-class audience, creating new public concert events in cities like London, Paris and Vienna.[5] Through the subscription concert, middle-class people could signal their own places, both economic and emotional, in the evolving tradition of music-making. Both aspects were important to their identities. Economically, by buying tickets they could collectively *own* performers and performances, collectively play the role of patron which was impossible to them as individuals, and thereby inhabit a specifically middle-class political economy of culture. Emotionally, as Richard Sennett has suggested, *identification* with particular, heroic performers like the pianist–composer Liszt and the violinist–composer Paganini was vitally important to an urban middle class trapped in codes of behaviour which denied them any public expressivity as individuals: reaction at concerts of these demonic performers was as hysterical as at those of today's rock concerts, and for similar reasons.[6] This identification was particularly important in the cities of England, to a middle class groping its way by the 1850s out of the gloomy fogs of Victorian 'respectability'.[7] Sennett's argument should be qualified in one respect. In the large amateur choirs which flourished in Victorian Britain, members of this group, and working-class families claiming their own 'respectability', could join in the performances of oratorios of Handel and later composers, and play, collectively, an ecstatic public role as musicians, without compromising their respectable status with the taints either of secularism or musical professionalism.[8]

Despite all this – despite the importance of music to the English middle class, as signalled by the rise of professional orchestras in the cities and the growth of the amateur choral tradition – and despite the growing importance of national identity through music signalled by the work of, for example, Mussorgsky in Russia, Wagner in Germany and Verdi in Italy – no music written by British people was accorded a place in this 'great tradition' of European composed music until late in the nineteenth century: at that point the last acknowledged representative in this Pantheon was Purcell (1659–95). To many Europeans, England remained 'das Land ohne Musik' (the land without music).[9] Even when British composers did emerge, their reputations, and, as importantly, their musical style, remained largely parochial. While in the first twenty years of the twentieth century Ives in the USA, and Mahler, Busoni, Debussy, Schoenberg and Stravinsky in Europe, were proposing their very different visions of the future of music, most British composers were still using, or tentatively developing, the musical language of the 1880s, the moment of the final re-emergence of British music after 200 years of virtual silence.

At that moment of busiest tradition inventing, the 1880s[10], we find the Irish Stanford, the Anglo-Welsh Parry and the Catholic Englishman Elgar forging a new language of musical 'Englishness', derived from the German models of Brahms and Wagner. This variant is most clearly exemplified in Elgar's use of the march, celebrating the solemn rituals of high imperialism – notably the first 'Pomp and Circumstance' march, which in its guise as the song 'Land of Hope and Glory' is still performed at the concluding moment of the only national musical celebration, the last night of the Proms concert season. At the same time English 'folk-songs' were collected and their melodies reworked into this nationalist concert music. Yet the 'folk-music' collected by Cecil Sharp and his followers was not that of the folk in the industrial towns (by far the majority of the population) but of the rural areas, especially the south-west.[11] Another common source was the composed music (for church and leisure) of the Tudor period, the 'golden age' also recreated by F.R. Leavis and his followers.[12] The ideology of Romantic anti-capitalism was clearly reinscribed in this construction, in a repetition of the paradoxical creation of a 'past' within modernisation which had seen the establishing of the classical music canon early in the nineteenth century. This paradox was a music whose presence demanded the facilities of the industrial and commercial city but which sought meaning in the rural and preindustrial.[13] Within this implicit denial of the economics of musical production, a vital tradition of specifically English composition was quickly developed from the music colleges. Early twentieth-century composers using folk and/or Tudor music included Cyril Scott, Rutland Boughton, Peter Warlock and Ralph Vaughan Williams (with others relying on Celtic sources, proclaiming their part in the creation of intra-imperial cultural nationalism: Arnold Bax using Irish music, Hamish McCunn Scottish, and Ethel Smyth Cornish, for example). This English style was developed especially after the Second World War by Michael Tippett, and by Benjamin Britten and his associates at Aldeburgh in Suffolk.

On Britten's death in 1977 his memory became almost instantaneously enshrined; because of the international success his music had enjoyed especially after 1945, he was seen as a great British composer, symbol of the fact that Britain had indeed played a part in this particular aspect of European heritage culture. Again, as I have argued elsewhere,[14] the particular construction of the musical tradition symbolised by Aldeburgh is of creative activity somehow divorced from socio-economic processes, including those of domestic life. (This implicitly masculine model of the lonely creator divorced from 'normal' society, is perhaps one of the reasons for the importance of gay men in twentieth-century English music; a construction only recently and tentatively explored in mainstream music criticism.[15]) The very place of Aldeburgh, a small town on the Suffolk coast, reinforces this sense of divorce from the everyday transactions of life, including the commercial. Britten was in fact a fully professional composer – by and large, his music was commissioned or it did not get written. Much of his success was due to the support he received in the 1930s from the new patrons, the BBC, and from the 1950s on from Faber music publishers and from the Decca record company, two London-based commercial organisations which marketed his work. But there is no place for these economic facts in this version of the theory of national genius.

An English musical 'tradition', then, had been both constructed and confirmed during the twentieth century – and in this chapter the musical products of this complex cultural moment will be called *traditional*. Precisely in its appeal to 'tradition' it is a crucial way through which many middle-class people have experienced modernity. The cultural confusion engendered by continuing transformations – of, for example, the steam and internal combustion engines, the chemical industries and microelectronics, with their massive impacts on lives and work experience – are offset by the creation of a past peopled with heroic figures and great works, which speak to them of essential national and local identities. The constant re-creation of musical tradition continues to offer a vital source of identity, one celebrated at national and local levels by a bewildering number of music festivals, including that at Aldeburgh.[16]

AN ENGLISH MODERNIST MUSIC?

And yet one shrine does not make a church. Aldeburgh is only one arm of musical tradition in England, if the most stable. Two other trends within British classical music should be noted. Firstly, in the interwar years, there were composers who used aspects of the international and especially the American popular music scene, notably jazz and related African–American musics. The products of this stylistic interaction will be called *modern* in this chapter. Sir William Walton, for example, used jazz rhythms and instruments, most notoriously in *Façade* (1922), his piece for reciters and musicians, setting the poetry of the Sitwells; the rhythms of jazz and dance music are never far away in his concerto for viola (1929) and even in the oratorio *Belshazzar's Feast* (1931). Similarly, Sir Michael Tippett's oratorio *A Child of Our Time* (1941) used spirituals as an equivalent for the chorale in the Bach cantatas. Tippett's music, while clearly indebted to Tudor sources, continues to show the clear influence of the blues, jazz and other African–American musics: his opera *The Ice Break* (1976) purveys a universalist message through an attempted mesh with the form 'rock opera' (launched in the 1960s with shows like *Hair*, and popularised in England and worldwide by Andrew Lloyd Webber's work from *Jesus Christ Superstar* onwards). Both Tippett and Walton turned to African–American music from within the musical languages and forms of the nationalist tradition: there was, then, a 'popular modernism' to complement the music of the English tradition – a popular modernism which had resonances in the work of European composers like Kurt Weill, Paul Hindemith and Ernst Krenek, and Americans like George Gershwin and Aaron Copland, in all of whom a mix of vernacular voices became part of the composing style, often for political reasons.[17]

Secondly, there was the gradual emergence in England of musical composition in the pan-European style of 'high Modernism', pioneered in Austria by Arnold Schoenberg and his pupils. This music involved a denial of *tonality*, the organising principle of all European music since the eighteenth century. European musical modernism thus parallels the rejection of perspective and other realist notions in modernist art, and the similar rejection of realist techniques in modernist writing; it was from the start deeply unpopular with audiences. Before the Second World War there was very little high Modernism in British music: thereafter this style gradually achieved a kind of hegemony within the arts establishment of programme directors and critics – the new patronage system. Here this style of music-making will be called *Modernist* – the capital 'M' denoting its difference from the Americanised popular modernism of Walton *et al.* After the Second World War the education system, the BBC, and the Arts Council combined to valorise this version of the European music tradition, a narrative of 'progress' based upon consequent development through the works of succeeding generations of German and Austrian composers (for example, Bach, Beethoven, Brahms, Schoenberg, Webern, Stockhausen).

The coherence of this Great Tradition of musical composition proved attractive to the meritocrats (influenced by Reith and Leavis) reordering British society after 1945. The pyramid structure of music education was based, in this post-1945 settlement, on the teaching of music performance and appreciation to all at junior level. In senior schools, however, the skills and techniques of classical music appreciation, performance and composition were taught only to those who were judged to display outstanding talent. Popular music was ignored. At the tertiary level, musicians with acceptable school qualifications were taught in state-funded colleges and universities. If judged by their elders to be successful, they graduated to work in a twilight world of state-funded support for performances and commissions for new compositions (from the central and local arts councils and from the BBC). The less 'successful', including those less committed to either Modernist or traditional styles, could find more financially rewarding work in film, radio and television. The unsuccessful, those who had studied music but had been weeded out either at school or college, were constructed as sensitive appreciators of music, much as students of English literature were constructed as sensitive readers rather than as writers. Most pupils were completely untouched by this process from secondary school onwards: classical music remained hedged by impenetrable boundaries of class and taste. The appreciation, performance and composition of music, indeed the very meaning of the word 'music', thus tended to be very different for the majority of the population than for the minority of trained musicians and appreciators.[18]

However, as the above analysis of traditional, modern and Modernist styles indicates, within that minority itself there were serious subdivisions. Between the university-educated composer and the A-level 'appreciator' there arose, from the 1960s on, increasingly bitter differences of emphasis. The general concert-going public, still wedded to the heroic, individualist notion of music implicit in the sonata models explored by Beethoven, and the subsequent tradition of emotionally engaged virtuoso performance, was uninterested in the technically able but (apparently) emotionally arid manipulations of composers given prominence throughout Europe after 1945, such as Karlheinz Stockhausen, Pierre Boulez and Iannis Xenakis. One explanation for the success of these *enfants terribles* will be hazarded: for forty years the products of this avant-garde had remained on the fringes of European music. This meant that they were unsullied with the taints of nationalism, and especially Nazism, and were therefore embraced as a new, pure, musical language after the Second World War.

Although this movement was late arriving in Britain,[19] musical Modernism became entrenched through the 1960s expansion of the universities (notably Sussex, York and Leeds), and by the late 1960s its apostles (for example, the composer Elizabeth Lutyens and the BBC Radio Three controller of music William Glock) were in high places in British musical life. Largely university-educated, possessed of the self-confidence of the expert, often indeed with contempt for the audience whose tastes they could bypass by means of subsidy, most of the new composers and administrators were suspicious of the folk-song derived musical traditionalism of the previous generation, and many thought of jazz and pop musics in an Adornoesque way as American mass culture;[20] so there was no interest in Walton–Tippett modernist music either. They were committed instead to the writing of music via the operations of pure mathematics ('total serialism') or pure chance ('aleatoric music'), and to the development of electronic musics. Glock enthusiastically championed the Modernists, appointing Boulez to the post of chief conductor of the BBC Symphony Orchestra in 1970 with a brief to perform as much of the new music as possible.[21]

The public remained unconvinced, and often actively hostile. Apart from the BBC Symphony Orchestra, 'new music' became the preserve of small, specialist performing ensembles, and equally small, specialist audiences. It continued to attract the support of the Arts Council and BBC, whose Radio Three network under Glock and his successors broadcast a great deal of Modernist contemporary music, arguably at the expense of the nationalist music of the 'tradition', certainly to the apoplectic rage of an increasingly vocal group of 'appreciators'.

The publication in 1991 of Glock's autobiography raised the public profile of the 'traditionalist' lobby group. Glock admitted that he had ignored the claims for air time of the composers they liked, putting forward the classic Reithian view that he had given the audience not what they liked but 'what they would like tomorrow';[22] while debate over these revelations was fresh, the then current director of the Proms season, John Drummond, repeated this position of contempt for the Radio Three audience.[23] The traditionalists, led by the conservative anti-establishment historian Corelli Barnett, argued for the continuity of music with the past, using a Burkean notion of the decisive role of tradition, rather than the Painean version of the use of first principles, in the creation of cultural products.[24] They demanded the dismemberment of Radio Three in recompense for this confirmation. One government response was to sanction the creation of a new national radio station to broadcast 'light' classical music (mainly of c. 1700–1850) in assumed opposition to the elitist BBC network.

Classic FM duly began to operate in September 1992, and quickly found an audience big enough for its advertisers, overtaking Radio Three within six months and by early 1994 regularly reaching 4.5 million listeners weekly against Radio Three's 2.75 million. Thriving in its populist mission to bring 'the world's most beautiful music' to an audience more convinced of the commodity value than the absolute status of cultural products, Classic FM established a national chart, along pop lines, with a weekly run-down show in which compilations of snippets rub shoulders with more arcane material that the channel has chosen to promote – most spectacularly, in 1992–3, the third Symphony of the contemporary Polish composer Henryk Górecki. Radio Three's response was to stress its own diversity and eclecticism in reworking the channel's output from mid-1992 in what its controller avowed was a more 'downmarket' direction, upsetting many regular listeners by running commuter-hour chat shows, and by making the composer of musicals, Stephen Sondheim, 'composer of the week' to signal this change.[25] Subsequent composers of the week have included Duke Ellington and Jerome Kern. Classical music on radio has changed, but not as some of its detractors wished.

In the venom of their attacks on Radio Three and the BBC's Proms concert seasons the conservative appreciators shared one obsession at least with the former prime minister, Margaret Thatcher. Certainly Thatcherism's stresses on privatisation, and on an imaginary national entrepreneurial spirit (an implication of the commercial with the cultural deeply imbedded within the new 'heritage culture' of the 1980s), helped to open the space within which the new musical conservatism could campaign against Modernist music. In their attack the musical conservatives could both call on their 'tradition' as an aspect of Englishness which should be continually available, and point to its recent, specifically commercial, successes.[26]

The Chandos record company, for instance, was astonished at the high sales figures for its recordings of symphonies by Sir Arnold Bax, a composer in the traditional style (making wide use of Irish folk music) whose music had been virtually ignored by the Glock BBC. Sales in the new, highly profitable CD format were particularly impressive, and the Chandos label has since embarked on another large-scale project to record the works of an underexposed English composer, Edmund Rubbra. By itself this success hardly falls within the purview of Thatcherism, at least in its populist sense. Chandos is a specialist hi-fi label. 'Hi-fi' in Britain is a hobby aimed primarily at middle-class men with sufficient wealth and leisure to search for and purchase equipment delivering the perfect sound – perfection usually (thus 'high fidelity') considered as the simulacrum of the voice and/or instruments making the recording (rather than the ability to remix, filter, distort or otherwise process the sound to one's own satisfaction, as with the reggae 'sound system', for example). The Bax symphony recordings, with their wide dynamic range, were rather good at demonstrating hi-fi, as the discursive constructions of hi-fi man, magazines like the *Gramophone* and *HiFi News And Record Review*, implied.

Even more commercially impressive during the 1980s was the revival of interest in opera.[27] Again, CD and video sales rose sharply, but there was also increasing demand for live performance. From about 1985, demand for tickets at the Royal Opera House began to exceed supply for even the most ordinary performances, while the rival English National Opera reached the height of its popularity. Touring opera companies were in increasing demand. In 1989 promoter Harvey Goldsmith mounted a production of Bizet's *Carmen* at the vast Earl's Court indoor arena in London. It made money, and further stadium promotions of Verdi's *Aida* and Puccini's *Turandot* were planned. Then the BBC chose as their signature tune for the 1990 football World Cup, the aria 'Nessun Dorma' from *Turandot*, sung by the Italian tenor Luciano Pavarotti. A concurrent single release of Pavarotti's rendition of this aria reached number two in the British pop charts; a concert by the three leading tenors, Pavarotti, Placido Domingo and José Carreras, broadcast worldwide live from Rome during the World Cup, realised enormous sales in follow-up recordings: a phenomenon repeated note for note (in both senses) during the 1994 World Cup held in the USA. We return once again to the basic paradox opened out at the start of the chapter: music from within the European tradition was fuelling the commercial modernity of the global leisure industry.[28]

The 1980s saw a renewed drive to achieve just this, as all the major record companies with classical recording interests began to market their products more aggressively, seeking markets other than the affluent, middle-aged, male, hi-fi enthusiast.[29] This incorporated image-making for performers. Young female performers like the singers Ute Lemper and Cecilia Bartoli and the cellist Ofra Harnoy were photographed as sexualised models.[30] The young(ish) male violinist Nigel Kennedy was remade as a punk(ish) populist, complete with spiked hair and cockneyfied accent seen and heard to good effect on one or two television advertisements; his chosen promotions included appearances at football matches. Kennedy's recordings of Vivaldi, Mendelssohn and Brahms concertos entered the pop album charts, despite the snobbish contempt of critics' reviews in the hi-fi magazines and broadsheet papers. An orchestra of young players, the London Chamber Orchestra, even tried to capitalise on Kennedy's success by promoting a series of concerts of classical music using the lights and amplification of the rock concert, promising that the result would be 'seriously loud' (it wasn't).[31] The Great Musical Tradition, so deliberately uncommercial in the hands of the BBC, the Arts Council and the Aldeburgh myth, was itself being used iconoclastically, against its elitist appropriation and for mass sales, in a way which Walter Benjamin would no doubt have noticed with satisfaction.[32]

OTHER PRESENCES: POP/ULATION CHANGES

As it happens, the high moment of nationalist music-making and the establishing of the great musical tradition with its implicitly anti-commercial ideology had already been subverted well before the 1980s, not by the institutional success of subsidised Modernist composition, but by two other aspects of British musical life: by the enormous, international, commercial success of British pop music since the early 1960s; and by the arrival in Britain since 1945 of musicians and musics from the former colonial and imperial territories, including the West Indies, India and South Africa. Both aspects involve moments of cultural miscegenation which have been massively productive for the development of British music; both involve continued negotiation with American culture, negotiation of the type which produced the modernism of Walton *et al.*, and had also produced a large part of the English light music scene in the interwar period.

British popular music displays its own continuities of tradition, its own engagement with American modernity and with technological modernism. Much work has been done on music-hall before the 1920s, but the popular musics of the interwar years await their historian. What follows is necessarily therefore only a sketch map of connections rather than a sustained analysis. Since it involves a tradition of songwriting which can be traced through bands like the Beatles and the Kinks in the 1960s, and Squeeze in the early 1980s, to Blur in the 1990s, the music-hall tradition is still alive.[33] Music-hall artists were important in the early history of the recording industry in Britain. Indeed, light entertainers like Flanagan and Allen (on radio) and then Morecambe and Wise (on television) stretched aspects of the music-hall format into the second half of the twentieth-century. Through the related development of the vaudeville theatre, connection can also be made between aspects of music-hall and the musical theatre of the 1920s and thereafter; from which the strongest survivals are the early shows by Noel Coward, perhaps the best-known example being *Bittersweet* (1929). For some, Coward's elegant music, including many standalone songs which owe a great deal to the music-hall tradition, comes under the catch-all banner of 'light music', which also includes the range of musics from the classically-trained Ketelbey's witty melodies to Americanised 'Tin Pan Alley' models of songwriting (as for example Burton and Kent's 'White Cliffs of Dover').

In the early 1950s there was a national light music industry based on the sale of sheet music, privileging the composer rather than the performer. Artists and writers alike benefited from the protectionism of the Musicians' Union ban on American performers which had been established in the 1930s – Americans could only perform in Britain if British performers visited the USA in exchange, a restriction reciprocated by the American union. Songwriters and publishers produced material which was delivered by photogenic youngsters; the real popular music rewards were in song-writing and publishing, for both writers and publishers gained performance royalties on songs performed live or broadcast over the national repository of popular music, the BBC Light Programme. This system survived the early years of rock'n'roll. The first generation of British 'teen idols', Tommy Steele, Cliff Richard *et al.,* sang other peoples' songs, and, with an eye to long careers, became general entertainers as soon as decently possible.[34] This was a comfortable system, which though it benefited American as well as British writers and publishers, was essentially an insular, protected market. It was disrupted by the success of the Beatles, in two ways. Firstly, their success in the USA undermined the effectiveness of the reciprocal union agreements, opening the Atlantic to trade in musicians as well as music and records. British popular music became an increasingly successful export. Secondly, by the establishing of Lennon and McCartney as *songwriters* as well as performers, the primacy of Denmark Street, Soho, was also under-mined, as the career of the independent songwriter foundered, while other bands which formed around songwriters (for example, The Rolling Stones and Mick Jagger–Keith Richards, The Who and Pete Townsend, The Kinks and Ray Davies) became similarly successful. The whole economy of light music production was fractured (though not entirely broken, as the more recent success of pop svengalis Stock, Aitken and Waterman indicates).

These newly independent bands operated in the early 1960s in a climate of assumed classlessness in which talent and youth were taken by many to be the answer to the ills of a nation in long-term decline. Pop seemed indeed to provide the required tonic, especially since this success was inter-national: British music was exported worldwide, and record companies and music publishers, recording studios and session musicians based in London became leaders of the world music market for a decade.

The musical transformations behind this success story are also well-known. The major impact of rock'n'roll in Britain, with its associated emergence of the teenager as folk devil, consumer category and socio-logical subject,[35] was shadowed by the emergence of a nightclub-based connoisseur's appreciation of both country blues and urban rhythm'n'blues. The Lennon–McCartney songwriting partnership emerged from a band which did not at first attempt to create original music, but played both rock'n'roll and rhythm'n'blues – copied American models, in other words. In the case of the similarly successful Jagger–Richards writing partnership, the Rolling Stones was a band which started life playing Chicago blues and rhythm'n'blues in an attempt to duplicate these specifically African–American forms rather than the more culturally hybrid rock'n'roll, but went on to develop a more Anglicised inflection on those basic elements. This sense of dialogue between African–American forms and British pop has of course continued – with the work of singers Joe Cocker and Chris Farlowe in the late 1960s, and the Scottish bands Average White Band (in the

1970s) and Wet Wet Wet (in the late 1980s), for example, attempting to recreate the soul musics of their times within the changing commercial imperatives of the British music industry.

And yet, while this particular British–American dialogue continues, with the emergence of British hip-hop, house and techno musics among others, the continuing story of British pop cannot be characterised so simply. It is and has been since the 1950s a *multilogue*, a mixture of musics intersecting in the various urban centres to produce among other things various forms of British reggae; two-tone; Bhangra and Indi-pop; and indeed skiffle, punk and Indi-pop; with all these being constantly subject to interactive evolution and reworking. British cities have been the site of these cultural developments for two related reasons.[36] Firstly, the very success of the early 1960s pop groups made first Liverpool and then London, in particular, into world musical centres. It was to London that Jimi Hendrix came in 1966, to escape from the stereotyped role of the black r'n'b guitarist which had been afforded him in the United States, and to forge a new expressive language of guitar playing. Hendrix developed this from r'n'b, the solo guitar voices of American urban blues players like B.B. King and Buddy Guy, and the more obsessive English blues guitarists like Peter Green and Eric Clapton. This solo voice was developed within a songwriting context which did not rely merely on blues harmonies or the controlled rhythmic repetition of r'n'b or soul, but also paid respect to white popular musics – as signalled by the use of white English musicians Noel Redding and Mitch Mitchell as fellow band members in the Jimi Hendrix Experience, and by the obvious debt to Bob Dylan as songwriter and especially lyricist. Hendrix's role as perhaps *the* pivotal musician in the emergence of 'rock music', the concert music developed from 1960s pop and other musics, has been emphasised (perhaps overemphasised) recently by Charles Shaar Murray.[37] Here the importance of London as the site through which Hendrix was able to operate during this transformation should be stressed.

Hendrix was not alone in this. The saxophonist Joe Harriott was one of the first wave of Caribbean immigrants to Britain. As well as playing in the accepted styles of the late 1950s and early 1960s, Harriott attempted in the middle 1960s to create a specifically post-colonial music using Indian musicians and instruments as well as Caribbean and white musicians and styles: the result he called Indo-Jazz Fusions. If the 1960s were positive for jazz, they were equally so for Indian 'classical' music, which, after the exposure given to the sounds of sitar and tabla on albums by the Beatles (*Sergeant Pepper*) and Rolling Stones (*Their Satanic Majesties Request*) in 1967, perhaps qualifies for the ambivalent title 'world music'. Harriott's efforts suffered in being compared with the Liverpool and Deptford bands' touristic appropriation. The Indo-Jazz Fusions tours received some Arts Council support, though at a fairly low level: jazz musicians were paid lower fees than classical musicians – presumably the Arts Council identified jazz creativity with poverty and was happy to keep it poor. Again, it was through London that this post-colonial interaction took place.

A more commercially successful post-colonial transformation of a music occurred in the early 1970s. It was from London that white Jamaican entrepreneur Chris Blackwell's Island label launched reggae as a worldwide musical form, principally through the elevation of Bob Marley as a 'rock' superstar. Reggae was transformed through Blackwell's investment, taking a music based on the economics of an impoverished island (cheap recordings quickly made and played in public, with hardly any live bands due to the expense of musical equipment) and imbuing it with the more ostentatious values of the global music economy (expensive studio recordings, world tours by groups of musicians, the album rather than the single as the most important form of production).[38]

The examples of Joe Harriott and Bob Marley point to the second reason for the importance of Britain as site for the transformation of pop musics: the nature and extent of post-war, post-colonial immigration. Since 1945, millions of people from the Caribbean, from India, Pakistan and Africa, have arrived and settled permanently in London and the other big cities. While there has been a black presence in Britain since at least the sixteenth century, and while there have *always* been musical cultures associated with black people in Britain,[39] the concentration of peoples in the last fifty years has produced specific responses, creating new markets for musical forms developed by and for specific ethnic groups, and providing the site for the interaction of these with existing forms and the consequent reproduction of musics. Reggae, for example, was recreated in Britain as a live form partly because there were substantial numbers of British people of West Indian origin prepared to buy the resulting concert tickets and albums. Yet while the international commercial success of reggae has not survived Marley's death, and many versions of reggae continue to address quite specifically a British West Indian audience, important points of crossover remain: the moment of punk in 1976, and the subsequent infusion of reggae in the Rock Against Racism movement of the late 1970s; the continuing importance of dance music of all kinds to the pop charts – in particular, the astonishing success in Britain of 'house' musics since 1988 is due in no small part to the presence of a reggae aesthetic making bass and drums the most important part of the mix. The typical house band name, Bomb the Bass, and typical acid house track title 'Bass: how low can you go?', emphasise this, while the revival of dub reggae in 1993 was often led by white DJs fascinated by the possibilities of detuned bass guitars, rather than young blacks who dismissed it as 'parents' music'.[40] The summer of 1994 saw the commercial popularity of 'jungle', a hybrid reggae/rave music, in which techno drum patterns, dub and techno bass lines and soul samples interact in a music claimed by its innovators to be specifically a London product; several emphasise the impossibility of such open black/white cultural interaction in New York, for example.[41]

Reggae and rave/dance musics remain, to an extent, on the margins of British pop music, however, because they are treated as marginal by the national broadcasting service, the BBC. This organisation, prevented by its Charter from advertising, and yet complicit with the commercial practices of the record industry (to the extent that potential chart material is still at the time of writing 'playlisted' by radio producers on a weekly basis), has enjoyed an official monopoly over the national radio broadcasting of pop music which only the last knee-jerk processes of Thatcherism have begun to break by the establishment of rival privately owned national radio stations – though the first of these, Virgin AM, explicitly set out to fill a different 'niche' by broadcasting 'album rock' rather than chart pop. The broadcasting of pop music on a dedicated network (Radio One) was established as late as 1966, and then only under severe pressure from illegal commercial 'pirate' radio stations.[42] As with Radio Three, every reorganisation of the Radio One schedules since has been driven by outside pressure. The BBC has consistently refused to countenance the broadcasting of reggae or indeed anything else not considered to be chart material except in a few 'ghetto slots', especially the hours of 10 p.m. to midnight. The story of pop music on television is similar, with, until the advent of the MTV video music channel (available on satellite and cable only), pop remaining confined to a few weekly programmes, despite the presence since 1957 of commercially successful rivals to the BBC.[43]

However, the basic constituents of successful chart material have continually changed, despite 'Aunty's' careful conservatism. Again, the presence in the bigger cities of large populations with cultural imperatives other than those of the BBC has helped to effect this transformation. The adoption by London gay men of the Eurodisco of the 1970s and its subsequent musical developments (hi-nrg, house, techno) led to the formation of a wider club culture, catering for virtually anyone aged from their teens to their early 30s, based around dance musics absent from Radio One airplay.[44] Pirate radio stations reappeared in the inner cities from the late 1970s to broadcast these musics – soul, funk, jazz–funk, hip-hop, rap and reggae. Despite opposition from both the record companies and the Home Office to stations which paid neither licence fees nor royalties, the pressure to provide air time for these musics eventually led to the granting of licences to several new stations, including in London the former pirate station Kiss FM.[45] One long-term effect has been to change the nature of the pop charts, so that the BBC, still wedded to the playlist, now (mid-1995) plays more black-influenced dance music than ever before.

The visibility of black music and musicians was improved by the 'jazz revival' of the 1980s. A great many young British jazz musicians emerged from around 1985; the big band Loose Tubes, for example, shot to fame

221

during a successful season at Ronnie Scott's. However, Loose Tubes was in its first incarnation all-white and all-male. A group of young black musicians, adopting both musical and ideological stances from the radical black American jazz of the 1960s (the music of Eric Dolphy, Archie Shepp, Albert Ayler and others, and the politics of the Afrocentric Chicago-based grouping the Association for the Advancement of Creative Music), formed a rival big band, the Jazz Warriors. In the saxophone section were Gail Thompson, Steve Williamson and Courtney Pine. Pine was then launched on a solo career. Like Bob Marley with reggae, his name and his first album (like Marley's, on the Island label) were used to help to launch this jazz revival to a wider audience, and both the album, *Journey to the Urge Within* (1986), and its single release, 'Children of the Ghetto', did well in the pop charts. Pine became in some ways a 'pop star', rather as violinist Nigel Kennedy became a 'pop star' – a curiosity, but an instant media personality, appearing on chat shows, modelling clothes, constantly pictured and interviewed. Behind him, a legion of young blacks put on zoot suits and hung around looking cool. This was not, precisely, aestheticised poverty *à la* Joe Harriott, but commercial success: it must be seen that the 'yuppie moment' of the late 1980s associated with Thatcherism had opened the space for the expression of this young, black and upwardly mobile grouping – the first even potentially upwardly mobile generation of blacks in Britain.[46] For a couple of years, black British jazz had a real social cachet, with advertising and television theme titles abundant, including credits music on the revived pop show *Juke Box Jury* and the first series of BBC2's *Late Show*. As it had been before the triumph of the electric guitar within pop, the saxophone became a cultural icon once more, signalling a successful, sexualised masculinity in a number of television adverts.

While the moment of 'jazz-revival' high fashion passed within two years, a number of long-term careers in jazz have been launched. Pine, Williamson, Philip Bent, Orphy Robinson and others have collaborated with American and European musicians and have produced music in dialogue with the American jazz tradition. Indeed, arguably the most significant achievement of these musicians is the insistence on its African–American roots, and their exploration of the legacy, notably of late 1950s 'hard bop', revalorising this as great music created largely by black people – and taught as such, by Gail Thompson among others, to future generations of musicians. A musical style created in the USA in the late 1950s and early 1960s (the moment of Civil Rights) and re-created in the Britain of the late 1980s and 1990s demands recognition as part of a Great Tradition; for British blacks, this is Heritage Culture, a proud re-creation of the past as intense and important in the formation of black identities within modern Britain as is the recreation of the past by middle-class white professionals which was discussed at the start of the chapter.[47] However, this is not a static position: black British jazz has moved outwards from the core hard-bop 'heritage culture' and begun to explore the musics of Africa and Latin America within a move towards a less aggressive and perhaps more commercial status. Bandleaders Orphy Robinson and Steve Williamson have incorporated aspects of 'world music'; the latter in particular also with a positive regard for the innovations in dance music of the acid house era and beyond, while Robinson is clearly influenced by English and Scottish folk musics, and has stressed this in interview.[48] Courtney Pine, meanwhile, produced *Closer to Home* (1990, remixed and re-released 1992), an album of Caribbean musics, mainly reggae.[49] Black British jazz musicians have confidently moved out from the African–American base.

Another black grouping to benefit from the entrepreneurial ethos of Thatcherism, and to an extent working within the same African–American Heritage notions of black music, was Soul II Soul, the recording ensemble and record company led by Jazzie B. Again the symbols of modernity and the musical references to the 1960s mixed happily. Jazzie B's constant companion in the early days of Soul II Soul's success (at least when there were photographers present) was a mobile telephone, perhaps the ultimate sign of the new confidence of the business classes in the late 1980s, the (very brief) moment of 'enterprise culture'. Jazzie B's dedication to the idea of a specifically black capitalism, so redolent of the example of Berry Gordy, has in fact led him to set up his own label within the Motown Corporation in California. Again, it must be said that the success of a black-owned British record company would have been unimaginable before Thatcherism; and ownership was crucial here. The chart successes of earlier black British performers such as Junior Giscombe, Light of the World, Imagination and Incognito in the early 1980s, was tempered by a (presumably) racist disbelief by the record companies in their abilities to produce long-term success.[50] Indeed, one implication of Jazzie B's move abroad in the early 1990s is that the British music industry is *still* fundamentally racist, hostile to and unwilling to invest in major black British talent.[51]

Meanwhile, the continuing and successful presence of black musics and musicians in Britain has prompted new waves of interaction within street-level musical culture, up to and including (so far) 'jungle'. As Dick Hebdige has shown, the black British presence has stimulated cultural change since the 1950s.[52] Simon Jones' book *Black Culture, White Youth* demonstrates powerfully the continuing attraction of reggae culture for young whites who choose to move within it.[53] There are white hip-hop bands, like the Stereo MCs, to match the early 1960s white r'n'b movement. And there is a long tradition of ethnically mixed bands from the Coventry two-tone bands like the Special AKA and Selecter, and Birmingham's UB40, in the early 1970s, through Culture Club and the Thompson Twins in early 1980s pop, to more recent bands such as the Bristol-based Massive Attack, who have used soul, jazz–funk and reggae samples as the bases for tracks which explore their places in the urban melting pot. Both musical style and ethnic identity are in this mix. Apachi Indian, raised in the Handsworth suburb of Birmingham, uses English, Punjabi and Jamaican patois interchangeably, rapping across language and dialect on the back of rhythm tracks owing more to dancehall reggae than to Indi-pop or Bhangra, for all their use of dhol and tabla drums.[54] At the time of writing, the most commercially successful of these syncretic adaptations is Bhangra, a form developed originally from a North Indian folk music but now driven by the rhythms of European/American dance music. Partly because of its continuing use of lyrics in Punjabi, Bhangra has a whole economic subculture of records, videos and live concerts;[55] the gradual emergence of this music into general awareness, helped by the first dedicated television series in 1991 (if only, again, in a 1.30 a.m. Channel 4 'ghetto slot'), promises much for the future interactive development of British pop.

Bhangra is not the only form to develop from within the British Asian communities: Najma Akhtar's careful fusing of the ghazal (Urdu ballad singing) style with rock and jazz rhythms and instruments has achieved commercial and critical success; Bengali pop musics drawing on rock, rap and rave have emerged in east London, with the band and associated DJs Joi fusing Bengali and rock rhythms. Other communities (the Greek, Turkish and Cypriot, for example) have produced fusions of their own drawn from rap, rock and their own rhythmic and harmonic systems; the success of pirate radio stations serving non-English-speaking publics in the cities (broadcasting in Greek, Turkish, Punjabi, etc.) has produced licences for new stations like Sunrise Radio, whose programming includes a great deal of what is often called 'ethnic' music – the popular music of Greece or Cyprus, say – but also fusions of these with the pop musics of other neighbouring cultures.[56]

THE USE OF DIVERSITY

Interactions with America and the former colonies have produced changes at every level of British musical life. The continuing presence of pop music, and the music of the Asian and Caribbean communities, on radio and in record stores, and the presence of the children of Commonwealth immigrants in the schools of British urban centres, have led gradually to the reformation of secondary school music teaching away from music appreciation, classical composition and instrumental technique, and towards the technologies and practices of popular music. The GCSE syllabuses introduced in 1985 stressed the learning of compositional and performance skills, including the use of synthesisers, samplers and recording equipment. A more recent consideration of this trend helped to draw attention to the acute tensions within the structure of British musical values. The Interim Report of the Working Group on the place of music in the national education curriculum was published in March 1991.[57] Enthusing in its multicultural brief, the committee's report assumed the equal value in education of musics as different as reggae and ragas, sambas and serialism. The skills of performance and composition were themselves stressed rather more than the learning of critical appreciation of the work of previous generations. Again, the use of synthesisers, computer-based composition packages and multi-track tape-recorders, African drumming techniques and jazz improvisation were placed alongside baroque counterpoint and sonata form. Only one composer from the European tradition, Mozart, was mentioned by name.

There followed a furore in the pages of the broadsheet newspapers. The Working Group was arraigned for betrayal of the classical music tradition, and in particular for its substitution of multiculturalism for the 'Englishness' of the post-Elgarian tradition. A series of letters and articles rallied the intellectuals of both old and new right in defence of 'traditional' musical education, in other words the appreciation of the techniques and achievements of previous generations of male Europeans. This musical tradition according to its defenders somehow encompassed the musical verities; others did not. Unsurprisingly, the authors of this anti-relativism polemic were among those engaged in the fight against musical Modernism in Radio Three programming.[58]

The conservatives' moral panic over the disappearance of 'their' tradition is no doubt underscored by the extreme fragility of the very notion of an autonomous tradition of music-making unsullied by cross-cultural contact. Whatever its internal hierarchical structure, the continuing power, status and authority of the European composed music tradition is one with which musics and musicians from 'outside' the culture continually negotiate – with those 'inside' it also parties to the negotiation. In the case of a composer like Bax, his use of Irish models is clear: listen, for instance, to the opening of the final movement of the Third Symphony (1929), with the violas playing a fiddle tune and the side-drum providing a reasonably effective version of a bhodran drum accompaniment – while the piece remains a symphony, using that material as the basis for its own transformations and developments. Even the most extreme avant-garde compositions of the 1950s are not hermetically sealed products of an autonomous European tradition, but of similar dialogue. Stockhausen's *Gruppen* for three orchestras (1957), for example, displays the mathematical fastidiousness of 'total serialism' – in which all musical parameters, pitch, rhythm, dynamic level, attack, vibrato, etc., are determined by numerical calculation – and it can be taught as such. And yet its orchestration (combinations of instruments and sounds, including in this case electric guitar, saxophones and many drums) owes as much to the then current popularity of rock'n'roll and the big band jazz of the Stan Kenton orchestra as to the symphonic tradition. This dialogue has always happened; musical hegemony is perpetually in flux, with the arrival of new rhythmic and harmonic processes, new instruments and new performing and recording techniques, changing the accepted parameters of composition and performance. Most innovations in 'classical music' have involved and do involve the acceptance of a popular musical form or practice. A few examples at random. The violin was a gypsy instrument from East Europe, the waltz a popular dance and the folk music of rural England, as used by Vaughan Williams *et al.*, was, well, folk music. Walton and Tippett were doing nothing radically new in incorporating African–American rhythms and harmonies into their music. Arguably the whole symphonic tradition, from the mid-eighteenth-century on, is based on the continuing trialogue between church music, popular songs and dance musics, and military music.

It is unsurprising, therefore, that the explosion of new musics resulting from urban interaction has also produced new voices within composed music who re-create British classical music along these multicultural lines, while simultaneously undermining the always fragile high/popular division.[59] More young composers work with jazz and rock instruments, and with computers and samplers. The Manchester-based pop and dance music label Factory launched its own 'classical' subdivision in 1989, headlining as its star attraction the aggressive jazz-influenced minimalism of Steve Martland (though it neglected to pay royalties, and went bust with the rest of Factory in 1993). There is increasing convergence of sound worlds, of audiences and indeed of appreciation of this by taste formers such as advertisers and journalists. The illustration reproduced in Figure 8.1 advertises a new production of Richard Strauss' opera *Elektra* as 'by the creators of the Pet Shop Boys' world tour': the potential opera-goer is assumed to be familiar with the latter. Similarly, when in a newspaper review a piece by composer Mark-Anthony Turnage is described as 'acid-house Bartok with attitude', the implication is that the reader can decode references to politicised rap, the hedonism of rave and the folk-derived modernism of the Hungarian composer, and imagine the resulting sound.[60]

Whatever the difficulties of the newspaper reading public in this regard, there is no doubt that composers are hearing their music in this way. Errollyn Wallen, born in Belize, is a graduate of Goldsmith's College and King's College, London. She was schooled in Modernist composition, but with a family background in popular music and jazz, found it easy to construct her own musical path from all three positions. Her band Ensemble X consists of session musicians who work happily in either jazz, commercial or classical music traditions, which is just as well as her compositions demand equal facility among all the possible permutations of these styles: strict observance of complex notation at one extreme, solo improvisation at the other, and in between the ability to interpret a written part with the right, but unwritable, groove or swing. Ensemble X has a growing reputation for its realisation of this particular 'crossover' music, but refuses to be bound within any such notion: 'we don't break down barriers in

Figure 8.1 A display of postmodern credentials
Source: Reproduced by kind permission of the Welsh National Opera

music ... we don't see any'.[61] Eleanor Alberga is another black woman whose music acknowledges and works within the rhythms of Caribbean music as well as the harmonic processes of European and American classical music. In a slightly different direction, Pritti Paintal's ensemble, Shiva Nova attempts to cross between Asian and European models of musical construction and realisation.

These examples are not the exception but the rule. Belatedly, most 'new music' made by trained composers now acknowledges once more the engagement with the popular which has characterised previous musical renewals: the continuities are with Walton's and Tippett's modernity, rather than Webern's and Lutyens's Modernism. Young(ish) composers like Wallen, Martland and John Lunn now work within the realms of reprocessing: for example, Lunn's string quartet 'Strange Fruit' (1988), inspired by the Billie Holiday song of the same name, is a creative reworking of an established form which owes as much to the repetitive drive of African–American musics as to the constant development of ideas finally legitimised by Beethoven. While the term 'postmodern' is as hackneyed a phrase in music as in any other of the arts – and while it can as easily be applied to the work of Charles Ives and Gustav Mahler as to any contemporary musician – it can serve here as a convenient label for the efforts of most younger composers. Certainly the open engagement with popular styles, and the questioning of any fixed hierarchies of value, often make their efforts explicitly anti-Modernist.[62] Festivals organised in July 1991 and 1992 by the pianist and composer Joanna MacGregor emphasised how far we have moved from both the traditionalist and Modernist traditions by programming jazz, minimalist and postmodernist musics. Simultaneously, the long-running Proms music festival also demonstrated this. In 1991 there were first performances of pieces by Martin Butler (openly acknowledging the influence of Latin American musics) and Mark-Anthony Turnage (with an acknowledged debt to jazz, specifically that of Miles Davis); in 1992 there was an evening of music by Rossini arranged for big band by jazz composer Mike Westbrook, and premières of a saxophone concerto by Richard Rodney Bennett originally written for the late Stan Getz, and a percussion concerto by James Macmillan, written for the young virtuoso Evelyn Glennie – a piece based on a plainchant melody but with worldwide rhythmic influences; and in 1993 a late night concert by trumpeter Wynton Marsalis' band which encompassed and celebrated the whole history of jazz.

One further barrier began to fall in the early 1990s, as modernist writing for string ensemble was heard as a part of rock music, and string ensembles began to play rock. Arguably *the* sign of the high, as opposed to the popular, the string quartet is an ensemble seemingly terminally appropriated by cultural elitism. It is taken for granted that training, performance, composition and even listening to the quartet and other small string ensembles requires the skills of the music academy and its subaltern studies, A-levels and the like. The generic term for small-ensemble classical musics, 'chamber music', is redolent of this elitism, implying the world of eighteenth-century patronage. Where Beethoven or Tchaikovsky may be to some extent popular musicians as symphonists, as quartet writers they remain firmly within the boundaries of trained appreciation; similarly, the orchestral music of contemporary composers like Bartok and Shostakovich is better known than their chamber music.

String ensembles have never been perfect strangers to popular music; the lush sound of a large string orchestra has accompanied countless singers, and was especially important to early 1970s soul. Though the intimate sound of the smaller ensemble is rare, it has been heard: George Martin's arrangements for the Beatles, 'Yesterday', 'Eleanor Rigby' and 'She's Leaving Home' are perhaps the best-known examples. There were attempts in the moment of 'progressive rock' to marry strings and rock band, perhaps least unsuccessfully with Barclay James Harvest and the more pop-based Electric Light Orchestra. More recently, Jimmy Somerville has toured with a small string group as part of the band. So the appearance of a string sextet as sole accompanist to one of the tracks on P.J. Harvey's 1993 album, *Rid of Me*, otherwise glorying in its self-propelling drums, bass and guitar sound, is not new of itself. What is surprising about this is the intensity of the arrangement, a Modernist emphasis owing far more to Bartok than to George Martin. Early 1993 also saw singer-songwriter Elvis Costello (an Irish Londoner) and the Brodsky Quartet collaborate to produce *The Juliet Letters*, an album and concert tour; again the arrangements crossed virtually every available musical boundary. These are not isolated examples: Lunn's 'Strange Fruit', mentioned on p. 228, is far from alone in its obvious homage to popular music. The 1990s have seen the emergence of what could be called the postmodern string quartet, with so many pieces being created that there are now ensembles dedicated to working against both the traditional quartet repertoire and its Modernist equivalents. Alex Balanescu is a Romanian Londoner, who among other credits has commissioned a concerto for violin and jazz ensemble by the American jazz composer Carla Bley, and played in both the Arditti string quartet, dedicated to the performance of complex Modernist musics, and his own Balanescu quartet, which follows the example of the American Kronos Quartet and plays pop arrangements as part of its standard repertoire.

What we have, then, is convergence, and at a faster rate than at any time since the classical music tradition was created. Given that music (and its teaching) crosses the boundaries of cultures and technologies, this convergence will continue[63]. Complex music for the concert hall and the hi-fi system will still, no doubt, be made; but the differences between this and other musics – jazz, ethnically-specific musics, the musics of the dance-floor – will be those of emphasis and scale rather than source material and process. The history of cultural interaction now being acknowledged in new music at the Proms series joins 'Land of Hope and Glory', and allows us to reread that sign of imperial grandeur as part of an ironic celebration of post-imperial global cultural and economic relations. As George Lipsitz has recently argued, new musics produced through the meeting and interaction of cultures are a positive outcome of the continuing processes of modernisation which are otherwise responsible for so much cultural and ecological destruction[64]. For all that music melts into air, the result is more often fusion (with its release of energy and power) than the gradual and irreversible loss of entropy.

This does not mean that all music is flowing towards the condition of postmodern irony, or that all music is converging. The search for an essential national tradition, for a music to match a limited, exclusive sense of national identity, continues. In the summer of 1994 Decca's heavily promoted compilation *The Essential Music of England* entered the Classic FM top 10.[65] Though at first sight it is like a lot of other Classic FM confections (other current hits included snippet compilations such as *Classic Moods: Passion* and *Classics from the Ads*) this is rather more generous: two full-length CDs, with a fair sprinkling of complete works along with the snippets. The CDs are themed: the second 'The Pastoral England', reflecting the country cottage on the cover, is a pleasant romp through, among other things, folk arrangements by Percy Grainger, folk-related orchestral music by Butterworth and Delius, Peter Warlock's mock-Tudor 'Capriol Suite' and Vaughan Williams' 'Lark Ascending'. The first CD, 'The Spirit of England', marches to a very different drummer. The 'spirit', apparently, is patriotism. There are a few hymns, including Parry's setting of Blake's 'Jerusalem'; there are excerpts from 'the Planets Suite', the 'Enigma Variations' and 'A Young Person's Guide to the Orchestra'. The predictable patriotism of ceremonial marches by Elgar and Walton are compounded by film music (from *The Dam Busters*, *Bridge Over the River Kwai*, Olivier's *Henry 5th*), and the final track, introduced by Churchill's 'fighting on the beaches' speech, is Vera Lynn's 'The White Cliffs of Dover' – the only bit of popular music on the album. All this stirring stuff commemorates, say the sleeve notes, the high points of empire and the Second World War. The *Henry 5th* extract is glossed thus: 'The year was 1944 and heroism was in the air as Britain was about to achieve total victory in the most arduous war in its history.'

This fantasy would be harmless enough by itself, perhaps. It isn't. We could go on: 'The story of England is one of regimental honour, daring exploits on the field of battle and great sacrifice. Thanks to these things there is such a thing as the English way of life' – thus Richard Johnson in a magazine released at the same time as the Decca compilation, the summer 1994 edition of the quarterly *This England*. This is a *Country Life* for the Eurosceptic, whose constant invocation of the Great Patriotic War matches that of Radio Moscow in the dying days of communism: a liturgy of past collective achievement hiding present national decay. In the summer 1994 issue the D-Day landings are commemorated, and the belief that the Second World War was won by the British, with the help of God, is repeated: with the additional liturgy, repeated in both articles and letters, that this victory will be worthless if Britain loses its sovereignty to a Europe demonised as bureaucratic and socialist. *This* England is the land of country cottages of the Decca front cover; it is the land of genteel whiteness figured in John

Major's 1993 vision of shadows on county grounds, warm beer and old maids cycling to communion. It is also an England of infinite regression, as authors, including the editor, remember their own childhoods as the golden age. The journal helps to maintain the regression by running a nice little line in musical souvenirs. But they are souvenirs from popular culture. Instead of the pastoral–traditional, or ceremonial marches, of Decca's high-culture effort, readers are offered the chance to relive the finest hour through nostalgic recordings of dance bands and singers of the 1940s. Many of whom, as it happens, were not 'Little English' but American (including the Ink Spots, the only black faces in the magazine), or tried to sound as if they were.

In precisely this way, musical cultures have a splendid habit of disrupting cultural isolationism. Whatever their point of origin, they emerge and develop through dialogue and interaction. As we noted above, the summer of 1994 was also the summer of 'jungle', a music which is more English in origin than anything the dance bands provided, the product of the continuing dialogue between black- and white-dominated dance musics. In discussing it, the journalism of the new streetwise cultures constructs an England which is very different from that of the plucky, embattled cottage gardeners of *This England*. It is an England of cultural and international dialogue, with the next good idea as likely to emerge from an Ibiza beach party as a Soho wine bar, and in which people and events in Newcastle, Manchester, Dortmund, Chicago and Los Angeles are all sites where more mixing will go on and from which more new sounds will emerge ripe for further transformation in metropolitan centres in Britain and elsewhere.[66]

BACK TO BUSINESS?

So we return to paradox, with this final emphasis. The urge to re-establish a musical tradition of appreciation through the education syllabus is matched by an urge to modernise that syllabus, to proactively work with the changes, for commercial reasons. The paradoxes of Thatcherite Conservatism (the desire to destroy cultural patterns in the name of market forces while maintaining, indeed strengthening, notions of patriotic pride) remain unworkable contradictions in the case of a British music which has been reconstituted through the interactions with America, the former colonies and the rest of the world. The equation enterprise, heritage, culture has a fourth term, education: the final paradox is that only if the terms balance will they not cancel each other, to leave precious little in the way of a future for music-making in Britain. Any return to the education of an elite of Leavisite appreciators would mean the loss of generations empowered actively to make music, as well as the creation of generations alienated from their own musicality, and others whose musicality will be expressed on the margins of an increasingly technologised and trained global entertainment

231

PLEASE Mr Major,
act to protect the musical future of our children.

"I find it hard to understand why England is to be denied the enlightened music curriculum that is to be adopted by Wales." PIERRE BOULEZ

21 FEBRUARY 1992

Dear Prime Minister,

Mr David Pascall, the Chairman of the National Curriculum Council has hailed the national curriculum for music as an exciting development which will benefit all our children. But his Council's work so far has served only to jeopardise it.

Earlier this year, the specialist music curriculum working group's proposals were wholeheartedly endorsed by the Welsh Curriculum Council. By contrast, the NCC made no less than 60 amendments to them, and superimposed a list of detailed prescriptions. On 3 February the Secretary of State for Wales published Draft Orders which incorporate the working group's proposals in full, including the three attainment targets - performing, composing, appraising - which already form the basis of the curriculum in Scotland. Yet on Mr Pascall's advice, the Secretary of State for Education has produced Draft Orders built on two attainment targets, with a half-hearted "weighting" towards practical work, and a mass of statutory requirements.

How has this divergence come about? The Welsh have decided to adopt a straightforward and logical structure, which is clear, practicable and easy to understand, for parents as well as teachers. The NCC, on the other hand, appear to have been pursuing the chimera of "curriculum coherence". Yet there is no relationship between their ideas for music history and the requirements for general historical studies. Rather, the NCC have arbitrarily imposed statutory requirements for studying particular musical styles, forms and periods. They have undoubtedly made one sort of curriculum explicit. But what virtue or sense is there in compelling all pupils to study "symphony" or "oratorio"? Why not "concerto" or "opera"? And how will parents from non-Christian faiths react to compulsory doses of religious oratorio music for their 11 to 14-year old children?

Now, the bulk of the NCC's misconceived and arbitrary suggestions are enshrined in draft legislation for England. But it is not too late: consultation runs until 4 March. Mr Clarke can and must think again, for the sake of music as a whole. His Orders as they stand are a recipe for divisiveness and confusion, and risk undermining the achievements of the GCSE syllabus. The only sensible way forward is for him to adopt the working group's proposals in their entirety.

Neil Hoyle

Chief Executive, The Incorporated Society of Musicians
10 Stratford Place, London, W1N 9AE

21 FEBRUARY 1992

Dear Prime Minister,

The music profession has been united in its condemnation of the National Curriculum Council's decision to overturn much of the original Music Working Group's report on the contents of the National Curriculum. Assurances given recently by the Secretary of State for Education about the marking ratios in his revised structure have not allayed genuine concerns that the balance between practical and theoretical music has been sufficiently established.

The Secretary of State for Wales has now adopted the Working Group's original proposal with its three attainment targets: Performing, Composing and Appreciating. This model provides a better structure for teaching music and for reporting accurately children's progress in music to their parents.

It is our belief that the more prescriptive Draft Orders for England, if implemented in law, will alienate many thousands of youngsters who might otherwise have come to love Western classical music and a wide variety of music from other traditions.

We urge the Secretary of State for Education and Science to adopt Orders for England similar to those proposed for Wales.

Ian Ritchie

Chairman, Association of British Orchestras
Francis House, Francis St., London, SW1P 1DE

Simon Rattle CBE, Alberni String Quartet, Thomas Allen, Norman Bailey CBE, Steuart Bedford, Alfred Brendal KBE, Jack Brymer OBE, Paul Crossley, Paul Daniel, John Dankworth, Sir Colin Davis, Peter Donohoe, Sian Edwards, Mark Elder CBE, James Galway, Lesley Garrett, Evelyn Glennie, Jane Glover, Sir Charles Groves, Richard Hickox, Elgar Howarth, Nicholas Hytner, Yvonne Kenny, Cleo Laine, Philip Langridge, Robert Lloyd, Benjamin Luxon CBE, Colin Matthews, Sir Peter Maxwell Davies, Jonathon Miller, Ann Murray, Roger Norrington CBE, Dennis O'Neill, Nigel Osborne, David Pountney, Andre Previn, Joan Rodgers, Mstislav Rostropovich, Sir Georg Solti, Michael Tilson Thomas, Roger Vignoles, Judith Weir, Willard White, John Williams.

21 FEBRUARY 1992

Dear Prime Minister,

I have followed the polemic surrounding the English National Curriculum for Music with interest.

Music is not the narrow field defined in the Draft Orders. Composers of today draw on the full diversity of culture available to them. Those learning should be exposed to practical experience of an equally wide variety of music.

To expect all children by the age of 11 to "understand the distinctive characteristics of medieval, renaissance, classical, romantic, recent and contemporary music" is totally unrealistic. To require by law that every 14-year-old in the land shall study "symphony and oratorio" is ludicrously arbitrary.

One cannot legislate for the taste of a nation. I join my colleagues who have already written to you in protesting that the Draft Orders for Music will do little to preserve your musical tradition. On the contrary, their narrow, prescriptive nature will drive many children away.

Teachers should be free to devise a curriculum suitable for each child within a challenging and flexible framework. I find it hard to understand why England is to be denied the enlightened curriculum that is to be adopted by Wales.

Pierre Boulez

Welsh National Opera,
Cardiff.

Over 80% of those who responded to proposals for the National Curriculum in Music wanted the same practical, non-prescriptive curriculum for English children as is to be adopted in Wales.

The most respected professional musicians working in Britain have repeatedly warned that plans for music in England will be disastrous for thousands of children.

This space was donated by Andrew Lloyd Webber who writes, "Over twenty years ago I composed "Joseph and the Amazing Technicolor©Dreamcoat" for a school performance. It was my first piece to be publicly performed and the consequence of its joyous, yet rough and ready premiere, was directly responsible for my career getting off the ground. Children should perform, compose, sing and then come to the theory of music through love of music".

Figure 8.2 A spectrum of musicians in search of reproduction
Source: Advertisement in *The Independent*, 24 February 1992

business. Conservative arguments for a return to traditional education in music, therefore, remain caught within the explicitly elitist, impractical and implicitly anti-commercial constructions of the post-war settlement.

The contradictions may well produce an equally contradictory, but potentially fruitful, alliance between the music business and the remaining cultural organisations of the corporate state. Since the 1960s, a great deal of music has been made in Britain, and a great deal of money has been made from it. The British music industry is aware that nothing of this can be taken for granted. The appearance of new musical technology, almost all of it developed outside Britain, and the continuing lack of training provision, has led to the realisation that structured training in the use of this equipment will be necessary in order to maintain Britain's role in the production of certain kinds of popular music.[67] These arguments for training in music technology are matched by those of supporters of training in the techniques of orchestral instruments, including the newspaper advertisement reproduced in Figure 8.2. Neither orchestral musicians nor pop musicians have the slightest interest in an educational curriculum dedicated to the manufacture of appreciators, rather than producers, of music. These arguments must be heard. Else, the solid aesthetic and commercial achievements of twentieth-century British musical production will melt into air, 'heritage' will be divorced from 'enterprise' and only the appreciators will remain inside an increasingly silent museum.

ACKNOWLEDGEMENTS

Many thanks for the time and advice given during the writing of this chapter by Alan Durant, Rory Forsyth, Gillian Moore, Errollyn Wallen and Colin Graham.

NOTES

1 The relationship between modernity, tradition and English culture is explored in P. Wright, *On Living in an Old Country*, London, Verso, 1985; R. Hewison, *The Heritage Industry. Britain in a Climate of Decline*, London, Methuen, 1987; J. Corner and S. Harvey (eds), *Enterprise and Heritage. Crosscurrents of National Culture*, London, Routledge, 1991. For a commentary on this type of work which exposes its closeness to the Englishness it ostensibly analyses critically, see P. Gilroy, *The Black Atlantic*, London, Verso, 1993. Gilroy's argument about the force of tradition in the experience of modernity is close to my own, which was developed independently.

2 I here use 'classical music' as shorthand for written European and American music from the foundation of the monasteries onwards, in the tradition identified and narrated from the eighteenth century on, and still to be found in such reference works as J. Westrup (general editor), *The New Oxford History of Music*, Oxford, Oxford University Press, 1975; G. Abraham, *The Concise Oxford History of Music*, Oxford, Oxford University Press, 1979; S. Sadie (ed.),

The New Grove Dictionary of Music and Musicians, London, Macmillan, 1982. The word 'classical' does *not*, in this text, refer only to music from this 'tradition' composed between *c.* 1770 and 1820.

3 E.A. Wrigley, 'The process of modernisation and the Industrial Revolution in England', *Journal of Interdisciplinary History*, vol. 3, pp. 1972, 225–59; M. Berg, *The Age of Manufactures*, Oxford, Oxford University Press, 1988.

4 See W. Weber, *The Rise of Musical Classics in Eighteenth Century England*, Oxford, Oxford University Press, 1992; R. Leppert, *Music and Image*, Cambridge, Cambridge University Press, 1988; C. Ehrlich, *The Musical Profession in Britain since the Eighteenth Century. A Social History*, Oxford, Oxford University Press, 1985.

5 For an interesting analysis of class, taste and the city, see W. Weber, *Music and the Middle Class*, London, Croom Helm, 1975.

6 R. Sennett, *The Fall of Public Man*, London, Faber, 1986, pp. 200–5. See also R. Walser, *Running with the Devil*, Hanover, NH, Wesleyan University Press, 1992, an exploration of heavy metal music and its very similar construction of demonic performers.

7 The vexed question of class and leisure is explored in P. Bailey, *Leisure and Class in Victorian England*, London, Routledge and Kegan Paul, 1978; H. Cunningham, *Leisure in the Industrial Revolution 1780–1880*, London, Croom Helm, 1980; H. Meller, *Leisure and the Changing City*, London, Routledge and Kegan Paul, 1976; D. Cannadine, 'The theory and practise of the English leisure class', *Historical Journal*, vol. 21, no. 2, 1978, pp. 445–67.

8 See Meller, *Leisure*, pp. 219–25; F.M.L. Thompson, *The Rise of Respectable Society*, London, Fontana, 1988, pp. 303–5; W. Mellers, *Vaughan Williams and the Vision of Albion*, London, Barrie and Jenkins, 1989, pp. 4–6.

9 An insult made popular at the start of the First World War in an eponymous book published in Germany by Oscar Schmitz. See the discussion in R. Stradling and M. Hughes, *The English Musical Renaissance*, London, Routledge, 1993, ch. 3.

10 R. Colls and P. Dodds (eds), *Englishness, Politics and Culture 1880–1920*, London, Croom Helm, 1986; E. Hobsbawm and T. Ranger, *The Invention of Tradition*, Cambridge, Cambridge University Press, 1983; C. Norris (ed.), *Music and the Politics of Culture*, London, Lawrence and Wishart, 1989; Wright, *Old Country*; Stradling and Hughes, *English Musical Renaissance*; Mellers, *Vaughan Williams*. See also Alan O'Shea, 'English subjects of modernity', Chapter 1 in this volume.

11 C. Sharp, *English Folk Song. Some Conclusions*, Taunton, Barnicott and Pearce, 1907; D. Harker, *Fakesong: the Manufacture of British 'Folksong' from 1700 to the Present Day*, Milton Keynes, Open University Press, 1990; G. Boyes, *The Imagined Village. Culture, Ideology and the English Folk Revival*, Manchester, Manchester University Press, 1993.

12 Mellers, *Vaughan Williams*, pp. 24–30; D. Laing, 'Scrutiny to subcultures: notes on literary criticism and popular music', *Popular Music*, vol. 13, no. 2, 1994, pp. 209–22; in general the authoritative account remains F. Mulhern, *The Moment of Scrutiny*, London, New Left Books, 1979.

13 In A. Blake, *Reading Victorian Fiction*, London, Macmillan, 1989, pp. 140–4, a general model of this seeming paradox was assembled from P. Anderson, 'Components of the national culture', *New Left Review* no. 23, January–February 1964; and M.J. Weiner, *English Culture and the Decline of the Industrial Spirit*, Cambridge, Cambridge University Press, 1980.

14 A. Blake, 'The death of a hero?', *Magazine of Cultural Studies*, vol. 1, no. 1, Spring 1990, pp. 32–5.

15 H. Carpenter, *Benjamin Britten. A Biography*, Faber, 1992. The domestic ideology has also marginalised women's compositional skills; see Leppert, *Music and Image*; and D. Hyde, *New Found Voices: Women in Nineteenth Century English Music*, Canterbury, Tritone Music Publishers, 1991.
16 See B. Appleyard, *The Culture Club. Crisis in the Arts*, London, Faber and Faber 1984, p. 97.
17 See M. Tippett, *Moving Into Aquarius*, London, Routledge and Kegan Paul, 1959; C. Lambert, *Music Ho! A Study of Music in Decline*, London, Faber and Faber, 1934. Lambert himself was a modern composer in the sense used here; one piece which has remained in the repertoire is his *The Rio Grande* for voice, piano, choir and orchestra (1927).
18 There is no space here to deal with the modes of listening which were ranged against the official model of 'appreciation'. See L. Green, *Music on Deaf Ears. Music, Meaning and Ideology in Education*, Manchester, Manchester University Press, 1988; J. Shepherd, *Music as Social Text*, Cambridge, Polity Press, 1991; K. Swanwick, *Music, Mind and Education*, London, Routledge, 1988; A. Peacock and R. Weir, *The Composer in the Market Place*, London, Faber and Faber, 1975.
19 Anderson, 'Components', is helpful, on the conservative nature of interwar immigration.
20 If they thought of it at all. The twenty composers interviewed by Paul Griffiths, *New Sounds, New Personalities: New Music of the 1980s*, London, Faber and Faber, 1985, mention popular music precisely twice. For Adorno's views, see for example, 'On popular music', *Studies in Philosophy and Social Sciences*, vol. 9, 1941, pp. 17–48, and 'Perennial fashion: jazz', in his *Prisms*, London, New Left Books, 1967, pp. 119–32; Adorno's views are sympathetically interrogated in R. Middleton, *Studying Popular Music*, Milton Keynes, Open University Press, 1990.
21 W. Glock, *Notes in Advance*, Oxford, Oxford University Press, 1991, p. 115.
22 ibid.: for example, 'It was this middle of the road policy I was determined to undermine' (p. 58); see also pp. 26, 35, 45, 49, 59, 197.
23 See reports and letters in *The Independent*: 10 June 1991, 11 June 1991, 12 June 1991, 14 June 1991, 15 June 1991, 16 June 1991.
24 Edmund Burke (1729–1797) and Tom Paine (1737–1809) argued over the French Revolution. Paine claimed that it was possible to begin society anew from first principles, and that, therefore, revolutions could be a good thing; Burke that societies are so constrained by their histories that radical departures therefrom will end in disaster.
25 Nicholas Kenyon interviewed in *Radio Times*, 4–10 July 1992. See also A. Blake, 'Summer's lists', *New Statesman and Society*, 7 June 1994.
26 See correspondence in *The Independent*, 17 October 1990, 31 October 1990, 10 January 1991, 11 September 1991. An earlier argument about the under-representation of English music at the Proms can be found in R. Simpson, *The Proms and Natural Justice*, London, Toccata, 1981.
27 See M. Kettle, 'Booming voices', *Marxism Today*, July 1991, pp. 36–7. A spectacular example of the new place of opera in popular culture is provided by the *Daily Mirror* front-page headline of 29 June 1991, 'You Tosca!', an attack on a government minister which contains several other operatic puns.
28 As a side-effect, the boom led to another, in the commissioning of new operas: the Covent Garden Venture put on four seasons of short works by young composers; several new operas were specifically commissioned for television; and there was an annual programme of new commissions for English National Opera.

29 The boom in classical music, and its move away from the existing connoisseur base, is signalled by the growth of magazines, most fronted by a 'free' CD sampler of new recordings (a complete performance in the case of the *BBC Music Magazine*); at the time of writing chain stores Woolworths, Boots and W.H. Smiths all have their own in-house labels, largely representing old recordings of mainstream repertoire works at prices significantly lower than the average; all these aimed at a broader market segment than middle-aged AB males. The successful television detective series *Morse* became a marketing opportunity for its composer, Barrington Pheloung, whose first CD of theme music from the series, along with snippets of Mozart, was another 'classical' CD to enter the pop album charts.

30 See *The Independent*, 9 June 1990, 11 December 1990; *Sunday Correspondent*, 4 March 1990.

31 *The Independent*, 27 June 1990, 28 June 1990.

32 W. Benjamin, 'The work of art in the age of mechanical reproduction', in his *Illuminations*, edited by Hannah Arendt, London, Verso, 1973.

33 For music-hall, see P. Bailey (ed.), *Music Hall: The Business of Pleasure*, Milton Keynes, Open University Press, 1987; and J.S. Bratton, (ed.), *Music Hall: Performance and Style*, Milton Keynes, Open University Press, 1989.

34 J. Rogan, *Starmakers and Svengalis*, London, McDonald Queen Anne, 1988, pp. 18–22; G. Melly, *Revolt Into Style*, Harmondsworth, Allen Lane, 1969, 26–9.

35 A process discussed by, for example, D. Hebdige, *Subculture: The Meaning of Style*, London, Methuen, 1979; P. Willis, *Profane Culture*, London, Routledge and Kegan Paul, 1978.

36 Discussed in Hebdige, *Subculture*; and I. Chambers, *Popular Culture the Metropolitan Experience*, London, Methuen, 1986, and *Urban Rhythms*, London, Macmillan, 1985.

37 C.S. Murray, *Crosstown Traffic. Jimi Hendrix and Post-War Pop*, London, Faber and Faber, 1989.

38 See S. Clarke, *Jah Music*, London, Heinemann, 1980; D. Hebdige, *Cut'n'Mix. Culture, Identity and Caribbean Music*, London, Methuen, 1987.

39 P. Fryer, *Staying Power*, London, Pluto, 1984; P. Gilroy, *There Ain't No Black in the Union Jack*, London, Hutchinson, 1989; P. Oliver (ed.), *Black Music in Britain*, Milton Keynes, Open University Press, 1990.

40 On black musics and cultural hybridity, see G. Stephens, 'Interracial dialogue in rap music', *New Formations*, no. 16, Spring 1992, pp. 62–79.

41 See the interview with Rebel MC, General Levy, DJ Ron and Jumpin' Jack Frost, all exponents of 'jungle', in *Mixmag*, July 1994, pp. 32–6.

42 This is the view of J. Hind and S. Mosco, *Rebel Radio*, London, Pluto, 1985; but note the qualifications offered in S. Barnard, *On the Radio*, Milton Keynes, Open University Press, 1989, pp. 40–1.

43 For the more recent phenomenon of MTV, see the very different accounts offered in E.A. Kaplan, *Rocking Around the Clock. Music Television, Postmodernism and Consumer Culture*, London, Routledge, 1988; and A. Goodwin, *Dancing in the Distraction Factory*, London, Routledge, 1993.

44 The independence of the rave scene was underlined in 1994 as the Conservative government sought new, draconian powers to criminalise such gatherings as outdoor parties.

45 *The Independent*, 30 September 1990.

46 An assertion borne out in interviews carried out in May 1992 with young black musicians Errollyn Wallen and Colin Graham.

47 Wallen interview; but note that there has also been a recycling of white pop in recent years, with bands like the Bootleg Beatles and Bjorn Again, a neo-ABBA, paralleling the continuing careers of the Rolling Stones, Genesis and the annual Christmas shows by that most pantomimic of pop performers, Gary Glitter.

48 Graham interview; *The Independent*, 4 September 1991; O. Robinson interviewed in the *Wire*, July 1992; Incognito interviewed in *Music Technology*, vol. 5, no. 10, September 1991.

49 For comment on this and on Pine's continuing career in general see *The Independent*, 22 August 1991; the *Wire*, July 1992. One problem here is the attempt, so far unsuccessful, to win over an American audience: the sleeve notes for Pine's album are Americanised; posters advertising his 1993 tour carried a pastiche photo of Pine as Charlie Parker.

50 Incognito, interview in *Music Technology*; Graham interview.

51 J. Street, *Rebel Rock*, Oxford, Basil Blackwell, 1986; BBC2 *Open Door*, 12 April 1991; the magazine *Hip-Hop Connection*, launched in 1988, had great trouble in persuading advertisers that young black people (the magazine's target audience) had money to spend (personal testimony).

52 The argument runs throughout Hebdige, *Subculture*.

53 S. Jones, *Black Culture, White Youth*, London, Macmillan, 1988.

54 *The Independent*, 19 September 1991.

55 Bhangra has yet to find its historian; one early approach is S. Bannerjee and G. Baumann, 'Bhangra 1984–8: fusion and professionalisation in a genre of South Asian dance music', in Oliver (ed.), *Black Music in Britain*, pp. 137–52.

56 There were two attempts to delineate some of this London-wide activity in two BBC2 television programmes in the *Rhythms of the World* series, April 1994. The outlook is not specific to Britain; the same *Rhythms of the World* series also contained a portrait of the ethnically mixed multicultural music group Zap Mama, whose source musics include medieval European as well as African and Asian. See also the Wally Badarou interview, *Music Technology*, vol. 1, no. 10, September 1987; Henry Threadgill, interview on BBC Radio Three, 18 May 1992.

57 *Interim Report of the National Curriculum Music Working Group*, London, HMSO, March 1991; *Final Report of the National Curriculum Music Working Group*, London, HMSO, October 1991.

58 See *The Independent*, 18 January 1992, 23 January 1992, 28 January 1992, 29 January 1992; 24 February 1992.

59 This is the basic editorial position of the series edited for Manchester University Press by P. Martin and W. Mellers under the general heading 'Music and Society'. See, for example, their preface to S. Frith (ed.), *World Music, Politics and Social Change*, Manchester, Manchester University Press, 1989, pp. ix–x.

60 *The Independent*, 29 August 1992.

61 Ensemble X concert programme, 24 July 1991.

62 Often aggressively so: see, for example, Steve Martland interview, 'New music's muscle man', *BBC Music Magazine*, vol. 1, no. 1, August 1992, pp. 31–3.

63 The debate on music in the national curriculum resulted in a fudge: music is not a compulsory part of the national curriculum; its attainments are measured in three key stages to age 12, rather than the more usual ten stages to age 14. Nevertheless, the stress on improvisation and composition as well as on appreciation remains. See *Music in the National Curriculum*, London, HMSO, 1992.

64 G. Lipsitz, *Dangerous Crossroads. Popular Music, Postmodernism and the Poetics of Place*, London, Verso, 1994.

65 Decca 443 936–2. This section of the chapter is based on A. Blake, 'Village Green, Urban Jungle', in *New Statesman and Society*, 12 August 1994.
66 See magazines such as *Mixmag, DJ, The Mix* and *Future Sound.*
67 See A. Blake, *The Music Business*, London, B.T. Batsford, 1992, pp. 93–107; and for a broader argument along the lines of this chapter, A. Blake, *The Land Without? Music, Culture and Society in Twentieth Century Britain*, Manchester, Manchester University Press, 1996.

9

WHAT A DAY FOR A DAYDREAM

Modernity, cinema and the popular imagination in the late twentieth century

Alan O'Shea

At the end of the twentieth century what is the place of modernity in British cultural life?

My earlier chapter in this book pointed to several connected senses of modernity: as a set of social aspirations and programmes ('the project of the Enlightenment'), as a historical period, and as a particular mode of experience (in which social agents engage with, as Berman put it, 'life's possibilities and perils').[1] Recent postmodernist writing has argued that the world, or at least the West, has moved on from modernity, in any of these senses: that those aspirations to harness the world's resources and to change political structures for a better humanity, whether as the expression of the philosophical tradition of the Enlightenment or as a feature of lived popular culture, have been abandoned, and that a new structure of feeling is now in place. Some of this writing laments this passing, some celebrates it. This chapter will suggest that many of the impulses of modernity, including those towards emancipation, equality and community, still register in popular culture in the 1980s and 1990s, particularly as represented by popular cinema and in those films most widely consumed by audiences in Britain (and elsewhere). It argues, incidentally, that it is possible to embrace much of the recent critique of modernity without abandoning these impulses, and explores, more speculatively, the political implications of both these arguments.

My line of argument has been provoked by the recent work of Fredric Jameson.[2] His particular significance for me is that he is both one of the leading proponents of 'the postmodern condition' and someone firmly holding onto a 'grand narrative' of (socialist) emancipation; but also that he has selected popular cinema as the paradigmatic site of a postmodernity which dissipates such an emancipatory project. Since my own capacity to imagine a less oppressive society is frequently refreshed by trips to the cinema, despite all the acclaim Jameson's argument has attracted, something needed to be unpicked.

239

ALAN O'SHEA

JAMESON, THE POSTMODERN AND THE CINEMA

Firstly, a summary of, and initial comments on, Jameson's account of the postmodern. Strongly influenced by Baudrillard, he likens the postmodern experience to schizophrenia in its breakdown of order in temporal, spatial and interpersonal relationships: isolated from the past 'the present suddenly engulfs the subject with indescribable vividness . . . with heightened intensity, bearing a mysterious charge of affect'.[3] There is no distancing, no possibility of putting things into any ordered perspective. He proposes a 'loss of distance' in two senses. Firstly, using examples of giant postmodern buildings, he argues that new developments in the built environment have 'finally succeeded in transcending the capacities of the individual human body to locate itself, to organise its immediate surroundings perceptually, and cognitively to map its position in a mappable external world'. Much less are we able 'to map the great global multinational and decentred communicational network in which we find ourselves caught as individual subjects'.[4] Secondly, he suggests there is a loss of *critical* distance – a place from which we can map out what is happening and mark out alternatives. Particularly significant for Jameson, as a Marxist, is the loss of an informed connection to the past and hence a sense of direction forward into the future. For him, 'the nostalgia mode' is omnipresent, particularly in the cinema, but this is more a question of pillaging the past for stylish images than an attempt to reconstruct historical processes. He sees this patching together of many disparate images – from the past and present, from high and popular culture – which characterises postmodernist aesthetic practice as not just one possible style out of many, but as the 'cultural dominant' of late capitalism – its form *corresponds* to the experience of consumer capitalism.

He identifies a desire for life to be different in many recent films, but points to the frequent nostalgic content of this longing (with a particular investment in the 1950s), and argues that in the process history is reduced to spectacle.[5] In the films he examines, history does indeed tend to be presented as spectacle; but, as I will elaborate (pp. 248–9), the problem with Jameson's methodology is that it reads off political effects too directly from his own (partial) analyses of texts. His selection of films and his apparently definitive reading of them merely confirm his political pessimism – which in turn derives from very inflexible political expectations. For at the very end of his book *Postmodernism*, he admits that the 'cognitive mapping' he has repeatedly found wanting in contemporary Western culture is 'in reality nothing but a code word for "class consciousness"'.[6] If only a class analysis will satisfy him, it is not surprising he can find no source of transformative politics in popular culture; as I will argue, this is not the place to look for coherent political argument.

This ineffectual corner into which Jameson and many other proponents

240

of the postmodern have talked themselves is largely an effect of a too un-critical acceptance of earlier theories of mass culture and the nature of popular modernity, and particularly those of members of the Frankfurt School, such as Adorno and Horkheimer.[7] As suggested in Chapter 1 (p. 9), they follow Weber in thinking that the project of the Enlightenment has been distorted by the subordination of all aspects of social life to the demands of instrumental rationality – the drive for efficiency to the neglect of everything else. In this view mass culture is written off as a possible site of critical ideas; hope is placed in the great modernist writers and theorists who escape the contamination of consumer culture and the demands of instrumental rationality (implicitly with the writer himself as an inheritor of that critical distance).[8] The different position to be taken here (also argued for in Chapter 1, p. 17 ff.) is that mass culture is itself contradic-tory and troubled, itself a site of struggle over the future direction of society. There is not a single, homogeneous mass culture or 'bourgeois ideology' which, imposed on the masses, renders them compliant with 'the system' – such that resistance has to arise from somewhere outside. Rather, what has been dominant in twentieth-century Western societies has been a *contra-dictory* formation of ideologies and practices, a battle over the realisation of the Enlightenment project, such that struggle arises from *within* mod-ernity. I will develop this argument from an alternative way of considering popular film.

CINEMA, UTOPIA AND MODERNITY

Postmodernity is an historical concept: it marks out something new and different from what preceded it. While my main focus will be on cultural material of the (postmodern?) past ten years, in order to problematise the idea of a fundamental transition, I will firstly examine material from the (modern) 1930s, so as to enable some discussion of what has persisted and what has changed.

It is the potency of the worlds conjured up in popular cinema, their centrality as material for the unconscious of culture, that makes them a paradigmatic site for the study of popular culture. Virtually all my instances will be from Hollywood cinema. So what of the English or British expe-rience? Well, the films examined are those which have been most readily available to English audiences and most popularly consumed: and part of the reason for this cinematic colonisation is that Hollywood has provided richer, more exciting and excessive dreams than, say, British cinema.[9] I am, therefore, concerned with the British experience, but acknowledging the powerful transatlantic influence on this sphere of popular culture.[10] But these films are consumed in determinate historical conditions, and the whole thrust of my argument suggests that a major determinant of their meaning is the specific political cultures into which they are inserted.

241

I will examine one film in some detail, and invite the reader to apply the approach more widely. It is the kind of film which Adorno and Horkheimer would have found most abhorrent – a 'formula' musical of the 1930s, *Footlight Parade*, directed in 1933 by Lloyd Bacon and choreographed by Busby Berkeley. Busby Berkeley musicals were usually set in the world of show business, frequently featuring Dick Powell as the romantic male lead, with a comic and romantic plot and building up to several fantastic (in every sense) dance sequences. In this example, James Cagney, playing the director of a musical production company, is placed, by various twists of the plot, in the position of having to devise new dance sequences and to perfect them with his company in a ridiculously short time. Since it is known that there is a spy among them who is leaking his ideas to a rival dance company, he locks everyone in the rehearsal theatre for several days, where they eat, sleep and work together, and achieve a burst of communal creative energy which transcends all the corruption, deceptions and hypocrisies of the outside world which had hitherto blocked their success. The dialogue and the action throughout are taken at a cracking pace; it is full of witty repartee, as much from the two female leads, Joan Blondell and Ruby Keeler, as from Cagney and Powell. These characters are precisely 'subjects of modernity' in Marshall Berman's sense:[11] battling though a fast changing world, living off their wits and energy on the edge of spectacular success or failure. In Chapter 1 we saw that the spectacular success of the cinema derived from the audiences' feeling that it took them out of the mundane routines of daily existence and put them in touch with the 'sensuous and immediate' 'pulse of life itself', 'life in its inexhaustibility'. In other words, although films such as this may be set in a contemporary urban metropolis, they proffered a transformed, utopian version of contemporary life: 'life' rather than life.

An approach which helps us to specify 'life' more concretely is offered in Richard Dyer's article, 'Entertainment and utopia', written in the 1970s but now rewarding a renewed attention in the context of the debates on modernity. He argued that classical popular cinema (and particularly musicals) offer utopias, but not by presenting blueprints of possible worlds: 'rather the utopianism is contained in the feelings it embodies. It presents . . . what utopia would feel like rather than how it would be organised.'[12] This sensibility is achieved through both representations and 'non-representational signs – colour, texture, movement, rhythm, melody, camerawork'. Dyer specifies five values embedded in this sensibility which can be summarised as follows:

- *energy* – the capacity to act vigorously: human power, activity, potential;
- *abundance* – conquest of scarcity; having enough to spare without a sense of poverty of others; enjoyment of sensuous material reality;

- *intensity* – experiencing emotion directly, fully, unambiguously, 'authentically', without holding back;
- *transparency* – a quality of relationships, true love, sincerity
- *community* – togetherness, sense of belonging.

In *Footlight Parade*, these values are carried in part by the film's story-line. But Dyer's insight that they are carried at least as powerfully through cinematic forms as through their content is borne out here. 'Abundance' is represented, not by wealth or profusion of goods, but by spectacular compositions, by the huge cast, by the massive sets through which the cast bustles in its vigorous activity, by excessive characters, by their verbosity and volubility and the noisiness of the soundtrack. 'Energy' and 'intensity' are represented through the acting (particularly Cagney's), by body posture and movement and by the pace of the dialogue or editing, as much as by the explicit themes of the film.

Particularly through the categories 'energy', 'intensity' and 'transparency', Dyer is probing the ways the cinema recognises the frustrations and inhibitions embodied in contemporary institutions and offers glimpses of transformed social relationships. The popularity of these films indicates that they have touched a chord – they celebrate instances of intense involvement which we only rarely experience in 'real life' but desire more of. Cinema offers escape to a transformed self in a changed relationship with others. But it is also an escape *from*: each of these categories also signify the transcendence of particular social malaises. 'Energy' triumphs over exhaustion and physical inadequacy, 'abundance' over scarcity and squalor, 'intensity' over dullness and monotony, 'transparency' over manipulation, exploitation and corruption, and 'community' over isolation. At least implicitly, and often explicitly, popular film represents existing social life as in many respects dystopian – with inhuman, unresponsive or corrupt bureaucracies, where money talks and the strong are able to exploit the weak, where we have to live a lie to survive, where there is no place for us to develop and express our physical, mental and creative capacities.

Dyer's argument centres around musicals, but he suggests that the same values can be found in other popular forms. In the Western, for example, 'energy' is present in the chases, fights and bar-room brawls, 'abundance' in the vast landscapes, 'intensity' in the suspense and the tense confrontations, 'transparency' in the straightforward, morally unambiguous characterisations, and 'community' in the townships or in the loyalties of the male group. It would be easy to extend his argument to the genre of crime thrillers also. Dystopian images of a harsh, unjust world loom larger than in the Western (metropolitan life is frequently represented as thoroughly corrupt), and there are fewer glimpses of transcendence, but the *search* for transcendence is central. The heroes and heroines who reach a sticky end do so because they will not settle for the world as it is: it offers no place

243

for their restless energy, or their desires to transform their lives.[13] At the beginning of this the book we considered a very similar depiction of contemporary urban life in Chaplin's *Modern Times* – in that case from a self-consciously socialist perspective (see p. 7).

To extend Dyer's argument a little: Bauman has suggested that the sweeping rationalism of modernity sees order as man-made and hence nature as unruly (and thus requiring to be tamed).[14] It is precisely the tension between a 'rational' society and the 'unruliness' of individual 'human nature' that has often been (and, I will argue, still is) explored in popular film.[15] Films frequently come down on the side of the quirky and the misfit, the side of spontaneity and the carnivalesque. As such they belong in the tradition of the Romantic critique of modernisation: the utopian resolution which is modelled is one in which rationality (community) is reconciled with the richness of spontaneous, affective and slightly chaotic humanity.

This is of course not the only problematic of popular cinema, or even the only problematic to be found within these films. *Footlight Parade*, for example, perpetuates the racism of its moment in deploying insulting images of blacks, and ends with a long dance sequence ('Shanghai Lil') which celebrates US nationalism and 'orientalises' most other national identities. Many Westerns of the period simultaneously promoted 'community' and legitimated the destruction of American Indian societies. Another fantasy offered by many films is that of male control – through physical confrontation or technological mastery – and unbridled individualism, rather than of a caring community in which oppressive power relations have been dissolved. For women, the dominant fantasy offered is the taming of male aggression, arrogance and stupidity through the power of love. The love story is undoubtedly *the* most recurrent theme – the (unachievable) desire for a perfectly fulfilling (hetero)sexual relationship. But the structure of feeling as marked out by Dyer recurs with remarkable frequency, and remains one powerful sensibility within the cinema and elsewhere in popular culture.

How do we relate these utopian elements to the question of modernity? The critique of existing social relations in these films, and also the moments of transcendence, tend to be fragmented, expressed through affective rather than cognitive modes, and often implicit. But, pieced together, these recurrent themes are too concrete to be dismissed as escape. Quite remarkably, they appear to mirror closely the Enlightenment project as represented by Habermas, in which emancipation from want and inequality is to be achieved through the development of 'science, universal morality and law, and autonomous art according to their inner logic'.[16] He argues that the project will be finally realised when these three separated spheres are reunited. In these cinematic utopias, not only is 'instrumental rationality' criticised, but material life, social and moral relationships and creativity are reconciled, and often in a non-hierarchical, collaborative form: the values of community and transparency offer precisely this. In other words, the very films portrayed by the Frankfurt School, and particularly Adorno and Horkheimer, as trivial and formulaic commodities for mass consumption and 'mass deception',[17] can also be understood as embodying critiques of the Western twentieth-century world which are similar to those emanating from this same group of intellectuals. Furthermore the audience is often invited to identify with precisely those rebellious characters who will not settle for the world as it is, even if this means self-destruction.[18]

Adorno and Horkheimer failed to see any contradictions within commodification. At least Jameson, despite working very closely within the same intellectual framework, has glimpsed this:

the works of mass culture, even if their function lies in the legitimation of the existing order – or some worse one – cannot do their job without deflecting in the latter's service the deepest and most fundamental hopes of the collectivity, to which they can therefore, no matter in how distorted a fashion, be found to have given voice. We therefore need a method capable of doing justice to both the ideological and the Utopian or transcendent functions of mass culture simultaneously.[19]

In rejecting the view that the meanings of mass cultural forms are intrinsically supportive of the interests of capitalism, I am not suggesting that this material is inherently anti-capitalist or even merely 'progressive'. Rather, it is politically *indeterminate*. Fiction films are (usually) not propagandistic – we are not fed an overt political line. Some Hollywood films have had a more overt politics: for example, those connected to New Deal populism, often vehicles for James Stewart (for example, *Mr Deeds Goes to Town*, Frank Capra, 1936) or Henry Fonda (*Young Mr Lincoln*, John Ford, 1939; *The Grapes of Wrath*, John Ford, 1940). But more generally, the most popular films offer many different modes of engagement to a varied (worldwide) audience. They can be read in very different ways and articulated to widely differing political projects. It is argued here that popular films make available, among other discourses, a utopian sentiment which *might* help to articulate a dissatisfaction with existing social relations and a transformative politics. But there is no guarantee that they *will*: this is a historically contingent matter – a matter which includes consideration of which political currents are in circulation and which discursive strategies they adopt.[20] It is also the case that the utopian mode of representation is defined precisely as a mode without a politics – in the sense that it represents a desired state of affairs, but no means of achieving it.

My reading is, however cautiously, more optimistic than Jameson's, not only because I see popular films as open to a range of readings, but also because of a different perspective on political change. As suggested above, Jameson seems doomed to dissatisfaction unless he finds signs of a (Marxist) cognitive map in the films – he is only interested in a politics already articulated. But a politics has to be built, and it can work on the most unlikely materials. Earlier this century, Gramsci, searching for the basis for a popular politics in an equally gloomy conjuncture (Italy in the early days of fascism), found it in the everyday 'common sense' – the often contradictory set of beliefs, feelings, images, practices and responses to be found in popular consciousness. He argued that political radicals should not expect to be able to politicise the masses by presenting them with, say, a fully-fledged Marxist theory of class exploitation. Rather, political movements would only have the energy and persistence they need if founded on this deeply grounded popular common sense with its unity of feeling, thought and action. More precisely it is the elements of 'good sense' within this culture (for him the aspirations and discontents compatible with socialism) which are the ground upon which political mobilisation must work.[21] The material of the popular cinema is precisely this 'common sense'. It chews over problems and explores attitudes which have profound political significance – the social function of the family, what counts as normal sexuality, the relation between the law and justice and so on.

Two other insights from Gramsci are relevant here. Firstly that a political project leading to change only has a chance of permanence when its aspirations are deeply embraced by a large section of society. Particularly in times of defeat and retrenchment, a slow building of this unity of thought and feeling across a broad spectrum of social groups is needed (a 'war of position').[22] Hence, even small shifts in perception, and small confirmations of either social critique or alternative visions, matter in the long run. A Gramscian analysis thus suggests, against Jameson, that we need to be looking at popular film for more than 'cognitive maps', particularly if only Marxist ones are valid. Much more inchoate forms of social dissatisfaction or aspiration might then be understood as potentially relevant to emancipatory projects, as containing elements of 'common sense' which they may be able to address.

Secondly, Gramsci argues that effective political action has to be conjunctural: that is, there is no abstract correct action; rather, strategy should depend on concrete, historically specific analysis of all the forces in play at a particular moment, and their relative strength.[23] On this view we must be wary of attributing any general significance to popular cinema. It will be its resonance in particular historical conjunctures that matters. Whether or not my particular reading of *Footlight Parade* accorded with the perceptions of 1930s audiences depends on the discursive frameworks they brought with them into the cinema. To speculate a little: one can perceive a correspondence between the celebration of the good-heartedness, spirit, wit, vitality and sense of community of the ordinary person in these films and the values carried in the populism of New Deal politics. It also shared much of the critique of big business corruption and of incompetent and arrogant officialdom represented in the films. The films may or may not have been read this way, but the point is that the two *could* be articulated and a popular pleasurable engagement with the films could enhance an affective attachment to the egalitarian and communitarian thrust of New Deal politics.

British audiences of the 1930s might have been able to articulate these sentiments to a similar popular resentment of poverty, decay and unemployment and critique of (incompetent) vested interests ('the old gang'), which developed during the Second World War into a more fully elaborated radical populism.[24] Evidence of the meanings derived by the audiences from the films they saw is not substantial, and, like all material concerned with cultural effects, extremely difficult to evaluate. For such effects usually operate unconsciously: what audiences *say* about their responses has to be reinterpreted.[25] Nevertheless, it is well established that British audiences found American films more pleasurable than those made in Britain (see also Chapter 1, p. 30). Contemporary sources identify the main reasons for this as their pace, their humour, their splendour and the glamour of their stars, while British films tended to be experienced as slow, 'wooden', middle class and 'old school tie'.[26] It has also been noted that while 'ordinary people' in American films are given individuality, careful social detail and active roles, in British films social groups below the middle class tend to be marginal and stereotypical, and not offering easy identification.[27] Evidence that American films fed social dissatisfaction and dreams of something better is hard to find directly. But, as Miles and Smith have noted, the problem which drove the plots of British film dramas along did not extend to questioning the rightness of the social order (to which we return unproblematically at the end); whereas in American films, however much they individualised social problems, these are nevertheless *endemic* to society, and we are presented, through the energetic attempts of the charismatic stars to put things right, with at least the aspiration of transcendence.[28]

In other words, these films offered some exploration of the deeply contradictory psychic formation of modernity outlined in Chapter 1. There is wide agreement that the fantasies of something more can enhance dissatisfaction with daily life. Whether this dissatisfaction, as many have argued, is channelled simply into the advertising industry's insubstantial invitation to transcend through consumption,[29] or remains an idle daydream, or whether it can be articulated to projects (individual or political) which do effect change, cannot be decided by theory. It is an empirical question, a question of the historical balance of forces in play for particular subjects at particular times. But the possibility of these fantasies feeding into a popular modernist politics should not be ruled out.

CONTEMPORARY CINEMA: POSTMODERN OR MODERN?

Yes, some will respond, but that was in the first half of the century, when people were still optimistic about removing want, inequality and oppression, when grand narratives of 'Progress' still had purchase in the popular imagination. But now, both the capitalist and communist routes to this end have been found to be both oppressive and dangerous. Many argue that positive expectations this kind have to a large extent been abandoned, at least in the West. And that whereas, earlier, intellectuals and artists at least were able to stand outside commodification, they no longer can: commodification has penetrated everywhere and obliterated all possibility of critical distance. Furthermore, the most characteristic films today do not contain those utopian glimpses; rather they recycle cultural material of the past in a playful but purposeless way, pastiche rather than parody.

For Jameson, the acceptance of this scenario is reluctant. He cannot accept it as 'the end of history', but as, hopefully, a transitional stage to a new purposive relation to history. Nevertheless, as has been indicated, he finds the case for it overwhelming, as he surveys architecture and urban space, writing, video, music, new therapies, cults, markets and consumption.[30] But he returns repeatedly to film as encapsulating postmodern culture. He picks out as characteristic a number of films which do not explore historical processes but rather lose themselves 'in mesmerised fascination with lavish images of the past'.[31] Films falling into this category include *American Graffiti* (George Lucas, 1973), *Rumble Fish* (Francis Ford Coppola, 1983) and *Chinatown* (Roman Polanski, 1974). This description, although somewhat differently, also characterises *Body Heat* (Lawrence Kasdan, 1981) which though set in the present is steeped in references to earlier genres (particularly the *film noir*), and hence depends on a knowing, nostalgic audience. These (and many other films) are clearly postmodernist in the sense of playing with existing cultural representations in pleasurable but rather purposeless ways. Other films are more self-consciously and radically postmodernist in that not only do they 'play' with genres, but they also refuse the spectator an easy and consistent position of knowledge and identification, while still retaining a popular appeal: *Blue Velvet* (David Lynch, 1986) and *Blade Runner* (Ridley Scott, 1982) are two frequently quoted examples.[32] But we can accept that these films deploy a postmodernist aesthetic, without also accepting the massive significance he gives them – as demonstrating a new 'mapless', postmodern subjectivity as the dominant cultural tendency in the West.

There is no doubt that in Britain and elsewhere political cultures have changed in many dramatic ways between the 1940s and 1980s. The popular support for a more equal and caring society of active citizens, which reached its height in the 1940s,[33] has gradually been displaced. The culture of consumerism has been fully extended to all sectors of society in this period; and by the 1980s Thatcherism had fundamentally shifted the grounds of political debate[34] and began to install a culture of private entrepreneurialism which stressed individual ambition and self-sufficiency. Though by no means complete, and not without resistance, there has been a major shift in the popular political imagination over this period. This New Right politics also, of course, took hold in the USA, the continuing source of most popular film, and it is quite easy to map the films Jameson selects onto a broader culture of cynical self-absorption.

But if we look more broadly at the output of the film industry over the past ten years, and particularly at the biggest box office successes, the story is not quite so straightforward. Popular cinema certainly has been transformed since the 1940s. It has been superseded by television as the dominant media form. Its audiences declined and became more differentiated: the prime audience is now aged between 16 and 30, and there is greater attention to genre-specific audiences (for martial arts movies, horror films, soft porn and so on). Cinema industries have had to undergo thorough restructuring to carry these changes.[35] Nevertheless, particularly since the spread of video-hire, films still hold a central place in western culture, and Hollywood still monopolises the market, if through different mechanisms. And recently cinema attendances have even been increasing: in 1993 they rose by 9 per cent to their highest point for twenty years. It is now true that, in many films, even those for children, a broad knowledge of other cultural forms and representations is (correctly) assumed. The audience is constructed as 'knowing', as cinema-literate; and much pleasure operates through allusion: simulacra rather than 'the real' are often the reference point.[36] But these postmodernist features are only one aspect of modern mainstream cinema. Jameson's selection is unrepresentative: it is not surprising that most analysts of the postmodern cinema tend to focus on the same few films, films which tend to play in a self-conscious way. This is because the majority of films hold onto a strong element of classic realism which invites audiences to suspend disbelief and identify with the social experiences depicted in them.

One might expect the films of the 1980s and early 1990s to mirror dominant political cultures, especially if one accepts the argument that commodification has now penetrated everywhere, including all aspects of culture and politics. But it is remarkable how much scepticism for the current direction of society is discernible in recent popular film, as well as the articulation of desires for different kinds of social relationships.

I will begin this examination of recent popular cinema by examining some films primarily addressed to a young audience. Firstly, a big box-office success of the 1980s, *Dirty Dancing* (Emile Ardolino, 1987). This could also be termed 'a nostalgia film': the heroine–narrator sets it 'back in 1963, when everyone called me Baby and it didn't occur to me to mind' – an age of innocence 'before President Kennedy was shot, before the Beatles came . . . and I thought I'd never find a guy as great as my dad'. Baby (Jennifer Grey) is on her way to an up-market mountain holiday resort with her parents and sister. Her father introduces her as 'the one who's going to change the world'; after the vacation she will go to college to study the economics of underdeveloped countries with the intention of joining the Peace Corps. But while she has mapped out a purposive and political direction for her life, it lacks a sensual dimension: at a dancing lesson she moves jerkily and self-consciously – she is not at ease with her body. The activities offered the guests are stultifyingly conventional and old fashioned, and the college-boy waiter–hosts are snobbish, self-seeking and sexist. But her energy and creativity (and her sexuality) are released when she is admitted to the forbidden quarters of the (working-class) enter-tainment staff, where sensuous, uninhibited and expressive dancing is the characteristic activity, where polite etiquette counts for nothing and where people can 'be themselves' and the inhibitions to direct, spontaneous and transparent relationships are removed. Again it is a glimpse of what trans-parency feels like (created cinematically by lighting, sound and movement), rather than a social model of how it might work. There, under the tuition of Johnny Castle (Patrick Swayze) she comes to terms with her body, her sexuality and her capacities for action and is able to return to her conven-tional, middle-class world with a new inner strength and confidence about her own identity. Not only are reason and feeling united, but she is now able, through her relationship with Johnny, to insist that she is not merely a mirror of her father's image of her. Johnny also gains. For despite his easy physicality and apparent confidence, he reveals his fear of being returned to the poverty of the urban streets. Anxiety about keeping his job forces him to humble himself before the camp management. Baby encour-ages him to identify positively with the skills he has, and he commits himself to standing up for his own way of doing things whatever the cost: Baby, he declares, 'has taught me the kind of person I want to be'. In the entertainment of the final night, he, with Baby as partner, dances the 'dirty' way. The other hired staff, delighted that their 'language' is given public expression, join in. The affluent, etiquette-bound guests, infected by the energy of the dancers, join in, and all their physical awkwardness dissolves away. As the camera draws back from the dancing crowd, the class differ-ences which the film had signalled strongly throughout can no longer be discerned.

This plot is pretty corny. *Dirty Dancing* is not a 'serious' film, nor is it 'realistic': the resolution is overtly unbelievable. Yet its audiences (largely young) loved it; no doubt the musical soundtrack – mainly early soul classics – contributed to this, but so too did the celebration of the under-dog, and a youth perspective in which adults are shown to be blinkered and convention-bound. But 'youth' also includes an identification with the values of justice, expressivity and community. And the final scene offers the fantasy of these values transforming social relations more generally.

Some years later, the Australian film *Strictly Ballroom* (Baz Luhrmann, 1992) reworked these same themes. The rigidity of the Australian ballroom dancing establishment, under a corrupt and tyrannical president, is challenged by a young dancer who wants to introduce an element of improvisation. The film is very different in tone – there are strong postmodernist elements: it is more knowing, and its characterisations are grossly cartoon-like. But the final scene is the same: the new dancing catches hold, and all the other dancers and spectators alike take to the floor in celebration of the overthrow of the old regime. Thus creativity, energy and integrity break through the fetters which hold these traits in check, and release them as part of an 'essential humanity' which, however long it is quiescent, in the end will not settle for the stifling and alienating conventions imposed by the powerful. Again dance is the form through which this emancipation is enacted, with youth once more posed against age.

Footloose (Herbert Ross, 1984) pleasurably enacts the same mythic structure. There are many very conservative assumptions built into this film, especially about gender roles, but we also see the middle-class establishment released by the young from the mindlessness and hypocrisy of authority and convention, and taught to renew their 'humanity' – a greater transparency in relationships, an openness to cultural difference. In *Breakfast Club* (John Hughes, 1984), another cult film for the young, an ill-assorted group of school students gather for a Saturday morning detention. Provoked partly by the oppressiveness of the teacher in change and partly by their own mutual antagonisms and repressed energies, they turn this situation into anarchy and, bound together by their transgressions, are able to break down their (class, gender, ethnic) prejudices towards each other, open up frank and transparent relationships by admitting their anxieties and frustrations and renew their relationship to their social world.

Many of the values Dyer found in classical Hollywood are in evidence here, but now organised rather differently. The utopian aspiration is still located in 'ordinary people', but it is a populism led by the young. 'The people' are differentiated by age, and the whole adult population tends to be seen as party to mindless convention and complicit with the corruption and hypocrisy of authority. 'Youth' has long had these connotations, and particularly so since the 1960s. The political expectations of that period – that the activity of the young might produce fundamental social change – now seem very distant, but *in film* they have remained the group which can see where adult society has lost its way, and whose refusals to conform result in social renewal. The figure of the moody, young (usually male) rebel, initiated by James Dean and Marlon Brando in the 1950s, is rearticulated in the 1980s by such actors as Micky Rourke and Matt Dillon – as in *Rumble Fish* and *The Outsiders* (both directed by Francis Ford

Coppola in 1983). Once again, the rebellion is against the stifling conformity of the parent culture and middle-class etiquette, against the hypocrisy which cripples the expression of 'true' feelings, prevents 'transparent' relationships and regards 'intensity' and 'energy' as dangerous. This refusal, this insistence on difference, has other features too. A repeated motif is the inability, or sometimes refusal, of the heroes to express their point of view *verbally*. This motif can convey different meanings. It could be that the character simply does not have access to the conventional articulacy required to participate in the parent culture. Or that contemporary language itself is too tied into cultural convention to be adequate to the expression of a different mode of social being. But it could also signify a more aggressive rejection of conventional language (and the culture it underpins) either for closed, subcultural verbal forms, or for non-verbal forms of communication – bodily gesture, dancing, musical performance.[37] The significance of this opposition which is opened up between verbal language and other expressive forms is explored in the final section of this chapter.

In this genre of film, Dyer's utopian categories are still in play, but, in a number of cases, represented as having to survive outside dominant social relations rather than as being latent values and desires of ordinary members of the society. As I will elaborate later, of all these values it is that of 'community' which becomes the most problematic, the hardest to sustain in contemporary film.

BUT WHAT ABOUT THE GROWN-UPS?

Social critique and utopian imagining are not confined to youth genres. Most popular films remain primarily concerned with adult relationships, and many of these offer a social distance from the New Right model of a thrusting, competitive, self-seeking society. But, compared with the earlier period, dystopian visions predominate over the prefiguring of transformed relationships. Late twentieth-century Western society is repeatedly represented as corrupt, totalitarian, violent, greedy and indifferent to 'human' values. As Judith Williamson has pointed out, so many of the biggest box-office successes of the past ten years – she mentions, among others, the *Die Hard* films (John McTiernan, 1988 and Renny Harlin, 1990), *Total Recall* (Paul Verhoeven, 1990), *Gremlins 2* (Joe Dante, 1990), *Pretty Woman* (G.K. Marshall, 1990), *Nine to Five* (Colin Higgins, 1990), *Big Business* (John Abrahams, 1988), *Dead Poets Society* (Peter Weir, 1989), *Regarding Henry* (Mike Nichols, 1991) and *Backdraft* (Ron Howard, 1991) – side with the forces of resistance to such social tendencies.[38] They promote the values of mutual trust, integrity, anti-militarism, social justice and personal autonomy, and do so fairly explicitly. So does the Enlightenment live on in the Odeon? Well, she rightly goes on to point out that these values are usually upheld by a tough, heroic masculinity. In some of these films, these dystopian features are challenged simply by the violence of an individual man (as in *Die Hard*, for example) or a man-made robot (for example, *Robocop*, Paul Verhoeven, 1987). One particularly overused plot structure is to open with an act of horrific violence which then legitimates an almost equally violent revenge. There may be some attempt to legitimate this violence as a defence of 'human' values, but there are few glimpses of what it might be like to live differently (and particularly outside a society energised by male aggression and violence).

Perhaps this marks out one significant shift in the representation of dystopia in film over the two periods we have been comparing. Crudely speaking, in the first half of this century, whether the cinema located the troubles with modernity in the insensitivities and disorders of families, townships or city life, there was a sense that rationality (often located within the law or democratic processes), human integrity and altruism, along with a good dose of (masculine) 'true grit', could eradicate or at least contain these troubles. In the past twenty years the dystopian discourse has been deepened to encompass anxieties about the future of Western civilisation itself and planetary survival, as in *Bladerunner* (Ridley Scott, 1982), *Brazil* (Terry Gilliam, 1985) and the *Superman* and *Terminator* (James Cameron, 1984 and 1991) films. In this scenario, the distortion of 'the project of modernity' is seen as so profound, so developed, that it is not surprising that only magical solutions – super-heroes and cyborgs – can be produced. There are significant implications for the representation of masculinity here. In the 1930s to 1950s, the lone male hero was much in evidence as our saviour, but he also could remain fallible and 'human'. This was the case whether he was upholding the values of citizenship (for example, James Stewart in *Mr Deeds Goes to Town* or in numerous Westerns), or whether he was the hard-boiled, cynical detective with his own code of honour (for example, Humphrey Bogart in *The Big Sleep*, Howard Hawks, 1946). More recent heroes are either mere mortals with miraculous powers of survival (for example, Bruce Willis in *Die Hard*, or Sylvester Stallone in *Rambo*, Ted Kotcheff, 1982) or are endowed with the indestructible qualities of a machine (Arnold Schwarzenegger in the *Terminator* films). As Judith Williamson suggests, their goal is to enable humanity to survive, and to restore civility and social justice. But means are sacrificed to these ends: we do not in the process glimpse (and enjoy) what that civility might be like. The textual pleasure is centred largely upon what it feels like to be a man overcoming massive odds.

If this were primarily a feminist analysis, searching for non-patriarchal imaginings, rather than for images of 'transparent', non-oppressive communitarian relationships, I would have a much tougher task. For all the critiques of hierarchy and competitiveness, women are generally marginalised in the challenge to existing structures. 'Boys with toys' predominate.

Some popular films problematise this kind of masculinity – at least partially (for example, *Nine to Five* and *Working Girl*, Mike Nichols, 1988). *Thelma and Louise* (Ridley Scott, 1991) more firmly displaces the male saviour. It locates the eponymous heroines in an oppressively patriarchal mid-Western USA: Thelma is trapped in a subservient marriage to a carpet salesman whose car registration is 'THE 1'. Her friend Louise, an exploited coffee-shop waitress, persuades Thelma to escape for a weekend in the country. In the opening sequences, through composition, sound and editing, we perceive contemporary America as harsh, thoughtlessly polluted, rushed, brutal and brutalising. Phallicism dominates the imagery. Early in their journey, Louise shoots a man who attempts to rape Thelma outside a bar. They take to the road, away from patriarchal power; and through various encounters, but particularly through their growing closeness and mutual pleasure in each other's company,[39] they gain such a revelatory glimpse of how relationships might be transformed outside existing society that they settle for staying outside: in the final shot, they drive through the (male) forces of law and order ranged against them off the edge of a high cliff above the Grand Canyon, and are freeze-framed floating in mid-air against the broad sky. Perhaps the most popular film of the 1980s, *ET* (Steven Spielberg, 1982), presents contemporary Western society as a dystopia in which prejudice, suspicion, meanness and a (masculine) bureaucratic militarism dominate, but are countered by the innocent, vulnerable, generous-spirited, creative, 'human' qualities of children, women and the eponymous alien.

When the output of even the most popular end of the cinema industry is examined in this way, it becomes hard to sustain the notion that the selection instanced here confirms or actually celebrates the status quo in any simple way, or that it merely plays listlessly with the signifiers of a commodified society. The dystopian reading of the contemporary world which emerges fairly relentlessly, rather than being a simple celebration of the consumer society, corresponds in many ways to the more elaborated arguments of left and liberal intellectuals (whether they embrace postmodernism or not) as they contemplate the failures of modernity in the twentieth century.

This is not of course pure chance. The intellectual formation of US film directors, writers and producers is a field of investigation in its own right; it would be remarkable if the elements of social critique I have identified was simply a cynical pandering to popular taste and not compatible with the political outlook of the film-makers. Just as, in the 1930s, anti-fascist intellectuals from Eastern Europe penetrated Hollywood (notably Fritz Lang, but also Robert Siodmak and many others), so in the post-war period the US left–liberal intelligentsia included many successful directors and writers: McCarthyism was not entirely wrong about dissent having a foothold in Hollywood. Furthermore, many of the current generation were formed in the radical 1960s.[40] The awareness that Hollywood (and still less the independent US film sector) has little respect for a smug endorsement of 'the American way of life' lies behind the recently renewed attack on the film industry led by Michael Medved; this attack focuses on excessive sex and violence, but is underpinned by a broader politics, a reverence for 'traditional' (i.e., New Right, Christian fundamentalist) America.[41]

It is not, then, the case that as soon as culture is commodified it is depoliticised. The market is indifferent to political expression – so long as it makes a profit. Nor am I suggesting that there is always a conscious political agenda in the minds of popular directors: more often than not the most powerful professional codes are aesthetic ones – the desire to deliver a product of which they can be proud and which will also be commercially successful. But to achieve this they need a feel for popular fantasy, the skill to articulate popular fears, anxieties and aspirations, including profound discontents with actually existing modernity.

But the significance attributed to these dystopian elements and fantasies of transcendence will vary according to the position taken on whether the values of modernity have a viable future. It will also depend on whether the utopian, nostalgic and 'humanist' form of these cinematic imaginings prevent them having any political purchase. Thirdly, it will depend on whether the frequently individualistic, masculine resolutions effectively close off the socially critical elements from more transformative political articulations. Let us tackle each of these questions in turn.

THE TROUBLE WITH(IN) MODERNITY

The first issue – whether modernity still has a political purchase – requires a detour from the cinema into a broader socio-cultural debate: how to conceptualise the transformations of the late twentieth century.

Both postmodernist critics such as Lyotard, and those such as Habermas who wish to hold onto 'the project of modernity' share deep concerns about the contemporary state of the world.[42] Firstly, the Enlightenment aspiration to rid the world of scarcity by developing productive forces ('harnessing nature') has had an increasingly unconvincing feel, and is now in deep crisis. The technology to feed, clothe and shelter the world is already in place, yet famine is on the increase, and even in the West homelessness is increasing. Faith in technology palls before the human and ecological damage inflicted at Chernobyl or in the sub-Sahara, before the unforeseen side-effects of many drugs and agricultural treatments and endless other instances. Science is now aware that it can deal only in probabilities rather than certainties, and risk, or even 'chaos', looms over all technological innovation.

The same can be said for social experimentation: the idea of a cumulative social wisdom, resulting in the gradual achievement of human rights and freedoms, is not borne out by a century which has included large-scale human destruction in the Holocaust, two world wars and many smaller ones; the proliferation of torture and other brutalities; the impoverishment and neglect of large sections of the population in the First World as well as the Third; and also many less sensational dehumanisations within social institutions and within industrial practices.

All this is not the outcome of simple human evil; it is structural. Giddens argues that societies have escaped human control through a process by which institutions have become 'disembedded' from relations of personal ties and direct knowledge, and fixed into more 'abstract' relations which depend on 'expert systems' – specialised knowledges from which most people are excluded and can only engage with through *trust*. Such a division of intellectual labour has produced not just feelings of impotence but social institutions which are 'careering juggernauts' – such that the world has in actuality become a more risk-ridden place[43]. In short 'instrumental rationality' has dominated, with devastating effect.

But does acceptance of this critique entail, as Lyotard suggests, an abandonment of 'the project of modernity', and the adoption of a postmodern perspective (see Chapter 1, p. 9)? Certainly, postmodern theory has forced an crucial investigation of the possibility of a qualitative sea-change in Western socio-cultural life during the second half of this century. But there are tendencies in many of its proponents towards sweepingly oversimplified narratives of historical change. One tendency has been to confuse theoretical innovation with broader, empirical historical changes.[44] While there has undoubtedly been a deep transformation of social and cultural conditions in the second half of this century, the argument that the culture and values of modernity have been destroyed is overdramatic.

What is overlooked is that 'the Enlightenment project' is shorthand not for a single dogma, but for a number of values and visions which not only have a degree of autonomy from each other but which can pull in different directions. Neither Lyotard's critique of modernity, nor that of the Frankfurt School (upon which the former is heavily dependent), reject all the elements of 'the project'. Adorno and Horkheimer's argument is that one particular element – the will for mastery and the drive for efficiency – has dominated and distorted it. This element, instrumental rationality, has outgrown its status as a *means* – to achieving emancipation, autonomy and self-development for all – and become an end in itself, such that people have been dominated rather than liberated.[45] Lyotard pushes the argument further and proposes that domination is a necessary consequence of any such totalising certainty. Thus Adorno and Horkheimer are not criticising the original Enlightenment principles wholesale but their distortion. And Lyotard's main attack is on the overweening *certainty* of the Enlightenment initiative and the consequent horrors that the attempt to impose rationality have produced – not on the idea of emancipation itself. On the contrary this is the very principle against which the failures of modernity are judged – that is, they have curtailed freedom.

To criticise the direction of history of the West (and of also 'Eastern' communism), we do not have to move *outside* modernity. Western modernity has been patriarchal, Eurocentric and totalitarian not in fulfilment of the Enlightenment project, but *against* its emancipatory principles. The history of the past 200 years (the period of modernity) should not be understood as a history of blind support for progress-at-all-costs, and thus now to be thoroughly abandoned. Rather, we should see that history as a struggle over the realisation of modernity, one which includes repeated powerful defences of those democratic and emancipatory elements of 'the project' which vested interests always sought to marginalise. This is not merely a question of how to name a period – it has political implications. Those who have conceptualised 'modernity' only through its bad side have rejected too much – particularly the possibility of continuing more universalistic struggles for democracy and expanded personal autonomy, as well as emancipation from hunger and want.

The postmodernist intervention has forced a valuable clarification of the dangers which future emancipatory projects need to avoid, in particular, that of arrogant *certainty*: such projects should be self-reflexive, provisional and careful to avoid 'othering' different social constituencies. In fact 'postmodernity' might be best understood not as the end of modernity, but as the end of its taken-for-grantedness – the moment when the historical contingency of its underlying assumptions, and their limits are made explicit.[46] But some of the more sweeping versions of postmodernism[47] can obscure the resources within existing cultures which can provide a basis for renewed emancipatory projects, particularly when they present a world conquered by consumer culture, if not content with itself then fatalistic – a flat sameness, an 'end of history'. Against this I have argued that, at the very *heart* of consumer culture, in the most popular narratives of our time, elements of a social critique are to be found, and imaginings of 'something better'.

But we still have to confront the question of whether these fragments of what Gramsci would call 'good sense' are couched in forms which can be articulated to political projects for change.

THE POLITICS OF POPULAR FANTASY

It is easy to exaggerate the political significance of these dystopian visions and utopian moments, but equally easy to dismiss them too decisively. These elements, particularly when expressed through nostalgia, could be understood to confirm precisely Jameson's view that postmodern culture has dissolved political purpose into a nostalgic play with the images of fantasy-land, and that fragmentary utopian fantasies are not the same as politically effective critique. The films can be understood as playing with pleasurable but directionless images of dystopia and transcendence – as inextricably bound into an idealist humanism, asserting an inevitable human transcendence which is comforting but unconnected to a political realism, and potentially distracting from political action rather than encouraging it. This takes us back to what Jameson would like to find in contemporary cinema – a 'cognitive map' which will enable effective political action. His perspective draws, implicitly at least, upon a Marxist critique of idealist, humanist and utopian thought as leading to misguided political action. He is absolutely right in this: an effective politics depends on a careful, materialist analysis of the whole conjuncture – of the balance of forces in play. But the fact that popular culture does not provide such a political analysis is not in dispute. Nor should we assume that popular cinema is likely to politicise in the direct way that other social experiences can. However we should not then draw the conclusion that popular utopianism is of *no* political relevance or use. The negative sense of 'utopian' denotes an impossible ideal; although, as David Purdy points out, Thomas More's original sense of the term was of a good but non-existent society, but one that was possible.[48] Utopian imagining is at the very least a way of creating a critical distance from the present, a resistance to the confinement of the imagination within existing social frameworks. To refer again to Gramsci's thinking on popular mobilisation, the presence of utopian aspirations could be a very significant element of a conjuncture, the element which clinches how vibrant a political movement is.

The term 'human' has been used rather freely in this chapter, and requires similar scrutiny. But it has always been allocated its inverted commas: my argument implies no support for a human essence which will one day fulfil itself. Althusser's argument for a theoretical anti-humanism remains as forceful as ever.[49] Humanism is, as he puts it, an 'ideology in the ethico-political domain'. Different versions of 'the human' are constructed in the context of different projects. While attempts may be made to legitimate them by claiming them to be 'natural' and located in an *essential* humanity, in fact they always express contingent aspirations and ideals of what social relations might be achieved. Humanisms are ethico-political statements, the expressions of projects, not statements of fact; and as such are future-oriented, even where their legitimating strategy is to make claims about ancestral foundations and essences. This means that their political effectiveness can only be discerned in relation to particular moments. Appeals to 'the human' can be articulated to right-wing discourses[50], but they can also be (and often are) projects on the side of emancipation, empowerment, democracy and communitarianism.

The 'nostalgia mode' is also politically indeterminate. It has become a taken-for-granted position within recent cultural studies that nostalgia, such as that for the mythical past of an 'organic community', is open to the criticism that it implies that the present has to be understood as loss or decline: that is, we have a *conservative* critique of the contemporary.[51] But perhaps this question should now be reopened. Firstly, there is a tendency to conflate 'conservative' with 'right wing': it is after all 'conservative' to wish to retain and indeed restore a state system of welfare in Britain, though not of course 'Conservative'. Secondly, nostalgia can be justifiably attacked as bad history, but it can also be a strategy for creating a distance from the present in order to think critically about it.

Thus nostalgia, myths of the past, humanism and utopianism may all be ideological in the sense of not recognising their own historicity and also in modelling a society which a materialist analysis can demonstrate to be unachievable in practice. Nevertheless each of these modes of representation allow an embryonic critique of existing social relations and a way of imagining of alternatives. These imaginings are not a political programme, but a political programme might be able to articulate them.

The other argument against the possibility of such an articulation is that the dystopian and utopian elements are already articulated within the narrative of the films themselves, and often to fantasies of male victory over all odds. But there is always a danger in equating narrative closure with ideological closure, a perspective associated with the early days of the journal *Screen*. A similar debate has taken place on how to interpret the meaning of the female heroines of the *films noirs* of the 1940s: whether the lesson female audiences learned was that women step out of a subordinate, domestic role at their peril (for the heroines who do so tend to end up dead, maimed or in jail), or whether the incandescent screen presence of the female stars were such that their moments of *autonomy* were what the audiences took away with them.[52] The initial *Screen* position – that the narrative structure imposed one single point of identification for the spectator – has long fallen into disrepute; it is now widely recognised that the audience reads the filmic text from within the cultural repertoire they already have available to them. They can thus read the film selectively and in effect recompose its meaning. It would therefore seem quite possible for a feminist and a male chauvinist to construct rather different meanings from these films. Likewise, whether particular film viewers connect the pleasures of communitarian transcendence they enjoy in a film to a communitarian politics will depend on the political culture they inhabit in that historical conjuncture.

To sum up the last few sections of the argument: postmodernism has tended to throw out the baby with the bath-water. The rejection of an overweening rationalism does not entail the rejection of the emancipatory and democratic dimensions of Enlightenment thought (nor the aspiration for a reconciliation of cognitive, ethical and aesthetic dimensions of social life). And popular utopian imaginings as reproduced and reinvented in the cinema could be a resource upon which emancipatory projects might draw. But because most filmic texts are open to different readings, they should only be seen as potential supports for political critique rather than as themselves politicising.

There are points of convergence between my argument and Anthony Giddens' attempt to renew the project of modernity in the late twentieth century. For him, an essential condition for the future avoidance of greater disasters and for social improvement is the 'heavily counter-factual nature of future-oriented thought' – in other words, the ability to imagine something that has not yet existed: 'for we can envisage alternative futures whose very propagation might help them be realised.'[53] Such a 'utopian realism' should centre on an emancipatory politics linked to a 'life politics . . . which seeks to further the possibilities of a fulfilling and satisfying life for all, and in respect of which there are no "others"'. The utopian sensibilities which have been identified in popular film sometimes overtly embrace, and are generally at least compatible with, the aspirations of such a 'life politics'.

The point here is not that the implicit social critique to be found in the popular cinema has stumbled on 'the truth' of what is wrong with the world, with Giddens and other intellectuals as the legitimators of that truth. Rather it is to propose the *possibility* of some kind of articulation between the sustained, theoretically sophisticated analyses and projects of 'progressive' intellectuals and the more fragmentary and affective utopian and dystopian elements of popular media forms.

THOUGHT, FEELING AND IMAGINED COMMUNITIES

The final stage of my discussion is to consider why, if this is the case, are there few instances of left or liberal political movements successfully drawing upon popular utopian sentiments?

We have examined one reason already: the tendency for intellectuals and radical politicians to set themselves up *against* popular culture.[54] Another is a predisposition towards rationalism, to the battle for *ideas*, at the expense of attention to feelings and psychic investments. Of course, political struggles are never won *without* a battle for ideas, but in concrete social situations ideas are always articulated to fears and desires. The neglect of this dimension in progressive politics is beginning to be recognised, prompted particularly by feminist interventions and a sense that the persistence of Thatcherism can be understood to have partly depended upon its success in addressing deep-rooted desires.[55]

The programmes of left–liberal social theorists such as Giddens exhibit this same separation of thought and feeling. Giddens' 'utopian realism' sets out the global goals of 'a post-scarcity system', 'the humanisation of technology', 'demilitarisation' and 'multilayered democratic participation'.[56] It is undoubtedly difficult to disagree with Giddens' imagined future (*of course* we all want global harmony). But, moral, rationalist and dutifully sensible as it is, it *does not quicken the pulse*. On the other hand, the 'film version' of a transformed world – so much more exciting and pleasurable, with its energy, its intensity, its excess, its refusals to behave – occupies the other side of the divide, presenting, to quote Dyer again, 'what utopia would feel like rather than how it would be organised'[57].

To some extent this divide, between rationalist blueprints and affective identifications, has opened up, or at least opened further, during the period under discussion, and this might be a understood as one of the key dimensions of postmodernity. It is illustrated in particular by the fate of imaginings of 'community' from the 1930s to the present day. As we have seen, images of community, togetherness, sense of belonging and mutuality are present in the classic cinematic genres. In 1930s musicals, for example, the members of the chorus not only sing and dance as a team, but support each other off-stage, lending each other clothes, money and emotional support. Another scenario from the Westerns of the 1930s and 1940s is the township of ordinary law-abiding people who manage to resist corruption, violence and tyranny only by banding together (in this case, men and women equally). The effectiveness of 'little people' collectively expressing their interests was a popular theme in American films of the New Deal era. But gradually this public, civic notion of community has become a rarer motif. A commoner form of 'community' has become the (usually male) group with a range of diverse skills who succeed by mutual interdependence (for example, *The Magnificent Seven*, John Sturges, 1960); perhaps even a majority of war films have been similarly structured – from *They Were Expendable* (John Ford, 1945) through *The Dirty Dozen* (Edward Dmytryk, 1952) to *Platoon* (Oliver Stone, 1986).

There are exceptions to this shift, particularly in overtly 'political' films. A recent reassertion of the possibility of public, civic action is John Sayles' *City of Hope* (1991), now acknowledging and exploring the *difficulties* of collective action, as well as insisting on its continuing possibility. *Blue Collar* (Paul Schrader, 1978) explores this theme in an industrial context. But some of these notions of community, such as the isolated self-sufficient township or the organic village, can now only be represented through nostalgia. Their material conditions of existence have been swept away by the rapid changes which have penetrated all 'communities' in the West at least: the nationalisation and then internationalisation of economic relationships, but also, increasingly, cultural ones – the presence of 'the global' in the 'local'.[58] Bauman has recently argued that one mark of postmodernity is the loss of modernist confidence that rationality or its institutionalised embodiment in the nation state or the law will solve our problems, and that as a consequence we resort to 'imagined communities'[59] which do not depend on physical proximity or traditional institutions but upon a perceived common interest (and often a 'single issue') which can intensify or wane equally quickly:

What it [the imagined community] lacks in stability and institutionalised continuity, it more that compensates for with overwhelming affective commitment of its self-appointed members. In the absence of institutional support, the commitment tends to be fickle and short-lived. At the moments of condensation, however, it may reach literally breath-taking intensity.[60]

For their effectiveness, they depend on gaining access to media attention and hence to the public imagination, by 'spectacular outbursts of togetherness' (demonstrations, festivals, riots), or by graffiti, terrorist acts and so on.

It is these new kinds of 'community' which are most likely to be portrayed in contemporary film: they articulate energy, intensity and transparency in the same way – the affective dimension looms large. And since popular films are working through the narrative codes of dramatic conflict, they tend to reproduce another feature Bauman identifies in this political form: 'displays of communal togetherness ... will remain perforce competitive and hence infused with inter-communal hostility'. These motifs occur particularly clearly in recent youth films – an intense and often desperate banding together against all odds, often against the threat of another group, or against the uncomprehending demands of adult society (as in *The Outsiders*, *Rumble Fish* or *Breakfast Club*). The Ninja Turtles films are one recent variation of this. However these are not quite celebrations of an aggressive, competitive neo-tribalism. The publicity material for *The Outsiders* (see Figure 9.1b) declares of the male gang from the wrong side of the tracks, 'They wanted to belong.' Their desire is to be part of a society which is freed of the hypocrisy, convention and class divisions which exclude them. Images of a present-day civic community cannot be plausibly represented, but the longing for one is, even though popular culture no longer seems to have clear images of what it might look like.

The question becomes whether 'sensible', rationalistic and altruistic models of community, which do not depend on competitive and aggressive intolerance of others, can be attached to the affective dimensions of modernity, the intense and vigorous psychic investments attached to desires for 'something different' which this chapter has been exploring. But there is more than just an opposition between thought and feeling operating here. We can also find a conflict between a desire for a just, stable and civil society and a celebration of spontaneity and, often, refusal. Berman characterised the experience of modernity as poised between possibility and growth on the one hand and danger and destruction on the other, and Bauman, as we have seen, argues that the project of modernity has been to impose order on what was seen as a naturally chaotic world. Perhaps what both (but particularly Bauman) fail to bring out is the *attraction* of the abyss, of chaos – particularly for those social groups who have good reason to resist the 'will to order' of those in power. The tradition of carnival within popular culture is one celebration of social disorder. This too has its place within popular cinema: the recent *Gremlins* films (Joe Dante, 1984

Figure 9.1 Two kinds of community, civic and neo-tribal. The township turns out to send off its delegate in *Young Mr Lincoln*, 1939 (above) and the young dispossessed band together in *The Outsiders*, 1983 (below)

Source: BFI stills, posters and designs

and 1990) represent orderly suburban America being thrown into chaos by creatures who follow their brute appetites. The creatures are represented explicitly as a threat to be contained, but the films only half-heartedly sustain that reading – the pleasure of disorder is what young audiences enjoyed most.

It is argued in Chapter 1 that twentieth-century Western popular culture is best characterised not as embodying a dominant ideology of 'bourgeois' aspirations, but as a contradictory synthesis of ideas, images and *feelings*. Raymond Williams' term 'structure of feeling' evokes this better than 'ideology'. There are dreams of stability – of rural independence in a self-sufficient homestead, of a suburban idyll, of balanced and just communities and more ambitiously of 'the family of man'. But there are also concurrent, and often simultaneously imagined, dreams of instability – of escape from social convention, routine and moderation into intense and perfect relationships untrammelled by social convention, into transcendence, into pushing the mind, the body, creativity beyond normal limits, into farcical or dangerous irresponsibility, 'naughtiness' or downright anarchy and, in the extreme, self-destruction. My argument has been that recent popular cinema continues to address this same range of, often contradictory, aspirations and desires, albeit now with very different emphases, imagery and resolutions. Social observers and politicians have picked up and addressed the desire for betterment, but not the more intense dreams of 'transparency' and transcendence.

Thus, on the one hand, we have massive psychic investments in desire for transformation which has only rarely been directed towards social change; on the other, we have political movements and parties which aim at social change but which touch none of this energy; rather they are perceived as part of the tedious, hypocritical and overly rationalist society in which we cannot be our spontaneous selves.

I have argued the following:

- that popular film continues to offer, alongside many other discursive effects, elements of social critique of unfreedom, hierarchies, power-mongering, bureaucracies, hypocrisy and unbridled competition, but also glimpses of what the transcendence over these oppressive features of society might feel like;
- that the values underpinning these features correspond to *some* elements of 'the project of modernity';
- that the popularity of these films suggests that these imaginings remain a vibrant element of Western mass culture;
- that the postmodernist critique of modernity leaves these same aspects of 'the project' intact and worthy of continued political struggle;
- that full identification with a political project needs an affective investment as well as a rational acceptance;

- that left political movements have tended to work over-exclusively in the sphere of the 'reason' and not on the terrain of feeling – fantasy, anxiety, pleasure and desire;
- and that this opens up the possibility that the psychic investments which these popular imaginings suggest might be articulated to a 'progressive' politics.

There is much speculation here and very little 'proof'. It points to the need for much more sustained and systematic work on the films than I have undertaken, but also on the subjectivities of their audiences. In the end my argument will only be upheld if and when it is seen to work in practice. It is based on a great deal of 'optimism of the will' and only small doses of 'pessimism of the intellect'. It would have probably been easier to stress the current weakness of transformative struggles in Britain and the unlikelihood of the kind of articulation I have imagined here. Or the fact that even in the context of a rising political movement, articulation is hard, and gradual, work, and has to be pragmatic, to acknowledge existing fixities;[61] or that it succeeds in some moments and not in others, and can equally easily be reversed. Nevertheless, in the context of the gloom of some postmodernist readings of present-day culture, it seemed more important to reassert the *possibilities* of renewal and the fact that, even at its most commodified heart, Western culture has *not* settled for the world as it is currently organised.

NOTES

1 M. Berman, *All That is Solid Melts into Air. The Experience of Modernity*, London, Verso, 1983, p. 15
2 Particularly his influential essay 'Postmodernism, or the cultural logic of late capitalism', *New Left Review*, no. 146, 1984; now reprinted in his book also called *Postmodernism, or the Cultural Logic Of Late Capitalism*, London and New York, Verso, 1991. For a more general critique of this book see A. O'Shea, 'Cultural logics, local and global', *Magazine of Cultural Studies*, issue 4, Autumn, 1991.
3 Jameson, 'Postmodernism', p. 73.
4 ibid., pp. 83, 84.
5 Jameson, *Postmodernism*, ch. 9.
6 ibid., p. 418.
7 In particular their influential 'The culture industry: enlightenment as mass deception', in their *Dialectics of Enlightenment*, London, Allen Lane, 1973.
8 Various attempts have been made to rescue the Frankfurt School from this monolithic representation; in my view these are not convincing. For example, Miriam Hansen's claim to do so, in 'Early cinema, late cinema: permutations of the public sphere', *Screen*, vol. 34, no. 3, Autumn 1993, still presents them as seeing the liberatory potential of the cinema evaporate in its 'alienating, conformist and manipulative use in Fordist–liberal capitalism'. Her claim for a critical, utopian edge in the cinema seems to be *despite* her inheritance of Frankfurt School traditions.

9 See J. Richards, *The Age of the Dream Palace*, London, Routledge, 1984, ch. 1, for evidence of this from the 1930s. Jackie Stacey has recently established similar evidence from the 1940s and 1950s in *Star Gazing: Hollywood Cinema and Female Spectatorship*, Routledge, 1994.

10 This argument is made in full in my first chapter in this volume.

11 Berman, *All That is Solid;* and see Chapter 1 of this volume for an extended critique.

12 R. Dyer, 'Entertainment and utopia', *Movie*, no. 24, 1977, reprinted in R. Altman (ed.), *Genre: The Musical*, London, RKP/BFI, 1981. The productiveness of this article is well illustrated in Stacey, *Star Gazing*.

13 See, for example, the James Cagney vehicles, *Public Enemy* (William Wellman, 1931) and *White Heat* (Raoul Walsh, 1949), or any number of *film noir* movies of the 1940s. In the latter, it is often the female lead whose desires for transcendence end in tragedy. See E. Ann Kaplan (ed.), *Women in Film Noir*, London, British Film Institute, 1978.

14 Z. Bauman, *Intimations of Postmodernity*, London, Routledge, 1992, pp. xiii ff.

15 See, for example, the analysis of Westerns in P. Wollen, *Signs and Meaning in the Cinema*, London, Secker and Warburg, 1969, ch. 2.

16 J. Habermas, 'Modernity – an incomplete project', in H. Foster (ed.), *Postmodern Culture*, London, Pluto, 1985.

17 Adorno and Horkheimer, 'The culture industry'.

18 This applies not only to male misfits, such as those played by James Cagney in the 1930s, or James Dean in the 1950s, but also to the women who struggle for autonomy from male dependence in the *films noirs* of the 1940s. Although such women tend to be forced back into their place or suffer violent consequences, the cinematic devices tend to position us in an empathetic relationship with them. Their world is unsatisfying, and their rebellious spirit is at least ambiguously celebrated (Kaplan (ed.), *Women in Film Noir*).

19 F. Jameson, 'Reification and utopia in mass culture', *Social Text*, vol. 1, Fall, 1979; reprinted in F. Jameson, *Signatures of the Visible*, New York and London, Routledge, 1992.

20 For an expansion of this argument see A. O'Shea, 'Television as culture: not just texts and readers', *Media, Culture and Society*, vol. 11, 1989, pp. 373–9.

21 A. Gramsci, *Selections from the Prison Notebooks*, London, Lawrence and Wishart, 1973, pp. 323ff., 'The study of philosophy'. Gramsci's fragmentary notes are usefully organised under themes in D. Forgacs (ed.), *A Gramsci Reader*, London, Lawrence and Wishart, 1988. The relevant section here is ch. 11. For a clear introduction to Gramsci's theories see R. Simon, *Gramsci's Political Thought: An Introduction*, London, Lawrence and Wishart, 1982.

22 See Forgacs (ed.), *Gramsci Reader*, chs 6 and 7.

23 ibid., pp. 200–2.

24 For a summary of the different articulations of such a populism, see the Cultural Historical Group, 'Out of the people: the politics of containment, 1935–45', *Working Papers in Cultural Studies 9*, Spring 1976.

25 See Stacey, *Star Gazing*, ch. 2, on the methodological difficulties as they apply to gendered readings.

26 Richards, *Age of the Dream Palace*, especially ch. 1.

27 ibid., ch. 1.

28 P. Miles and M. Smith, *Cinema, Literature and Society. Elite and Mass Culture in Interwar Britain*, London, Croom Helm, 1987.

29 Aside from Adorno and Horkheimer, see, for example, W.F. Haug, *Commodity Aesthetics, Ideology and Culture*, New York, International General, 1987; and

C. Campbell, 'The desire for the new', in R. Silverstone and E. Hirsch (eds), *Consuming Technologies*, London, Routledge, 1992.

30 Jameson, *Postmodernism*.

31 ibid., p. 296.

32 See Jameson's analysis of *Blue Velvet* (*Postmodernism*, p. 288ff.). See also S. Connor, *Postmodernist Culture*, Oxford, Blackwell, 1989, pp. 173ff.; and N.K. Denzin, *Images of Postmodern Society: Social Theory and Contemporary Cinema*, London, Sage, 1991.

33 Cf. A. Calder, *The People's War*, Granada, 1971; and the Cultural Historical Group, 'Out of the People'.

34 S. Hall and M. Jacques, *The Politics of Thatcherism*, London, Lawrence and Wishart, 1983.

35 See Thomas Schatz, 'The new Hollywood', in J. Collins, H. Radner and A. Preacher Collins (eds), *Film Theory Goes to the Movies*, London, Routledge, 1993; and Jim Hillier, *The New Hollywood*, London, Studio Vista, 1992.

36 See J. Baudrillard, *Simulations*, New York, Semiotext, 1983, for his exposition of 'simulacra' (signs without a referent).

37 This motif parallels the development of popular music over the second half of this century: the further towards the rebellious end of this form we look, the more we find lyrics obscured and meaning refused. Punk certainly demonstrates this, and the earlier 'Talking about My Generation' by The Who dissolves in the end into pure 'noise'. This strategy of challenging 'logocentrism' is in part borrowed from Afro-American and Afro-Caribbean cultural forms (D. Hebdige, *Subculture: the Meaning of Style*, London, Methuen, 1979). For black strategies of engaging with modernity through various forms of performance, see P. Gilroy, 'It ain't where you're from, it's where you're at . . .: the dialectics of diaspora identification', *Third Text*, vol. 13, 1990 (also collected in his *Small Acts*, London, Serpent's Tail, 1993).

38 Judith Williamson, in her 'Second sight' column in *Guardian*, on 13 September 1990 and 24 October 1991.

39 Though Judith Williamson (*Guardian*, 24 October 91) finds this relationship unsatisfactorily represented: 'annoying as male-bonding scenarios often are, they do hit on deep-lying issues of loyalty, selflessness, friendship and human values at a level which makes *Thelma and Louise* merely silly'.

40 This point is noted in Michael Ryan and Douglas Kellner, *Camera Politica*, Bloomington and Indianapolis, Indiana University Press, 1990, which seeks to construct a correspondence between changing cinematic representations and changing political cultures in the USA from the 1960s to the mid-1980s. Since they tend to read off the politics of a film from its narrative closure (for example, rampant masculinity winning through), at the expense of, say, its utopian moments, their conclusions are relatively gloomy. But they do note an opening up of more liberal narratives from the late 1980s, and connect this in part to the increasing influence of former 1960s radicals in the industry.

41 M. Medved, *Hollywood vs America: Popular Culture and the War on Traditional Values*, London, Harper Collins, 1993.

42 Habermas, 'Modernity – an incomplete project'; J.-F. Lyotard, 'Defining the postmodern', in L. Appignenesi (ed.), *Postmodernism: ICA Documents*, London, Free Association Books, 1989. See also Chapter 1 p. 9.

43 A. Giddens, *The Consequences of Modernity*, Cambridge, Polity Press, 1990.

44 For example, postmodern cultural theory, drawing on poststructuralism and psychoanalytic theory, asserts that subjectivity is decentred, fragmented, multiple, contradictory and unstable. This, in my view, does grasp a wide-

spread contemporary experience. But it is a category mistake to see this break within cultural theory as necessarily mirroring a change in typical *historical* subjectivities – from ones which are fixed and singular to ones which (since the establishment of postmodernism?) are multiple and incomplete. Such an assertion is frequently made without the empirical historical research needed to establish this. Such research produces a more complex picture: for example, the case-studies in this book tend to suggest a much longer history of contra- dictory, unsettled subjectivities, with respect to a range of social groups. For an example of a text which falls into the above trap, see M. Poster, *The Mode of Information*, Cambridge, Polity, 1990.

45 Adorno and Horkheimer, *Dialectics of Enlightenment*.
46 Many commentators have taken this line. See, for example, Keith Tester, *The Life and Times of Postmodernity*, London, Routledge, 1993, p. 157.
47 Lyotard and Baudrillard in particular. As Angela McRobbie points out (*Postmodernism and Popular Culture*, London, Routledge, 1994, especially ch. 4), life is not so simple as being for or against postmodernism or modernity. There is in fact a subtle spectrum of arguments about the depth of the cultural shifts in which we are embroiled, which the modernity/postmodernity oppo- sition is too clumsy to elucidate.
48 David Purdy, in a book review in *Renewal*, vol. 2, no. 3, July 1994, p. 85.
49 L. Althusser, 'Marxism and humanism', in his *For Marx*, London, New Left Books, 1977.
50 See A. O'Shea, 'Trusting the people: how does Thatcherism work?', in *Formations of Nation and People*, London, Routledge, 1984.
51 See the final section of Chapter 1 (p. 28) for how this has operated in English cultural criticism during the first half of this century.
52 Kaplan (ed.), *Women in Film Noir*.
53 Giddens, *Consequences of Modernity*, p. 154.
54 See also Chapter 1 in this volume.
55 See J. Rose, 'Margaret Thatcher and Ruth Ellis', *New Formations*, no. 6, Winter, 1988.
56 Giddens, *Consequences of Modernity*, pp. 164ff.
57 Dyer, 'Entertainment and utopia', p. 177.
58 Cf. Doreen Massey, 'A global sense of place', *Marxism Today*, June 1991.
59 Borrowing the term from B. Anderson, *Imagined Communities*, London, Verso, 1983.
60 Z. Bauman, *Intimations of Postmodernity*, London, Routledge, 1992, p. xix.
61 See S. Hall, *The Hard Road to Renewal*, London, Verso, 1988.

INDEX

269